HUDSON TAYLOR

&

CHINA'S OPEN CENTURY

Book Four: Survivors' Pact

19.25

By the same author:

Hudson Taylor and China's Open Century
Book 1: Barbarians at the Gates
Book 2: Over the Treaty Wall
Book 3: If I Had a Thousand Lives

HUDSON TAYLOR

&

CHINA'S OPEN CENTURY

BOOK FOUR
Survivors' Pact

A J Broomhall

HODDER AND STOUGHTON
and
THE OVERSEAS MISSIONARY FELLOWSHIP

British Library Cataloguing in Publication Data

Broomhall, A. J.
 Hudson Taylor & China's open century.—(Hodder
 Christian paperbacks)
 Bk. 4; Survivors' pact
 1. Taylor, Hudson   2. Missionaries—China—Biography
 266'.0092'4   BV3427.T3

 ISBN 0 340 34922 0

Foreword to the Series

China appears to be re-opening its doors to the Western world. The future of Christianity in that vast country is known only to God. It is, however, important that we in the West should be alert to the present situation, and be enabled to see it in the perspective of the long history of missionary enterprise there. It is one of the merits of these six remarkable volumes that they provide us with just such a perspective.

These books are much more than just the story of the life and work of Hudson Taylor told in great detail. If they were that alone, they would be a worthwhile enterprise, for, as the *Preface* reminds us, he has been called by no less a Church historian than Professor K S Latourette 'one of the greatest missionaries of all time'. He was a man of total devotion to Christ and to the missionary cause, a man of ecumenical spirit, a man of originality in initiating new attitudes to mission, a doctor, a translator, an evangelist, an heroic figure of the Church.

The historian – whether his interests be primarily military, missionary, or social – will find much to interest him here. The heinous opium traffic which led to two wars with China is described. The relationship of 'the man in the field' to the society which sent him is set before us in all its complexity and (often) painfulness. And the story of Biblical translation and dissemination will be full of interest to those experts who work under the banner of the United Bible Societies and to that great fellowship of men and women who support them across the length and breadth of the world.

Dr Broomhall is to be congratulated on writing a major work which, while being of interest *primarily* to students of mission, deserves a far wider readership. We owe our thanks to Messrs Hodder and Stoughton for their boldness in printing so large a series of volumes in days when all publishers have financial problems. I believe that author and publisher will be rewarded, for we have here a fascinating galaxy of men and women who faced the challenge of the evangelisation of China with daring and devotion, and none more so than the central figure of that galaxy, Hudson Taylor himself. The secret of his perseverance, of his achievement, and of his significance in missionary history is to be found in some words which he wrote to his favourite sister, Amelia:

'If I had a thousand pounds, China should have it. If I had a thousand lives, China should have them. No! not *China*, but *Christ*. Can we do too much for Him?'

Sissinghurst, Kent   Donald Coggan

PREFACE

(See also the General Preface in Book One)

This book begins a record of the most stormy period of Hudson Taylor's life. It follows and depends for understanding on the three preceding volumes, *Barbarians at the Gates*, *Over the Treaty Wall* and *If I Had a Thousand Lives*. Again it is a record of events and statements, rather than a narrative.

Survivors' Pact takes up the story from the launching of the 'China Inland Mission'. It continues the study of Hudson Taylor's personality and eventful life, in the perspective of contemporary Chinese and world history, of other missions and missionaries, and of the individuals with whom he was in close contact. As before, new features are given in some detail, but the conditions of life and travel in China experienced by Hudson Taylor and others, the background to the opium scandal, the 'unequal treaties' between China and the Western nations, and the horrific Taiping rebellion, to name a few examples, are 'taken as read'.

This fourth book shows Hudson Taylor in his first two years as a leader of men, one of the most crucial periods of his life. Some detail is necessary to portray the widely differing personalities he had to cope with. It shows him facing circumstances which would have defeated many men, yet keeping his goals in sight with a resilience of mind and spirit explained only by his 'practice of the presence of God'. The paucity of source material showing his shortcomings is a matter for regret as it makes a balanced picture of him difficult to attain, but nothing is suppressed.

The team of colleagues he began with was as varied in nature as could be held harmoniously together in far more favourable conditions. The 'Ningbo five', sent out to China during Hudson Taylor's enforced stay in England (1861–65), could understandably feel only loosely linked to him and to the mission he formed in their absence. This volume tells how they were slow to co-operate but before long found they could not do without him. The young men and women he took with him when he returned to China in 1866, and those who joined him shortly afterwards, were so diverse in temperament and social background (from Scottish blacksmith and Kingsland draper to Swiss governess and Irish colonel's sons, and from Presbyterians and Baptists to Anglicans and Brethren) that incompatibility could be expected. Their interaction is an interesting study, but Hudson Taylor's success and failures in leading them are as telling.

From the arrival of its first shipload in 1866, the China Inland Mission (CIM) was one of the largest missionary bodies in China (CIM:24), exceeded in membership by only the London Missionary Society (LMS:27) and American Presbyterian Mission (APM:30). But apart from Hudson and Maria Taylor, all except James Meadows were inexperienced novices, and Meadows had no more knowledge of China than four years in the treaty port of Ningbo had given him. So, single-handed, Hudson Taylor's first aim was to weld his team together while they learned the language and made that vital acquaintance with Chinese thought and culture which would keep them out of trouble of their own making, and give them the tools of competence. An inevitable time-lag while nothing appeared to be happening caused the eyebrows of uncomprehending observers in Britain and China to be raised – but that was nothing in comparison with the predictable opposition to the policies and practices of the Mission. Chinese clothes, Chinese home life with a minimum of Western comforts; young unmarried women going into the little-known 'interior' and living close to the Chinese people, all without a home committee or visible means of support – eccentricities in such contrast to the conventional isolation of most Westerners in their semi-foreign 'stations' could be counted on to bring down a hail of vituperation, as they did. It was a battle from the start, to establish the cross-cultural characteristics of the Mission, to wean the members from their foreignness and to make them feel at home in the land of their adoption. To give in and sue for peace would have been all too easy, since to keep such principles firmly in view was to so many rank stubbornness or madness. Yet there was no written contract between them, only the word of friends. How Hudson Taylor coped and how the Mission survived holds many lessons.

This volume differs from the others as a study in personalities: from Mr and Mrs William Berger in the United Kingdom, and the two girls, Jennie Faulding and Emily Blatchley, so deserving of credit that they must be given prominence, to Lewis Nicol, a thorn in the flesh, and a variety of friends and critics sometimes more well-meaning than helpful. It describes attempts to discredit Hudson Taylor and to extinguish his fledgling Mission. Careful enquiry has led to only one source outside the Hudson Taylor archives, which goes far to establish the motives of the honoured missionary who led the criticism, a man whom Hudson Taylor and the CIM otherwise admired (p 263). Like the opposition to his marriage (in Book 3) these encounters throw strong light on Hudson Taylor himself, providing what can now be recognised as indispensable training for his role as leader of such a heterogeneous international society.

Because in the text itself an attempt is made to state the documented facts with a minimum of interpretation or gloss, perhaps some comment here may be allowed, to assist the reader in his own assessment of those facts. That Hudson Taylor had no hold on his colleagues beyond their own choice and agreement to be led and directed by him is the measure of his gift of leadership. That they loved him and Maria says more. To see *how* he wrote to them, dealt with their difficulties and differences of opinion, and how they addressed him, is informative. In the dangerous stage when they were gaining fluency and self-confidence but still had so much to learn, his control combined firmness with respect and affection. When their follies threatened the whole venture he tempered forthrightness with friendship. How he himself acted when physically or emotionally at a low ebb – with good cause – speaks volumes.

Through it all he steered the Mission, consistently applying its few declared principles in such a way as to evolve what over the years became known as the *Principles and Practice* (P and P). Commentators should note that the chronological progression of his thinking, and of the Mission's policies, render generalisations suspect or invalid. (Instances could be cited of even a passing remark in his youth being mistakenly used to assess him in his maturity.) His own attitudes to money and to 'faith in God' changed considerably through different periods of his developing years, even in the brief period covered by this book. His faith and understanding were growing all the time. The first chapter contains examples.

Similarly, K S Latourette's remark that Hudson Taylor's faith 'thrived on advertising', if taken out of context, may be misconstrued. Going on to say that the Mission's financial principles were faithfully adhered to in practice, Latourette was referring to Hudson Taylor's delight in declaring how God honoured reliance on his, God's, faithfulness.[1] Hudson Taylor was no orator, but he was a good communicator. And he burned with zeal to awaken the Church to China's spiritual need and claims upon Christendom. He well knew that this publicity by word of mouth and by his pen could not but bring financial returns. And he held strongly that the Church at large and local churches in particular ought with conviction to send and support their missionaries to the world. If he had indulged in deliberate oblique solicitation he would soon have reaped the bitter fruits of hypocrisy. When the Christian public forgot China and the Great Commission they also forgot Hudson Taylor and the CIM; and when he inspired them again, or new hearers, both China and missions benefited through more lives dedicated to serve in them, and more prayer and funds to make it possible.

Even in the earliest stages (described in Chapter 1) this inseparability of spiritual concern and practical response is demonstrated. As the years passed, his principles and how they were applied impressed and attracted so many Christians that the CIM grew far beyond Hudson Taylor's early dreams, expanding deeply into 'inland' China and bringing more and more of the Christian world under their influence. That theme is to be continued in the final books.

Concentration upon Hudson Taylor and the CIM would present too restricted a view of the great missionary movements taking place in East Asia. So before we return to the narrative, a sketchy prologue follows as a necessary backdrop to the drama and to remind readers of the contents of the first three volumes.

The spelling of Chinese names varies so much in the sources as to defy attempts at uniformity. In this fourth volume I have resorted more to the *pinyin* system, except for Peking, Canton and the treaties of Nanking and Tientsin – as they are spelt in most encyclopaedias. But in quotations, intelligible spelling has been left unchanged apart from dialect variations in some. The *pinyin* then seems the sanest way out. Otherwise, who would take Wu-tsiu to be Huzhou, or Nyin-tsiu to be Yanzhou?

Lastly, the temptation to depart from a chronological record of events, to discuss at any length the burning issues they raise, has again been resisted. To readers who look for comment on recent criticism of Western aggression in China, or of the Taiping rebellion as a 'people's movement' against imperialism, I offer my apologies. In the last volume I expect to lace the history and romance with some assessment and opinion. For the present I stand fast to my aim of presenting the contents of the Hudson Taylor archives in the perspective of contemporary events and personalities.

AJB

ACKNOWLEDGMENTS

Most of the substance of this book is from the Hudson Taylor archives, but Stock's *History of the Church Missionary Society* and Latourette's *History of Christian Missions in China* again supply indispensable background information. I am grateful to the CMS and the Bible Society in particular for help received from their archivists, and to the librarian of the National Maritime Museum and the master of the *Cutty Sark* who made my visits most worthwhile. The source Notes and Bibliography name those authors and publishers from whom I have drawn facts and brief quotations. I am also indebted once again for invaluable criticism and advice by Jane Lenon, Leslie Lyall, Pauline McIldowie, Howard Peskett, Dr Harold Rowdon and Dr and Mrs James H Taylor. Bishop Stephen Neill's encouragement has spurred me on, although his own writing has precluded his reading this manuscript. As usual it has been for me to harmonise the variety of viewpoints and opinions, from 'Tedious! Delete?' to 'Valuable insight! Retain!' Responsibility for the result is mine, but full credit is due to my tolerant friends for delivering me from unseen pitfalls. Val Connolly's artwork is always greatly appreciated, and the mountains of typescript in my 'den' again stand as monuments to the skilful industry of Mollie Robertson and my patient wife. Thanks too to Professor C F D Moule for his magnanimity, and to Rob Warner and Hodder & Stoughton for their continuing belief in the value of this series.

KEY TO ABBREVIATIONS

ABMU	= American Baptist Missionary Union
American Board (ABCFM)	= American Board of Commissioners for Foreign Missions
APM	= American Presbyterian Mission
Bible Societies	= American Bible Society, B&FBS, National Bible Society of Scotland
Bible Society (B & FBS)	= British and Foreign Bible Society
BMMF	= Bible and Medical Missionary Fellowship
BMS	= Baptist Missionary Society
Bridge Street	= Wugyiaodeo premises in Ningbo
CES	= Chinese Evangelization Society
CIM	= China Inland Mission
CMS	= Church Missionary Society
FES	= Foreign Evangelist Society
Gleaner, The	= *The Chinese Missionary Gleaner* of the CES
HTCOC	= Hudson Taylor & China's Open Century
JHT	= James Hudson Taylor
LCM	= London City Mission
LMS	= London Missionary Society
MRCS	= Member of the Royal College of Surgeons
New Lane	= Xin Kai Long, Hangzhou
OMFA	= Overseas Missionary Fellowship Archives
P & O	= Peninsular and Oriental Steam Navigation Company
P & P	= Principles and Practice
Paris Mission	= Société des Missions Étrangères de Paris
RBMU	= Regions Beyond Missionary Union
RTS	= Religious Tract Society
SA	= Salvation Army

SPCK   = Society for Promoting Christian
                              Knowledge
SPG (USPG)   = Society for the Propagation of the Gospel
The Mission   = China Inland Mission
UMFC   = United Methodist Free Church
WMMS   = Wesleyan Methodist Missionary Society
YMCA   = Young Men's Christian Association

GLOSSARY OF CHINESE TERMS

Aimei   = 'beloved sister'
baojia   = government by graded responsibility,
                              each to the next
daotai   = Intendent of Circuit over 2 or 3
                              prefectures
dibao   = local constable, police sergeant
fengshui   = 'wind and water', harmony of nature
                              governing decisions
fu   = happiness; a prefecture
futai   = provincial governor
fu, zhou   = prefectures and cities
hong, hang   = merchant house, warehouse
Hua Yuan   = Academy of Arts
laoban   = 'old plank', foreman, boss
Nianfei   = rebels in north China
Panthay   = Muslim rebels in Yunnan
pugai   = Chinese duvet, bed quilt
sanban   = 'three planks'; skiff with oars or scull
Taiping   = rebellion led by Hong Xiuquan
yamen   = official residence of any mandarin
xian   = county town, district magistrate
Zongli Yamen   = Chinese Foreign Office

Book Four: Survivors' Pact

CONTENTS

PART 2   THE *LAMMERMUIR* PARTY   1866

MAPS

ILLUSTRATIONS

PART 1

THE PACT: A TEAM AGREED

1865–66

MILLIONS ON THE MOVE
1860–70

Phoenix from the ashes

In early Chinese mythology the *feng huang*, closest in our thinking to the phoenix, was a powerful, giant bird with eagle-beak and talons, symbolic of the strong-omened South, of heat and fire. As if immune to the fires of war and disaster, the phoenix of the Qing (Ch'ing) dynasty rose again – and under the strong hand of Ci Xi, the young Empress Dowager, the empire of the Manchus slowly regained its prestige.

The forty years after the sacking of the Summer Palace and the surrender of Peking have (incredibly) been called 'a quiet period', in the sense that to foreign advantage-seekers they were relatively uneventful. Only twenty major international incidents occurred.[1] For China they continued to hold devastating rebellions, vast famines, more humiliations at the hands of the Western and then Japanese powers, and the loss of millions of lives.

By the Treaty of Nanking (1842) the five ports of Canton, Xiamen (Amoy), Fuzhou, Ningbo and Shanghai had been opened to foreign trade, and the island of Hong Kong had been ceded to Britain. After 1860, by the Treaty of Tientsin (1858) and the Peking Convention (1860), nine more ports were declared open.[2] Foreign shipping at last had access far and wide. Beyond the ports, the 'interior' of the country was legally open to travel and residence, with the right of navigation on the Yangzi. A customs tariff was agreed, and opium trading was legalised. By the 1860 treaty 'Kowloon' on the mainland opposite Hong Kong was also ceded to Britain; diplomatic representatives were to be admitted to Peking and formally took up residence on March 25, 1861, though still without access to the emperor; the offensive term *yi* (barbarian) was no longer to be used to designate Westerners; and the propagation of the Christian gospel was to be allowed. Lord Elgin had fulfilled Lord Clarendon's directives.

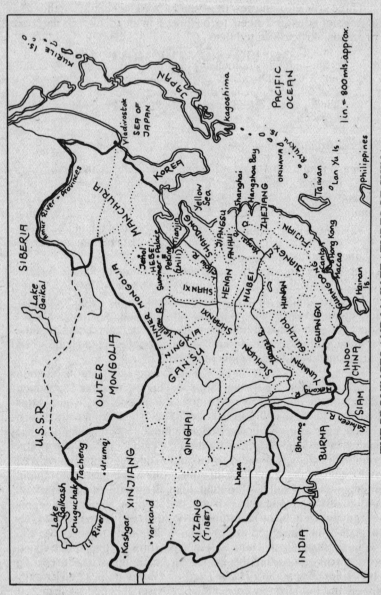

THE PROVINCES AND MAIN FEATURES OF CHINA

Three articles of the new treaty had a marked bearing on the work of missionaries and need to be borne in mind as this narrative proceeds. Article 8 stated that,

> Persons teaching or professing the Christian religion (Protestant or Roman Catholic) shall alike be entitled to the protection of the Chinese authorities; nor shall any such, peaceably pursuing their calling, and not offending against the laws, be persecuted or interfered with.

Article 9 went on,

> British subjects are hereby authorised to travel, for their pleasure or purposes of trade, to all parts of the interior, under passports which will be issued by their Consuls, and countersigned by the local authorities . . . and no opposition shall be offered to (the bearer) hiring persons or vessels for the carriage of his baggage or merchandise.

Article 12 went further,

> British subjects, whether at the ports or at other places, desiring to build or open houses, warehouses, churches, hospitals or burial-grounds, shall make their agreement for the land or buildings they require, at the rates prevailing among the people, equitably, and without exaction on either side.

The American treaty was comparable, but through the devious action of the Abbé Delamarre, the Chinese version of the French treaty included the annulment of edicts of persecution and confiscation of Roman Catholic property. Too late the Chinese found that claims based on this clause would lead to endless trouble. Properties which had changed hands many times would be claimed back from innocent owners, damaging litigation would sour relations, temples erected on sites confiscated long, long ago would be destroyed and indignation would lead to extreme violence.

Phoenix or not, the ignominious flight of the imperial court at the approach of the Allied forces in 1860 had discredited the Manchu dynasty and a stigma clung to it for fully thirty years. On the court's return to Peking after the emperor's death and the failure of the Jehol plot (Book 3, *If I Had a Thousand Lives*, p 260), the Empress Ci Xi and her strongly conservative advisers blamed the Emperor

Xian Feng's brother, Prince Kong, for his realistic surrender and the treaties he had negotiated with such dignity and skill. Although the Empress was time and again to show how misguided and unscrupulous she was at heart, she had a few wise and able ministers. Prince Kong was one. They ensured that her administration in the child emperor Tong Zhi's name was largely successful. Prince Kong established an enlightened offshoot of the Grand Council known as the Zongli (Tsungli) Yamen, in effect a Foreign Office to maintain good relations with the conquering powers. The period of recovery following the second opium war (1858–60) and the end of the Taiping rebellion (1850–64), became known as the Tong Zhi (T'ung Chih) Restoration. In spite of the obscurants, the Zongli Yamen worked towards some modernisation, and the heroes of the victory over the Taipings, Zeng Guofan and Li Hongzhang, promoted westernisations such as the building of the Nanjing arsenal and of shipyards and, belatedly, the development of coal-mining, railways and telegraphy.

'Foreign mud'

It was a sad day for China when the English newspapers began to carry headlines such as 'TEA, SILK, COTTON, AND OPIUM RETURNS' blazoned across their papers. Dr J G Kerr in Canton was to write,

> With regard to the extent of opium-*smoking*, there are no data from which to make a reliable statement. It is, indeed, a matter of no consequence to have the accurate statistics on this point. It is sufficient to know that in addition to native production [the growing tragedy], $58,200,000 worth of opium is annually imported, all of which is consumed, partly by smokers, and partly as a poison for self-destruction. Hundreds and perhaps thousands of lives are lost annually in this province by suicide, and many of them merely because the poison is so easily obtained. Perhaps for all China 10,000 deaths annually would not be too high an estimate.[3]

The opium traffic was booming, but 'The Society for Suppressing Opium Smuggling', with its object 'the suppression of the Opium Monopoly in India, and of the contraband traffic in the drug in China', had to change its name and stated aims. They could still with good reason quote Mr Marjoribanks, one-time President of the Select Committee at Canton, on their official notices,

The misery and demoralization occasioned by the use of opium are almost beyond belief. Any man who has witnessed its frightful ravages and demoralizing effects in China, must feel deeply on this subject.

The Earl of Shaftesbury was its president, the Hon A Kinnaird and Sir E N Buxton, Bart, among its vice-presidents, and on its committee four stalwarts of the Church Missionary Society (CMS) including Henry Venn and Joseph Ridgeway, who unfailingly voiced their indignation through the Society's periodicals. The London Missionary Society (LMS) was represented by Dr Arthur Tidman, the Wesleyans by William Arthur, the Baptists by Frederick Trestrail, the British and Foreign Bible Society by S B Bergne, all influential people of the day with whom Hudson Taylor had dealings. Other members were Captain Fishbourne RN of the East Asian fleet, known for his heroic rescue of massacre victims at Amoy, and John Eliot Howard, the manufacturing chemist soon to become a Fellow of the Royal Society. Legalisation of the infamous traffic only strengthened the determination of its opponents, who now adopted the new name, 'The Society for the Suppression of the Opium Trade'! 'Trade' or 'traffic', it was only a matter of dress.

What had begun as emigration from China of fortune-seekers and manual labourers to the plantations and gold fields of California and Australia, and turned into a kidnapping and slave-trading scandal known as the 'coolie traffic', at last became the subject of an Anglo-French agreement with China, on March 5, 1866. Although the 'convention' was not ratified, the worst abuses were controlled.

Of lasting benefit to China was the customs inspectorate, called the Imperial Maritime Customs. Horatio N Lay, HBM Consul in Fuzhou and Canton, became Inspector-General on January 21, 1861, but when serving as a volunteer against marauders at Shanghai was severely wounded, leaving Robert Hart and G H Fitz-Roy (*sic*) in temporary charge.[4] A year later, however, the bizarre affair of the Lay–Osborne fleet began. Rightly advising that a customs service must have its fleet of vessels for inspection and law enforcement, Lay was instructed on March 14, 1861, to equip such a fleet of steamships and to man them with Englishmen. Without proper credentials or undertakings from the Peking government he proceeded to Britain and, convincing some gullible authorities out of their depths in such exotic waters, succeeded in buying the naval

ships he thought necessary and enlisting the services of a Captain
Sherard Osborne and crews to take them out to China.

On the arrival of the fleet on the China coast in September 1863
the whole project was repudiated! Li Hongzhang attempted to
divert the crews to the ships he was equipping semi-surreptitiously
on the Yangzi, and Lay became the laughing stock of Chinese and
foreigners alike. He was dismissed, and on November 15, 1863, to
the discomfiture of other foreign powers looking for positions of
advantage, Robert Hart, at twenty-eight, was appointed Inspector-
General in his place. Maria Dyer's disappointed suitor thus
embarked upon the life work in which he quickly became a world-
famous figure, the 'great I-G', trusted servant of emperors,
Empress Dowager and the princes for forty-four years, 'a Mandarin
many times honoured' for his unblemished record, but abused by
the British merchants for his incorruptibility and efficiency.[5] Robert
Hart's promotions had followed quickly one upon another. Within a
few weeks of Maria's marriage to Hudson Taylor in Ningbo on
January 20, 1858, Hart had been sent to Canton as secretary to the
Allied Commission governing the city, under Harry Parkes. In
October he was attached to Sir Rutherford Alcock at the Canton
consulate, and in May 1859 became an assistant in the Imperial
Customs, taking charge a few months later.

Stability regained

After the capture of Peking and the conclusion of the treaties of
1860, the aggressor nations were satisfied for the present. France
took advantage of Delamarre's deceit but no further territorial
gains were sought, except by Russia. By her treaty she had added
possession of the maritime province of Manchuria to the Amur
provinces already conceded to her, half-encircling Chinese Manchuria. There, on the Pacific coast, Russia proceeded to construct
the great naval base of Vladivostok and to threaten Japan.[6] In
1864–65, in China's far western dependency of Turkestan, Russia
occupied more large territories, thus threatening Afghanistan and
Iran. Her aggression coincided with the Muslim uprising of Yakub
Beg (or Bey) in Ili, against Chinese domination. The Taiping
rebellion had bled China too white for Peking to be able to resist it.
Yakub Beg set up his kingdom of Kashgaria, over Kashgar and
Yarkand, for thirteen years. But the Russo-Chinese protocol of
Chuguchak delimited and for a while stabilised the frontier between

these great nations. Other European countries signed treaties with China, Spain in 1864 and Belgium in 1865, and slowly mutual understanding and co-operation between the Empire and the West began to develop.

By tacit agreement the foreign settlements in the treaty ports were governed by their Western occupants, although no transfer of sovereignty from China had taken place. Chinese merchants and refugees who had crowded into the settlements were still taxed by their own government (until 1869), but governed as 'tolerated aliens' by the foreigners. In Shanghai the foreign merchant community recognised the injustice of so many Chinese being disenfranchised. So in 1866 Chinese representation on the municipal council was introduced, only to be disallowed by the foreign diplomats at Peking, as guardians of the Westerners' 'rights'.[7] This state of affairs which persisted until 1929 was not as extraordinary as it appears today, for Disraeli's Parliamentary Reform Act of 1867 only extended the franchise in Britain beyond the middle classes (who had received it in 1832) to include certain householders and lodgers of the labouring class paying appreciable rents or rates.

Into the unhealthy scene of China's unwilling submission to the will of outsiders, came a breath of fresh air in the form of a friendly American envoy, the Methodist Anson Burlingame. His predecessor, the Hon John E Ward, had resigned in despair of understanding and finding patience for dealing with his Chinese counterparts. Anson Burlingame, in contrast, liked and was liked by the Chinese, and brought in a brief period of co-operation which was to influence his own and European governments, not least Lord Clarendon at the Foreign Office in London. Burlingame's untimely death in St Petersburg deflated a bubble which would have brought him grief when it burst. But that story belongs to 1868 and after.

Of more immediate concern to China was the harrowing end in 1864 of the Taiping rebellion. After fourteen years of appalling suffering, with the fall of Nanjing it was largely over. By a generally agreed assessment, twenty million men, women and children had died by the sword, fire, pestilence, starvation or their own hand, as a direct result of the ravages of war.[8] About one third of these were natives of Jiangsu province. At once the millions of displaced survivors sold what possessions they could not take with them and began the great trek back to their forsaken homes. In every well-populated region of China the countryside had previously been covered by smallholdings, hamlets, villages and, surprisingly few miles apart, market towns, county towns (*xian*), prefectures and cities (*fu* and *zhou*), all stoutly walled. Those who travelled through the regions which had been devastated first by rebels, then by imperial armies, often by both repeatedly as hostilities surged back and forth, told of mile upon mile devoid of standing dwellings. Once the corpses were no longer lying where they had fallen, claimants to the land would erect whatever shanties they could, and begin to build from the rubble around them. Deeds, witnesses or proofs of any kind were almost impossible to find, even if courts existed to establish rights of ownership. The unscrupulous laid claim to what they wanted and 'might was right'. The '*baojia*' system of government under the Tong Zhi Restoration took time to establish control (Book 3, p 351). Temples, palaces, the *yamens* of the rulers were in ruins. Much of the ancient glory and beauty of the famous cities (of Hangzhou, Suzhou, Nanjing and many more) had gone for ever. Through the fallen remains, returning refugees struggled in their tens of thousands, weighed down by what they could carry. Anhui, the first province inland from Nanjing, once densely populated with 39 million inhabitants 'though rather smaller than England (with) more than twice England's population', at that time, had been reduced to 9 million.[9] Many had died but millions were on the move, trekking homewards.

Overcrowded Shanghai, where foreign arms had afforded some hope of safety from the rival Taipings and imperial troops, was suddenly half empty. From a population of 500,000 in the Settlement in 1862 and 1½ million outside, it had fallen to 70,000 in the Settlement by 1865 and 20,000 in the suburb of Hongkou. The thronged streets were quiet and property values had never been so low. After a decade of danger and anxiety the foreign residents of the Settlement relaxed. Sports clubs were organised, for those from the right social drawer, to counter the boredom of the foreign merchants' lives.[10] In 1863 there were no more than seventy-four foreign women in Shanghai, and at a ball in 1864 the men outnumbered the women present by ten to one. With peace, suburban homes became possible, women increased in number and the keeping of Asian concubines or mistresses carried a social stigma. The *North China Herald* (1850) found a rival in The *North China Daily News* (1864), and the Hong Kong and Shanghai Banking Corporation opened its doors. The big merchant houses ended their collegiate 'factory' or '*hong*' system, and trade enjoyed increasing momentum. 'As a rule . . . in each port the foreigners were in two

reciprocally suspicious camps,' merchant and missionary.[11] Some
on each side successfully crossed the divide, but while most merchants and consuls (with conspicuous exceptions) 'were severely
critical of the missionary and his work', the missionaries as a whole
thoroughly disapproved of the lives led by the average expatriate,
'beyond the range of the Ten Commandments'. A Union Chapel
was erected on LMS ground. In the Chinese city the temple of the
god of war was restored to its original purpose – as a Catholic
church. At a time of persecution it had been seized and desecrated.

The central Taiping rebellion was over, and its associated southern Triad revolts reduced to impotence, but the Nianfei rebels in the
north-east, the Muslim 'Panthay' rebellion in Yunnan province in
the south-west (1855–73), and the new Muslim rising in the far
north-west (1862–76) remained a serious menace to the dynasty.
Each must be considered for its bearing upon the story of Hudson
Taylor. At this point we need only note their continuing existence in
the mosaic forming the China to which Hudson Taylor was preparing to lead his first team of colleagues. The ranks of the Nianfei were
being swollen by fleeing Taipings, but relief at last from the demands of the Taiping war made a determined campaign against both
Nianfei and Muslims possible.

In spite of these preoccupations, China could neither forget nor
forgive Britain, France, America or Russia for battering their way
to the gates of Peking and forcing the Son of Heaven and his court to
flee in ignominy. The unruly barbarian had flown his flags on the
walls of the capital, ravaged the beautiful Summer Palace and
exacted unreasonable concessions. Reactionary xenophobia was
the natural outcome.

The history of China had for centuries been the history of a
civilisation rather than of a nation or people. So great a country with
so many ethnic components made her not so much a racial as a cultural unity.[12] Her reaction to the crude impact of Western aggression for its own ends, however much outlets for industrial expansion
were needed, was one of revulsion. The limitation of Western
influence to the coast, 'like a modern hem sewn along the edge of an
ancient garment',[13] had been tolerable. The five treaty ports had
been ghettos comparable to the 'Factory' at Canton. But after the
Peking Convention in 1860 that influence began to penetrate far
inland – innocently led to a large extent by missionaries on their
very different, well-meaning enterprises. For China was open, at
least theoretically. How truly open would have to be put to the test.

Griffith John had started work far up the Yangzi in the new treaty port of Hankou. Captain Blakiston and T T Cooper were to make for the Tibetan border in the name of commerce. But it was Hudson Taylor who was to meet with ferocious opposition from the old-style literati who feared innovations, abetted by Zeng Guofan and Li Hongzhang, the very men whose xenophobia was expressed, in contrast, by modernising China in order to strengthen her.

Worlds apart

While China suffered the misfortune of closed minds in the courts of Peking, Japan was changing fast. The British bombardment of Kagoshima in 1863 came as a shock to the Tokugawa shoguns, military dictators unaccustomed to any challenge to their authority, and this new reminder of the power of the Western states encouraged plots against the shoguns, in support of the emperor. Only five years later an alliance of nobles, samurai and merchants succeeded in establishing the sixteen-year-old Meiji emperor under the banner of Shinto and bringing in the new era of Japanese modernisation. Sir Rutherford Alcock was well received as British minister in 1864, and within twelve years Japan was asserting her new vitality by challenging China's hold upon Korea. The 1860s were years of disturbances in Japan with many local outrages against foreigners, some of whom discreetly withdrew.

Farther away, in mid-century America, the United States had been locked in civil war. On Good Friday, April 15, 1865, an assassin shot Abraham Lincoln who had been the 'architect of victory and emancipation' and advocated reconciliation 'with malice toward none'. These were the headlines and comments in the press when Hudson Taylor was approaching his crisis of June 25, and staking so much on his understanding of God. By 1866 the Southern States had abolished slavery. Britain had been intimately involved in the Civil War. A cotton famine came close to ruining the textile industry of Lancashire, and there was anxiety as to whether war with the States could be avoided. America, like China, was nursing her wounds. The wealth of the South had been spent or lost in the war, and the North was drained of energy. Her weakness gave the new thinkers of China courage to contemplate recovery of her sovereignty, and many others to take violent action against foreigners. Supplies to American missions were drastically reduced and their capabilities curtailed. American foreign policy towards

Europe of necessity became conciliatory and relations with Britain improved.

June 1864 had seen Napoleon's great gamble to place Maximillian of Hapsburg on the throne of a Mexican empire, until in 1867 the United States government forced France to withdraw her twenty-five thousand protecting bayonets. After that France's world-wide prestige quickly waned. Italian unity had been achieved under Victor Emmanuel I in 1861. France's weakness was apparent when she had to withdraw her protectorate of the Pope in 1866 to defend her own capital against Prussia, and Garibaldi attacked Rome in 1867 and deprived the papacy of its capital, with the exception of the Vatican buildings. In China she continued to be assertive, however, and overplayed her hand.

Prussia's Otto von Bismarck was saying, 'The great questions of the day will not be decided by speeches and majority votes but by blood and iron.' In 1864 he fought Denmark and took Schleswig-Holstein. In 1866 it was Austria's turn. In July 1870 France was to blunder into war with Prussia and have Paris besieged, the royal château of Saint-Cloud a smoking ruin like the Summer Palace of Peking, and the Tuileries in flames. The price of Napoleon Bonaparte's annexation of half Prussia in 1807 had been paid, by the inculcation of a German national consciousness and pride.

Britain had her own problems, with a period of gloom in public affairs. Queen Victoria, who had grown up 'vivacious and natural', had lost her adored Prince Albert when he died of typhoid on December 14, 1861, and shrank into herself in dark seclusion, while the whole nation mourned. Disraeli drew her out when he became Prime Minister in 1868 (and again in 1874), and encouraged her to use her full influence for the good of the nation, especially by her appointments. Lord Palmerston had been Prime Minister for ten years when he fell dead over an unfinished despatch on October 18, 1865, at the age of eighty-one. His mistakes in China since 1834 had been monumental. Nothing could erase them. Other foreign ministers and premiers had followed his precedents, but he had chosen the path of aggression and poisoned relations for a hundred and fifty years with the ancient, intelligent and potentially immense Chinese market. With Palmerston's death a period of political agitation began and Lord John Russell's government was quickly followed by Lord Derby's, before Disraeli and then Gladstone in 1868. Reversals of policy were to confuse the issue surrounding Hudson Taylor and the Yangzhou riot (1868).

At the third jubilee of the Society for the Propagation of the Gospel (SPG founded 1701) the Prince Consort had said, 'This civilisation rests on Christianity, could only be raised on Christianity, can only be maintained by Christianity.' And referring to the Church, 'I have no fear . . . for her safety and ultimate welfare, so long as she holds fast to what our ancestors gained for us at the Reformation – the Gospel, and the unfettered right of its use.'[14] Christian officials in the Indian Government even appealed to the CMS to send more missionaries, but this was at a time of apathy in the Church, which affected the Oxford Movement as much as the then dominant Evangelicals.

Industrialisation was still accompanied by grinding poverty among the masses of working people. John Stuart Mill's essay *On Liberty* in 1859 was a plea for the rights of minorities, and when within a decade a million labourers received the vote, he urged in 1867 that women paying tax should also be enfranchised.[15] It was also in 1867 that Karl Marx finished his first volume of *Das Kapital*, advocating violence to secure for oppressed manual workers the full rewards of their labour. 1866 saw the first conflict in Ireland with the Fenians, members of an Irish revolutionary organisation founded in the United States to fight for an independent Ireland.[16] And 1868, the year of the Yangzhou riot, witnessed the last public hanging in Britain.

Disraeli's social reforms brought in slum clearance and public sanitation, with sewers replacing cesspits. The great cholera epidemics, worst of all in 1866, led to public health education and a fashionable obsession with hygiene. Following Pasteur, Robert Koch discovered the bacillus of tuberculosis, and a stride toward the control of this lethal disease was made, but not before its ravages tragically reduced the ranks of the China Inland Mission. Joseph Lister introduced antisepsis in 1865, and 'some sort of training was given' in the nursing schools begun in this decade, including the London Hospital where Florence Nightingale was a life governor, Mrs Gladstone was a regular ward visitor, even during the cholera epidemic, and the nurses petitioned to be allowed one week's holiday each year.[17] This too was when Tom Barnardo started as a medical student at 'The London' while living with the Hudson Taylors.

In many ways China and Britain were similar, and travellers from one country to the other did not have to adapt as much as might be imagined. In 1840 there were less than five thousand miles of railway track in the world, two thirds of it in America and the rest in Europe, but by the end of the century it had increased to a total world-wide, of one million miles.[18] Yet because of a strong belief in *fengshui* (*see* p 381 and Appendix 8) the first railroad in China was not laid until 1876, to be torn up within a few months. The bridging of the Atlantic by telegraphic cable posed major problems between 1858, the first attempt, and 1865, but at last Lord Kelvin's success revolutionised communication over long distances, in time for Faraday, the pioneer of electricity, to see this achievement before he died in 1867. Telegraphy did not reach Hong Kong until 1870, but was extended soon afterwards to Shanghai, towards the end of Hudson Taylor's second period in China.

China's millions and Christian apathy

China's vast territory and population had so impressed Marco Polo on his return to Venice that he could not stop singing her praises. He prejudiced the effect of his own accounts by so much hyperbole that he became known as 'il Milione' and 'messer Milione'.[19] The site of his house in Venice to this day is called Corte de Milione. But he was more right than wrong. The thronging streets and market places, the busy roads and waterways, the riversides packed even thirty-deep with junks, wherever he went, all told unmistakably of a teeming population.

It was this impression that weighed upon Hudson Taylor's spirit after he returned home and as he prepared magazine articles on China for William Garrett Lewis (Book 3, p 409). It was not multitudes in the mass or population statistics that impressed him. It was 'multitudes, multitudes in the valley of decision' (*Joel* 3.14); individuals, every one a person for whom Christ had died, but ignorant of the fact and condemned by his own sinfulness. Christ had provided for this, telling his people to go out into all the world and publicise what he had done, so Hudson Taylor's concern lay in their failure to obey, to China's great loss. Christians had responded in a small way to 'China's need and claims', but very inadequately. In Britain the Church seemed unable to stir herself to act realistically. The Empire and commerce drew a flood of enthusiastic young men, and women, to remote continents, while the Churches' best was only a handful here and a handful there.

The reason was not far to seek. Spiritual vitality was at a low ebb in the Church as a whole. The Evangelical Awakening, as it came to be called, infused new life into Christians and added to their numbers tens of thousands of newly converted people. Most of these entered the denominational churches and new groupings like the Brethren, but were not taught to look beyond their own small world to the non-Christian world beyond. Many local churches resisted the revival movement, debarring its preachers, and gave no encouragement to their own denominational missions. The movement itself directed attention to Britain's heathen, not those abroad. Henry Venn protested in 1865 that only one in four or five Anglican clergy permitted the CMS to make appeals to their congregations. The SPG and SPCK fared no better. So, even if new missionaries had been forthcoming, funds were scarce. Interest in missions was low, concern for the non-Christian world appeared to be lacking.

Twenty-three years after China was opened by the Treaty of Nanking (1842), fewer than one hundred Protestant missionaries were at work in China. Five years after ratification of the Treaty of Tientsin (1858) by the Peking Convention (1860), declaring freedom to travel and reside in the interior with the right to believe, worship and teach without molestation, Henry Venn told the Islington clerical meeting that while 'the extent and influence of evangelical truth in the Church had very largely increased', missionary zeal had distinctly 'retrograded', as seen in 'a failing treasury and a scanty supply of candidates'.[20] Another reason was the preoccupation of evangelical clergymen with the growing controversy over 'Rationalism, Ritualism and Radicalism', three threats against which Biblical truth had to be defended.

Henry Venn himself was ageing rapidly and giving weak leadership.[21] By 1861 there were only seven CMS men in China[22] and when the newly knighted Sir Harry Parkes urged the CMS to expand its work in China, W H Collins was moved from Shanghai to join John Burdon in Peking, leaving the Anglican work in Shanghai under the supervision of the American Episcopal Church. But the American Civil War soon crippled the Episcopal Mission so that they asked the CMS to take over their work.[23] When the Loochoo Naval (Medical) Mission had to close down, and asked the CMS to adopt this stepping-stone to Japan, it had to be disappointed. On October 11, 1850, Venn had written in his private journal that King Frederick William of Prussia had sent a sixteen-page letter urging his ambassador in London, Baron Bunsen, 'to arouse the Bishops and clergy of the Church of England to vigorous action for the evangelisation of China'.[24] But the policy of recruiting ordinands had met with scant success. Fifteen years had passed and the same truth held. The need was recognised, but apparently could not be met.

The London Missionary Society (LMS) suffered similarly, protesting in 1866 that the mission was not receiving the support owed to it by the Churches. The CMS, LMS and Wesleyan Methodist Missionary Society (WMMS) enlisted artisan types for appropriate work overseas, but for church-planting they wanted ordained men with more education. Charles Simeon and John Venn had proposed the use of lay missionaries to serve as catechists, in the early days of the CMS, but could not carry the policy against the opinion of their colleagues.[25] By 1865 laymen were being accepted, only to be directed in many instances to study for ordination, even in the case of medical men. W H Collins was a case in point. The same was true of other denominational societies.

Another strong reason for the inertia of the Churches was explained by Hudson Taylor in 1886, looking back beyond his Mission's infancy – no more nor less than the tendency of Christians to equate 'human facilities for preaching the Gospel (with) God's providences' – waiting until human intervention made it safe to proceed. Such reasonable caution had paralysing effects.

> When I began twenty years ago [in fact it was thirty] to urge inland work, I was met by this, 'We must not go before God's providence' – in other words, 'We must not go until we have gunboats and passports and treaties'. It was so difficult to get people to realise that it was our duty to go forward, notwithstanding there were no treaties – nay, rejoicing in the fact that the power of Christ would have to be the more manifested.

He was harking back to 1856, before the Treaty of Tientsin when most missionaries stayed within the five treaty ports, and to 1866 when the new treaties were still not being put to the test to any degree. Assurances on paper of freedom to travel, reside and preach in the interior were empty until shown to be valid in practice.

How end the inertia?

Five long years had passed since those treaties had been ratified. Someone had to act on them. How it was done is the subject of this book and those to follow. In 1865 when word had got about that the China *Inland* Mission had been inaugurated, fear of the outcome led well-meaning advisers to urge extreme caution, and critics to condemn the venture. Wait until the treaties are seen to be effective! Hudson Taylor begged to differ. Caution (call it 'prudence' or 'wisdom' if you will) could be evidence of maturity, but faith, courage, daring, could be no less so. To take new colleagues inland could be eccentric, foolhardy or culpable – or might demonstrate the fact that China was truly open to messengers of the gospel, paving the way for many more to follow. The Roman Church had lost no time. Many recently arrived priests were in Peking, W A P Martin reported, and many inland. The Protestant Church must shake itself out of its torpor. The treaty ports were self-inflicted restraints, confining them as Canton had caged the merchants. To expand from the first five treaty ports to the nine new ones fell far short of accepting the freedom to travel and reside anywhere in the Empire. But the societies 'felt unable to spread their activities much further than they were doing'.[26]

To those who had eyes to see and ears to hear, of whom there were several in the records, the moment for which Robert Morrison had looked, James Legge had been persuaded to wait, and everyone had been hoping and praying, had come – and now was in danger of not being recognised, or of being recognised and allowed to pass unexploited. W A P Martin had made one attempt to reach Nanjing and in the mid-fifties had written to his directors, 'My heart is set on going to some place in the interior where the Gospel has not yet been preached.' But he had found his increasingly valuable niche in the capital. In China opposition to Christianity down the centuries had been due to its incompatibility with ancestor worship, with the practices of guilds and festivals connected with community life, and to the transference of loyalty from priests and temples and idols, when devotees were converted. Christian 'intolerance', seen in unwillingness to compromise, and dogmatism in its message, were unpalatable. Contempt for everything foreign, because it was alien, prejudiced Chinese against the foreign religion.[27]

All these barriers had now been shaken to their foundations. Foreign power was impressive. Temples, priests and idols had been impotent in the face of the iconoclastic Taipings and irreverent imperial troops. Not only families and communities but the whole social structure of the war-torn provinces had been disrupted. Tombs had been desecrated and destroyed. Sons had disappeared and no one remained to venerate the ancestors. The hearts of tens of thousands, millions of Chinese, were open to whatever comfort and hope could be offered to them. Many had been protected, fed and housed by Christians, when driven to destitution. Faith in their old creeds being so shaken, they were receptive to new ideas. Although confused by the Taipings' false claims to Christianity, and by the schism between the Catholics and Protestants, they were prepared to listen. Large crowds thronged around any preacher, and colporteurs had no lack of customers for their tracts and Scriptures. If ever the nation was to be evangelised it was after the rebellion ended and before the old ways were revived. But the Church was asleep.

Hudson Taylor had seen much of this situation before he was. invalided home. Following the news of events while he recovered, and studying his large map of China, his vision had broadened from concern for Ningbo and the coastal provinces to a devouring passion to hasten the evangelisation of the whole empire.

> While (in China) the pressure of claims immediately around me were so great that I could not think much of the still greater needs of regions farther inland; and . . . could do nothing for them. But . . . in England, while daily viewing the whole country on the large map upon the wall of my study, I was so near to the vast region of inland China . . . I saw that the Apostolic plan was not to raise ways and means, but to go and do the work . . .[28]

Of all the societies he had consulted, the Baptist Missionary Society (BMS) had shown the strongest signs of striking while the iron was hot, but the old enemy, lack of funds, had quenched the initiative. Greater determination must be shown by the Church as a whole, and greater numbers of missionaries be sent, if a start with any promise of success was to be made. By June 1865 five had gone to Ningbo at Hudson Taylor's instigation, in answer to five years of prayer, and more would be ready to follow in the autumn. For the whole of China many, many more, predominantly Chinese, would be needed.

Hudson Taylor's concept of 'a new agency', channelling a new type of missionary to China, was taking shape. Products of the Evangelical Awakening, drawn from the artisan class of society, and those of a better education (if they were forthcoming without depriving the denominational societies) were the type he had in mind. In the tenth anniversary meeting of the CIM, in 1876, he said,

The problem was – how to attempt wisely an auxiliary effort that
should not in any degree interfere with the operations of those
Missionary Societies whose agents were already in the field, and on
whose labours God had put His seal of approbation. There were
Societies already seeking in vain for additional labourers; where,
then, (1) were new missionaries to come from? There were agencies
in need of increased funds; how could pecuniary supplies be drawn
(2) without diverting contributions from established channels? – a
procedure greatly to be deprecated. Again: were men and means
forthcoming (3) would the interior of China be found open to their
labours? (4) would they have needful protection? and should they
succeed in penetrating the remote provinces of central and western
China, (5) could pecuniary supplies be transmitted to them? . . . It
was concluded that these difficulties might be largely met by forming
a Mission on a catholic basis, for evangelistic purposes; one in which
members of various evangelical churches, sound in the faith on
fundamental points, might work together in spreading the knowledge of the blessed Saviour . . . It was believed, in answer to prayer,
suitable agents would be raised up; and that by adopting the plan of
making no collections, interference with contributions to existing
Societies could be avoided; which, if we only had God-sent workers,
there could be no doubt as to His faithfulness in supplying their
pecuniary needs.[29]

On June 1, 1865, he asked a meeting of friends at Saint Hill, East
Grinstead, to pray for suitable men for each of the unevangelised
provinces. By the 13th he was writing of 'my new project for China'
and the goal of twenty-four Western and twenty-four Chinese
missionaries travelling together two by two, in the manner of
Wesley's preachers and of Charles Gutzlaff's vision of fifteen years
previously (Book 1, p 333). They were to specialise in the dialect of
each province and to demonstrate the practicability of working in
the far interior. If this could be done, 'The Church of God in Europe
and America would be encouraged to more adequate effort.'[30] *To
create the momentum, to get the Church to break out* of its inertia was
a deliberate aim, second only to the prime purpose of his mission,
the evangelisation of China.

After two or three months under considerable pressure, during
which sleep often forsook him, Hudson Taylor was driven to accept
the onus of leading the men and women God sent to him, on 'God's
responsibility, not mine'. The name, China Inland Mission, had
been chosen in discussions with his friend William Berger of Saint
Hill. He opened a bank account in this name, and the Mission was

launched, to preach the gospel of Jesus Christ, to turn Chinese from death to life, and to train them to become stable Christians bearing witness to others of their faith in him.

So far so good. This 33-year-old had staked everything on a project to penetrate the long-impenetrable interior of China. Wife and children, a score of young men and women who trusted him, and his own life and reputation were to be thrown into the teeming expanses of a still hostile empire with its thousands of cities and towns, and its endless succession of villages, to offer the people an alien religion – with no visible means of support. His doubly 'mad venture' could end in disaster before they set foot in China or at any time after landing there.

From the day of his decision to obey what he believed was God's assignment to him, and his prayer 'Thou, Lord, shalt have the responsibility. At Thy bidding, as Thy servant, I go forward, leaving all to Thee', a new dynamism filled him. His certainty, his confidence, the heat of his conviction, the drive behind all his actions revealed it. In photographs taken in the spring of 1865 with the young men he was sending ahead to Ningbo on their own responsibility, he appeared relaxed. After his mission was launched his shoulders are held back more firmly, his stance is stronger, he is the leader of men addressing himself to an expedition into the unknown, realistic about the hazards but confident of success.

But how was a decision of such complexity to be translated into action?

CHAPTER ONE

ACTION
1865

Watchman   *July–August 1865*

High city walls and towering massive gates manned by troops of the Manchu garrison had often confronted Hudson Taylor on his travels in China. Before he put off his strange foreign clothes and dressed as a respectable Chinese, he had known those guards to sound an alarm and the gates to clang shut against him. He had stood with Triad sentries on the ancient walls of the city of Shanghai and watched an attack developing from the imperialist camp. When he read in the Bible Ezekiel's impassioned allegory (ch. 33) and saw what Ezekiel saw, the galloping enemy, the flashing swords, the terrifying rank upon rank of advancing infantry, and the sentry above the gates sounding the alarm, Ezekiel's words lived for Hudson Taylor not as a dream or parable but as a vivid memory. The warning, 'If the watchman sees the sword coming and does not blow the trumpet to warn the people . . . I will hold the watchman accountable', was not for Ezekiel only. In China he had seen appalling wickedness, the work of foreigners as much as of Chinese. But Westerners had all the opportunity they needed to repent. The Chinese outnumbered them incalculably and had almost no one to give them God's message, 'Turn! Turn! from your evil ways! Why will you die?' – no one to sound that trumpet and make them look to their safety.

He had been sent to the Chinese and had regained health to be sent again. His eyes had been opened to the millions out of reach of the gospel, and his mind to the need to act radically if this situation was to be changed. He saw the need for at least two Western and two Chinese missionaries to go to each inland province with the good news of forgiveness and life through Jesus Christ. Under no illusions as to how difficult it would be to attain this first goal, he had burned his bridges by declaring his intentions, and there was no going back. His friends held their breath. Some expressed surprise or disapproval, others shared his and the Bergers' faith, and wrote encouragingly.

Those who held the view of the main societies, that expansion into China should be from secure bases in the treaty ports, saw danger, failure and wasted resources in an impatient attempt to penetrate far from the support of colleagues, the supply of neccesities and protection by the consuls. Never mind that slow penetration had been given sixty years of trial, and more than twenty since the five free ports were opened, with little progress to be seen. If it must be looked at from the angle of treaties, the terms of the new treaties of Tientsin and Peking had declared freedom to go, live and work anywhere within the empire and, far more convincingly, God himself had made it increasingly plain to him that this was a matter of obeying a divine command. 'I have made you a watchman . . . I will hold you accountable' was a reverberating echo of that awareness.

He needed now to crystallise his intentions and plans. Maria, William and Mary Berger, his own parents and he were praying for those '24 willing, skilful laborers' (sic) and the means to send or take them to China. Close friends like the Howards and Miss Stacey of Tottenham, George Müller of Bristol, George Pearse, Frederick Gough and Mary Jones in London, were heart and soul with them. But the time had come to speak out, to share the whole concept with the Church at large, to carry others with him, making this not a thing in a corner but an expression of the new life of the revival movement in Ireland, Scotland, the West Country and London. Five years before, when he and Maria had arrived home from China, praying for five new missionaries for Ningbo, the time had not been fully ripe. The Churches on the whole were apathetic, and he did not wish to poach on others' ground. The Great Awakening was still young. New converts were finding their spiritual feet. James Meadows, Jean Notman, Stephan Barchet and the Crombies, the five he had sent, were maturer Christians. Now, in 1865, products of the new turning to God in Britain were looking for ways to serve him. There was a reservoir of young men and women of the right type, ready to be faced with the fact of China and Christ's command to go into all the world as his witnesses.

It was high time for Hudson Taylor himself to return to China, and he had less than a year for everything that needed to be done, to find, train and outfit his team, and to complete with William Berger a system of co-operation between them when thousands of miles

apart. The autumn and winter were bad times for a voyage to the far
side of the world, with Atlantic gales and Pacific typhoons. Spring or
early summer were best. Instead of arriving in the great heat they
would arrive after it, and get settled in before the winter cold. It was
time to overcome his reluctance to draw the limelight on himself,
and to face the Christian world in Britain with the issues that had
galvanised him to action.

His course was clear. This was a spiritual venture, however
inseparable material matters might be from it. The twenty-four
companions he needed must come in answer to prayer, not persuasion; to the call of God, not recruiting. And yet the message of God
must be proclaimed, not muted. Years of work on the revision of the
New Testament in the Ningbo vernacular had taught him plain
lessons. Prayer and prophecy, prayer and the Word, each had its
place.

> I learned that to obtain successful labourers, not elaborate appeals
> for help, but first, earnest prayer to God to thrust forth laborers (sic),
> and, second, the deepening of the spiritual life of the church, so that
> men should be unable to stay at home, were what was needed.[1]

Because he had not prayed sooner, as he had known he should be
praying, early in June,

> The feeling of blood-guiltiness (had become) more and more intense.
> Simply because I refused to ask for them, the laborers did not come
> forward – did not go out to China – and every day tens of thousands
> were passing away to Christless graves.[2]

So he enlisted the prayers of those whose effective praying he had
come to trust. The ones he always turned to first were his father and
mother, whose prayerfulness he had known intimately since childhood, and after them to Amelia, his sister and confidante, and her
husband, his own boyhood friend Benjamin. The prayers of his firm
friends he could also count upon. They had proved their worth for a
decade and more, and been privy to his deepening convictions.
Apart from them his circle of acquaintances was largely limited to
the ministers and mission leaders he had been working with. He was
little known and had to start from obscurity.

In Ningbo he had seen how effective women missionaries could
be. Maria herself had been so fluent and at ease in Chinese homes
that she was always in demand. Her good friend Mrs Bausum was

the equivalent of at least one good man. Mary Gough and Mary
Jones had both shown their worth. William Burns had emphasised
the value of lay evangelists, a Biblical order, and the need of women
to work among Chinese women whose secluded lives made them
inaccessible to men. Few societies provided scope for women except
as educationalists. The China Inland Mission was to be open from
the outset to women of the right kind. The younger they were, the
sooner they would be fluent in Chinese. For the present, however,
only men would be able to penetrate untried territory.

> It was seen (from the first) that . . . grave difficulties would be
> inevitable. Men of faith, therefore, and of sober mind, as well as of
> earnest piety were sought for . . . and these were found.

Men and women who knew the grace of God in their own
experience, and were prepared to step out on to the sea of the
unknown and to walk in trustful dependence on God, were the kind
needed. They would have to accept Hudson Taylor and Maria as
their leaders, the only ones among them with experience and
knowledge of what they were going to. So a relationship of leaders
and led would mean mutual confidence and commitment. If they
believed God had called them to go with Hudson Taylor and if he
agreed, on the ground of their suitability – their personality, health
and spiritual fitness, so far as these could be assessed – he would
give them the essentials of preliminary training, equip them with a
minimum outfit, and take them with him. The best training would
be given and gained in the face of practical circumstances, on the
voyage and living among the Chinese.

Then *how* were they to be found? How could the Christian world
be aroused and young people know what was happening? And
whom should he approach? How could he avoid intruding upon
denominational territory unless invited to do so? The trans-
denominational Evangelical Awakening had weakened individual
links with the divided Churches by strengthening the attachment of
Christians to each other, whatever their background, and *The
Revival* magazine, voice of the movement, had already carried some
letters on the subject of 'China's Need'. The people who read *The
Revival* were the type he had in mind, those who were zealous for
the spread of Christ's kingdom and looking for a part in it. Beyond
them he saw many Christians who needed only the right information

and stimulus to jolt them out of complacency or mistaken ideas of the facts, to support their own missionary societies.

In the role of 'watchman' it was his duty to do this. And already his work on a 'pamphlet', as any essay intended to influence opinion was called, was well advanced. The significance of it had come vividly home to him. All that had stirred his own soul must be shared, to stir others. It was a manifesto, a public declaration of his motives and intentions, but more, it must be persuasive propaganda to change the readers' lives.

The revival movement had also given rise to meetings and conferences 'for the deepening of spiritual life', the very climate he had seen to be necessary 'so that men should be unable to stay at home', and would be impelled to carry the gospel overseas. He must take his message to such concourses of godly people. Evan Davies, author of the *Memoir of the Rev. Samuel Dyer* (1846), Maria's father, had written another book on *China and her Spiritual Claims*. China's *need* was more prominent in Hudson Taylor's thinking. He must inform people about China so that that need would be obvious to them, and the wide-open possibility of helping. 'We do not need to say much about CIM,' he said. Concern would lead to inquiries. China and China's need were paramount. The Churches were tired of appeals for money; money should be left out of it. A Father God must be trusted to provide for the work he commanded. No solicitation was to be the rule. And no debt, for going into debt implied failure by God to supply enough. Hudson Taylor saw his duty as the watchman's duty, to impress upon his fellow-Christians the urgency and immensity of China's need, and to impel them to act. He would make it known that the type of man and woman usually passed over could, as a missionary, do in China the kind of Christian work he or she was already doing in Britain, and far more. Others who could not go themselves would help in a hundred and one ways at home, especially by praying and providing the funds needed in growing amounts. That would be between God and themselves.

Manifesto   *July–September 1865*

Coborn Street was in one of the newer residential parts of Mile End Old Town. Its well-built three-storeyed Georgian houses were set back about thirty feet from the road with a little garden at the front and another at the back. Number 30 was the Taylors' own home, rented for their personal use, but as always it was 'open house' for all their friends and for all purposes.[3]

Until the pressure on space became too great, all the activities of Maria, her children, a nurse and a cook-housemaid, of Hudson Taylor and Frederick Gough revising the Ningbo New Testament in the study, and of their many callers, were concentrated within its walls. After Stephan Barchet and George Crombie sailed from Plymouth and Anne Skinner followed them a fortnight later, James Vigeon the accountant and his wife, who lived elsewhere, came and went freely, at first for consultation and then for Chinese language lessons. John Stevenson and in July his fiancée Anne Jolly, and George Stott the Scottish schoolmaster, also learning under the Taylors' guidance, made up the household.

Invariably every Saturday the meeting to pray for China was held there and friends from far and near would crowd into the living room. Jennie Faulding, and from July her student friend Emily Blatchley, would be present if they could. Emily had just finished her teacher training at the Home and Colonial School in Gray's Inn Road, to start work under a Madame Halliday after the summer break. Jennie saw that Emily had the abilities the Taylors needed in a personal secretary-cum-governess and suggested her to them. On July 5 the two of them spent the night at Coborn Street, and on the 7th Emily Blatchley wrote from Jennie's home at 340 Euston Road, agreeing to come and help initially for the six weeks of the school holidays. 'Arrangements had better be left open, until you have had a better opportunity of judging whether I am capable of doing what you require' she said. 'The work you offer me, and the home, are far more congenial than school-teaching . . .' When Jennie offered to take her place until a permanent substitute was found, Mme Halliday released Emily and so began a partnership that was to be at the core of the Mission. Grace Ciggie was another with whom Hudson Taylor had been corresponding since meeting her at Glasgow before Barchet and Truelove sailed on the *Corea*.[4] These were the sort of girls he could see making their mark as missionaries in China.

Since April when he had made the acquaintance of the Dowager Lady Radstock and her son the Hon Granville Waldegrave, Lord Radstock, (a year younger than himself but a veteran of the Crimean war and commander of the West Middlesex Rifles which he had raised) they had been meeting more and more frequently. After telling the Welbeck Street congregation on July 2 about China and the preparations for the Stevensons, Vigeons and possibly George Stott to sail soon, he had breakfast at 26 Portland Place with Dowager Lady Radstock the next morning, spoke on China to friends at young Lord and Lady Radstock's home in Bryanston Square on Friday, and dined with his mother at Portland Place on the following Monday. There he talked with a Russian guest about China. He received a donation from them on the Saturday and an invitation to tea the next week, at which he and Lord Radstock addressed a meeting. Afterwards Hudson Taylor went on with the Hon Miss Waldegrave to her 'refuge for boys'. Back then to Lord Radstock's for dinner and tea, and another address on China. Dowager Lady Radstock had asked him during one of his visits to pray with them for her sister who was to undergo an operation, so hazardous in those days. On the Saturday he heard from the young Lady Radstock that all had gone well, and she invited him to dine with them the next Tuesday. So it went on. Speaking at more meetings, dining with the Dowager Lady Radstock's sister when she was well again, declining some invitations and accepting others, his relationship with the family was closer at the time than with any other mentioned in his journals, and was to lead to greater things as the time of his departure drew nearer.[5]

His days were very full and time for research and work on his 'pamphlet' was scarce, but he was reading Rhind's book on China, and came home from the Royal Geographical Society one day armed with 'some valuable information about China'. Sunday afternoons and evenings were often his least disturbed times for writing, with Maria at the table while Hudson paced up and down dictating to her. 'China's Need' and 'The Work of God in China' were his normal subjects when he preached or lectured, as on July 11 at Welbeck Street when he 'spoke on China's need and our duty'; so *China's Spiritual Need and Claims* became his text and title as the book grew.

The theme of his manifesto was: China, that huge empire of such fine people, is 'without hope and without God'. Until the Christian Church takes action on a far greater scale, the present fearful toll of 'a million a month dying without Christ' will continue. Millions upon millions in province upon province, eleven provinces apart from Manchuria and Mongolia, have no one to tell them about Jesus who alone can save them. Our duty is to go, our guilt is that we do not. But something is projected, a team is assembling and soon will sail, to penetrate to every corner of the empire.

His readers needed no reminding of the fate of unbelievers. New thinking on 'universalism' and 'conditional immortality' had made little headway in 1865. When attacks were made on the Bible and the teachings of the Church of England in 1862, high church and low united to declare their common beliefs. Eleven thousand clergymen and a hundred and thirty-seven thousand others gave their signatures to the statement,

> the whole catholic [in the sense of a universal] Church maintains without reserve or qualification the inspiration and divine authority of the whole canonical Scriptures, as not only *containing*, but *being*, the Word of God, and further teaches, in the words of our blessed Lord, that the 'punishment' of the 'cursed', equally with the 'life' of the 'righteous' is 'everlasting'.[6]

The current deviation was, as now, to give 'natural religions' a place alongside the Bible and biblical doctrine, so that Bishop J C Ryle answered it with the apostle Paul's declaration at Athens, the city full of idols. Paul's spirit was stirred 'not with admiration for the beauty of temples and statues, but with compassion for the idolators and zeal for their conversion'. So Paul preached 'Jesus and the resurrection'. None but deviants and unbelievers would wish anything else to be the ground and message of Hudson Taylor's manifesto. The unsaved were lost and only through this gospel could they be saved, by faith in Christ.

His 'pamphlet' plunged straight in by quoting from *Proverbs* the stern warning beginning in the King James version universally used,

> If thou forbear to deliver them that are drawn unto death, and those that are ready to be slain; if thou sayest, Behold, we knew it not; doth not He that pondereth the heart consider it? and He that keepeth *thy* soul doth not He know it? and shall not He render to every man according to his works? (*Proverbs* 24.11,12)

The effect of reading those words, it went on, must be 'effectual, fervent prayer, and strenuous, self-denying effort for the salvation of the benighted Chinese', or the penalty of the warning to the reader. Did Jesus himself not say most emphatically, 'Go – into *all* the world and preach the Gospel to *every creature*'? He taught his people that they were to be the light, not only of the Jews but of *the world*, and put 'Thy will be done' before any personal petitions in their prayers.

Expanding the articles he had been writing for William Garrett Lewis of Westbourne Grove, Hudson Taylor painted word pictures of the wonderful nation of China, 'its great antiquity, its vast extent, its teeming population, its spiritual destitution, and overwhelming need'. A million being an unimaginable amount, he looked for visual aids, to help his readers to see what he himself saw and to understand the gravity of his theme. He wanted to shake the complacent into action. He found the answer in mental pictures of armies of Chinese marching in single file along the stone-flagged country trails. How often he had waited interminably for such a body of men to pass. Over many years this device became familiar, then hackneyed, and lost its power to impress, but within his own lifetime it possessed a persuasive power that moved thousands of Christians to respond, and hundreds to give their lives to serve God in China.

He used the official Chinese census figures, those taken 'for regulating the assessment of a capitation tax throughout the empire, and estimating the amount of rice to be stored as a reserve in case of famine'.[7] The 1812 census, cited in Wells Williams' *Middle Kingdom*, gave 360 million as the population of China proper. That of 1852, found in the official residence of Commissioner Ye when the British shelled and occupied Canton, gave 396 million. By 1858 it was 415 million, probably including Manchuria, but omitting in each census the millions of aboriginal peoples in the mountains. Allowing for millions of deaths from the Taiping war, Hudson Taylor took the round number of 400 million for his purposes. 'Four hundred millions! what mind can grasp it?' Marching in single file one yard apart they would circle the world at its equator more than ten times. Were they to march past the reader, at the rate of thirty miles a day,

> they would move on and on, day after day, week after week, month after month; and more than twenty-three years and a half would elapse before the last individual had passed by . . . Four hundred millions of souls, 'having no hope, and without God in the world' . . . an army whose forces, if placed singly, rather more than four hundred yards apart and within call of each other would extend from the earth to the sun! who, standing hand in hand, might extend over a greater distance than from this globe to the moon! The number is inconceivable – the view is appalling.

And the mortality rate was said to be thirty-three thousand a day, outnumbering the population of London in three months, and of England in eighteen months. What were his readers doing for them? Saying, 'We didn't know'? What did God who weighs men's hearts see their attitudes to be?

He reviewed the heroic efforts of the Nestorian and Roman Churches, and the late arrival, in 1807, of the first Protestant missionary Robert Morrison. By forty years later a mere handful of others had reached China, and the one hundred and fifteen who were there in 1860 had been reduced to ninety-one by 1865. Results of their work were to be seen, but 'much, very much' remained to be done. Giving the census figures of York, Canterbury, Oxford, Cambridge, Durham, Exeter, Lincoln and Ripon, whole dioceses, he showed the combined inhabitants to be as many as one of those missionaries would face in trying to present the gospel to a quarter of a million Chinese.

Then he examined the coastal provinces of China, one by one. The population of Zhili, in which lay Peking and Tianjin, was ten times that of Scotland. Yet Scotland had thousands of Christian ministers, not one too many, and church workers of many kinds, as well as Bibles and books. Who could be complacent? 'Do we really believe that "This is life eternal, that they might know Thee, the only true God, and Jesus Christ whom Thou has sent" – and that "The wicked shall be turned into hell, and all nations that forget God"?'

He told the story of the reformed Buddhist at Ningbo who, after hearing him preach the gospel stood up in the audience and said, 'I have long sought for the truth – as my father did before me – but I have not found it . . . I have found no rest in Confucianism, Buddhism, Taoism; but I do find rest in what I have heard to-night. Henceforth I believe in Jesus.' A few nights later he had asked how long this good news had been known in England. When told 'some hundreds of years' he had looked amazed. '"What!" said he, "is it possible . . . and yet (you) have only now come (to tell us)? My father sought after the truth for more than twenty years, and died without finding it. Why did you not come sooner?" Why indeed . . . ? Now that (China) is fully open, why are we so slow to enter . . . ? While we hang back the multitudes perish.' He blamed no one. Only so recently he himself had baulked at the responsibilities involved in taking action.

Moving on from consideration of the coastal provinces with their handful of missionaries, he examined those in the deep interior of China. France, he said, was four times the size of England, and Spain almost as large. But Gansu, in China's far north-west, was larger than both together, with 'No missionary'. Sichuan province and Yunnan, bordering Burma and reaching almost to Assam, with 30 million Chinese and unnumbered millions of tribal people (about 10 million); Shanxi the size of England and Wales; Shaanxi, larger still; on and on one after the other, adding after each, 'No Protestant missionary', and finally, 'Should not these provinces immediately be occupied?' Eleven provinces, averaging 18 million and totalling 197½ million, without a single bearer of the pure gospel. Add to these the 185 million in the coastal provinces yet out of reach, and more than 380 million were seen to be waiting still for the gospel Christ commanded his Church to take to 'every creature', all creation. 'Is it not *your* duty to carry the gospel to these perishing ones?'

He told the story of 'Man overboard!' – the drowning of his Chinese companion, Peter, and the delay while fishermen stood haggling over the sum he would pay them for bringing him up (Book 2, pp 371ff). Do not condemn them, he told his readers, 'lest a greater than Nathan say, "*THOU* art the man!" . . . "If thou forbear to deliver them . . . He that keepeth *thy* soul, doth He not know it?"' It was powerful pleading, and as he went on to examine the death rate in China, he pointed the moral without mercy.

> Do you *believe* that each unit of these millions has an immortal soul? and that 'there is none other name under heaven whereby they must be saved'? . . . It will not do to say that you have no special call to go to China. With these facts before you, and with the command of the Lord Jesus to *go* . . . you need rather to ascertain whether you have a special call to stay at home.

Filling several pages with geographical facts and figures, followed by the text of Articles 8, 9 and 12 of the Treaty of Tientsin (*see* p 27), he showed the feasibility of travelling throughout China. From his own experience of being manhandled by mobs and obstructed by mandarins, he knew the significance of these legal concessions. They proclaimed not merely toleration of Christianity but official protection. The Church was duty- and honour-bound to move in. 'The rough plough of war' between Taipings and Manchus had left many Chinese homeless and bereft. Their temples destroyed, pagan priests had been forced into secular occupations. Many rich people had become poor. War-weary and heart-sore, the attitudes of millions had changed. 'The missionaries tell us of such willingness to hear the gospel as never was found before.' The Bible had been translated into the literary and vernacular languages, and aids to learning Chinese had been prepared. So while

> there is ample room for those whom God has endowed with special philological talent, there is no reason why men 'full of faith and of the Holy Ghost' who have enjoyed but few educational advantages, should not be engaged (in pioneering the unevangelised regions).

Not only China was involved. 'India is by no means adequately supplied by the 520 or 530 Protestant missionaries . . . among her teeming millions.' And how about the vast regions of Manchuria, Mongolia and Tibet, larger in area than Europe? Could not all the Protestant Churches of America and Europe send 'a single ambassador of Christ to carry the Word of reconciliation, and to pray men in Christ's stead, "Be ye reconciled to God"? How long shall this state of things be allowed to continue?'

> We do not hesitate to ask the great Lord of the harvest to call forth, to *thrust* forth twenty-four European and twenty-four (Chinese) evangelists, to plant the standard of the Cross in the eleven unevangelised provinces of China proper and in Chinese Tartary. To those who have never been called to prove the faithfulness of the covenant-keeping God, in supplying, in answer to prayer alone, the pecuniary need of His servants, it might seem a hazardous experiment to send twenty-four evangelists to a distant heathen land with 'ONLY God to look to'. But to one whose privilege it has been for many years past to put that God to the test . . . at home and abroad, by land and by sea, in sickness and in health, in necessities, in dangers, and at the gates of death – such apprehensions would be wholly inexcusable . . . For more than eight years and a half he has proved the faithfulness of God, in supplying . . . means for his own temporal wants, and for the work he has been engaged in.[8]

He told the story of the Ningbo massacre plot; and about the unexpected arrival of his box of clothing from Shantou (Swatow), just after he had burned everything contaminated by virulent smallpox through nursing his American friend John Quarterman, and had no money to buy more. He quoted at length from his own letter about the early arrival of $214 with which to feed seventy destitute people, when he had less than one dollar left to meet his own needs and those of John Jones and his family, and how ample funds kept coming to enable him to run the Ningbo hospital for several months after Dr William Parker's enforced return home from China. In answer to prayer, James Meadows had gone to Ningbo, and the story of his success as a missionary was the story of 'God's grace'. Without naming Richard Truelove, he told of how he had backed out of his commitment to go, and how George Crombie sailed away instead, when Anne, the bride he was on the point of marrying, said 'Go! and show that you love the cause of God more than me.' To bring that story up to date he quoted from Anne's letter written on the China Sea shortly before she too arrived. All five for whom he and Maria had prayed, had reached Ningbo, and 'the same God . . . . can raise up others to follow them . . . "Willing, skilful men" for every department of service.'

The dangers, privations and difficulties might concern some who contemplated going.

> (They) will be neither few nor small, (but) while leading to a greater realisation of our weakness . . . will also constrain us to lean more constantly . . . on the strength, the riches, the fulness of Jesus. 'In the world ye shall have tribulation, but in Me ye shall have peace,' will be the experience of those engaged in the work. If it be for God's glory, for the benefit of His cause, and for the true interest of those labouring, the times of greatest trial and danger will be the times when His delivering power will shine forth most conspicuously; and if otherwise, His sustaining grace will prove sufficient for the weakest servant in the conflict.

Pure prophecy was what Maria wrote as her husband paced the room and his words flowed. He went on to give the account from his journal of how John Burdon and he were mobbed on Chongming Island and emerged unscathed, little knowing that that experience had been child's play in comparison with what was in store for him and for the women and children he was preparing to take back to China. Nor had he any inkling of the precise way in which his words were to apply in his old age.

> There are other difficulties to which (missionaries) in the interior of China may be exposed . . . Their funds may become exhausted . . . and communication with the free ports may be difficult or impossible. Or they may be robbed of all they possess, and may find themselves

> destitute in the midst of strangers. But they cannot be robbed of His
> presence and aid, whose are the gold and the silver, and the cattle on
> a thousand hills . . . *He* can soften the hardest hearts, and give help
> to His servants, by means through which it was least expected.

And he gave the full story of his own robbery on the way to Ningbo,
and of how complete strangers went surety for him and secured a
place on a fast boat back to Shanghai.[9]

> Let but faithful labourers be found, who will prove faithful to God,
> and there is no reason to fear that God will not prove faithful to them.

Only the plans for the next stage remained to be outlined.

No 30 Coborn Street   *July–September 1865*

The pencilled journals which Hudson Taylor kept, in little penny
notebooks, are a window on the life of that most unusual household
in Coborn Street. Entries skip from item to item just as they
occurred, or as he recalled them late at night or the next morning. A
maximum of *aides-memoire* in a minimum of space gives us far more
detail than can be used, each throwing light on the rest. Apart from
his meetings, lectures and social obligations, of which there were
many besides those with the enthusiastic Radstocks (for Hudson
Taylor supported his friends as well as promoting his own cause), his
correspondence was heavy. On July 17 he told his mother in his
tenth letter of the day, 'Our work is growing. Each week brings new
applications, new responsibilities, new claims. The good Lord
supply all our need, to the glory of His own name.' She had offered
to make two copies of Maria's drafts of the manifesto, as far as he
had reached.

Apart from new developments, the men and women he had sent
out to Ningbo had the first claim on his attention. In the same letter
to his mother he lamented that China news was chequered. Mrs
Fuller, of the United Methodist Free Church, was very ill and not
expected to recover. Jean Notman, on the voyage out, had surprised everyone by transferring from her cabin to a more expensive
one and referring the bill to the Foreign Evangelist Society who had
paid for her ticket. At Ningbo she was adapting slowly to the world
she had entered, and showing more interest in marrying a correspondent in Malaya whom she had never met – and then someone in

Ningbo who began courting her. It was not long before she forsook her calling. James Meadows was a fully fledged and effective missionary, building up a strong congregation. He was courting a friend, Elizabeth Rose, of Barnsley. Stephan Barchet and George Crombie had sailed in the *Corea* in April and news of their safe arrival could not reach home until October or later. On August 11 word came of the loss of the *Corea* and Hudson Taylor hurried off to Lloyds and the P & O Office, to find that it was a P & O ship of the same name, wrecked off Shanghai. Letters had to be sent immediately to Glasgow, to Crombie's father and to Mr Berger. Mr Denny's *Corea* had made a quick voyage and delivered Barchet and Crombie in China by the end of July.

Stephan was showing great promise under E C Lord's guidance, and Thomas D Marshall, minister of Bryanston Hall, the independent church at Portman Square which had sent him out, conferred from time to time with Hudson Taylor about Stephan's financial needs. In August he was living in a village with a Chinese companion. Home was four walls, a roof and two partitions, with a mat for a ceiling, blown down if a strong wind sprang up. As for rats, 'I mind them no more than the ticking of my watch.' His bed was a mat, with his mosquito net suspended on two bamboos. In the central 'room' between the partitions were a table stacked with books and a table for meals and studying Chinese. Unable to preach, Stephan was the curiosity whom people came to see, and the evangelist would then preach to them.

George Crombie was learning the language in Ningbo, unable to be much help in James Meadows' work, and Anne Skinner was still at sea, not arriving at Ningbo until September. Hudson Taylor left supervision of local affairs to E C Lord and Meadows but, although under no formal obligation to any of them, he felt bound to do all he could to send funds at regular intervals, when he had them in hand. Even when the pressure of demands on his time and thought were heavy, he included entries in his journal of remittances despatched.

From time to time he lectured or preached at Bryanston Hall, dining or staying the night with Marshall or one of the deacons, and so struck up a lasting friendship with two of them: William Hall, a manufacturer of footwear, and John Challice, a businessman of Dover Street, Piccadilly, later to become honorary treasurer of the China Inland Mission. But Hudson Taylor was as often at the chapels and churches of other friends: J M Denniston's Presbyterian Church in south Hackney; Mr Kennedy's Congregational chapel in

Stepney where he paid a pew rent for his household; frequently at Brook Street, Tottenham, with the Howards and Miss Stacey, and sometimes at the Brethren chapel in Hackney village. He co-operated with Henry Lance of Berger Hall in Empson Street, Bromley-by-Bow, the chapel W T Berger had built for the employees at his starch works, or St George's Mission in Tower Hamlets. Occasionally he spoke for the CMS at St Andrew's Parish Church or Mission Hall, or met with the Association of East End Evangelists who used the Freemasons' hall. At other times he travelled farther afield to Mildmay, Islington, where William Pennefather was now vicar of St Jude's, after nine years at Christ Church, Barnet, or to Regent's Park Chapel, where the Fauldings and Emily Blatchley were members and William Landels drew evening congregations of eighteen hundred.

Charles Haddon Spurgeon, two years younger than Hudson Taylor, had already become established as a superlative preacher with a gift of oratory to enhance his Biblical expositions. At a cost of thirty thousand pounds, a great deal at the time, his congregation had built the magnificent Metropolitan Tabernacle (1859) at the Elephant and Castle, to hold the five thousand who flocked to hear him. It was characteristic of him to say at a Bible Society anniversary when the Bible was under attack in the sixties, 'Defend the Bible! How would you defend a lion? Open the cage and *let him out*!'[10] When Hudson Taylor spoke at Spurgeon's prayer meeting, Spurgeon invited him to return and address a meeting on China. So began many years of friendship between them. Landels and Spurgeon, under George Müller's influence, increasingly shared Hudson Taylor's views, especially with regard to monetary matters. When the BMS was in debt, Spurgeon urged more faith and more direct involvement of the churches, more trusting in God and teaching of the congregations on their spiritual responsibility.

Closest of all was the friendship deepening between the Taylors and Bergers. At his fine house, Saint Hill, near East Grinstead, with its many acres of land which William Berger farmed through a manager, and its lake and rolling lawns, they had worked out how to run their little mission once Hudson Taylor and Maria had sailed away to China. Mr Berger would represent him in Britain, helped by Mary Berger ('all love and gentleness' but competent too) and Mr Aveline his personal secretary, an ex-missionary. Meanwhile the starch factory was near enough for Mr Berger to look in at Coborn Street or for Hudson Taylor to go round to discuss matters

SAINT HILL, EAST GRINSTEAD, 1865

of business. He could consult the factory manager, Mr Mears, about packing cases, and William Berger could interview applicants to join the CIM. They were agreed that small beginnings were best and, in Berger's simile, to let the Mission grow like a tree, a sapling adding slowly to its size and reach if conditions allowed.

So on July 3 after Hudson Taylor returned from breakfast at Portland Place, they were consulting about plans and principles. Mr Berger came in for afternoon tea and stayed till seven in the evening. Before leaving he promised a hundred and fifty pounds for the Mission and eighty or a hundred pounds for a printing press and type for use in China. It arrived on the 25th, press, inking table and rollers, and with the help of *Every Man His Own Printer* they learned to use it. On the 14th they agreed that all Mission receipts should pass through the bank. It had already been decided that the Taylors should receive no money from Mission funds for their personal use. On the 17th Hudson Taylor was proposing an *Occasional Paper* to inform friends of progress, and on the 25th he sent part of his 'pamphlet' for the Bergers to criticise. A few days later he and Maria took John Stevenson and Annie, George Stott and the Vigeons to Saint Hill to be 'commended' to God for service in

China. By then only a few weeks remained before they must sail.

On June 27 he had tried to see Henry Venn, but finding he was in committee had gone on to the Bible Society, where he discussed with S B Bergne the difficulty of completing the revision of the Ningbo New Testament. Back at home again he dropped Bergne a line saying, 'We *could* finish it in six, four, or even three months, according as we include or otherwise the Epistle to the Hebrews and the Pastoral Epistles, in the portion we thoroughly study and correct.' The old problem of co-ordinating work with the unpunctual, unpredictable Frederick Gough continued, and Hudson Taylor's sighs can be heard between the lines of his journal: 'Wednesday, 28th. Mr Gough busy with Mr Russell all day. Thursday, 29th. Morning doing various little things waiting for Mr. G. till long after 11 a.m. (from 9.00 a.m.).' He himself had the Foreign Evangelist Society (FES) committee meeting to attend in the afternoon and a lecture to give at Portman Square in the evening. Most of Friday and Saturday was spent revising, but on Monday 'Mr Gough did not come for work morning or afternoon.' So their New Testament revision dragged. By mid-August they had completed all stages of *Colossians*, but were having to despatch unrevised New Testaments to Ningbo. In his *History of the CMS*, Eugene Stock threw light on this difficulty, though in connection with the work F F Gough was to do a few years later. 'Gough was a thorough scholar, and became a perfect master of classical Chinese, exasperating the Bible Society, says Bishop Moule, by his minute and elaborate corrections from the Delegates' Version.'[11] Personal relations between Gough and Hudson Taylor continued as warm as ever.

Most time-consuming but perhaps most rewarding, as the fulfilment of his prime purpose, were the correspondence and interviews with candidates, and the training of those whom Hudson Taylor believed to be called by God and fit to go to China. Not all were proposing to go with him. In August when Hudson Taylor was preaching at the Wesleyan Chapel in Bow, Lieutenant Dodds, of Captain Roderick Dew's little naval force which had driven the Taiping thousands out of Ningbo and the surrounding area, introduced himself and they spent the afternoon together.

John Stevenson was proving all they had hoped of him. Tall, broad-shouldered and straight-backed, his personality was in keeping with his bearing. A quiet, reserved Scotsman of twenty, he 'believed in work and unwasted days'. Between his arrival in London in October 1864 and his sailing for China in October 1865, besides working as Henry Lance's assistant pastor and transcribing the whole of the romanised dictionary of the Ningbo dialect, and the whole manuscript of Hudson Taylor's book, *China: Its Spiritual Need and Claims* for the printer, he worked so hard at the language with Maria's coaching, that before he sailed he could read and understand the romanised New Testament. His fiancée Anne Jolly arrived at Coborn Street on July 12. In August Hudson Taylor took them to Bristol for four days to be approved and advised by George Müller, who intended, he said, to contribute toward their expenses as he was able from the missionary fund of his Scriptural Knowledge Institution.

James Vigeon was in trouble, but on July 3 he was 'fixed in purpose'. He needed to be, for he had a wife and three children. Her parents were objecting to their going to China, and Vigeon himself was articled to a firm of accountants who had not yet released him. An upstanding, able man like Stevenson, he was the kind Hudson Taylor wanted to deal with the business affairs of the Mission, a task for which the artisan types whom he also welcomed would be less fitted. When Hudson Taylor and George Stott arrived back from Bristol, Vigeon came round to Coborn Street, 'told us his difficulties' and asked Hudson Taylor to intercede with his employers. They refused. 'He was greatly distressed.' Still James Vigeon would not give up. He went on getting their outfit together and joining the household at Number 30 when he could.[12]

George Stott had his own problems throughout the same period. He had had a 'white swelling', tuberculosis of the knee joint, for which amputation had been performed, and while incapacitated for nine months 'had responded to the love of Christ'. Then he had taken up teaching for a livelihood, but reading about China had said, 'I do not see those with two legs going, so I must.' He had written to Hudson Taylor on June 15 of leaving his work as a schoolmaster and coming to London without delay. And Hudson Taylor, recognising 'a marked answer to prayer', had sent him his expenses. On July 7 came his announcement that he had proposed to his landlady's daughter, Agnes Lamont. Stott arrived in London on July 21, only to fall ill with dysentery, but on his recovery was included in all the preparations for sailing in September.

In the midst of Stevenson's and Vigeon's difficulties Hudson Taylor was painstakingly arranging for Stott to be fitted with an artificial limb. On the way to the Royal Geographical Society he called on Jonathan Hutchinson, the London Hospital surgeon, for

Augt 1865.

Monday 21st. Went to Bristol with Mr. Stott. Stevenson, Annie & Mrs. T. following. Mrs H. Groves took tea with us, & took us to Bethesda. After the meeting was opened by Mr. Müller, I spoke of our past & present walk & of China's need. After the meeting, a brother gave me £2.0.0

Tuesday 22nd. Went to see the suspension bridge. Thence to the Orphan House No. 3, where we had an hour with Mr. Müller. He spoke most preciously on the call & the spirit of the Missionary; on the consecutive reading of the Scriptures; on prayer & faith in God; on obstacles & thorn-hedges. Then we went over No. 2 & took tea with the teachers there, & I conducted service with the Orphans. We returned with Mr. Harne, & spent the evening there. Mr. H. gave Stevenson & Stott Angus' Bible Hand-book each.

advice, and from there went on to Dowager Lady Radstock for
lunch, and so back to the weekly prayer meeting. On Monday he
was off to a Mr Biggs about Stott's leg, then to Portland Place,
looking without success for the umbrella he had left somewhere.
Miss Waldegrave gave him one pound toward 'Stott's leg or outfit'.
After that to Baker's in High Holborn inquiring about artificial legs,
and so back home again, very weary. On Saturday he went again
and placed an order for 'Mr Stott's legs', for which Mr Berger said
he wished to pay, and on the following Wednesday to the City to get
a pair of 'trowsers' made to go with them. Together they went on the
25th to have the leg fitted – yet another incident in days full of far
weightier matters, for this was the day when James Vigeon learned
that his firm would not release him. For his part Stott deputised for
Hudson Taylor by preaching at Bryanston Hall, and was at once
enlisted to preach twice on the coming Sunday and again a week
later. But the climax of Hudson Taylor's difficulties was reached
when he went to Scotland the next day.

Grace Ciggie was a unique Glasgow girl of twenty. When both her
parents had died, her grandmother had cared for her, and when her
grandmother died a friend had become a mother to her. Slight in
figure, she was strong in character and independent in spirit. At
sixteen through gratitude to Jesus for having 'bought' her she had
proceeded to point many other people to him. When Hudson
Taylor was in Glasgow seeing Barchet and Truelove off on the
Corea, she had heard him speak about 'China's need' and say 'Why
do *you* not go and tell them of a Saviour's love?' That had touched a
chord in her own heart. She had never heard of women going out as
missionaries, but she asked Hudson Taylor, Could a girl go? and he
could see no reason why not. He was impressed by her openness.

Mrs Faulding's objections to Jennie going to China were reced-
ing, and not only she but two aunts, her son and her other daughter
Ellen, always called 'Nellie', occasionally visited Coborn Street.
Cheerful and outgoing, an enthusiast about the cause she had taken
up, Jennie was its tireless ambassador. She was being taught
Chinese by Maria and sometimes Hudson Taylor and began
teaching Emily Blatchley what she herself had learned. Having
known him since she was nine, and loving Maria from the first,
Jennie's relationship with them was more that of a young sister than
a friend. Mary Bausum, now fourteen, was another whom Maria
made one of the family. Before long Mrs Faulding agreed to
Jennie's going, on condition it was with them.

The incessant round of daily events against the background of revising the Ningbo New Testament and writing *China: Its Spiritual Need and Claims*, also included keeping the cash and ledger account, acknowledging donations and disbursing money for all that was needed. 'Got to our accounts with Maria,' is a typical journal entry. Family life and social events had to be fitted in, as when their old friend and brother-in-law John Burdon introduced his new wife at a reception for the Taylors, Frederick Gough, Mary Jones and other Ningbo friends. News of the death of old Benjamin Hudson, his grandfather, reached Hudson Taylor on July 24, but neither he nor Maria could get to the funeral. The children were a problem as the house filled up, but the hospitable Howards had Grace to stay with them sometimes 'at their House Beautiful', and so did Miss Stacey, always a faithful friend.[13]

Doctoring and teaching medical essentials had dropped out of Hudson Taylor's journal entries, apart from an occasional reference, such as the purchase of another Gray's *Anatomy* for three shillings and sixpence. But on the day Hudson Taylor was about to start for Scotland, his infant Samuel sat on 'a pin which broke off deep in the nates' and was lost to sight. A quick decision had to be made. 'After prayer decided to cut it out [without anaesthesia]. The Lord enabled me to reach it by the first incision' although it was deeply buried and only three quarters of an inch long. He left by the night train for Aberdeen.

'Modus operandi'   *September 1865*

Two urgent matters were taking Hudson Taylor to Scotland. It was the end of August and George Stott was due to sail with Stevenson in September or early October. He had hoped to marry before then, as John Stevenson and Annie were doing. But Mr Lamont had put his foot down. His daughter was not marrying a missionary! George could do nothing. Perhaps Hudson Taylor could help. In *The Revival* magazine, notice had been given of a conference 'for the deepening of spiritual life' to be held at Perth from Tuesday, September 5 to Friday, September 8.[14] This was too good an opportunity to be missed. If Hudson Taylor could get a hearing by the conveners, he might be allowed even a few minutes to plead before hundreds or thousands the burning message of China's spiritual need, her claims upon them, and the fact that something far-reaching was being done about it.

He had clear plans, all worked out with William Berger by slow degrees, and agreed with the missionaries about to sail the germ of a 'Principles and Practice' of the composition, aims and financial policy of the new mission. And he knew precisely what he had in mind for making up the team and launching them into the interior of China. Any at the conference, young or old, who asked for information could be given it. Ministers and church members who could not go to China would be made alive to what was happening, and young men and women could judge for themselves and decide on what action to take if God told them to leave all and go. He believed that his prayer for pioneers was being answered, and that eastern Scotland, home of spiritual revival, would supply more. He had not thought of attending the conference sufficiently early to approach the organisers in advance, but George Stott's predicament settled the matter. With the help of Mr Berger and one or two others with Scottish connections, he was carrying letters of introduction, and looked forward to meeting several of William Burns' friends. Personal interviews with the conveners might succeed where a request in writing could be declined without further thought.

The broad principles of the China Inland Mission were easily outlined. In nature it was to be as simple and free from regulations as possible. As long as its members were of one heart and mind in the essentials of the faith, any differences of interpretation and church government were to be accorded the secondary place they deserved. The great revival that had 'swept across denominational lines'[15] made this a natural relationship. Hudson Taylor spoke of it as 'inter-denominational', but only in the sense of harmony and co-operation at a personal level.[16] In China missionaries of the same persuasion were to work together and build up congregations according to their own conviction. Already those who had gone to China and others preparing to go were drawn from most of the major Churches, and living and working together harmoniously. They were also from a variety of social backgrounds. In *China: Its Spiritual Need and Claims* Hudson Taylor was writing,

> There is ample scope for the highest talent . . . for men filled with love to God, whose superior education would enable them to occupy spheres of influence into which others could not enter, (yet) the proposed field is so extensive, and the need of labourers of every class so great, that 'the eye cannot say to the hand, I have no need of thee' . . . therefore persons of moderate ability and limited attainments

are not precluded . . . There was need of and work for a Paul, an
Apollos, a Luke, as well as those who were manifestly 'unlearned and
ignorant', but of whom men 'took knowledge that they had been with
Jesus'.[17]

Existing missionary societies looked predominantly for educated
men, and Hudson Taylor's innovation was to throw the doors wide
open to others *also*. For this reason he prepared to make the fact
widely known, while no less looking for men and women from the
professions and universities. In K S Latourette's words, 'While
persons of education were preferred, those were also welcomed
who were without much learning but who were otherwise
qualified.'[18] Their most important qualification, whatever their
origins, must be spiritual, 'men who believe that there is a God, and
that He is both intelligent and faithful, and *who therefore trust Him*';
and whose love for Christ made them love people and exert
themselves to bring them to him. Women would find different ways
of working among the women of China, but would have no less
valuable roles than men.[19]

The aims of the Mission were indicated by its name. The geographical goal was the whole of the Chinese empire, and the purpose
to preach the everlasting gospel far and wide, to as many as possible,
so that all might hear it, rather than to win converts. The CIM
would sow the seed hoping also to reap a harvest. Believers would
be gathered into local churches and taught as disciples to spread the
gospel to their own people in multiplying numbers. But if others did
the reaping, the CIM would be as glad. Common in the thinking and
writing of many missionaries over the years had been the transformation of all China by a 'Christianising' process, involving
cultural changes. The literati were the chief objects of such missionaries' efforts, along intellectual paths. Hudson Taylor saw the same
and greater spiritual results arising from direct preaching of the gospel, while Christianising could leave men's hearts unregenerate.
Valuing the work of the others, and sometimes contributing to it, he
and the CIM were called to share with William Muirhead and
Griffith John of the LMS, John Burdon of the CMS, and John
Nevius the Presbyterian, as evangelists and church-planters.

The cardinal policy of trusting in God as a Father unable to forget
or neglect his children, meant that the Mission would look to him
and not appeal to churches or church members for its necessities. So
no collections would be taken by the CIM or at meetings organised

by the CIM, and no appeals for funds would be authorised. At the same time, Christian stewardship as a Biblical principle should be taught and encouraged, as with all other teachings of Scripture. On the same principle, congregations should send and support their own missionaries. It was enough for the Mission to inform the Christian world about China and what was being done to meet her spiritual needs. How God moved his people to respond could be left to him.

> The rights and interests of donors were considered as well as those of future workers. That it would in future be impossible to convene the donors for conference, rendered necessary the determination of certain questions of mission polity, and these were publicly announced before contributions to any extent were received or workers invited.[20]

Not knowing from where funds might be coming, or how much, meant that no salary could be promised. Income would be shared; that was as far as it was possible to go. And, no less fundamentally, no debts would be incurred.

> It is really just as easy for God to give *beforehand* . . . And what does going into debt really mean? It means that God has not supplied your need. You trusted Him, but He has not supplied your need. You trusted Him, but He has not given you the money; so you supply yourself, and borrow. That would be to put the blame on God when the fault had lain in your running ahead of His will.[21]

As for the administration of this Mission, both Hudson Taylor and Mr Berger had seen the Chinese Evangelization Society falter and fail through control from a distance by members of a committee who had no knowledge of conditions in China. Neither wished to repeat that mistake. Hudson Taylor had reached the conviction while still in China that leadership at the site of action was essential. The unpredictable circumstances demanded a flexibility and finality in decision-taking that made committee rule inadvisable and often impossible, even if the members were within reach of each other in China itself. For several years he and Maria would be the only ones in a position of experience to assess the situation and give a positive lead. It was imperative that anyone deciding to join them in this venture should, before leaving Britain, accept him as their leader and director. This 'was determined from the very outset'.[22] Mr

Berger should have sole charge at home 'looking prayerfully to God for guidance, to act without unnecessary delay in every matter as it arose', while similar responsibility was to rest on Hudson Taylor in China. Members of the Mission would go on their own initiative, advised and led by him as his colleagues.

Long discussions over the past few months had led to these decisions and, on August 5 in particular, to an agreed '*modus operandi*'[23] so 'the operations of the mission were from the first both systematic and methodical'. Continuing to use Ningbo as the base for extension into the interior, although few of them would actually live there, they would proceed in two stages. From their arrival in China they would all adopt Chinese clothing, as a courtesy to the people of China and as the most expedient measure. Until the new arrivals could speak some Chinese, had some knowledge of Chinese customs and viewpoints, and had adapted to the climate and unfamiliar diet, they would stay together and work with the Taylors or, later, with James Meadows. Then they would travel with Chinese Christians to towns and cities in the same province of Zhejiang or neighbouring Jiangsu, and attempt to rent premises and live quietly where no foreigners had lived before. Gradually, as their experience grew, they would move out, deeper and deeper into China's inhabited expanses, however distant, until all the eleven unevangelised provinces had resident teams.

Just as the apostle Paul went to the great strategic centres of the Roman empire, while not neglecting smaller towns en route, so they would try to get a footing in provincial capitals and prefectures, even though they tended to be difficult places in which to establish churches. From these centres they would deploy and expand their work to smaller cities, towns and villages.[24] They hoped within a decade or so to be able to locate two missionaries with two or more Chinese colleagues in each of the unevangelised provinces. This leap forward would be necessary because of the dialect differences making specialisation essential. Whenever a congregation of believers came together, they should as soon as practicable have a Chinese pastor of their own, and worship 'in edifices of a thoroughly Chinese style of architecture'. No quasi-Gothic imitations of foreign church buildings should be erected, let alone steeples and towers such as already marked Christianity as alien in Shanghai, Ningbo, and other ports, and offended against the Chinese sense of propriety by overshadowing the mandarins' *yamens*.

These principles had been agreed, and discussed at length with

Stevenson and Stott, so soon to sail away. At the Perth conference, however, it was not the structure or even the aims of the China Inland Mission which Hudson Taylor wished to announce. He wanted to make an awareness of China and her spiritual need become part of the deepening spiritual life of those present. An awareness that bred concern would lead to prayer and the offer of more lives to serve the Lord either in or for China.

Scotland[25]   *August–September 1865*

The nine fifteen night train from King's Cross to Edinburgh on August 28 was full. Travelling third class, as usual, Hudson Taylor shared a hard seat with two others. It was only possible to sit upright, and when they reached Edinburgh at nine a m he had had little sleep. He found a buffet, had some breakfast and a wash, and set out to call on five strangers to whom he had introductions.

Again that evening his train to Aberdeen left at nine fifteen p m and arrived at three forty-five a m on Wednesday 30th, but this time he had been able to stretch out and sleep. He sat in the station guards' room until five a m and then wandered on the sands and through the city until seven. After another hour over 'some coffee and a bun' he took the eight o'clock train to Whitehouse, twenty-five miles out in the Grampians, and presented himself at Bridge of Bent, the home of the Rev John Milne, an old friend of William Burns and one of the conveners of the conference, to whom he had been recommended. His warm reception at a second breakfast of oatcakes and an egg augured well for his prospects. But his attempt to intercede for George Stott with Agnes Lamont's father failed completely.

> In the afternoon I called on Mr Jas Lamont and found him in the harvest field. He said he had not time to spare for conversation; was annoyed at my coming to see him on such a subject, but that his mind was fully and finally made up. That if I were not a stranger, he could give his reasons; but that, (I) being a perfect stranger, he did not intend to do so. After leaving him, I walked to the top of one of the highest hills and returned somewhat composed in spirit and well wearied in body.

Agnes could marry the schoolmaster, but not a fanatic heading for China!

Saturday came, September 2, and he returned to Aberdeen, made the Forsythe Hotel his base, and called on the parents of Dr Gauld of Shantou (Swatow). They insisted that he fetch his bags and stay with them. His appointment with George Crombie's parents was difficult to keep. By the six a m train on Monday he went to Ellon, twenty miles to the north of Aberdeen and 'prayed God to help me and make my way plain'. At Ellon a gentleman was boarding the train, and his coachman, 'a pleasant Christian', took Hudson Taylor half the way to Slains, his destination. Crombie's parents and brothers received him warmly and, to everyone's great joy, soon after his arrival a letter from George Stott was delivered, announcing the safe arrival of the *Corea* and George Crombie at Hong Kong, in the remarkable time of a few hours less than three months. 'They borrowed a gig and horse and Mr C drove me to Ellon,' for the train back to Aberdeen.

There 'a young man, George Duncan . . . spoke to me about going to China' and 'a long interview' led to his asking a fortnight later to join the China Inland Mission. A letter from Vigeon had arrived to tell Hudson Taylor that the shipping agents, Killick and Martin, had found a ship for the Stevensons and George Stott – to sail on the 25th! So instructions about the passage money and what kind of accommodation to secure had to be written in the Ellon to Aberdeen train – a cabin for the newly wed Stevensons, and a berth somewhere for Stott. The wedding could now be safely arranged for the 12th, but outfitting would have to be hurried on. With so many uncertainties the Vigeons would have to admit that they could not sail on this ship.

Feeling lonely and helpless Hudson Taylor set off from Aberdeen on Tuesday, September 5 to attend the Perth conference and try to get a hearing. The scheduled speakers were all notable men, Brownlow North, Andrew Bonar (another friend of William Burns) and Stevenson Arthur Blackwood of the Treasury among them. It was unlikely that a young missionary would be found time to speak, even if considered suitable.

Again he travelled by the six a m train, 'looking to the Lord to open up my way and use me for China's good and God's glory'. Writing to Maria 'between Forfar and Perth' he said, 'I have much reason to hope that I have got one labourer for China, if not more; a very nice, earnest and intelligent man.' The impossibility of getting on with his New Testament revision until the Stevensons' ship sailed was worrying him. Could Maria perhaps arrange a sewing party of

Hackney and Bromley ladies to finish off the outfits? She and
Amelia were making the wedding dress and trousseau. Then,

> it is not pleasant to me to go to strange places and push myself
> forward, but the Lord helps me . . . Through God's goodness I have
> got some letters of introduction to Perth. May the Lord help and
> guide me, and use me there. My hope is in Him. I do not desire to
> please myself, but to lay myself open for Christ's sake. I much need to
> add to faith *Courage*; may God give it to me.

He left his carpet-bags at the station and went straight to the
conference in the City Hall. It was the third year it had been held
and its timetable was stereotyped. After the morning session he
handed his letters of introduction to his Aberdeen friend John
Milne, who passed them on to the chairman, Hay Macdowell Grant
of Arndilly. The request for a chance to speak about China shocked
this godly gentleman. 'But, my dear sir, it is quite out of the
question! You surely misunderstand. These meetings are for
edification,' he protested.[26] Embarrassed by what he was doing,
Hudson Taylor saw that it was now or never. He pleaded that the
claims of Christ upon every Christian to be a disciple taking the
gospel to 'every creature' lay at the very heart of holiness and
consecration. Here was a conference of two thousand Christians. In
the time spent in one session, as many Chinese would die without
even hearing of Jesus. Who would tell this to the congregation if he
himself could not? He presented his case so urgently and succinctly
that the chairman seemed moved; they agreed to consult together,
and talked with him about William Burns. When later they gave him
their reply it was Yes, he could have twenty minutes the next
morning to speak on China, and at this evening's meeting to lead in
prayer.[27]

He enjoyed the conference sessions after that, and when the
evening came, 'in answer to prayer, God enabled me to pray' – 'for
Duff town and surrounding valleys and for a fresh revival to
Dundee', the conference report said. Dowager Lady Radstock had
been struck by this young man's way of praying, as if he were at
ease, speaking to his Father. After the meeting, General Sir Alexander Lindsey invited him to go and stay with him, 'but (I) could not
get there till too late'. Instead the conveners asked him to be the
guest of the conference, and a young minister took him home.

He was up at four a m on Wednesday to pray, for his address was going to surprise everyone and a great deal hung upon it. After breakfast they 'had a Scripture reading', which in Hudson Taylor's vocabulary meant that he read and expounded passages on world mission to his friend and another guest from Argyllshire. Then they went to the City Hall. In his journal Hudson Taylor wrote, 'The Lord answered prayer and gave me a word to the consciences of the people. Mr A Bonar spoke . . . on the necessity of working.' But although he had addressed audiences as large as this before, Hudson Taylor felt unusually nervous.

Andrew Bonar finished his sermon, R C Morgan, editor of *The Revival* prayed, and Hudson Taylor was announced. He went forward and stood in silence, finding it hard to begin. Then he too said, 'Let us pray,' and for five minutes poured out his heart to God. After that he had no difficulty. He took up Bonar's theme – 'Work out the faith that is in you; freely you have received, as freely give it out.' Giving the essence of his 'pamphlet' he started with the story of Peter's drowning and the apathy of the boatmen who bargained before trying to save him, 'stating the claims of (China) with its countless millions in heathen darkness'. 'A deep impression was produced,' *The Revival* reported in a resumé over the initials of a special correspondent, 'JM' (John Milne?). As he ended Hudson Taylor said, 'We want lay men to come out to China, to teach Christ, and to live Christ before the people. Some four months of study will prepare anyone to be a labourer there.'

George Duncan who was probably present, James Williamson of Arbroath who certainly was, and William Rudland of Cambridgeshire who read the verbatim account in *The Revival*, were three direct products of that address who went to China with the Taylors a few months later. Many in the meeting came to inquire further and promised to pray for China. One was William Mackintosh 'of Egypt' who with John Fraser had started the movement which gave rise to the Foreign Evangelist Society and indirectly to the CIM (Book 3, p 393). Decades later people still referred to the occasion.

That evening, Wednesday, September 6, General Lindsey captured Hudson Taylor at last, took him home to dinner and kept him as his guest until he left Perth on Saturday. So many had questions to put to Hudson Taylor on the 7th that he quickly arranged for a special meeting on China the following day, after the close of the conference, and supported by John Milne had it announced in the afternoon and evening sessions. As a result the big St Leonard's

Free Church was 'well filled' when he took all the time he wanted to describe his companionship with William Burns in Black Town (Wuzhen) (Book 2, p 326) and to enlarge on China's need of the gospel.

From the Lindseys he made his way to Glasgow. Grace Ciggie came to breakfast the next day and agreed to travel with him to meet William Berger in London, insisting that she had the money to pay her own fares. Two days passed in visits to Professor Islay Burns, William Burns' brother, and then to their mother and sister and others, before meeting Grace Ciggie and her brother at the night train. It was noon on the 13th when they reached Coborn Street and he could tell 'poor Stott' about his visit to Agnes Lamont's father – a bitter blow, for the whole of the next day was given up to the Stevensons' wedding.

Apart from the men and women who became pioneers of the China Inland Mission as a result of these two weeks in Scotland, Hudson Taylor had made new friends who were to be faithful to him through the years ahead. William Scott was one of the staunchest, after they first became acquainted at Perth. A manufacturer at Dunedin, his name recurs in the accounts with gifts of twenty or fifty pounds at a time. A Christian merchant from Shanghai, Thomas Weir, heard him in Glasgow, either on this occasion or the previous one when seeing Barchet and Truelove off, and was impressed that 'he spoke very quietly, every word was carefully chosen and told. He spoke with deep feeling of the great need' of China, giving details of what the various missionary societies were doing at each port, including Hankou, and going on to show how much remained to be done in the interior, beyond consular protection and medical aid. Among those influenced with Weir were John R Caldwell, a silk merchant, and Thomas McLaren, who also kept in close touch with the CIM for many years. Weir wrote, 'The quiet unostentatious start, and dependence on God for everything, commended it to me and to the brethren.' There was no rhetoric, romanticism or fund raising to tarnish the spiritual impact.

London and Norfolk[28] *September 1865*

Hudson Taylor was back to the increasing tempo of ceaseless activity: the business matters that had been waiting for his return, doing his accounts, chasing Mr Berger from the starch works to the station to introduce a candidate to him; getting a group photograph taken on the 15th with the Vigeons, Mary Jones, Grace Ciggie, Jennie Faulding and Emily Blatchley all in it; and paying Killick and Martin the deposit on passages by the *Antipodes* for the Stevensons, Stott and Kying-hae, Mary Jones' adopted boy, due to sail on the 25th. Unaccompanied by any but the captain and crew, they were emulating Hudson Taylor on the *Dumfries*, and John Stevenson, at twenty-one, was the same age. The cabins on sailing ships were still entirely unfurnished. Furniture, bedding and hand-basins had to be bought and taken aboard. Even the supply of water was limited. George Stott was still feeling shaken by the news about Agnes, and uncertain whether to go, but soon became resigned to it.

After a quiet Sunday Hudson Taylor worked hard all through the next week, seeing about the travellers' outfits and stores and carting them down to the ship, writing to accept Lady Beauchamp's invitation to visit Norfolk for a week, celebrating his sister Amelia's birthday, and dealing with George Duncan's application from Aberdeen to join the CIM. A gift arrived, of '£25 from Mr Berger for my own use. This came in just as I was asking the Lord for funds which are urgently needed. Thank God.' Another of twenty pounds received in Glasgow he had allocated to the Mission. On Saturday 23rd, most of the remaining baggage was taken to the ship and a farewell meeting at No 30 was crowded to the doors.

Sunday was busy with a communion service for the travellers and letters to write to Mr Burns and others, so that his journal entry ended with 'Forgot to go to Twig Folly in afternoon' – a mission hall where he was often the speaker. All of Monday and Monday night until six thirty a m were then spent on completing the outfits, as he himself had to travel to Norwich on Tuesday.

Jennie Faulding was in the thick of the preparations. When the time came to go home to Marylebone on Monday evening, Hudson Taylor escorted her to the station. He had something to say. From his reading about Burma and the 'mass movement' of Karens embracing Christianity, he had formed a plan and written to consult William Burns in Peking – asking for more information and comment, and inviting Burns to co-operate. British India, governing southern Burma since 1826, had opened trading relations with King Mindon of Upper Burma in 1862, at Mandalay, and had shown that river steamers could get as far upstream as Bhamo, less than fifty miles from China's Yunnan province. The agreement included trade with China, for half the population of Bhamo was Chinese and caravans of traders constantly came and went across the border. Farther south there was the possibility of entering China from the Shan states. And close to the border was the Karen Christian Church already numbering thousands. Yunnan was a thousand miles from any Protestant church in China, a thousand miles of dangerous travel through the mountains, among hostile people. To reach Bhamo through Burma, on the other hand, although nine hundred miles from the sea, involved an easy journey by river boat. His innovative, pioneering spirit felt the lure of potential success. He wanted Jennie to know what was brewing.

During their visit to Bristol in August, Hudson Taylor had discussed with John Stevenson the idea of their going together, with one other missionary, to explore the possibilities in Burma. By the time the next party of men and women arrived in China, Stevenson would be more at home in the language, and once the newcomers were safely settled at their Zhejiang base under Maria's supervision, with James Meadows and other missions near at hand, Hudson Taylor could accompany John Stevenson to Burma. Together they would survey the situation. If its promise was confirmed, John and his companion would stay and prepare to enter Yunnan from the west, while Hudson Taylor returned to Zhejiang and began the penetration of inland China from the east.[29]

Jennie's maturity made her a valuable friend. As for her mother, the more she saw of the Taylors the more willing she became for Jennie to go with them in the spring or early summer. Seeing the Burma project from the woman's point of view (and with scant regard for punctuation) Jennie opened her heart to Maria.

> 340 Euston Road
> 27 September '65, Wednesday

My *precious* Sister,

Dear Mr Taylor was telling me on Monday as we walked to the station of his having written to Mr Burns about the Burmah project and of your grief at the thought of separation and I felt so sad for you, all the afternoon and evening I felt oppressed because I could realize something of what your trial would be, to part from such a treasure would be to you no small sacrifice.

This morning as I was working and feeling full of joy to think that Jesus was going to count me worthy to follow Him fully, that He was going to let me have all my time to use in His direct service . . . as my heart was glowing with love, my thoughts turned to you and I almost envied you in the power to make such a sacrifice for the Master. He calls you to be a heroine, to lay on His altar your most precious treasure and if He lets you give up so much what blessings must there not be in store for you . . . oh I feel sure that those who give up most for Jesus are the happiest, the most blessed, oh is not any sacrifice that will honour Jesus and that He will accept worth making? No, it isn't too much to give up for Jesus is it?

Dear one . . . you both have helped me so much to get nearer to Jesus that it would be a great joy to me to be able to comfort you . . . with warmest love I am in Him your sister.
                                    Jennie.

Meanwhile Hudson Taylor worked right through Monday night, snatched a little sleep and hurried away to Liverpool Street station. On the train, travelling second class to preserve his best suit, he wrote to Maria, posting his letter in Norwich. His apologies, please, to Stevenson and Stott for not managing a last farewell, not only because in haste, but as

> I hardly felt equal to saying goodbye after so fatiguing a night. I should have lost my train, too, if I had delayed . . . Don't forget the looking-glasses, calico for cabin, socks, shirts, drawers, things for Mrs Knowlton, letter scales . . . money for Stott, letter weigher for Crombie. If they like to take three more chairs let them have them. Tell Annie about the enema and the use of the lemon kali [potassium citrate. On and on he went] . . . Give them a word from me, 'Be kindly affectioned one to another in brotherly love; in honor preferring one another.' Give them all three much love from me . . . may all our party in China be kept right in heart and head – [words of greater consequence than he knew].

From Norwich he went out to Buckenham, a few miles to the east on another line, to advise a Mrs Haslam 'about Li-li' [a Chinese girl?]. 'Then Sir Thos Beauchamp came in and took me home with him to Langley Park, where I was most kindly received by Lady Beauchamp, D Lady Beauchamp and Miss Waldegrave.'

His old friend of Shanghai days, the surgeon William Lockhart, was in Norwich, speaking at meetings of the Bible Society the next day. After two years in Peking as surgeon to the British legation, and a brief stay in Japan, he had left in 1864 and was serving the LMS in Britain for three years. In Peking he had set up a hospital, as he had done in Hong Kong, Zhoushan (Chusan) and Shanghai, and his brother-in-law Sir Harry Parkes wrote in 1864, 'Your hospital I look upon as the most marked incident in our relations with China

. . . since the signing of the last treaty.'[30] The Beauchamps took Hudson Taylor to hear him in the morning, speaking on conditions in both countries. He shared the platform in the evening, telling about Ningbo and his work on the New Testament, and stayed the night with a Norwich minister who helped him in the morning to seek out James Meadows' family. Back at Langley Park he addressed the villagers, and on Friday afternoon a large drawing-room meeting for the Beauchamps' 'wealthy neighbours' with 'upwards of 50 ladies and gentlemen and clergy' present.

A letter had come from Maria. The departure of the *Antipodes* had been postponed until Monday, October 2, so now he could hope to see his friends again before they sailed. It would not be right to come home before Monday, 'for there seems to be work to be done for the Lord and for China'. He would reach Stratford at three twenty-eight. Could Sarah, the housemaid, or Collyer, a 'cabby', meet him there 'and bring me my second best frock-coat, for fear this [best one] should be spoiled with tar'. Whoever came could take it and his carpet-bags home with them, while he went on directly to Gravesend for the final 'goodbye to our friends'. 'The candles are in a separate box marked "cabin". The other goods are stored in tin box, and soap in wooden case' . . . fifty-six pounds for each, including J Meadows. He had written to Mrs Pennefather for tickets for the Mildmay Conference in October. As for Langley Park itself, appropriately for a baronet, 'the Hall is not quite so large as Stainboro' Hall near Barnsley, but is of that class. The Park is very large and beautiful.'

On Sunday morning he 'spent some time with the (Beauchamp) children' before addressing 'Lady B's class of boys'. He had taken his Chinese clothes, bowl and chopsticks and other curios, and dressed up as a Chinese to demonstrate their customs. One of the Beauchamp sons, Sir Montagu, recalled the occasion long after Hudson Taylor's death. He also recalled that his father had already distributed a tithe of his income but wanted to give Hudson Taylor a donation, so he withheld the insurance premium on his conservatories and gave that sum instead. When a storm wreaked great damage in the neighbourhood and his own property suffered little harm, Sir Thomas welcomed it as the reward of faith. Twenty years later, in 1886, when Montagu Beauchamp mentioned this to him in China, Hudson Taylor said, 'I knew that that particular sum of money came in a very special way, but did not know the details.' But Hudson Taylor's work on that Sunday was not over. A Bible-exposition in the garden and an address on China in another village followed.

They saw him off on Monday with the handsome gifts (at that time) of ten pounds from Sir Thomas, five pounds from Lady Beauchamp and ten pounds from Miss Waldegrave, half for China and half for his own expenses, and he arrived at Stratford to learn that the ship would not sail for another twenty-four hours. So Tuesday, October 4, was spent with five others on board 'as far as Gravesend with them'. 'And left them on their way,' the hardened traveller was content to say, although this was the first party to launch out since the China Inland Mission was founded. His journal for Wednesday went on, 'Worked at the accounts, etc, and prepared to finish paper on China. Took house number 34 Coborn Street, Bow.' He was back at work.

For Gracie Ciggie it was another matter. 'As I saw them slowly sail out of the docks a great hope welled up in my heart that I should soon follow . . .' It was to happen, though not 'soon'. Through the sheer force of spiritual self-discipline and courage she was first to equip herself for China by befriending the lowest of Glasgow's women to lead them to Christ.

CHAPTER TWO

SUBSTANCE
1865–66

A team takes shape   *October 1865*

When William Berger, James Vigeon, Hudson Taylor and others stood in the saloon of the *Antipodes* and prayed with the Stevensons and George Stott before going ashore at Gravesend and watching them 'on their way' to China, all expected the Vigeons and Grace Ciggie to follow before long. And when Hudson Taylor went straight back to Welbeck Street to tell his faithful friends that three more had sailed to join the Ningbo five, he would naturally have added his hopes for the Vigeons and Grace. James Vigeon was a man of quality, and an accountant was needed in the team. It was not to be. Insuperable obstacles from his employers and in-laws finally prevented him from going. Within a month Hudson Taylor was asking his parents to pray for some well-educated colleagues to help with the accounts, editorial work and public speaking. But Vigeon would not give up and continued learning Chinese throughout the winter. For the present Grace Ciggie stayed on at Coborn Street proving her worth.

The tempo of applications from candidates to join the Mission began to increase, and expecting to take possession of No 34 Coborn Street by the end of October, Hudson Taylor invited a young widow, Mary Parsons, to come as 'matron', housekeeper and Bible-teacher for the recruits.[1] He heard from George Duncan, the tall Scotsman from Banff, a mason by trade, that he would come down to London in early November, and two days later another Scotsman, a brawny blacksmith of twenty-three named Lewis Nicol, 'well recommended from Arbroath', wrote answering questions put by Hudson Taylor. Only with hindsight could his colourful language be seen to betray the fatal flaw in his character which came close to wrecking the Mission. He was a Sunday-school superintendent, he said, active also during the week, visiting 'the low dens of iniquity' and holding prayer meetings in them. Engaged to a girl named Eliza Calder, he was willing to go abroad single or married. Lewis Nicol duly arrived at Coborn Street on October 27, the day the Mildmay conference was ending, and settled into the household for a month.

Another young hopeful was Josiah Alexander Jackson, a carpenter-turned-draper in Kingsland, near the new middle-class suburb of Mildmay in Islington, who began coming to Coborn Street on Saturdays. Jennie Faulding and Emily Blatchley, deeply involved, had a hand in every activity open to them. Jennie was living at home, but learning Chinese, reading A H Francke's *Life*, about living by faith in God, and coming to help when needed. No 30 was home to Emily, already working as Hudson Taylor's secretary and teacher of the older Taylor children. So when the new hand-printing press, two founts of type[2] and then a lithograph stone arrived, they helped Hudson Taylor to get them going. Jennie was setting type for the first print run when Jackson arrived. And she it was who collected the group photographs from the photographer and distributed them, and who helped to proof-read *China: Its Spiritual Need and Claims* as it came sheet by sheet from Elliott's steam-printing press in Paddington. Emily, it seems, had been ignorant of George Stott's proposal to Agnes Lamont, and her father's blunt rejection of him. Though shaken by his rebuttal, Stott had recovered quickly and, by casting around for another potential wife, had shown that in his thinking love was to follow rather than precede any marriage he might arrange. For, five days after Stott sailed, Hudson Taylor decided he must act, and 'spoke to Miss Blatchley of Mr Stott's marked attention to her'. If she had been rising to the bait she should know, presumably, that his interest was so recent. Attitudes and customs varied from place to place and decade to decade and Hudson Taylor had not forgotten his own experiences.

William D Rudland, an agricultural 'engineer' and blacksmith, was another candidate. Back in 1859–60 a certain Annie Macpherson was running her own boarding-school for girls at Eversden, seven miles south-west of Cambridge. Hearing of how the young evangelist Henry Grattan Guinness and others were addressing great crowds at their 'revival' meetings in London, she and her sister and brother-in-law, a genial young farmer named Merry, had gone up to London to hear him. They were inspired. Annie Macpherson, already an evangelist to Cambridgeshire coprolite diggers, opened a night-school for boys (after teaching her girls by day) and a Bible class to which about thirty came. As they grew up Joseph Merry used to gather half a dozen young men at a time around a big log fire in his old farmhouse to read the Bible. One of them was Rudland. Conversion in 1860 for him had also meant sharing his discovery with others and from the beginning he too had been an evangelist. When he read Hudson Taylor's Perth addresses in *The Revival* he was impressed.

Shortly before William Pennefather began his conferences in Mildmay, in July 1864, Annie Macpherson had moved to London, teaching in Bishopsgate and working as an evangelist among the semi-pagan population of Whitechapel and Houndsditch. From caring for 'matchbox makers', waifs and strays (before Thomas Barnardo came to London) she developed her life work – sending the boys and girls she rescued to the care of good people in Canada where they could put down roots. When the first Mildmay conference was announced in 1864, she had sent tickets to Rudland and others at Eversden. Coming from a place where it would be the talk of the village if the vicar and non-conformist minister were to be seen talking to each other, 'Mildmay was like heaven on earth. I cannot tell you what it was to us young men,' Rudland said. Christians from every denomination attended, 'all one in Christ Jesus'. So when Annie Macpherson sent him a ticket for the second Mildmay conference in October, 1865, he pressed his employer to accept it and taste the experience for himself.

Annie Macpherson had been to the Saturday meetings at No 30 Coborn Street to pray for China, and she knew what William Rudland was thinking. In answer to Hudson Taylor's appeal for men to go to China without a promised salary, doing God's work while banking on the words of *Philippians* 4.19, 'My God shall supply all your need according to His riches in glory by Christ Jesus,' Rudland had said, 'If we can trust God with our souls, why not our bodies?' He talked so much about it that his friends nicknamed him 'China'. Now, knowing that he had given away his Mildmay ticket, Annie Macpherson invited him instead to meet Hudson Taylor at Coborn Street.

Only a pamphlet?   *October 1865*

Meanwhile October was as full as ever for Hudson Taylor. The day after the *Antipodes* had sailed he worked on his accounts and turned to his 'pamphlet', determined to have it in print for the conference beginning on October 25. That meant giving every available moment to it. But the other demands of life were incessant: recruits to train, FES committees to attend, endless callers to be entertained and letters to write, dealing with candidates' applications and keeping Mr Berger informed about everything. Yet day after day 'worked on paper' is his first journal entry, and the early pages of the book were already at the printer's while he continued to write.

On October 9 he addressed an open letter to *The Revival* referring to the eight already in China or on the way, and saying that others were preparing to follow them.

> We fully believe that in His own good time the Lord will open the way for some of these (to go) as well as continuing to supply what is needed for the support of those who have already gone forth without any earthly promise of support, leaning on the more secure promises of *His* Word, who never fails or changes.[3]

Direct solicitation of funds, the usual practice of church societies, was one of the methods he and William Berger had agreed with the first missionaries not to use. But 'trust in God and let the facts be known' was reasonable and a bold departure. As he wrote the final pages of his 'pamphlet' in the next five days, he stated his estimate of costs, 'a yearly expenditure of about £5,600'. Within four months, however, he learned what he saw as a better way, and defined a new attitude to declaring financial needs.

After a lecture at Welbeck Street on October 11 he went to Paddington to discuss the printing with the proprietor of the steampress, John Elliott. He saw that he must finish his writing by the 15th, and left what he had with him to be type-set. Each day after that he was collecting proofs, sheet by sheet, correcting and returning them, helped by Jennie Faulding. On Saturday 21st he 'Brought home sheet 6, & took it back with 20 (corrections) at 11 p.m. Got home soon after 2 a.m.' On Monday evening he 'went to Mr Elliott's but found we had crossed on the way. Got home & found 7 and 8 waiting. Sat up all night & corrected them . . . Sent back the sheets & went to bed at 8 a.m.'

At lunch-time the following day, October 25, the first bound copies of *China: Its Spiritual Need and Claims* were delivered to him. 'Gave some away in the afternoon and evening' (at the conference) is all he wrote in his journal, but this was a high point in his hopes and plans. It was an unveiling, the first time the name

'China Inland Mission' had appeared in print, and a crystallisation of all he had said in his lectures and addresses from Brighton to Aberdeen. William Berger had undertaken to cover the cost of the first issue of three thousand copies, to be sold at sixpence a copy or distributed gratis as unblushing propaganda to jolt as many readers as possible out of complacency and into activity on behalf of China. Today it would be called a 'paperback', of over a hundred pages with a flexible card cover.

The impact on the Christian public was immediate. Latourette said that it 'had an effect not unlike Carey's *Inquiry* written more than seventy years before'.[4] *An Inquiry into the Obligations of Christians to Use Means for the Conversion of the Heathen* (1792) had challenged the prevalent hyper-Calvinist teaching that God would act on behalf of the heathen without the Church's intervention. Together with his Northampton sermon and the aphorism 'Expect great things from God; attempt great things for God', the impact of that paper had resulted in the prompt foundation, in the same year, of 'the Particular Baptist Society for Propagating the Gospel among the Heathen' (BMS). Not surprisingly, William Carey himself had been sent as the society's first missionary to India. Hudson Taylor's manifesto had as dramatic an outcome, in a different form. His society was already in embryo and he was set on sailing to China in the coming spring. Offers from men and women to accompany him immediately began to flow in. In Bishop Stephen Neill's words, 'Almost from the start his success was sensational. Recruits crowded to his door.'[5]

As vicar of St Jude's, Mildmay, William Pennefather, 'the George Müller of the Church of England',[6] naturally drew Anglicans to the annual conference he convened, but in the climate of the Evangelical Awakening, Christians of all complexions attended.[7] Busy as he was, Pennefather had his friend Hudson Taylor to breakfast with him on the morning of the 26th, and 'gave permission for the pamphlet to be sold at the doors and for me to plead for China in the evening'. As a result eighty-two copies were disposed of on that day and many more requested. After the close of the conference Hudson Taylor 'dined with D Lady Radstock. Sir Thos & Lady Beauchamp and Lord Cecil were present.' From Portland Place he went on to Thomas Marshall and sold him fifty-two copies. Back at Coborn Street Mr Berger took ten, Vigeon seven and Gough four but he 'let Miss Faulding have 20'. She, the enthusiast, sold them all and was back for more.

Within three weeks the book had to be reprinted. A second edition had to be published two months later, in February 1866, a third in 1868, and a fourth in 1872. In 1884 a large-format fifth edition of five thousand copies with maps and illustrations was exhausted between June and September. A sixth, of the same kind, followed in the same year, and in 1887 a seventh presentation edition of ten thousand copies in green and gilt, with a statistical table of Protestant missions in China.[8] Three years later, in 1890, an eighth edition was needed. After the fourth edition the title by which it had long been known in speech was adopted in print. Instead of *China: Its Spiritual Need and Claims* it became *China's Spiritual Need and Claims*, the form most used today.

Lord Radstock wrote from the Isle of Wight,

> I have read yr pamphlet on my way down here in the train – I have been greatly stirred by it . . . (I) have received a fresh stimulus to work for the Lord in England . . . Dear brother, enlarge your desires & ask for 100 labourers & the Lord will give them to you. I enclose a cheque for £100 . . .
> Ever yours in Him,
>
> Radstock.

'A very encouraging note', Hudson Taylor called it. Apart from one gift of two hundred pounds by Mr Berger at the inauguration of the CIM, and one hundred and fifty from the Foreign Evangelist Society as the passage money for three adults to China, this gift from Lord Radstock was by far the largest received. Most were in single figures and very few exceeded twenty-five pounds, so that the total still fell short of seven hundred pounds. (To multiply these sums by twenty in the late twentieth century may give a very approximate idea of sterling values at that time.) As for raising his sights to ask for one hundred new missionaries, many more than that would be needed to fulfil the sweeping aims of the Mission, but whether even an initial twenty could be trained, deployed and directed successfully was in question. No society had even attempted it in China. To take so many novices into the 'interior' was already being judged foolhardy by men well qualified to know. Radstock, the young regimental commander, knew that well enough. He was only saying in effect, 'Don't stop at twenty-four. "Ask and you will receive!"' But Hudson Taylor, the realist, had no illusions about the difficulty of finding accommodation and language teachers for a handful, let alone a score, and guiding them through adaption from brash foreignness to behaviour acceptable to cultured Chinese, whether in a treaty port or the interior. To be so adventurous meant that all were strong-willed men and women. And all were free to reject his leadership. He would proceed one step at a time.

But the conference was over and the book was on its way into homes in every part of the United Kingdom, soon to give the world some outstanding missionaries, Britain its Dr Thomas Barnardo and a new training college under Grattan Guinness. Lewis Nicol had arrived from Scotland, George Duncan was soon to follow, Jackson was preparing to take leave of his employer and move to Coborn Street, and Mrs Parsons was to come soon to run the second house, No 34.

Monday, October 30, saw Hudson Taylor back at revising the Ningbo New Testament with Frederick Gough, and in the evening with a bundle of his books at a meeting of the Open Air Mission to hear 'Mr Offord on the nature, distinctions and relations of Justification and Sanctification'. The Earl of Cavan was there, and also young Jackson, probably on Hudson Taylor's advice. They and others received copies. 'Revision' and interviews with missionary candidates filled this historic month of October 1865. It had seen the departure to China of the first pioneers to sail under the 'China Inland Mission'. The dynamic 'pamphlet' had been completed and published, and the first signs of its powerful influence were appearing.

Everything at once[9]   *November–December 1865*

November was much the same, with the pressures of life increasing. No 34 Coborn Street had to be furnished and supplied with all the household equipment Mrs Parsons and her lodgers would need. That meant shopping expeditions, for Hudson Taylor had no one yet to whom he could confidently delegate such work. After a full Friday, November 3, he was balancing his books and checking his available cash at one a m when he discovered that he had none to draw. 'Awoke M. (Maria) to join in prayer,' he recorded on Saturday. 'This morning recd. £20 from Mr Berger. Thank the Lord!'

Inquiries and offers to join him were multiplying, from young men and women to go to China. A Mr and Mrs Manning had been to see him on October 31. 'He seemed a *very* suitable man, but his wife has not faith.' A Mr Saddler of the Highgate Missionary Institute came on November 3. Thomas Phillips was sent by the FES the next day, but making for Assam. George Duncan wrote declining his fare from Aberdeen. 'I will manage fine to get there,' a reply consistent with the personality of this brave pioneer of the future. He arrived on the 10th. On November 6 it was W Smith, who 'had heard me at Mildmay conference and was stirred up to offer himself for China'. James Vigeon, Lewis Nicol and Grace Ciggie were having Chinese lessons. On the 10th he wrote, 'saw Mr Richards for some time'.[10] The next day he was writing to an Elizabeth Tapp, as well as to Jackson and Smith, and soon afterwards to a Swiss governess, a Miss Gruber, and her friend Anna Towne, aged twenty-two and twenty. There was no knowing which of these would go on to reach China.

On November 15 Annie Macpherson told him about William Rudland, the 26-year-old Eversden mechanic 'desiring to labor for China'. She had sent Rudland a copy of *China: Its Spiritual Need and Claims* three days before bringing him to Coborn Street. He had shown her letter to his employer, saying 'I won't finish this work just now, I must go to London for a few days.' The older man had heard Hudson Taylor speak at Mildmay, and replied as he read the letter, 'As sure as you cross that threshold you are on your way to China.'

William Rudland's first impression as he entered No 30 that Saturday afternoon was of 'a small room full of people'. Of Hudson Taylor he saw 'nothing noticeable' except to say to himself, 'Here is a man in real earnest.' But he was struck by the fact that when they began to pray, no one was asked to do so, they followed one another spontaneously. If the report of the Perth conference had stirred him, and *China's Need* renewed that interest, meeting Hudson Taylor and his friends now 'attracted' him all the more. Before Rudland returned to Cambridge Hudson Taylor said, 'Don't throw up your employment. Come for a month or so, and see if you are fit for the work.' Rudland was back the next Saturday to stay for a week initially, and after a brief visit home began serious training.

On that Saturday, November 18, Hudson Taylor wrote to his parents explaining that the letter must be brief or would not get done at all.

> The (New Testament) revision is now going on; we have reprinted the pamphlet; have got the missionary boxes on the way. I am

preparing for a Magazine for the Mission; furnishing a house; completing and setting up two fonts of type for China; teaching four pupils Chinese; receiving new applications from candidates continually; lecturing or attending meetings daily (except one night *only* for the last month). I am also preparing 'a new year's address on China' for Sunday School Teachers & Scholars – and a Missionary Map of China.

The magazine was to be a news bulletin or 'occasional paper'. He was giving many evenings to work for the FES, and spoke twice for the CMS at Streatham. As for 'receiving applications', it was an understatement of the daily correspondence and frequent interviews with young men and women whose offers to join him were exceeding his expectation. Knowing of the scarcity of offers to the main missionary societies he had thought to draw upon the 'untapped reservoir' of the revival movement. So far his writings and speeches could have touched only its fringes, but more and more letters were flowing in.

I ask you to pray . . . that the Lord will give us a few *well-educated helpers* to assist in accounts, writing for press, editorial work, public meetings, etc . . . [cf p 67 quotation.] The Lord is very good to us and supplies our every need. Apart from my own support and expenses, and the money sent direct to China for our work [by George Müller and others] I have received upwards of £770 since June in answer to prayer. Will you join us in praying . . . for the *right* kind of laborers; that others may be kept back or not accepted; for many are coming forward.

Patently unsuitable applicants were taking precious time, for he would not simply brush them off. A few days later he was writing to his parents again. Between twenty and thirty men and women were now in touch with him. 'The number of candidates is almost weekly increasing, and many important questions arise respecting them. The expenses are great and ever increasing.'

The second impression of *China's Need* was in the binder's hands and completed copies promised for the 23rd, but stock was running low. Jennie Faulding came back for more, reporting that a gentleman on reading his copy had undertaken to find nineteen friends jointly to support a missionary in China. With William Tarn's help an engraver was working on the map of China. But the need to issue a formal report of the year meant extra work during December.

Then Lewis Nicol went home to Scotland, to bring his fiancée, Eliza Calder, and the other Arbroath man, James Williamson, back with him.

Hudson Taylor had enough on his hands without domestic worries, but in the midst of everything came serious illness overshadowing it all. Maria had written while he was in Norfolk that her pregnancy was threatened. In any case her perpetual cough and fever indicated progressive lung disease, though medical men still knew too little to be able to identify and treat it. Her busy part in the Coborn Street community, supervising the household, the servants, the children, the catering and laundry, while still working on the Ningbo New Testament because of her expert knowledge of the dialect, and as amanuensis to her husband, all had to be set aside when she was confined to bed with clear signs of *placenta praevia* endangering the life of her child and herself. On November 18 he had told his mother,

> (Maria) has been failing for the past 4 months, and each time worse than the preceding . . . I fear that if spared till her confinement, we shall have a very trying time. If she gets over that, it will be well if a tendency to Phthisis is not established in the meantime. She has been confined to her room or bed for three weeks, so I have had very little help from her.[11] God has sustained me or I should have broken down. [He sometimes used this expression for physical as well as emotional health] . . . Mr Lord is spoken of as ill, with little or no hope of recovery . . . Meadows is well, but the work is outgrowing his strength.

Then on November 29 Kate, one of the servants, came to Hudson Taylor looking ill and running a fever which steadily worsened. Hudson Taylor had to lecture on China at the YMCA, Euston Road, with his mind preoccupied by the emergency at home. He had prepared for such a crisis and sent his three elder children, Grace, Herbert and Howard (Freddie), in the care of Sarah the nurse, to his mother at Barnsley. After breakfast at the Fauldings he brought Jennie back with him to help for forty-eight hours. But she had already returned home when things went from bad to worse. On December 3 he asked his mother if she could come and help. Even so his letter was full of business matters. He felt a moral obligation to complete the translation work entrusted to him by the Bible Society in 1861. 'Revision and re-printing' were 'above all' taking his time. 'I scarcely know how to get through.'

Grace Ciggie, often affected by the London smog, fell ill and needed to get away, and Maria was so much 'worse, very prostrated' that her husband 'felt very serious alarm about her; also very uneasy about Kate'. On December 5 Dr Barnes, a London Hospital obstetrician, came to see Maria and advised immediate induction of labour. The baby would be born prematurely but the risk to Maria of delaying was too great. Hudson Taylor carried out the procedure himself, and at two a m wrote urgently 'to Mr Müller, Mr Horne (of Clevedon), Mr Berger, Amelia and Mother to pray for us'.

> My dear Maria is in a very precarious state. I called in Dr Barnes (the first authority in London in these cases) to-day. . . . It seems very solemn to feel that all our married happiness *may* be so near its close.

It was after three a m before he got to bed.

He called Mr Pope, the local doctor, to take charge of Kate, now known to have typhoid, and because Kate was too ill to be moved, carried Maria to No 34, putting their own home, No 30, into isolation. Dr Woodman, another London Hospital obstetrician, came at eleven pm and presided at a doubly hazardous breech delivery soon after midnight.[12] Jane Dyer Taylor, the baby, lived only half an hour. Hudson Taylor stayed up attending Maria, and at six a m scribbled a note to tell his mother about the horrific night.

In a postscript he added, 'I have just been elected Fellow of the Royal Geographical Society.' The notification from 15 Whitehall Place on 29 November 1865, signed by Clements R Markham and Laurence Oliphant, stated that he had been proposed by 'E B Underhill, Esq. and seconded by Lord Radstock and Major-General G Balfour CBE', HBM consul and architect in 1843 of the Shanghai Settlement. By the standard of the time this was a considerable honour, so his passing reference to it is a measure of the stresses on him.

Only disconnected records of the rest of December appear to have survived. Lewis Nicol, Eliza Calder and James Williamson arrived by ship from Aberdeen on Friday, December 22. With sick people in each house accommodation was badly taxed, so Hudson Taylor rented half of No 33 as well, to house the men, keeping No 34 for the women under Mary Parsons' care. It increased his financial obligations to £110 per ann. for rent and tax alone. Before long he had to take the whole of No 33.

On Christmas Day – the day Evangeline Booth was born to

William and Catherine in Hackney, not many streets away – Hudson Taylor wrote to one of those wanting to go to China. This frank letter, shirking no pastoral duty and demonstrating his care in selecting colleagues, gives a glimpse into his correspondence. The copy is in Emily Blatchley's hand.

> The dangerous illness of my dear wife . . . compelled me to defer writing to you. [Then, after referring to satisfactory testimonials] But I was much pained by rumours which reached me . . . Into these rumours I do not wish to go more deeply unless you wish it . . . If based on facts . . . it would be very undesirable (so soon after such a fall) for you to go to China, where temptations and dangers abound . . . If you feel in your conscience, before God, that such has not been the case, and court investigation in this matter, I will write for definite charges and furnish them to you and to your Pastor for investigation . . . If the charges were disproved, we might wish to see you in London; and then it would be an open question as to whether you had the physical, mental and spiritual qualifications requisite for work in China. Here, as elsewhere, many are called but few chosen . . . It would have been easy to give you no reasons for the conclusion that, for the present at least, you had better serve God at home. But it seems more candid to let you know the reasons for doing so, tho' more painful perhaps . . .

Also on Christmas Day he drafted an open letter to all friends and supporters of the CIM, saying that the Coborn Street households would be keeping Saturday, December 30, as a day of thanksgiving, fasting and prayer for China and the Mission.

> We have now arrived at a very momentous stage of our work. Besides the eight of our Brothers and Sisters who are in China or on their way there, between twenty and thirty others are desiring to serve the Lord there in connection with us. How much we need the Lord's guidance both for them and for ourselves! We have undertaken to work in the interior of China, looking to the Lord for help of all kinds. This we can only do in His strength; and if we are to be much used by the Lord, we must live very near to Him. We propose, therefore, to seek the Lord, both in private and unitedly, by prayer and fasting (see *Acts* 13.3) during the earlier part of the day. We shall meet unitedly from 10.30 a.m. to 1.30 p.m. and from 4 p.m. to 5.30 p.m.

It was the first of such observances which have continued annually ever since, wherever the CIM has been represented.[13] Between

December 20, 1864, and June 3, 1865, Hudson Taylor had received £221.12s.6d. for the Ningbo mission. Between then and December 30, 1865, £908.16s.8d. had come in, a total of £1182.3s.2d. Confidence in God to provide necessities in response to prayer was not being disappointed. But with the rental and rates for three houses to meet, an increasing flow of cash for day to day needs, large payments looming up, and Ningbo to supply when he was able, he entered the new year with only £210.3s.8d. and a stock of materials for future travellers' outfits valued at £120.

One other incident encouraged Hudson Taylor as the year ended, for it showed that the circle of interest in his venture was wider than appeared superficially. From the Junior United Service Club, London, S.W. came a note which ran,

> Having a Magnetic Electric machine by me, I thought that perhaps you might find some use for it . . . It is a large one and is a machine used by medical men . . . It also serves as an amusement to those who have not been able to attend lectures on Scientific subjects. I left it today at the Charing Cross station Booking office, and enclose a ticket . . . it is addressed to you on the outside. . . . Hoping your family has been restored to health, Believe me, yours sincerely,
>
> C G Gordon

At the time 'Chinese Gordon' as an engineer brevet lieutenant-colonel was relegated to 'an obsolete fort at Gravesend', with responsibility for modernising the defences of the Thames. He was also beginning his work among outcast and destitute boys of which the Gordon Boys' School at Woking is the national memorial. Years later at a meal in Shanghai, when Hudson Taylor was asked why he did not use such a letter in the Mission magazine, for 'it would have been of great interest', he replied, 'Yes, if we depended on the influence of great names.'

'The momentous stage'[14]   *January 1866*

At the rate *China: Its Spiritual Need and Claims* was going out, the reprint would soon be exhausted. The first priority was to re-edit the book and get it through the drudgery of publication again. Maria was fragile and unable to help. Emily Blatchley was mourning the rapid advance of her brother's tuberculosis, but doing all she could to take Maria's place in the household. Jennie Faulding was away in

Yorkshire, but Mary Bausum, approaching fifteen, was proving useful. The children and Grace Ciggie were all at Barnsley, with Hudson Taylor's parents, but Duncan, Nicol and Eliza, Williamson and sometimes Vigeon and Jackson had to be taught Chinese language, history and customs, and as much theology, English grammar and practical medicine as Hudson Taylor could find time for. His New Year address for Sunday schools, *China and the Chinese*, with a photograph of William Burns in Chinese dress on the cover, had all been distributed.

On January 6, 1866, he wrote again to his longsuffering mother, approaching her fifty-eighth birthday, asking her to say candidly if the children could stay with her a week or two longer. He was taking Maria to recuperate with the Bergers at Saint Hill for a week, and then to George Pearse at Brighton if she was well enough. At three a m with more letters to write, he continued, 'We shall (D.V.) leave for China not later than the end of May next, whether our work is finished or not. (In confidence) I may say that we *may* need to return to England after (a year or two). But go soon I must, to set matters there on a safe and permanent basis.'

That Saturday, January 7, Frederick Gough and James Vigeon, Emily Blatchley and Miss Gruber, the Swiss candidate, Maria and Hudson Taylor descended on the hospitable Bergers for the weekend at Saint Hill, East Grinstead. And on Monday the girls stayed with Maria while the men returned to London for the Evangelical Alliance Week of Prayer in the City. Hudson Taylor was to be the speaker on Thursday night. When word came on Thursday morning that Maria was coughing blood, he had not yet prepared his address. He was also dining that day with Robert Baxter, the Parliamentary lawyer who rented Queen Anne's Chapel Royal in Queen Anne's Gate to preach in, and was chairman of the Foreign Evangelist Society. So Hudson Taylor, unable to go to Maria, could only send medicine.

William Rudland was going with him to the Freemasons Hall each day and recalled that, probably after the Thursday address, when one person after another prayed for China to be opened to the gospel, Hudson Taylor stood up and said quietly, 'China I believe *is* open. We need to go . . . and enter the open door. May we not confidently expect that the Lord will open the door more widely if we do so?' 'I don't know what missionary life may involve of privation or difficulty,' Rudland said to himself, 'but I know I can follow that man.' What Rudland, 'a man of absorbing purpose',

WILLIAM BURNS IN CHINESE WINTER CLOTHES

reality, simplicity and intensity, went through before he became the
pioneer founder of a Chinese church and translator of the New
Testament into the local dialect, is part of this unfolding story.

Hudson Taylor returned to Saint Hill for the weekend and each
weekend of the month, but had lectures to deliver here, there and
everywhere – at Dorking, in London at Grafton Street, Soho, at
Baxter's chapel, at Harley Street, the YMCA, Canonbury Presbyterian church, and soon farther afield. Lady Radstock pressed him
to come to 30 Bryanston Square on Monday evenings to pray with
them, '(we) shall be *so* glad to see you. Tea is at eight o'clock', but
he seldom managed to go. So although Maria continued to cough
blood and was anchored at the Bergers, he could not stay with her.
'It makes me very anxious,' he wrote on the 17th.

A note from Maria on the same day said Emily Blatchley was sick
with grief over her unconverted brother who had not long to live.
She was refusing food and unable to sleep. But a cryptic comment
by Hudson Taylor to Maria permits the inference that a broken
romance was as much to blame. On January 24 Maria and Hudson
Taylor gave Emily a new polyglot Bible with alternating Hebrew or
Greek and English pages, with their love and, in his hand, *Joshua*
1.7, 8, 'Be strong and of a good courage . . .' quoted in full. Dating
the pages from cover to cover, with two or three chapters to read
each day, she used it as a spiritual diary, a log of her spiritual voyage
through the next six or seven years. Storms, riots, heartaches,
despair, each has its date beside passages of topical meaning to her.

Hudson Taylor had lost the secretarial help of both Maria and
Emily and was writing by hand instead of dictating his many letters.
May 15 he named again and again as the date by which he must sail
with the next party of pioneers. After a night back at Saint Hill, and
an early morning start to London, he scribbled a hurried note
saying, 'I have not breakfasted yet beyond what I got at East
Grinstead, so am ready for tea.' Ten unanswered and more un-
opened letters were waiting for attention. On the following day he
had sixty more letters to write when he asked his mother to order
another dress coat and trousers from his tailor. In that letter he said
that Maria was 'steadily improving. I am now sure her lungs are
diseased.' In fact, if pathology had been better understood at the
time, he would have known how desperately ill she already was. The
severity of symptoms still held priority over their cause, and medical
text-books of the period still groped after the truth of unexplained
conditions, as they do today.

The time had come to admit that his commitments were too many and he must bow out of the Ningbo New Testament revision. Frederick Gough's visits with him to Saint Hill were partly to allow them to consult and pray with William Berger about approaching the sponsoring CMS and the Bible Society again. On January 25 they had an interview with Henry Venn and Charles Jackson, the Bible Society Secretary (1862–79), and Hudson Taylor wrote, 'The B & F and CMS have agreed to let me go, and Mr Gough to finish the New Testament.' A year had passed since he had written from Glasgow to prepare them for this moment. Even now his urge to complete the work and put the vernacular version into the hands of the Christians of Ningbo drove him on. He continued to give all the time he could to helping his friend, until they had consigned *Thessalonians* to Spottiswoodes the printers, and finished revising *Timothy*.

On March 29, 1866, Hudson Taylor formally resigned, writing,

> I greatly regret that I should be unable to see the work to its close. From Sepr. 1861 to March 1865 with the exception of about three months in 1862, and an annual rest of a few weeks, I gave myself very fully to the work, spending from 5 to 7 hours daily upon it – [a striking understatement] . . . From May to August 17 (1865) I was able to give up from 9 or 10 a.m. to 2 p.m. to the work, but since that time a constantly increasing pressure of work has made my co-operation with Mr Gough more and more difficult . . .

While Frederick Gough had been working alone on the text as far as *Titus* 3, he explained, Maria and he had done the marginal references.

In June the Bible Society minuted that having decided to vote him a hundred pounds they had been thanked for their 'liberality' but he had declined any remuneration. (*See* Appendix 1.)

'Chequered news' from Ningbo   1865–66

Soon it would be six years since Hudson Taylor and Maria had had to leave Ningbo and China, he in poor physical condition and doubtful of ever returning. More than five years had passed since the Peking Convention had given merchant and missionary the freedom to travel and live in inland China. Missions had been 'caught on the wrong foot'. The only deployment possible had been at the expense of the barely viable churches in the five treaty ports.

The Ningbo missions had suffered severely. Many of the familiar figures were no longer there. Some had moved to the new treaty ports of Yantai and Tianjin. Others had left China. Of the CMS all three experienced men had returned to Britain. R H Cobbold had taken the parish of Broseley in Staffordshire, F F Gough was with Hudson Taylor in London, and W A Russell was beginning a protracted absence of seven years while his directors and the Anglican Church debated his future. George Moule, who had arrived in China very shortly before the Taylors departed, was left in charge. He himself moved to Hangzhou in 1865, leaving his brother Arthur, who had joined him in 1861, in charge at Ningbo. T S Fleming had lasted less than three years before being invalided home in 1863, and J D Valentine was still a novice, having reached China in 1864.

Of the American Presbyterians, W A P Martin had moved first to Shanghai and then to Peking, and his brother Samuel and the R Q Ways were in the States. American missions were being severely disrupted by the Civil War. Dr McCartee alone of the veterans was in Ningbo, helped by two recent arrivals, D D Green and Samuel Dodd. Miles Knowlton of the American Baptist Missionary Union (ABMU) had returned, but Horace Jenkins, his colleague, was another beginner in 1862, joined by Carl T Kreyer in 1866. Each mission could barely hold the line. Expansion was impossible. Edward C Lord had left the ABMU in July 1863 to work on his own, calling his independent enterprise the American Baptist Mission.

Dr John Parker, who took his brother William's place after his tragic death in 1863, had become a representative of the United Presbyterian Church of Scotland in 1865. The tally of Ningbo missionaries was completed by Hudson Taylor's protégés, William Fuller and John Mara of the United Methodist Free Church (UMFC), also newcomers, and those whom Hudson Taylor had sent out to the Bridge Street church. Jean Notman had ceased to be a missionary when she married in December 1865. Stephan Barchet was attached to the Lords, and George and Annie Crombie, married on October 1, 1865, were sharing the old Bridge Street premises with James Meadows, and learning Chinese. Of all the seventeen missionary men and fifteen women, Hudson Taylor had sent nine, five men and four women, and the Stevensons and George Stott were due at Shanghai any day.[15]

The churches had suffered from the depletion of missionary staff but picked up again. After losing ten members, to his own discouragement, James Meadows had watched the Bridge Street congregation climb back to fifty and then sixty. Mrs Lord (as Jemima Bausum, the Taylors' staunch friend through their stormy courtship) wrote of hundreds responding to the gospel in and around Ningbo. But at the end of 1865 the total number admitted to church membership in the year was 141, making 656 in all. (They were witnessing the nascent stage of the virile Church of the post-Mao period.) Helen Nevius reported that the people of Ningbo called Christianity the *dabudaode daoli*, the invincible doctrine, because of the resilience of the Christians under persecution and adversity.

Since 1857 when Hudson Taylor and John Jones had begun work together, one hundred had been baptised at Bridge Street. Some had died and some had lapsed, but several were so zealous as amateur evangelists, at work and in their spare time, that the Foreign Evangelist Society elected to provide enough for the livelihood of three and then five of them, while the redoubtable Mrs Ranyard offered support for two more Bible-reading women. Two of the most promising men, Feng Nenggui and Fan Qiseng, were to play a part in the move 'inland' from Ningbo. Wang Lae-djün, who had had three years of personal training by the Taylors in London while helping them with the New Testament, was still working with W R Fuller.

As Hudson Taylor forwarded remittances from the FES at intervals, and sent what he could to Meadows, Crombie and the others, he followed their progress. Telling the Lords about his own developing venture and the plan to have a mission base in a city or town not too far from the Ningbo church, Hudson Taylor asked them to rent suitable premises for him. Instead of a reply came the news that in September Mr Lord was ill, with little or no hope of recovery. 'Stevenson and Stott [their ship, that is] have not been heard of . . . Meadows is well, but the work is outgrowing his strength; the recruits are needed to keep pace with the blessing (in Ningbo).'

Since the end of the Taiping rebellion and second opium war, national recovery meant that standing properties were everywhere in great demand. When Lord recovered he launched into forthright advice typical of him as the efficient American consul.

> If you have as many missionaries here (in China) as you seem to expect, your permanent presence at home will be almost necessary

[to direct them and raise funds, so he thought] . . . I shall be ready and glad to do anything in my power to aid you in the great and good work contemplated.

Mr Barchet is a young man of unusual promise (progressing finely with the language) . . . I would earnestly advise you to encourage him to turn his attention . . . to the ministry of the Word (and to ordination) . . . (Meadows) has not done or said anything to give me the least cause of complaint . . . Should it be your wish I will gladly retire and leave him in charge of (the Bridge Street) church. (But Barchet) is more intelligent and teachable . . . (and in a few months could be the better man for it, while Meadows is) a good man and a zealous worker, but one a good deal inclined to have his own way.

E C Lord did not wait for Hudson Taylor's approval, and on January 30, 1866, wrote to James Meadows saying that he himself was retiring in favour of him as pastor of the congregation. Then he wrote to Hudson Taylor again on February 20. The *Antipodes* had made its perfect voyage in only four months and delivered the Stevensons and George Stott safe and sound at Shanghai on February 6. They had come on by coaster and reached Ningbo two days later. John and Annie Stevenson were with the Lords in the north suburb, working hard at the language with Mr Tsiu as their teacher, and John Stevenson was spending several hours of each day with him in the city, the temples and villages. John's hard work at home and on the voyage were paying dividends as within a few weeks he began the rudiments of preaching in Chinese. A letter from George Stott on February 17 showed the same spirit.

On arriving at Ningbo, I had no plan of operation in view; but after consulting with Mr Lord and Brother Crombie, we have determined (DV) to proceed to Fenghua, a town about twenty miles from Ningpo, and if possible pitch our tent there . . . I intend to plant a school at once; and to enable me to effect that design, I have in view to engage one who has had experience in teaching.

We intend to set out for Fenghua tonight, about six o'clock . . . We may have some difficulty in gaining a footing, as there has never been a foreigner living there. Mr Lord approves very much of the course we are taking . . . [16]

So when E C Lord wrote, Meadows, Crombie and Stott were on their way by river boat to Fenghua, hoping to rent premises. Anything suitable as a base for a sizeable team would be very expensive. Lord agreed with Hudson Taylor:

A missionary on his first arrival does not know what he wants, nor how to supply the wants he feels. He has a longing to get some resting place, and get to work, but his wants and his means seldom correspond. Under these circumstances the best way perhaps is to encourage him to occupy some temporary quarters until he has time to find out what he needs, and to become a little accustomed to his new life. This of course is what you have had in mind in establishing a *head-quarters*. (A house for two or three families will cost $500 to $1000 for the first year and $200–300 in succeeding years, and even so it will be very inferior.)[17]

Then Lord made an offer typical of his generosity knowing the size of party Hudson Taylor expected to bring: 'Your missionaries on their arrival can always find a home for a short while with us.'

To Hudson Taylor this statement must have come as an immense relief when it reached him at the end of April, less than a month before he sailed from Britain. His own experience time and again, from 1854 onward, had been of the difficulty of finding essential accommodation for himself and even one family. No hint appears anywhere that the thought of arriving with a score or even a dozen colleagues, with nowhere to live, was a nightmare to him. While not banking upon others' hospitality, he had learned from William Burns that a houseboat could be a good alternative, but having the Lords' home and school premises available assured him of enough initial housing should he need it.

William Burns' advice[18]   1866

Early in March a letter reached London from William Burns in Peking, dated January 5, 1866. News of his friends in Scotland and of how they had welcomed and assisted Hudson Taylor had warmed his heart, but even more the news that,

> though you have delayed so long your return to this land, your heart has been meditating good things for its unenlightened millions . . . Your plan of seeking to plant two missionaries in each of the unoccupied provinces is a noble one; and if, by the help of our God, it is but half accomplished, a great step will have been taken in advance, and the necessities of China will become more visible and clamant in the view of all the Protestant churches.

Hudson Taylor had said that one of his main aims was to arouse the Churches to awareness of China's need. William Burns went on,

The only part of your proposed scheme that strikes me as happily [*sic* ?haply] unsuitable is that which contemplates entering China from the Burmah frontier. Now that we can obtain passports to travel in any part of China that is not the seat of a rebellion, the way is open to proceed at once from any of the open ports, if desired, to the boundaries of Burmah and Thibet. We hear that very lately a Protestant missionary has reached Shanghai, after having gone as far in Sze-Chuen (Sichuan) as the borders of Thibet. We have not heard the name of the individual, but he is supposed to be a self-supported young American named Bagley, who last year paid a visit to Peking. He was in the United States a local preacher, connected with the American Episcopalian Methodists.

Being in Peking, Burns had the latest news of the bloodthirsty Muslim rebellion in Yunnan, bordering Burma, and saw that it would be impossible to enter west China by that route. To Hudson Taylor his remark was enough. He accepted the advice and deferred the Burma project until the rebellion ended in 1873. What Burns had to say about penetrating the rest of China must have given him great hope, carefully worded though it was.

The difficulty, as far as I can see, of carrying out your plans will not be so much in peregrinating the country, as in getting the new missionaries permanently located, and then afterwards in supplying them in positions so distant and isolated, with the outward means of support. However, the command is plain, 'Go ye into all the world, and preach the gospel to *every* creature;' and He who gives the command, adds for our encouragement – 'Lo I am with you alway, even unto the end of the world.' Let us then go forward, assured that 'no good word shall fail of all that the Lord hath spoken.' Whether it shall be the Lord's will, that I should take a part with you or not in this blessed work, I am at present unable to form any conjecture. Human probabilities seem to be against such a course; my brethren in the south having been for some time urging my return to Amoy, Siraton, and the new field opened by Dr Maxwell on Formosa.[19] However I shall keep, if spared, the matter before the throne of grace; and who can tell but that the Lord may, notwithstanding all obstacles, open up my way to join you in some part of your exploratory journeyings.

William Burns had been publishing his Mandarin vernacular translation of *The Pilgrim's Progress* in Peking by the time-honoured Chinese method of carved blocks, assured of popularity.

The printing of the first part of the 'Pilgrim's Progress' in Mandarin colloquial, is just completed, and the second part (Christiana, etc), for the first time put into Chinese, is now in the course of being cut on blocks. While this is going on I have other work on hand with my teacher. During the year just finished, I have on three occasions paid missionary visits to places in this province in company with some of Mr Edkins' assistants. The time occupied thus was, in all, fully three months.

Burns did not live to share in the work of the China Inland Mission, but his *Pilgrim's Progress* was still widely in circulation at the close of China's 'open century' over eighty years later.

The postponement of the Burma plan left John and Anne Stevenson free to develop their own pioneer venture in Zhejiang. The immensity, perhaps the impossibility, of Hudson Taylor's far-reaching aims came home to them when faced by the difficulties of their own limited area. No handful of missionaries could ever carry them out, nor any but heroes. Anne wrote, 'We are increasingly impressed with the solemnity of dear Mr Taylor's service for the Lord . . . May God raise up and send forth many laborers in the gospel to China . . .' Meanwhile Stephan Barchet, out among the villages, met Meadows, Crombie and Stott on their way home. They had found and rented a small house at Fenghua, suitable for their own purposes but not for a Mission base. His letter and Anne Stevenson's probably reached London just before the main party sailed. Expansion beyond the treaty ports had begun.

CHAPTER THREE

'GOING IN MAY'
1866

Who is to go?   *February 1866*

Blackwood's 'Shilling Scribbling Diary' for 1866 is a museum piece, apart from Hudson Taylor's entries. The Almanack on the cover recorded the execution of five pirates at the Old Bailey in the City of London on February 22, 1864, and the assassination of President Lincoln on April 14, 1864. In its postal information it stated, 'Within about 3 miles of the General Post Office, there are twelve (hourly) deliveries of Letters daily . . . Within 12 miles . . . there are seven despatches daily' at the cost of one penny per half-ounce. A map inside showed postal districts and railway stations but no trains crossing the Thames, so no Victoria or Charing Cross stations. A wages table only went up to £50 per annum, that is 19s 2¾d per week, and foreign exchange showed the American dollar to be worth four shillings – five dollars to the pound sterling. 'New Dress Fabrics' were advertised by Peter Robinson's of Oxford Street and Regent Street: 'yeddo' poplin of pure Llama wool, corded silk poplins for 'a most useful and elegant dress, 35s to 3 guineas'. Again 'Rich Silks' and 'Rich Plain Silks in 48 New Colours' cost £2 19s 6d to 5 guineas for a 'full dress of 14 yards', but 'silk poplinettes' were only '35s the full dress'.[1]

Life was too full for Hudson Taylor's journal entries. Yet the first week of February was historic. With the firm decision to sail in May, only three and a half months away, the names of the ship's party were being listed. How many would join it was still uncertain. Of forty definite offers, fifteen or sixteen had been invited to Coborn Street for interviews, and with the Bergers' and Taylors' concurrence ten believed that God had called them to go. Several more were approaching a decision or were dependent on being set free by parents or employers. Others corresponding with Hudson Taylor were hoping to be included.

James Meadows had written proposing marriage to his dead

Martha's friend, Elizabeth Rose. On February 1 Hudson Taylor thanked his mother for her comment, saying, 'I am glad to hear that he has chosen so well and so wisely,' and on February 7 he was to go up to Barnsley to meet her and to lecture on China. If she was willing, and suitable for the life of a missionary, she would be added to the list. James Vigeon, the accountant, was tenaciously hoping and praying for his firm to release him so that he and his wife and children might also sail. Lewis Nicol, the Aberdeen blacksmith, and Eliza Calder planned to marry soon and go together. William Rudland the Cambridgeshire mechanic, and George Duncan the Banffshire mason, James Williamson and Josiah Jackson the two carpenters, from Scotland and North London, were in no doubt.

Jennie Faulding was as certain, but Emily Blatchley's health and family troubles still posed a problem. On the 10th she was to write to Maria, 'You cannot think, dear, dear Mrs Taylor, how bitter to me is the thought (the possibility) of having to part from you and dear Mr Taylor.' And two days later as she steeled herself to take disappointment in the right spirit, one of making any sacrifice that God might require of her, she wrote 'Feb. 12th. 1866' beside the words in the new Bible they had given her: 'You pay tithes of mint and anise [the trivial things] . . . and have omitted the weightier matters . . .' In this company of devoted people, at Coborn Street and Saint Hill, her spiritual maturity was growing visibly, to her friends' delight.

Hardly had it been decided that Grace Ciggie should go than her health gave way. At home in Glasgow she seldom had a day of illness, but in London bronchitis plagued her. 'Bow does not suit her' was Hudson Taylor's first note, and after medical consultation a month later, 'Grace Ciggie . . . I fear must not go just now.' If London fogs were too much for her, how would she stand up to tropical heat and humidity? Years later she recalled her bitter disappointment.

One night, when upon my knees, with tearful confession of selfwill, it seemed as if I heard a voice saying, 'If you still want to serve Me go back to Glasgow, and take My message to the Salt Market and the district round about.' My heart almost stood still: the Salt Market was one of the vilest and most wicked places in Glasgow, inhabited almost exclusively by thieves and women of ill-repute. It was hardly fit for a man to go into such a place – could it be God was sending a young girl there . . .? I then told the Lord that as I could not go alone

I should refuse to go any day I did not feel His presence and power with me.[2]

Time was to show how vital this experience would be to her in China. Not telling anyone about her transaction, she stayed to help the travellers to prepare their outfits – and her health improved. Miss Gruber, the Swiss governess, was on the list, and Mary Bausum. Although barely fifteen, Mary had become a valuable member of the Coborn Street family and, as Maria well knew from her own journey to China and work as a missionary at the same age, deserved to be considered one of the party and not as a child. Hudson Taylor recognised this and listed her as going to assist her truly missionary mother.

After Maria's father, Samuel Dyer, died in 1843, her mother had married J G Bausum of Penang, only to die herself soon afterwards. Mr Bausum had later married Mary's mother, and then in the grim sequence of missionary fatalities he too had died. Maria and Mary were like sisters although fourteen years apart in age. With the Taylors and their four children, and a children's nurse, if a suitable replacement for Sarah could be found, the number of tickets to be bought was at least eighteen, at fifty pounds for each adult. Mary's mother, now Mrs E C Lord, would pay for her. Hudson Taylor would pay for his own family and the nurse. But the rest would have to be met from Mission funds. 'Pray for us,' he wrote to his mother. 'We shall need £1200 to £1500 more than we now have in hand for outfit and passage money alone by May 15. The Lord will provide.'[3] Continuing expenses for the Coborn Street premises and households constituted needs over and above those sums. Yet by February 6 he had received less than two hundred pounds since December 30.

A family pact   *February 1866*

More important to Hudson Taylor, believing as he did that God who had told him to take them would supply all necessities, was the need to weld the growing team into one. Socially it was happening already. No hint of disharmony between Cockney and Highlander, governess and shop-assistant, Baptist and Presbyterian, had been worthy of mention. They were one in heart and mind, keyed up to the adventure drawing daily closer, and sharing in the spiritual exercise of praying for their daily bread. Agreement on how to meet the unknown in China, and how to work together in a completely strange environment and strange language, must however be reached before they embarked. Every one of the party had the quality of independence which had led them to consider joining this young visionary on the terms he proposed – trusting God, not Hudson Taylor, to feed, clothe and house them. All knew the risks, at sea and on land, and the average life expectancy of perhaps seven years. He thought a written agreement would be wise but, perhaps remembering the trouble such documents had produced for the Chinese Evangelization Society, William Berger advocated full consultation and agreement without binding rules and signatures. As a wholesale manufacturer accustomed to dealing with employees and customers of all kinds, Mr Berger was far from naive. It was his considered judgment. A verbal pact involving loyalty based on mutual confidence and love could be stronger by far than any written bond.

On February 2 they met with the men, Duncan, Nicol, Rudland and Williamson, to discuss the principles of co-operation already accepted by Stevenson and Stott (p 70). Mr Berger was the chief spokesman. No minute or resolution was drawn up at the time, but when memories needed to be refreshed after they had reached China, Hudson Taylor drafted a memorandum which all accepted.

It stated that Hudson Taylor had felt called by God to do work in China which required helpers, that those who offered to help him must be satisfied that God himself had called them individually to work 'for Him' and for the good of the Chinese, 'and must look to God for their support and trust to Him to provide it, and not to lean on me.' They must be prepared to go and work without any human guarantee of support, 'promising to work under my guidance and direction,' while for his part he would 'in the event of my having funds at my disposal minister to their need as the Lord might direct me.'

Recognising that Hudson Taylor and Maria were the only ones with personal knowledge and experience of the conditions they were going to meet, and that their very safety might depend upon it – but not referring to the fact, or to the possibility that others in China might dispute his leadership – it was reiterated, with Mr Berger emphasising the point,

> that in every respect what I deemed requisite must be complied with. That where we should go to, where and when different individuals

should be located, the positions they should occupy must be left for me to determine . . .

That it was not for the brethren themselves to decide what they were fit for, or when they were to go, but that in all points save those of conscience on which Christians of various denominations differed, it was to be fully understood that I should direct.

That it was most needful for all to seek to assist me in the great work contemplated in every way in their power, above all supporting my hands by prayer [a reference to Moses' hands being held up by Aaron and Hur until the Amalekites were routed in the Sinai peninsula] seeking especially from God that I might be directed by Him in my direction of the affairs of the Mission . . . And finally, in the event of anyone being unable to work longer under my direction, he must quietly resign his connection with the Mission . . . that the relation between us was this: that as far as possible they should feel responsible for affording me all the help in their power in the work of the Mission, and that I should feel myself responsible for guiding, directing, and helping – pecuniarily and otherwise – as I might be able, and deem advisable . . . No human foresight could anticipate the various contingencies which might arise . . . and that my decision, *as such*, was to be accepted, whether those helping me could or could not see the necessity of the step . . .[4]

This was the agreement reached that day, February 2, 1866, at No 30 Coborn Street, though only committed to writing a year later. Each of the young men assented to it, and all who were included in the party during the next few weeks entered into the same unique pact on the same grounds.

Learning from experience   *February 1866*

The next day, Saturday, Hudson Taylor went down to Saint Hill and over the weekend completed his draft of the first *Occasional Paper*, to serve as an interim report of progress since the founding of the Mission and an announcement of their impending departure. Its main interest lies in its revelation of how he thought at this point about mentioning financial needs, and how, before it was published, his attitude changed dramatically, so that he had to insert a coloured slip of paper in explanation. In the second issue, before he sailed, he told the full story.

Summarising the financial arrangements made for the nine he had already sent out (including Martha Meadows), he said of James Meadows, 'His outfit and passage money were provided by a friend,' not naming William Berger. Miss Notman's expenses had been carried by the FES. The owner of the *Corea* had given free passages to Stephan Barchet and George Crombie, and all Stephan's other needs had been and were being met by the congregation of Bryanston Hall with whom he had worshipped. The FES had provided twenty-five pounds towards Anne Skinner's outfit and passage, fifty pounds for the Vigeon family, which they still hoped to use, and a hundred pounds for George Stott and the Stevensons whose tickets had cost one hundred and fifty pounds and their outfits a total of eighty-eight pounds. Between June and December 1865 a little over nine hundred pounds (£908 16s 8d) had been received in donations, all but two hundred and ten of which had been expended on outfits (£200), passages (£150), remittances to China (£160), printing presses (£69), printing *China's Need* (£25), rent, board, domestic salaries (£52) and sundry stores, stationery and travelling costs.[5] (*See* Appendix 7.) So 1866 had begun with £210 2s 8d in hand, together with a miscellany of goods in kind.

> Several valuable parcels of worn clothing and bed-linen for use on the voyage, have been sent to us [expendable because of ship's tar]; and we have received some articles of new clothing made at ladies' working parties. The cost of outfitting has been lessened by means of these contributions; and through the kind help of many ladies, materials purchased have been made up almost free of cost to the Mission. Most of the materials required have been supplied by Christian tradesmen, either at the trade price or at a considerable reduction on the ordinary selling price. Thus, in many ways, the Lord has been supplying the needs . . . As will be observed, the sums entered in the accounts as supplied to missionaries are very small, remittances having been frequently made by donors direct, thus leaving no necessity for their being passed through our accounts.

This referred to George Müller's and Thomas Marshall's practice of sending remittances from donors to the Scriptural Knowledge Institution's missionary fund and from Bryanston Hall, either direct to the missionaries abroad or by banker's drafts forwarded by Hudson Taylor. He also remitted the FES's provision for Chinese evangelists. Another source of incidental income had been the sale of 'pamphlets' published at William Berger's expense, 'bound in cloth, for one shilling, or paper cover, sixpence'. Because missionary boxes were convenient for some and popularised by the older societies, many donors asked for CIM boxes. They cost six pounds to produce, and were supplied on request, gratis.

> It only remains to speak of the prospect immediately before us . . . We are now preparing to leave England by the fifteenth of May, or as soon after that time as a suitable ship can be found. A party of ten brothers and sisters will accompany us, if the Lord provide the means . . . In the case of six others we have not yet arrived at a definite conclusion as to their accompanying us at this time or not. In addition to them we are in correspondence with several persons, of whom we have strong hopes that they will eventually have their way opened to labour in China . . . To meet the expenses of the outfit and passage of so large a party, funds (in addition to what is needed for current expenses) to the amount of from £1500 to £2000, according to the number going, will be required.
>
> In conclusion we may adopt the language of the Apostle Paul, and say, 'Who is sufficient for these things?' Utter weakness in ourselves, we should be overwhelmed with the immensity of the work before us, and the weight of responsibility lying upon us, were it not that our very weakness and insufficiency give us a special claim to the fulfilment of *His* promise who has said, 'My grace is sufficient for thee; My strength is made perfect in weakness.'

The simple, open statement of estimated expenses was to be a short-lived practice. He had also followed it in the final pages of his book:

> For the carrying on of the work, on the plan and to the extent proposed above, a yearly expenditure of about £5,600 would be needed. And for outfits and passage-money, considerable additional expense may be anticipated. . . . The support of a native brother will probably vary from about £15 to £20 per annum; a native Bible-woman will require about £12 per annum for her maintenance.[6]

There was a distinction in his mind between the needs of the China Inland Mission and those of Chinese who discarded their own means of livelihood to devote all their time to the gospel. He did not hesitate to encourage people to undertake the regular support of such a worthy cause. When those Christians became part and parcel of the pioneering existence of the Mission, he was to stop advocating their support. Hudson Taylor left this manuscript with Maria for her to edit while he was away in the north. This she did, but a fire at the printer's was to delay publication for another month.

In the second number of the *Occasional Paper*, Mr Berger made doubly plain what Hudson Taylor could not repeat without drawing attention to himself, that he had always,

> studiously refrained from appropriating any of the funds sent for the Mission to his own use or that of his family, or for his own house-keeping. Those sums only which have been sent for his own expenses has he felt free to appropriate to himself; and this practice he intends, by God's grace, to continue.

The principle of 'no personal solicitation', 'no collections' and 'no debt' was being adhered to. The anticipated costs had been stated and no more would be done to raise the sums needed. William and Mary Berger were ready to do all they could to help, but they wished neither the new mission to depend on them nor that Christians in Britain should be deprived of the blessing of a share in the spiritual enterprise. The Bergers as much as the Taylors and their team were placing their faith for its success in the Lord alone. Who or what God worked through was for God to show.

Money was only one element, and at that a small one, in the Mission's needs. Safety on sea and land and from hostile people, access and freedom to stay in remote Chinese cities, wise judgment in perplexing situations, harmony between themselves, with other societies and Chinese colleagues – an unending list could be drawn up of needs no Bergers or Müllers could supply. As James Meadows put it, Hudson Taylor 'did not trust in Mr Berger's nor in any man's gifts, he knew full well that there was no permanent help in princes,' citing the psalmist, 'It is better to trust in the Lord than to put confidence in princes . . . Put not your trust in princes, nor in the son of man, in whom there is no help.' (*Psalms* 118.9; 146.3). In God alone could they put their trust if they were not to be confounded. Not one would dare to set out on so solemn, perilous and distant an adventure looking for enough support to spring from a bland statement or two of anticipated costs, or from the small circle of friends they knew. God alone, through prayer to him as children to a Father, was their only hope.

So when the Mission's income during January and the first six days of February was £170 8s 3d, barely enough to sustain those already in China, Hudson Taylor's reaction was characteristic. Even a hundred pounds were not to be taken for granted.

We felt much encouraged by the receipt of so much money in little more than a month, as it was entirely made up of donations unsolicited by us – save from God. But it was also evident that we must ask the Lord to do yet greater things for us, or it would be impossible for a party of from ten to sixteen to leave in the middle of May.

On his return to Coborn Street from Saint Hill, when he opened his mail and found no fat cheques to change the picture, he called the three households together at noon specifically to pray for the money needed 'for the outfits and passages of as many as He would have go out in May'. The money received would dictate the number to sail. He stood where he had stood with John Jones in Shanghai when they resigned from the Chinese Evangelization Society. He would not embark upon borrowed money, or make his decision as to how many he should take with him, until God had shown him unmistakably by providing for their journey in advance. In this he differed markedly from the practice of the CES, and from a CMS report of the same period, 1853. He is seen to be less original in his declaration of faith than in his application of it. The CMS had said,

> The Committee state . . . before the Church at large, their willingness to accept any number of missionaries, who may appear to be called of God to the work. They will send out any number, trusting in the Lord of the harvest, whose is the silver and the gold, to supply their treasury with the funds for this blessed and glorious undertaking.[7]

The CIM were praying for at least twenty-four Western pioneers for the unevangelised provinces of China, and as many Chinese. The number who could go in May (and this was the crux) would be revealed in answer to 'daily united prayer'. Such prayer continued as the normal practice of the Mission.

That evening he had a meeting to address at Pimlico and afterwards was detained so that he reached home after midnight. The evening mail deliveries had been heavy. But he had an early morning train to catch to Barnsley, and so he must reply to them at once. At five forty-five a m he wrote finally to Maria at Saint Hill.

> I leave at 6.15 so must soon pack . . . (When I got home after midnight) I found a pile of letters which have occupied me ever since. I have written to McDougall. Have sent the cover [a design for the *Occasional Paper*] to Mr Elliott. I have told him that he may send the

proof of pamphlet sheet 'A' at any time. If it comes, read it carefully and return it. I am too sleepy to write more.[8]

The second edition of *China: Its Spiritual Need and Claims* was on the press. Not one donation was in those waiting letters, but a copy remains of his reply to the young Lady Radstock. Dating it February 7, he wrote,

> I think I may venture to accept your kind invitation for the 16th., my only fear is lest I should be so weary as to be unable to enter, as I should wish, into the important question to which you refer. I leave London for the North in about two hours and have engagements for each intervening day in the West Riding of Yorkshire, Liverpool, Birkenhead and Manchester until the 15th., when I lecture in London. But the Lord often gives physical strength, as well as grace, in answer to prayer, and I must look to Him. May I ask your prayers for God's help in endeavouring to lay China's need on the hearts of God's people in various parts of the country? . . .

His faith was to be honoured in such a way that his attitudes and practice were to become drastically changed.

The 'perfect stranger'   *February 1866*

More hung upon this seemingly unnecessary week of travel and incidental meetings in Barnsley, Liverpool and Manchester than anyone involved foresaw. It appears that a Mr T Matheson had invited Hudson Taylor to address a meeting of the English Presbyterian Mission in Liverpool on Tuesday, February 13, and another in Manchester at Dr Monro's church the next day. This was William Burns' own society and no one could speak more intimately of his Shanghai and Shantou (Swatow) period than Hudson Taylor. Liverpool was the home of his friend William Collingwood, the water-colourist and a leader of the Brethren (father of W G Collingwood, biographer of Ruskin, and grandfather of R G Collingwood, the Oxford philosopher and expert on Roman Britain). William Collingwood had seen him off to China on the *Dumfries* twelve and a half years previously and kept in touch. As a result of Charles Gutzlaff's visit to Liverpool in 1850, William Collingwood had been prepared before Gutzlaff died to go to China to pursue his art in the cause of missions. Hudson Taylor also had other acquaintances in Liverpool, so he decided to go early and look them up. The

Christians of Liverpool were missionary minded. The city had been the venue of the strategic missionary conference of 1860. (Book 3, pp 251–2).[9]

As he had seen little of his parents, or of his children since the dramatic days of Maria's confinement in early December and their hurried despatch to Yorkshire, he had arranged to interview James Meadows' fiancée, Elizabeth Rose, at Barnsley, her home town. He asked his parents to arrange for him to give a public lecture on China while he was there, saying 'it would last two hours', and early on the 7th he was on his way.

His father had taken the Mechanics' Hall for the lecture on February 9, and after they had gone early together to set up his display of Chinese curios and hang a large map, his mother wrote to Maria, 'He has had an interview this afternoon with Elizabeth Rose, and is very much pleased. She bears a most excellent character.' Another first quality member of the team, from good village stock, would be ready to sail in May.

He travelled on the next day to Liverpool and stayed the first night at the Collingwoods, cementing their friendship. Several times a year from then on they sent him donations of ten pounds. Perhaps by Collingwood's arrangement he moved to the home of a new acquaintance, John Houghton, and was introduced to the young orator-evangelist of the Evangelical Awakening, Henry Grattan Guinness, still drawing large audiences. A chain of remarkable developments at once began.

Grattan Guinness, then aged thirty-one (Hudson Taylor's junior by two years), had read his Perth address in *The Revival* magazine which, as he said, 'first drew my heart to him'. 'From that interview (at the Houghtons) sprang the friendship and fellowship of a lifetime,' crowned in the next generation by the marriage of Howard Taylor to Geraldine Guinness. The immediate result of their acquaintance was that Grattan Guinness invited him to Dublin to address a tutorial group of young men 'studying the evidences of Christianity with a view to preparing for home and foreign missionary work'. Hudson Taylor told Maria,

Please send immediately . . . four pamphlets to the Rev H G Guinness, 31 Upper Bagot Street, Dublin . . . 'He who opens and none can shut' has opened my way to Ireland. I've promised to go, D.V. on Monday the 19th to address (Mr Guinness' young men), on Tuesday . . . a meeting in Limerick, on Wednesday at Cork, Thursday Merion Hall, Dublin, [changed to the Rotunda], Friday Belfast, perhaps on Saturday going to Glasgow. How wonderful are His ways . . . if we *only* want to do *His* will, He will not leave us to walk in darkness.

His sense of Divine overruling was not mistaken. This appointment and its numerous outcomes have had historic effects continuing to the present day, as will be seen.

On Monday, February 12, after a satisfactory meeting specifically to tell about the China Inland Mission, Hudson Taylor was taken home for the night by another new acquaintance, Mr Robert Lockhart. Both Presbyterian meetings followed on Tuesday, the first in Liverpool and the second in Manchester, where he was the guest of David Bannerman. On Thursday, February 15, he arrived in London only just in time for his lecture to a working men's club at Grafton Street, Soho, arranged by another friend, Joseph Weatherley, and reached home at Coborn Street after midnight.

A letter written that same day by John Houghton followed him to London. Only his travelling expenses and a few minor gifts, none of more than five pounds, had been handed to him in the north. Another week had passed, a week of daily praying for '£1500 to £2000', and expenditure was still not matched by income. So John Houghton's note came as a breath of encouragement.

> It is my intention to contribute to the China Inland Mission and shall endeavour to interest my Friends in the Work . . . In the meantime I have sent £25 to the London and County Bank . . . When you come to Liverpool, I shall be glad to see you and give you a Prophet's Chamber.

William Collingwood's wife was Swiss, and had 'like one of the family' a Swiss governess for their children. Louise Desgraz shared the Collingwoods' concern for China, and after Hudson Taylor's visit offered to go with him. She too came to Coborn Street, another member of the fast-growing community, and another needing an outfit and a ticket to the far side of the world.

Even at Liverpool Hudson Taylor was working on proof sheets of the second edition of *China's Need*. To Maria, an invalid barely convalescing, he wrote with a long list of emendations.

> You may go to press with sheet 'B' of the pamphlet if you can. See what Mr Berger's suggestions are, and if you judge them suitable

adopt them. You know the reasons which led to the use of almost
every sentence in the book . . . We need to get out the edition as soon
as possible, or we shall be out of them. I am sorry to hear that you
have been overdone. Do take care of yourself Darling, for the Lord's
sake and for China's sake. May He strengthen you, Love, and spare
you to me and the dear little ones and His own work.

He had to see her, however briefly, so after a little more than a cat
nap and a change of clothes, before most of the household at No 30
even knew he had returned, he was off again at five a m to Saint Hill,
'just to spend an hour or two with Maria and stayed till dinner time'.
He had hoped to be able to bring her home to London, but the
cavity in her lung was still bleeding and the Bergers insisted that she
stay with them.

He dined with the Radstocks at Bryanston Square that evening
(of Friday, February 16) and, it appears, addressed a number of
their friends who came in afterwards. Probably at table that evening
the conversation took place to which Lord Radstock referred when
he spoke at the annual meeting of the CIM in 1880. In answer to a
question as to how many would be sailing in May, Hudson Taylor
said, 'If the Lord sends money to send out three or four, three or
four will go. If for seventeen, then seventeen.'[10] He would not
presume to know the will of God without an adequate indication of
it, nor would he incur a debt by buying what he could not pay for.
Recurrent obligations, such as rental of premises, had to be viewed
differently. The need and the provision to meet them initially, he
treated as justification for the obligation incurred.

He was to catch a seven fifteen a m train to Ireland on Monday
morning, February 19. So he packed on Saturday and after the usual
weekly hour of prayer for China at Coborn Street he went to Euston
Road to spend a quiet Sunday with the Fauldings. A letter from
Grattan Guinness arrived on Saturday. The Dublin men were to
meet them on Monday evening. He himself would then travel with
Hudson Taylor to Limerick and Cork and take part in the meetings,
'being better known at present in Ireland than you are'. This was
sheer humility and courtesy, for at both places he had addressed
huge audiences. 'I feel profoundly impressed with China's need,' he
continued. He would meet the ferry at 'half past six Irish time, seven
o'clock English, and bring you on to our house. May you come in
fulness of blessing.' How quiet that Sunday at the Fauldings was
may be doubted, for long after midnight Hudson Taylor was writing

to his mother, 'Pray for me, for I am tired; but God will help me, He never fails me.'

Ten days in Ireland   *February 19–28, 1866*

The effects of this visit to Ireland were out of all proportion to appearances. Three generations of some of the CIM's best missionaries throughout the rest of the 'open century' were to spring from this brief meeting of dedicated minds. New missionary societies and the training and sending of many hundreds of missionaries to widely scattered parts of the world were to be a direct outcome. Barnardo's Homes were to owe their germination and sapling growth to it.

Grattan Guinness was a big man in every sense. Tall and striking in appearance, a man of vision and big ideas, he drew others as if magnetically by his firm convictions and the enthusiasm of his devotion to God. His father had been an officer of the East India Company and had fought in the Mahratta campaign.[11] When Grattan Guinness himself and his younger brother Robert were midshipmen, and his vessel was short-handed through desertions, he had known 'the exaltation of battling single-handed with the top-gallant sail when sent aloft to furl it before the rising storm'. Robert served with a Christian first officer and was converted at sea. Arriving home at two a m one night when the house was full, he climbed into Grattan's bed with him and talked at length about finding Christ, in such a way that 'from that night he (too) was a changed man'.

No less could Grattan keep his new life to himself. He began going from house to house in Tipperary speaking about Jesus. The priests denounced him. He was threatened with violence and death. But he wrote to his mother that the wider world needed him as a missionary. She advised him to study for the ministry and he went to New College, London, for two years. Academic life was so deadening to his spirit that he left and, declining the pastorate of Moorfields Tabernacle, gave himself to evangelism. In the great revivals of 1859 thousands in England, Wales and Ireland flocked to hear him. 'Grattan Guinness was the most popular evangelist in Ulster during the 1859 Revival and on one occasion he addressed twenty thousand people from the top of a cab.' '(He won) multiplied thousands of converts.'[12]

After five years, when he was twenty-seven, he met Fanny

Fitzgerald. Her father, Major Edward Marlborough Fitzgerald, and her mother, daughter of an Admiral Stopford, were both dead, and Fanny was making her home with a Quaker couple at Tottenham. Three months later Grattan and she were married in the Quaker meeting house at Bath and sailed at once to America where he drew more crowds.

They had no home of their own, moving frequently and living as guests or short-lease tenants in place after place, as now in Ireland.

On February 19, 1866, Hudson Taylor caught the Irish express to Holyhead. Grattan Guinness met him in the evening at the Kingston pier, Dublin, and took him 'home' to No 31 Upper Bagot Street. The Guinnesses and the men in their study group had read Hudson Taylor's book, and been strongly influenced. Charles T Fishe and his brother Edward, the sons of a retired colonel of the East India Company's Madras Horse Artillery, well-disposed to Hudson Taylor,[13] had already corresponded with him. A letter from Charles Fishe dated December 6, 1865, was not the first. John McCarthy, mature and thoughtful, was older and married with three children. Another, like the Fishe brothers not yet twenty-one, was Thomas Barnardo, short, slight and bespectacled. At fifteen he had read books by Voltaire and Tom Paine and been captivated by their socialist and agnostic arguments. So when he was converted at seventeen through the testimony of a newly Christian actor, and of his own brothers, he wrote to George Müller for advice, saying, 'Seven members of my own family and myself within the last five months (have turned to Jesus Christ.)' To study the Bible and Christian doctrine with Grattan Guinness was the best thing for him.

That Monday night of February 19, 1866, he and his friends were sitting in the Guinness home. When the door of the room opened and the commanding figure of Grattan Guinness filled the doorway, eclipsing Hudson Taylor, for a moment they thought he was alone. 'Where is the great man?' exclaimed Barnardo in an undertone to John McCarthy. Then they saw Hudson Taylor, so much shorter than Guinness, 'fair-haired . . . with an abundance of white tie and in a dress coat'. (A fair inference is that they were amused. Was he still at the height of 1852 fashion? Or right for London but not provincial Dublin? cf p 125). Disappointed, McCarthy was saying to Barnardo, 'I suppose he's not come,' when Barnardo interrupted with 'There's hope for me!'

Standing by the mantelpiece and pointing to a map, indicating province upon province, Hudson Taylor urged upon them 'the claims of China' as their personal responsibility. He had found fertile soil. Four of them, McCarthy, Barnardo, Charles Fishe and another, probably Edward Fishe, afterwards asked for an opportunity to talk with him personally. It was 'long after midnight' before Hudson Taylor got to bed.

> The night [wrote John McCarthy in retrospect] was a very memorable one for me. I there heard the answer from God to many prayers . . . I see him now, so quiet, so very unassuming in his manner and address, but so full of the power of God. I found that night that I had not only heard the answer from the Lord as to my sphere of service, but that I had found the God-given leader in the work to which God had called me, and the little talk in his bedroom after the meeting and the simple prayer to God for guidance are among the most treasured memories of my life.
>
> (He had) a wonderful fund of sympathy which led (us) to feel that he considered these matters under discussion to be of primary importance, so that for the time being he evidently [visibly] gave them his undivided attention.[14]

Many people had told McCarthy that having a family was an insuperable barrier to his being a missionary overseas. When Hudson Taylor told him there was scope for married as well as single men and women, it was the first encouragement he had received.

The fact that Hudson Taylor prayed with him first (as with each of the men) before discussing his problems, made the deepest impression on Charles Fishe. Years later when he knew Hudson Taylor intimately he wrote, 'His plan always was, prayer first, talk afterwards.' Of these four, three followed Hudson Taylor to China. The Brethren of Merion Hall, Dublin, deterred young Christians from going abroad, saying there was enough to be done at home, Charles recalled, but Colonel Fishe, his father, warmly approved, only requiring that he should delay going until more mature.

Grattan Guinness and Hudson Taylor set off for Limerick after an early breakfast on the 20th, and as they travelled on each of the next three days had time to talk. His wife and he, Guinness said, were no less concerned than McCarthy and his friends, and were weighing up what they should do. 'Is it God's will, God's call?' 'Shortly afterwards, we ourselves were led to . . . a decision I have never regretted,' to offer to go to China. Hudson Taylor, however, advised that at their age they would find the Chinese language exceptionally difficult and frustrating, and that with his gifts as an evangelist and expositor Guinness could do more for China by staying in Europe. How fully this proved to be true will emerge as this saga unfolds. Of their own three children, Harry was to step into his father's shoes, Geraldine and Whitfield to spend their lives in and for China, and some of the grandchildren after them.

At Limerick they were the guests of a Mr Boyd, connected with the Howards of Tottenham. 'Limerick is very excited at present,' Hudson Taylor wrote to Maria that night. 'They are today arresting about sixty leaders of the Fenians here.'[15] But the meeting was well attended, the book *China's Need* sold well, and at least one person, Susan Barnes, offered to sail with him in a few weeks' time. Again at Cork in the far south the next day all went well.

At his own expense a good friend, Henry Bewley, had hired the Dublin Rotunda as a denominationally neutral venue for a major meeting, and on Thursday, February 22, Grattan Guinness and Hudson Taylor travelled back to address an 'influential and representative audience' who 'well filled' it.

Then he set off alone for Belfast ('I know no one there') and on arrival at a hotel wrote of southern Ireland,

Some hundreds know more of China's need than they did before . . . Some fine young men and several females desire to go to China. Fishe, I think, is *now* too young . . . One medical student (Evans) desires to go . . . [In Belfast on Saturday] I commenced the day fearing . . . lest I might not get on well among strangers and rather stiff Presbyterians (but) I thought, if my wife were here, leaning on my arm, led on by me, she would not feel anxious. And I leaned more heavily on (the Lord's) arm and went on. . . . I am to speak of China (in lieu of the sermon) in the Rev Dr Knox's church . . . at 11.30 a.m. Then to take the whole service for Rev Dr Morgan (of the principal Presbyterian Church) at 1.30 p.m.–3 p.m. Thence to dine with a gentleman immediately, and afterwards to address a Sunday-school at 5 p.m. Then a full service (for Rev Dr Cook) at May Street Church at 7 p.m. So you see how wonderfully God has opened my way here. Now for grace to trust Him for wisdom and strength . . .

Sunday the 25th was as full as promised, and as rewarding. Apart from five and a half hours of actual services there were the social intervals with many questions to answer. He took it in his stride. Taxing his strength of mind and body to the limit, as he so often did, only someone in essentially robust health could have stood the pace he maintained day after day (often night after night) and week after week. The diseases that had brought him home from China were things of the past. He could write from Belfast, 'I . . . am, I think, quite as fresh as when I left London.'

But he was anxious about Maria. Why was there no letter from her either at Dublin or Belfast? They had an arrangement that she should address him at the post office wherever he was going, if she had no address. Was she very ill again? And had the proofs of the *Occasional Paper* reached her; and of the second edition of *China: Its Spiritual Need and Claims*? He felt he ought to get home without delay and wrote a full page in the Ningbo vernacular, a way of committing his tenderest remarks to paper.

Although on Sunday he had addressed 'some thousands of hearers', he had himself booked the large Victoria Hall for a lecture on China on Monday night, and the mayor of Belfast had agreed to preside. Another meeting was being arranged for him in Dublin on Tuesday night, so he discarded the contingency plan to cross over to Glasgow.

The earliest he could return to London was Thursday, March 1, in time for a meeting of the Foreign Evangelist Society. He would try to catch the last train out to East Grinstead, he wrote, but he would have to go on to a drawing-room meeting in Brighton the next day, and then back to London 'for our own meeting' on Saturday afternoon. He was writing to Maria on the train between Belfast and Dublin while waiting at Moira for the derailed engine of a freight train to be cleared from the track.

> I feel very little doubt that the result of this attempt to stir up the Presbyterians here will be the sending of several missionaries to China. If the English Presbyterian Mission will only follow up the interest, they will easily get funds for the support of three or four men. Belfast is the centre of Irish Presbyterianism. The expense of this effort cannot have been much less than £4.0.0. But we must not consider as loss what we expend in the service of God.

Two years later, in response to William Burns' dying appeal, two Irish Presbyterians took his place in Manchuria.

Back in Dublin Hudson Taylor appears to have consulted further with the Guinnesses and others, advising Tom Barnardo to come to London. He joined the Coborn Street family a month later. A Mrs Gainfort, who ran a study group like the one at Upper Bagot Street, also had two young men who spoke of going to China. Robert White and Thomas Harvey were both to train briefly at the London Hospital and join Hudson Taylor in China, with bizarre results. True to her word, Susan Barnes, the Limerick girl, also came to Coborn Street and sailed in May. Travelling overnight to reach London on Thursday, March 1, Hudson Taylor told his parents, 'I think we shall get about ten labourers for China from (Ireland), and support for most of them eventually.' Shortly after he had gone, Fanny Guinness wrote to him,

> We see our way clearly now, I think, to aid the work not *directly* but indirectly . . . *Here* we may do much and be the means of sending you many more efficient labourers than ourselves . . .
> We feel we must make a beginning, by striking while the iron is hot; and propose to establish at once an 'Irish Auxiliary of the China Inland Mission' . . . to disseminate information and stir up interest . . . to promote prayer and liberality on its behalf . . . to assist in the way of counsel, training, etc, suitable candidates, and provide funds for passage and outfit money.

Hudson Taylor could be forgiven if he became anxious as he read. This high-powered couple could be valuable friends, but did they intend to start raising funds? She enclosed a 'notice' which they proposed to disseminate through Ireland, and urged that two of the six or eight candidates willing to go at once should join the team to sail in May, even if it meant leaving two English ones behind, and continued,

> It is something tangible to say, Here is the opening and here are the men, funds are wanted now for this definite purpose . . . [Again she showed that they themselves had much to learn of Hudson Taylor's principles.] It would add to your staff a different style of men also . . . McCarthy was here last night; full of calm purpose but of patience too, ready to go but willing to wait. His wife's confinement will be over before you sail . . . She is a trained teacher.

Hudson Taylor's reply has not been preserved, but that he made his views plain and carried the Guinnesses with him in thought is seen times without number in their subsequent dealings with each other.

Rank and influence *March 1866*

The excursions were over and he was back at work in London. The nominal sailing date had come all the closer. For three weeks they had been praying together for two thousand pounds (forty thousand today?) with little apparent effect. For the younger members of the team at Bow it was becoming a severe test of their fledgling faith. The Bergers and Maria exercised their own stronger faith as they waited for God to act. Hudson Taylor himself made no reference to the matter in his letters from Ireland. Miss Stacey sent twenty pounds, and a Birmingham couple the same amount, but until February 24 only six gifts of a pound and one of £12 10s had come in. When Hudson Taylor reached Saint Hill and Maria on March 1, he learned that on the 24th Lord Congleton had sent a hundred pounds for the Mission and George Müller twenty-five pounds for the Taylors' own needs. At last the tide showed signs of turning.

Lord Congleton was John Vesey Parnell, the second baron. In 1829 when he was twenty-four he had arranged for Anthony Norris Groves and his missionary party, of which Parnell himself was one, to travel in a friend's yacht to Saint Petersburg en route for Baghdad. Three years later he had married an Iranian Christian from Shiraz, disowned by her family, and from 1837 they lived very simply at Teignmouth in an uncarpeted house, that he might give all he could to good causes. In 1849, seven years after succeeding to the title, he had moved to London and become the leading member of the assembly at Welbeck Street, where he came to know Hudson Taylor. He was not a wealthy man, leaving seven thousand pounds when he died.[16]

On March 2, the day after Hudson Taylor arrived back from Ireland, William Berger made a gift of three hundred pounds to pay for the printing presses and founts, and told him of twenty pounds from a friend in Southport. The Brighton lecture had been postponed, so at least he had Friday with Maria, no better in health, before going that evening or on Saturday to Coborn Street to share his news with the rest of the team. Finding Grace Ciggie down with bronchitis again, it seemed clear to him but to her great distress that she ought not 'to go just now'.

He was due in Birmingham the following Tuesday, but the week's chief appointment was the Radstocks' reception at 30 Bryanston Square on Thursday, March 8. Writing to his mother he said, 'A hundred and sixty or more persons of influence or rank, or interest in China, have been invited, in the hope of their helping this work by prayer and effort.' This of course meant monetary help as well and Hudson Taylor, while not himself taking action to raise funds, was grateful for whatever the Radstocks or anyone else did in their own name as distinct from the CIM's. He told his mother that in addition to the two hundred and ten pounds in hand at the close of 1865, he had received since then about seven hundred and fifty in all, of which five hundred and fifty pounds were toward the goal of two thousand.

Tuesday, March 6 was cold and wintry. He went to Birmingham as the guest of one of the Howard family and her husband, E R Lloyd, of The Shrubbery, Spark Hill – Anglicans who had once been Friends. By the time of the meeting it was so stormy that Hudson Taylor was advised not to go out, no one would be there. His own sense of duty and experience of rough living left him no option. He made his way to the schoolroom and found eight or nine waiting, joined shortly by others. Thirty-four years later he told a friend in Switzerland that that occasion was one of the most influential in his experience. Half of those present either became missionaries themselves or gave one or more of their children to be, and the rest became permanent supporters at home. In the morning he called on Dr Benjamin Hobson, Robert Morrison's son-in-law, Liang A-fa's colleague in Canton, and his own good friend in Shanghai, the first to translate books of Western medicine into Chinese. He was introduced to the newly appointed chaplain of Fuzhou, George Hamilton, and with ten pounds from the Lloyds in his pocket he returned home to find that in his absence a William Rawlinson of Taunton had sent two hundred and fifty pounds to Coborn Street. A month later the Lloyds were asking for 'two or three dozen missionary boxes and a supply of literature' to follow up the interest in China his visit had aroused.

Sending an outfit list for Elizabeth Rose to Hudson Taylor's mother, Maria wrote on March 8, 'We have received £1,000 this year: to God be *all* the glory.' These were very large amounts and new experiences for all of them. The theory of trusting God and praying to him instead of asking people for money was working out in practice. Awakening interest and a sense of responsibility were delighting those who responded and leading them into the additional pleasure of a deeper commitment to God which expressed itself in generosity. The pattern was plain, and evident from all corners of

Britain. Many friends were dressmaking for the team and helping with the children's outfits, Maria said. Mrs Berger had a working party at Saint Hill every week, and Miss Stacey was about to start one at Tottenham. Outfitting had begun well before funds for the costly passages began to come in.

Thursday evening arrived, and Lord and Lady Radstock were at home to their invited guests. The rooms were full and Hudson Taylor too much in demand to meet everyone. The following Wednesday, while he was in Brighton, a gentleman from Berlin (whose name Emily Blatchley spelt as Prince de Talm Harstman and elsewhere as Harzmann) found his way to No 30 Coborn Street and asked her, she wrote, 'to give you his very very kind compliments, and expressed his regret at not having the pleasure of shaking hands with you. He could not get an opportunity of speaking with you at Lady Radstock's the other evening, he said.'

The Guinnesses had come over from Dublin and were at Lord Radstock's evening to share the limelight with Hudson Taylor. Grattan's sparkling wit and 'marvellous power' were of a different order from Hudson Taylor's measured presentation of fact and transparent conviction. But it was also a social occasion, as the invitation made clear. Dublin was out of step with London, apparently, for 'to her horror' Fanny found the ladies so *décolletée* that her own neck and shoulders were unfashionably covered. No report of the speeches has come down to us, so the main light on the occasion and the guests is thrown by a succession of notes from Lord Radstock to Hudson Taylor in the days after the event. By normal timing of the China mails, William Burns' letter of January 6 was due and Hudson Taylor would have been glad to refer to it, and to Burns' opinion which led to the postponement of his Burma project. But it did not arrive until the next morning, so he probably referred to Burma as a potential door to western China.

On the day of the Radstocks' reception Hudson Taylor entered in his cash book the sum of twenty pounds from a Captain Browne of the Royal Artillery, Woolwich, and five pounds from the Earl of Cavan. After Eton the earl had served in the 7th Dragoon Guards, for six years as lieutenant-colonel.[17] As a member of the general committee of the Chinese Evangelization Society he had known Hudson Taylor for fourteen years, and more recently as a trustee of the Mildmay Conference. The Rev W Hay Aitken, curate to William Pennefather at St Jude's Mildmay, and widely known in later years as Canon Hay Aitken of the Keswick Movement, was the next donor listed. Like three of the van Sommer family who followed, he gave ten shillings.

Entry No 81, on March 10, was of a gift of greater magnitude. A letter from John Houghton of Liverpool stated, 'I have now to inform you that I have this day remitted to the London and County Bank £650.0.0. on account of the China Inland Mission, being a donation from my Father Mr Richard Houghton . . . who on reading your work on China feels the importance of making Efforts to preach the Gospel in the Interior of that vast Country.'[18]

On the same day Lord Radstock wrote enclosing cheques for one hundred pounds from R C Bevan of 25 Princes Gate; six pounds from Mrs Braithwaite of Gloucester Place, Hyde Park; five pounds from their neighbour Miss Erskine of 29 Bryanston Square and another hundred pounds from himself. Robert Bevan, a partner in Barclays Bank, was an Anglican, deeply involved in numerous Christian societies, especially the CMS, London City Mission and YMCA.[19] Previously a member of the general committee of the Chinese Evangelization Society, he also had followed Hudson Taylor's progress for fourteen years.

Suddenly the heavens had opened and funds were flowing in. All doubt about how many should sail in May was evaporating. At this rate any who were fit and ready could be included. Hudson Taylor sent off remittances to Ningbo, and more a fortnight later.

With pardonable vivacity he wrote from Saint Hill on the 12th acknowledging the gifts, only to have his letter cross another from Lord Radstock enclosing fifty pounds from Francis A Bevan, a son of Robert Bevan, and a partner in Barclays, becoming chairman in 1896. He too was an Anglican, primarily supporting the CMS. Thanking Lord Radstock for the £211 he had sent, Hudson Taylor went on, 'May the Lord abundantly bless you, and all the kind donors, for His dear Son's sake,' and told him about each of the other gifts received. Six hundred and fifty pounds 'from a perfect stranger' whom he had never met! Twenty-two pounds from Presbyterians in Scotland. And this morning three more donations, bringing the total receipts and balance brought forward from 1865 to £2154 17s 10d. Of this, little more than two hundred pounds had been used in expenses at home and remittances to China. He did not say that until a few days ago the barrel had been very nearly empty. In addition Grattan Guinness received more than a hundred pounds for the CIM, and at the soirée another hundred had been promised. From the fact that a hundred pounds came shortly afterwards from the Beauchamps of Norfolk, Lord Radstock's sister and her husband, it may be assumed that one or both were present on the 8th. 'Is not the Lord working wonderfully for us? He seems to say, "Ye shall see greater things than these."'[20]

The lesson learnt   March 1866

While Hudson Taylor was away in Ireland, Maria and the Bergers had steered the draft of the first *Occasional Paper* through its first editing and despatch to the printers, and had checked the proofs with Hudson Taylor's help and handed them over for the final printing. But the fire at the press (mentioned on p 110) and the engraving of the title page had delayed production, so that the printed sheets only reached the publisher for stapling and distribution on March 10. Yet he delivered the completed papers in 'bales' to Coborn Street on the 12th in time for the German prince to take half a dozen to his friends in Berlin.[21] Meanwhile Hudson Taylor wrote to his parents from Saint Hill on Sunday, March 11, saying that the whole of the two thousand pounds named in the *Occasional Paper* as being needed, had in fact been received by the 10th, Mr Richard Houghton's six hundred and fifty pounds completing the estimated sum.

> Of course *he* knew nothing, either of the amount required, or of the sum in hand towards it. Of this £2000 I do not think more than £450 are given by those personally known to me, and none of it save a few small sums amounting to less than thirty shillings is given anonymously. Thanks be to God! [PS] This morning £210 *additional* has come in. I return to London tomorrow. Maria remains.[22]

He arrived at No 30 on March 12 in time for the daily session for prayer from noon until one p m, and reported progress. For a month and six days from February 6 the households, 'eighteen of us', had been praying like this. Afterwards, in the presence of the young men and women, and saying, 'Let us now see what God has done . . . before this paper is circulated,' he brought out his cash book and did a quick calculation.[23] In the equivalent period before February 6, only £170 8s 3d had been received. During the period since that date £1974 5s 11d had come in. When Hudson Taylor made a similar comparison a month and six days after March 12, 'the receipts were £529, showing that when God had supplied the special

BEHOLD! THESE SHALL COME FROM FAR; AND LO! THESE FROM THE NORTH AND FROM THE WEST; AND THESE FROM THE LAND OF SINIM. ISAIAH XLIX. 12.

JEHOVAH-NISSI.

1866-67

China
Inland Mission
Occasional
Paper.

以便以設耳

耶和華以拉

NISBET & CO., BERNERS STREET.
S. W. PARTRIDGE,
9 PATERNOSTER ROW, E.C.

EBENEZER

JEHOVAH-JIREH

COVER DESIGN OF THE *OCCASIONAL PAPER*

(*Reduced facsimile*)

need, the special supply also ceased. Truly there *is* a LIVING GOD, and He is the hearer and answerer of prayer.'

To every one of them this was God's demonstration that he would provide for them in China. But in those bales of *Occasional Paper* No 1 was the statement in print: 'To meet the expense of the outfits and passage of so large a party, funds (in addition to what is needed for current expenses) to the amount of from £1500 to £2000 according to the number going, will be required.'

The policy of trusting God and letting the facts be known (not 'personal solicitation', but indirectly an appeal) had been dramatically shown to be unnecessary. More than enough for those purposes was in hand. To Lord Radstock he wrote,

> Before we could get the *Occasional Paper* into circulation stating that £1500 to £2000 would be needed . . . the *Lord* had sent the whole sum. None can now say the 'Paper' has done it. No! The *Lord* has done it – His alone is the glory. And I am so thankful that three fourths of it is is given by persons who are strangers to me.
>
> P.S. Perhaps I should add . . . that the number of those going out is likely to be increased by two, and perhaps four labourers, from Ireland. Is not this cause for gratitude? and ought we not with the fullest confidence to leave the care of all these dear Brothers and Sisters in the Lord's hands, who has *shown* Himself both able and willing to do *more* than we asked or thought?

He was sensitive to what critics, even friends, were saying about his financial prospects and also about the risks he was leading a bunch of innocents into. But if God provided for their material needs in this way, could they not equally count on God's protection?

The *Occasional Paper* could not be sent out as it stood. Quickly he had a letter printed (probably on the Mission's hand press already in use), for insertion in copies to be despatched to all donors, and a coloured slip in all the rest, stating what had happened. A difficulty remained, however. To say that these needs had been met might be misconstrued as meaning that no further donations were required. It would be wise to say more. In solving his problem he still did not abandon his previous stance. Thanking the donors again, he pointed out that individual donations were acknowledged by number on the cover of the *Paper*. Then he said that unsolicited contributions had already more than covered the needs stated inside, 'leaving a small surplus towards the current expenditure of the Mission, and the somewhat heavy initial expenses which may be anticipated on our arrival in China'. He had covered the danger of misunderstanding, but had again deliberately brought other needs to their attention. He was learning step by step, but had not yet reached the point of being silent about monetary needs, except to God, until after they had been met. His practice at the time was summed up by a nephew in these words:

> Although Mr Taylor did not hesitate, when he thought it desirable, as the early records of the Mission will show, to publicly state what financial outlay certain developments involved, there was to be no solicitation of money, but a simple dependence upon God to move the hearts of His stewards, as His servants obeyed His bidding.[24]

The change was not long in coming.

His companions were learning too. William Rudland, the Cambridgeshire mechanic, later recalled that through reading of George Müller's experiences he himself became confident that God would supply his own personal needs as well as the Mission's. As an only son he believed he should go and see his mother in Somerset.[25] But the earnings he had brought to London had all been spent. He could not even afford a stamp to let her know he was coming. So he asked God to make it possible, and told no one of his predicament. One Saturday Hudson Taylor put a sovereign into Rudland's hand saying, 'If you need more please let me know.' It was not enough, but a friend at Annie Macpherson's refuge for children where he was helping gave him ten shillings, and a friend of Mrs Merry two pounds more. Ungrammatically he wrote, 'Instead of asking Mr Taylor for more, the Lord so abundantly heard prayer that I was able to give a donation to the Mission'! Recording these reminiscences he also remembered that when Mr Berger and Hudson Taylor together interviewed him before formally receiving him into the CIM, Hudson Taylor said, 'Remember this. You are going out to serve the Lord Jesus, not the China Inland Mission. The Mission might fail. Look always off to Him (*sic*). He will never fail you.'

A succession of meetings continued to keep Hudson Taylor busy, speaking for Dr Landels at the Regent's Park Chapel and with his good friend George Piercy of Canton on two occasions at Wesleyan chapels. On March 14 and again on the 22nd, this time joined by Maria, he was the guest speaker at social events in Brighton.[26] At the first, 'a drawing-room lecture', he received several contributions from 'titled ladies', and after a second a succession of donations from the same and others. Many in the upper strata of society were not ashamed to be zealous evangelical Christians. Lady Aberdeen and her daughters donated five pounds.[27] Lady Georgina Bailey, a close relative, was another, and Lady Abinger, widow of the first Baron Abinger, a third. A later donation from Lady Abinger was accompanied by gifts from two of her servants. The most enthusiastic friend made at Brighton, however, was A Cuninghame who gave Hudson Taylor twenty-five pounds after his first meeting, asked for two hundred copies of the *Occasional Paper* to distribute, sent to him the next day, and forwarded gifts from his friends on subsequent days.

The money mattered, though most amounts were small, but the chief aim of all these meetings was being achieved – the Christian public were becoming increasingly alert to the facts about China, and were being moved to care about China and to identify themselves with what was being done for China. The recognisable quality common to true men of God and being seen in Hudson Taylor by those who came to know him, commanded their attention. And more – many loved him for what he was, so that the affection and admiration of Lord Radstock, for example, remained as strong in 1913 as in 1866. Others responded while his influence on them lasted, until wider interests put their first impressions into a new perspective. The early Brethren particularly approved of his conciliatory, supra-sectarian attitude toward 'all who loved the Lord Jesus in sincerity and truth'.

March was coming to an end. Lord Radstock forwarded more incidental donations, writing 'May the Lord guide you and may you follow His leading.' The Howards and Miss Stacey made Maria and Hudson Taylor feel loved by having the children to stay with them and by substantial donations for their own use. On the 27th and 29th he paid the last amounts in rent for their own house, No 30 Coborn Street, and for Nos 33 and 34, intending to be away on the high seas within two months. On the 28th Grattan Guinness called at Coborn Street to confer with him, probably about the Irish recruits coming to London, and at East Grinstead for interviews with the Bergers and Hudson Taylor together. John McCarthy, Tom Barnardo, Susan Barnes and a Miss Walshe arrived on or just before Saturday, March 31, and went with Hudson Taylor to Saint Hill for the weekend. Years afterwards, Grattan Guinness remembered the scene at No 30.

I think I can see now that lowly dwelling as it was in those days, its narrow front passage encumbered and crowded with boxes and baggage . . . and I well remember the wonder and joy felt at the speedy and liberal answer to (their) prayers, the beginning of the inflow of the funds by which that Mission has been sustained in all its growth and development.

And John McCarthy too, writing thirty-five years after the event:

I was particularly struck with the careful instructions given me by Mr Taylor in his letter. He knew that I had not been to London before and gave me such minute directions so as to save me trouble, that if I had been blind almost, I might have gone direct to his house by asking a few questions. With all the large and important matters that filled his mind, he never forgot to go into any minute matters . . . to help (those) he had to deal with.

We found him in the midst of busy preparations for returning to China . . . It must have been clear to the most careless observer that the fundamental principles of successful leadership had been very clearly grasped by our brother for certainly as much as any man I had ever met, he did seem to be the servant of all those who, in their inexperience, made such demands upon his time and patience. With the whole weight of the responsibility of the movement resting upon him, a movement thought by many good men . . . to be rather wild and quixotic, with meetings and correspondence and all the arrangements for the departure of the largest bodies of missionaries that had ever sailed at one time for China . . . with no one but his dear wife whose experience could . . . help him, he was still ever ready to help in any possible way, and willing to answer the various questions by which he was often overwhelmed.

The manifest dependence upon *God* for guidance, shown in the frequent reference of all matters to the Lord, was no doubt the secret of the calm, steady perseverance to attain the object in view. One could not fail to be struck by the way the Lord had prepared His servant for the work to which He had called him. Questions on printing, lithographic or common engraving, purchase of materials, and the thousand and one things that come up in connection with a large party leaving home for a foreign land, and for the first time, (would) all seem to have light thrown on them by reference to a leader who was supposed to know everything and who really did seem to have learned something about every matter that was however remotely connected with the work.

John McCarthy had to return home soon afterwards and wait for his wife's confinement, but Tom Barnardo moved in with Rudland,

Williamson, Nicol, Duncan (and probably Jackson) at No 33. For his practical training Barnardo was attached to Annie Macpherson's rescue work for destitute children, in connection with the Friends' Bedford Institute near Bishopsgate. It opened his eyes to their existence in large numbers in East London. At the Westminster Chapel on August 4, 1876, Hudson Taylor threw more light on the community life at Coborn Street. They 'had a short period of testing – testing rather than training – training in some measure, but rather testing than training'.[28] Life in such rough circumstances was to some extent potentially as revealing of personality and spirituality as life in China would be.

Soon it was clear to Hudson Taylor that Tom Barnardo would benefit by longer preparation before going to China. In consultation with Mr Berger it was agreed that he should study medicine, and Hudson Taylor introduced him to the London Hospital Medical College. After returning to Ireland he came to stay at Coborn Street again at the end of April and began preparing to take the entrance examinations. In his Bible he wrote 'Tom Barnardo, China', and in 1869 his heart was still there – as well as in London. As far as can be judged, Susan Barnes joined Grace Ciggie, Eliza Calder (Mrs Nicol), Louise Desgraz (and Miss Gruber?) under Mary Parsons' care in No 34, while Emily Blatchley and Mary Bausum held the fort with the nurse and children at No 30 while the Taylors were away. Maria had been ill since September, and in danger of her life through November until her confinement was over in December. At Saint Hill from January 16 she had been an invalid under serious threat, cared for by Mrs Berger and her maid Ann Boffey as if she were their younger sister. At last in April she seemed fit enough to venture out, but not to go back to the pressures of London life. A sea voyage, good sea air, was considered ideal for patients with tuberculosis, so no apprehension, no reference to a possibility of her being unfit to travel appears in the records. She was to face China and all that the future held as if she were well and strong.

'Wit, intellect and learning'   *April 1866*

Only six weeks remained until the date Hudson Taylor had set himself for sailing. A mountain of work lay before the whole growing team and the small army of friends already straining to make or find bedding, clothing, personal effects and furnishing for the cabins and saloon of the ship they had yet to engage. Hudson

Taylor had visited and made his mark in Scotland, Norfolk, the West Riding of Yorkshire, Lancashire, Ireland, London and Brighton. Only to the western counties where he had many friends had he not given as much time. In Brethren circles he was well loved, particularly by George Müller at Bristol and Robert Chapman at Barnstaple. His links with friends from China formed another strong bond. R H Cobbold of the CMS in Ningbo, rector of Broseley in Shropshire, wanted Maria to come with Hudson Taylor. He had escorted her to China in the *Harriet Humble* in 1852 when she was fifteen, less than fifteen years ago. And as one of the original translators of the vernacular New Testament he had authorised and followed with interest Hudson Taylor's revision from its inception.

The Evangelical Awakening had made a strong impact from Shropshire to Devonshire, which meant that there were men and women there who might respond to the claims of China. Dr Edward Cranage, through whose 'prayer meetings' at Wellington, Salop, thousands turned to Christ, welcomed him to come and speak. 'Leo' Hay at Malvern wanted Maria too. The town halls of Cheltenham and Bath were to be booked for him. Philip Gosse, the naturalist, father of Edmund, and one of Hudson Taylor's early friends at Hackney, had moved to Torquay. A visit there would allow him to call on Anne Crombie's mother at Callington in Cornwall. At Exeter were the Chancery barrister Henry W Soltau whom he had come to know at Welbeck Street in 1865, and a Lieutenant-Colonel Stafford who was to be his host. So he had arranged an itinerary from Shropshire to Exeter, Torquay and Plymouth, ending with a return visit to Bristol on the way home. How much he himself initiated and how much was at the instance of his friends is not clear, except that he himself co-ordinated the plans. Painstaking preparations at each place, with printed posters and handbills advertising his lectures and church services, led to full halls and quick results. In 1872 he was to repeat the tour to report on the intervening years in China.

Hudson Taylor and Maria left London together on Wednesday, April 4, and he returned three weeks later. It was a long absence at such a crucial time. Reliable mails and an efficient secretary in Emily Blatchley made it possible. Leaving Maria at Broseley[29] he was the guest on Thursday of Dr Cranage at the Old Hall, Wellington, and addressed 'a good meeting'. After witnessing the Ulster revival in 1859, Dr Cranage had returned to Wellington and called his friends in all denominations together to pray for God to bless

Wellington as he was doing in Ireland. Unconverted people began to attend in growing numbers. Forty-five thousand attendances at his meetings in the next two years resulted in six or a dozen conversions nightly.[30] A loyal Anglican himself, he had built a hall for the community in 1862 regardless of denomination.

Hudson Taylor had come to the heart of the spiritual movement, and was well received. He returned to Broseley to lecture on Friday, lectured again to a full house in the historic 'Meet-room' at Hereford on Saturday, spoke three times on Sunday and again on Monday. Between meetings he was writing business letters, confidently committing work of all kinds to 'dear Miss Blatchley'. In view of the part she was to play in the next few years, these glimpses into her personality at the age of twenty-one are illuminating.[31] From dealings with the bank and despatching books to addresses he supplied; from 'give Mr Vigeon's shirts to Rudland as proposed,' to 'stir up Mr Elliott about the *pamphlets*,' he counted on her efficiency and was not disappointed. Signing his letters on April 9 'Affly yours in Jesus', he followed the first to her on that day by a later note about entries in the invoice book, apparently expecting it to reach her by the late delivery on the same day. 'The Lord be with you and bless you,' he wrote. 'Do retire soon.' She worked long hours and late at night, hence, Go to bed! He also wrote to Maria at Broseley enclosing two pounds their host had given him after seeing Maria's poor state of health. He wished her to travel by first class on her return to London.

Emily was no less engrossed that day at Coborn Street. As the co-ordinator of outfitting she wrote to Jennie Faulding at her Euston home. 'Dearest Jennie' had mobilised forty women to work for them,

> a goodly number, and I am glad they promise to *finish* [Emily scrawled]. I heard from dear Mr Taylor this morning . . . He feels he is being prospered – of wh. thing we who know him have but little doubt . . . Yesterday I cd. not come, having to 'pay out' as dear Mr Taylor said I shd. have to do, sooner or later, for the night work of the previous week. Well, I don't want to *rust out*, you know, dear. [And in a PS] Please, dear, get the white petticoat done off today; as I want it to take as a pattern to get more of the Indian long-cloth . . . Be sure, dear, leave Miss Bowyer's drawers if anything is left: they are not cut out . . . Get someone else to cut the shirts, dear. I shd. think they can; and you'll not have time; I cd. not possibly send them before; I've done my utmost – been at work since soon after mid-

night, and have to go to Wickham's (the outfitters). What is not taken in hand, I had better have back at once – others are wanting work, faster than I can supply it . . . Better not let the ladies pull the packets apart, dear; or the things will get into confusion. It would be well to have them all laid out *as they are* on a table with tickets uppermost . . . please impress upon them the importance of keeping all the pieces of one article together. [The next day it was about shopping and discounts, and ended with:] This morning's letter from dear Mr Taylor tells me he is getting on well – and working; 3 lectures per diem; yet so dear and kind and thoughtful of me. 'Do go to bed early.' But I really do not see how I can possibly get to bed at all tonight; I'll try . . .

To Maria she gave news of the family in all the bustle. 'The dear children are all quite well. Gracie got feeding her brothers with Mr Taylor's morphia lozenges.' Herbert had had most, treated with castor oil, two or three days before. She was looking for more work to give the forty ladies 'of our church' (at Regent's Park) and for Mrs Jones, Mrs Lane and the ladies of Epsom Street. Also, in a glimpse of their frank relationship: Was one of the dresses Maria had bought intended for anyone in particular? 'I do not hesitate to ask you,' she added, 'because I know you will kindly say "no" if you had in mind another to whom to give it.'

From Hereford Hudson Taylor went to Ross. In apologising to his mother for writing infrequently he said Maria was to join him at the Hays' home in Malvern Wells and stay while he went on with his journey.

Has Miss Blatchley ordered a black suit for Meadows through you? . . . Lecturing and travelling, and being in strange places fill all my time, and require all my strength. Besides which I have an *immense* correspondence . . . [But] our outfits are getting fast forward to-wards completion.

This day's letter to Emily was about detailed money matters and printing. She should address him on the 16th c/o General Bell, Abberton House, Cheltenham. Would she please send a dozen copies of each of the five different photographs of members of the team. And 'continue to pray for me. It is rather hard work.'

After Ross it was Ludlow Market Hall, by favour of the mayor, and then Malvern, where 'all classes (were) invited' to the meeting

CHINA AND THE CHINESE.

REV. J. HUDSON TAYLOR,

M. R. C. S., F. R. G. S.,

MEDICAL MISSIONARY FROM NINGPO, CHINA,

WILL

LECTURE

UPON THE

PRESENT CONDITION OF CHINA,

EMBRACING THE GEOGRAPHY, ANTIQUITY, AND
POPULATION OF THE EMPIRE,

ON THURSDAY, APRIL 12,

AT HALF-PAST THREE O'CLOCK, AT THE

WINTER PROMENADE,

SOUTHFIELD, MALVERN.

DR. GRINDROD IN THE CHAIR,

ADMISSION FREE. NO COLLECTION MADE.

All classes are invited to attend the Meeting, when subjects of intense
interest will be brought before them, not only as it regards the spiritual
destitution of 400,000,000 of their fellow-creatures, but in reference to
their manners, customs, religions, languages, &c. Maps, drawings, idols,
and costumes, will be exhibited.

A similar LECTURE will be given at Malvern Wells, at half-
past 7 p. m. on the same evening.

PRINTED AT THE "ADVERTISER" OFFICE, MALVERN: W. BARNES, MANAGER.

A POSTER FOR THE WEST COUNTRY TOUR

in Great Malvern followed by a lecture at Malvern Wells. Arrangements had been made for a missionary-minded local girl, Mary Bell, to sail with the Taylors to China as their children's nurse. Then on to Bath, where he wrote 'affly and tenderly' to Maria. He had already had two lectures, one in the town hall, and had three services ahead of him on Sunday. The Bergers were to be with him at Bristol. 'Mr and Mrs Berger wish you to go to Saint Hill whether they are at home or not. In haste with much love (as train almost due) Hudson.' Ann Boffey would mother her there. Maria told his mother,

> He generally has to rise early and travel early and does not get much rest except in bed . . . Dear Hudson still speaks of the 15th of May, but I doubt whether we can possibly manage all by that time. We shall be glad if you can come, to make up in some measure for his being able to spend so little time with you. . . . Dear mother, I do admire the grace of God in you, in enabling you to give your son, your only son, whom you love, to God and His service. A lady says 'your dear husband has won the hearts of many in Bath'. God does seem to be giving him favour with those he meets.[32]

On the 16th he was lecturing at Cheltenham town hall. At Stroud the next day he was not disappointed that no meeting had been arranged. In a letter from the train he told his mother,

> Some interest has been excited in places where the need of China was little realised and where our work for it was unknown before . . . Through a misunderstanding I had a holiday yesterday at Stroud. The Lord saw I needed it and gave it to me . . . It is a joy to work for such a Master. If the labour is great, and the difficulties numerous, and formidable, the strength – 'all might according to His glorious power' – is greater. No service can be happier . . . But the reward is not yet. It is eternal. Miss E. Rose need not come to London before May . . . My soul is often filled almost to overflowing . . . We shall be ready to sail by the 15th if we get suitable shipping . . . I question whether (Maria) will be able to get to Nottingham. I *must* do so. D.V.

From the railway station on the way to Devon he advised Maria, still suffering from the effects of her traumatic confinement, to go home. On the 20th she went to Amelia at Bayswater. Apparently after breaking his journey at Bristol to see the Bergers, he went straight on. At Teignmouth or Torquay an undated note from the

saintly Robert Chapman of Barnstaple reached him, saying he
expected to see him there on the 18th, and giving him this invitation:

> My dear brother Taylor,
>   Consider our claim on you. We desire fellowship with you in your
> work. Oh! come and speak to us your brethren here. Say when you
> can come. . . . God delights to fill our open mouths [a reference to
> *Psalm* 81.10] . . . If by His Spirit we know Christ aright, we know we
> have favour with God . . . 'The time is short.'
>   Yours affectionately in Christ,
>   Robert C. Chapman.

They had dined together at George Pearse's on September 20, 1863,
and were warm friends as long as both lived. Hudson Taylor went to
Barnstaple on April 24, 1866.

What transpired at Teignmouth, Torquay and Plymouth, which
he visited on the 17th to 19th, was largely obscured in the records by
his preoccupation with correspondence. But Henry W Soltau was
there, and the effect on him and his whole family is a keystone in the
history of the CIM. Hudson Taylor stayed at the home of Leonard
Strong in Torquay, visited Plymouth, and spent a night at Anne
Skinner's home in Callington, Cornwall. He met Philip Gosse
who gave him a donation, and was taken to Exeter by his host
Lieutenant-Colonel Stafford of Southernhays. A *cri de coeur* had
reached him from Emily Blatchley.

> I would rather tell you thus than when you return. Yesterday came
> the telegram that I have been looking for, hourly, all this week. My
> brother is being brought back to London, while I write, – *not* living.
> And he *would* not believe that he should die: bade father go down
> next week and take him for a walk.
>   God is laying the strain terribly tight, and on many chords at
> once – touching my soul to the very quick. For *this* is one of the many
> swords that are piercing just now; that have come all together. Will
> you plead just this for me, – that I may *be strong*, and await with
> more patience and *submission* the issue of these anxieties.
>   If you are writing to any friends here, make no mention of my
> brother's death. Bear with me, but I could not endure the well-meant
> vacant commonplaces of friends – not just now. Pray that my sister's
> life may be spared, – and that somehow the blood of Christ may
> cleanse black stains. And that if I have to bear the thing I dread, I
> may do so bravely.

>   And that God will rectify all that is wrong – to His own glory and
> to the salvation of those I love.
>   Yours very affectionately,
>   Emily.
> P.S. You must not fear to trust me with directions and commissions,
> dear Mr Taylor: sorrow is no new thing to me that it should stagger
> and bewilder me.[33]

His reply has not come down to us. All his letters to her were
solicitous, even affectionate, without being familiar.

At Exeter station on Saturday, April 21, he had time for a note to
Maria, outlining his movements as far as London on Thursday.
'Before (then) I hope to meet – you, darling, and to find you better
. . . as for His work's sake we are now often separated, may He
spare us to, and for each other, in His service, and give us more real
love and happiness in each other than we should have by *selfishly*
seeking for such enjoyment.'

Pulmonary tuberculosis, the killer of many thousands every year,
had its grip on his Maria. Although many contracted it and recovered, effectively immunised against further tuberculosis, he
could not but have strong premonitions of fatal progress in her
intractable disease. Every moment with her was precious to him.
Still at Colonel Stafford's two days later, he referred to going to
Brighton,

> to speak for the CMS, but most likely return the same night. That I
> must complete my own outfit and prepare for China. On Thursday or
> Friday I must take passages. Three ships are before me. Pray for
> guidance. . .
> P.S. Have (advised) McCarthy (that his wife come to London and be
> confined there) . . . She might be well enough to go from our house
> to the ship, tho' unequal to come from Ireland . . . Barnardo is
> coming up to stay with us till we leave.[34]

He was looking ahead. At Exeter more was happening than he was
aware of.

Henry W Soltau, a barrister of 'sparkling wit, keen intellect, and
extensive literary acquirements' and in 'his full vigour', had nine
children. Three grown sons, George, William and Henry, and three
daughters, Agnes, Lucy and Henrietta were to serve the CIM in one
way or another. Agnes was to marry the architect Richard Harris
Hill in a few weeks' time.

Father came home at midday [on Saturday, April 21, Henrietta wrote], and the first thing he said was 'I have seen a missionary from China . . . Go to Mr Cole and secure the Athenaeum for him tonight and ask him to get out bills as quickly as possible in order to fill the hall! We three sisters went off and told everyone we could . . . and when the evening came the hall was crowded. [At Colonel Stafford's, Hudson Taylor] looked so slight and young, with light hair. He gave us a warm welcome and asked us if we had ever prayed for China. We said 'No' . . . That evening he spoke on *Proverbs* 24.11 and 12 ('If thou forbear to deliver them that are drawn unto death . . . if thou sayest, Behold, we knew it not . . . He that keepeth *thy* soul, doth He not know it? . . .'). My sister Agnes and I hardly slept that night, and in the morning she said to me, 'If only I was not going to be married next month, I should go to China, but you must go, and Richard and I will help support you.' The next day I offered to go, with my parents' support.[35]

What had Hudson Taylor said at Teignmouth to capture the barrister's heart and mind? He was not an orator. The impact of his words lay in their precision and sincerity delivered carefully in dependence on God to use them. James Meadows was to write,

I was never charmed with Mr Taylor's eloquence; he was a man of fluent speech, well chosen words always, but he never stirred one's soul by eloquence of speech, but the eloquence of his life of Faith in God is a continuous power for good.

For what remained of his life, H W Soltau 'took the deepest interest' in Hudson Taylor's venture. Henrietta was to recall that people thought it 'a tremendous risk' to take a defenceless team 'to such a country', but 'some said a prophet had risen up amongst them.'

On Sunday after he had preached in the morning, the Soltau girls took Hudson Taylor to their Ragged School in 'a low dancing-room' in Cheek Street. He talked about idols and idol worship so vividly that the impression made on them and others 'was never forgotten'. They asked him to preach the gospel to the very poor and in the evening he took as his subject the man possessed by evil spirits and delivered by Jesus who then said, 'Go home to your family and tell them!' What struck Henrietta was the insistence that those who owe their freedom to Jesus should go and tell others. On the Monday he lectured again, with the Bergers joining him overnight at the

Staffords. Then he went north to Barnstaple and spent the evening with Robert Chapman. Six or seven years later Robert Chapman greeted Hudson Taylor with patriarchal affection, saying, 'I have visited you every day since you went to China!' meaning that he had prayed for him daily by name.[36]

He could never tell where or when there would be a response or how profound it would be. Looking ahead, that weekend at Exeter brought to him all three Soltau sons, Henry, William and George, who with Agnes' husband Richard Hill became his mission advisers and administrators in London a few years later. In 1875 Henry joined John Stevenson as a pioneer at Bhamo, Burma. Henrietta, after nursing Lucy and her father through their last illnesses, opened a home in London for the care of missionaries' children, and later for training new missionaries – herself one of the most outstanding women in the China Inland Mision.

So ended Hudson Taylor's fleeting visits to various parts of the country, none providing more than a weekend's contact with people who previously had been strangers, yet radically shaping the lives of numbers of them. Word reached him that his Brighton appointment had been postponed, so he broke his homeward journey to have a few hours with George Müller and other friends in Bristol.

He reached home later on Wednesday, April 25, picked up the reins of management at Coborn Street, balanced his accounts, entering gifts sent in by William Collingwood and J M Denniston, had his books audited, and handed them over to William Berger. In the first *Occasional Paper* he had requested, 'As far as possible, letters and communications should, after the 30th of April, be addressed to W T Berger Esq, Saint Hill, East Grinstead, who has kindly agreed to carry on the home department of the work after our leaving England.' That same day, April 30, the first farewell meeting was held in Kingsland, near Mildmay, Josiah Jackson's home ground. From the first of May until they sailed, preparations of all kinds and goodbyes to their now extensive circle of well-wishers were the order of the day. They had no time to lose.

PART 2

THE *LAMMERMUIR* PARTY

1866

CHAPTER FOUR

BON VOYAGE!
1866

'I must take passages'   *May 1866*

If six hundred and fifty pounds from a new reader of 'the pamphlet' was a remarkable windfall, and if sizeable gifts of fifty or a hundred pounds from several others ensured passages to China for ten travellers, the effect on Hudson Taylor may seem astonishing. In modern values we see those figures in terms of thousands instead of hundreds. Yet he was no more surprised than satisfied. The gift of missionaries for China was in answer to prayer, and more men and women were hoping to sail than even such generous funds so far made possible.

It was time to book passages. The party need not be all in the same ship, but to have his whole team under instruction for four, five or six months at sea, would have considerable advantages. He had been too busy to teach them very much in London. The educated members had been reading standard books on China and the Chinese and, like John Stevenson, learning the language through the romanised script. The rest needed personal tuition and all ought to make good headway with Chinese 'character', the ideographs. They would do this better with his and Maria's help than on their own in another ship. Before facing a foreign land together with all the cultural adaptations they would need to make, they must adapt to one another in unfamiliar circumstances. They must be welded into a working team. More even than that, in the life they were going to lead they would need not only to tolerate but to love each other. His inquiries were well advanced, and his shipping agent, Captain Killick of Killick and Martin, Moorgate, was keeping him informed.

Travelling conditions had changed since Hudson Taylor first went to China. Steam had come in, making steamships increasingly independent of wind and current, but steamers were relatively scarce. Not until 1883 did the registered tonnage of British steamships exceed that of sail. On both sides of the Atlantic and on the Pacific coast of America during the sixties and seventies, shipyards were turning more and more to iron. Steel replaced iron only in the eighties. Not until the late fifties did screw-driven vessels usurp the proud place of the side-wheel marvels. Then Jardine, Matheson's ships outpaced other companies' and arriving ahead of most mail ships could manipulate the China market. The design of sailing ships had reached its peak in the fifties, with 'Yankee clippers' from New England and Nova Scotia the fastest and most breathtakingly beautiful. Long, sleek, tall-masted, carrying a huge spread of sail, one had logged four hundred and sixty-five nautical miles at twenty knots one day in 1854. They were by no means outmoded in 1866.

The five years of 1864–69 were the heyday of the Oriental tea-clippers. Forty sailed to Britain each season with fresh tea from China's spring harvest. While the old sail, with poop and deck structures impeding progress, lumbered slowly across the oceans with inferior produce, taking five or six months between China and England, the new flush-decked greyhounds were cutting the time taken to four months or less. These were the days of competition between ship and ship, company and company, days of tremendous *esprit de corps*, of seamen's shanties at their best, and of nail-biting finishes at London and Liverpool. Clippers would load alongside each other at Fuzhou, Xiamen (Amoy), Canton and Shanghai. The Shanghai vessels would be towed by steam tugs to the mouth of the Yangzi estuary near Gutzlaff Island, and at crack of dawn up-anchor and head for the Cape and home and the five-hundred-pound bonus for the ship that berthed first. Big bets were laid on them and first cargoes fetched top prices from tea-fanciers.

Of all famous races, that of 1866 while Hudson Taylor's team prepared to sail, was most historic and exciting. Five clippers of between seven hundred and eight hundred and fifty tons left Fuzhou within three days of each other. They reached the English Channel so close in each other's wake that at the Downs roadstead, beside the Goodwin Sands, the *Ariel* was ten minutes ahead of the *Taeping*, only to lose to her by eighteen minutes at docking. A captain earned two hundred pounds a year and twenty-five shillings weekly for his board, the first officer or mate no more than six pounds a month. Such were the currency values. Prestige mattered more, so that crews were not hard to enlist.

The *Cutty Sark*, showpiece of the era, was built in 1869, at the end

THE *CUTTY SARK* AT SEA

of the clipper era and the apogee of its glory, a wooden ship on an iron frame. The Suez Canal had opened to shipping in 1867, though not officially inaugurated until 1869. So while steamships passed freely from the Mediterranean to the Indian Ocean, sailing ships could not afford the towage and kept to the high seas. Their voyage curtailed, the steamer could charge four or five pounds per ton of cargo to the sailing ship's seven. So sail progressively declined. In its heyday, when the Coborn Street party were preparing for tar stains on everything, the fast clippers had cabins and gilded saloons, with red plush or velvet upholstery, showers, ice-rooms, and the rigorous etiquette of the captain's table. Fares were correspondingly impressive, not far short of two hundred pounds per passenger, wines included. In contrast, the Stevensons' and George Stott's passages had cost fifty pounds each in a very different type of vessel.[1]

The 'overland route' was still the fastest, involving trans-shipping at Alexandria and crossing Egypt to the Red Sea by camel before and by train after 1858, but only on hard benches in cattle trucks. To ensure the safe transit of much personal baggage could be the last straw in the difficult journey. To transport all the luggage of a large party such as Hudson Taylor's, the women and children, would be too difficult an undertaking. The cost of a journey by that route, from London to Shanghai, was prohibitive. Three thousand pounds would not have covered it. By the average ship round the Cape he should be able to buy passages for a total of one thousand pounds.

With all their advantages, the P & O Steam Navigation Company still had to traverse poorly charted waters. Little advance had been made since the voyage of the ill-fated *Dumfries*. Between 1850 and 1870 sixteen P & O ships were wrecked or disabled on the treacherous coral-reefs of the East Asian routes, or overwhelmed by unheralded typhoons of ferocious strength. Only the previous year, 1865, the P & O *Corea* had vanished in a typhoon with the loss of one hundred and three lives. Navigation by eye and hand, in all weathers, still could not avoid the unknown or anticipate the unpredictable. To take your life in your hands was an expression in every traveller's mind. To Hudson Taylor and his companions the dangers of the sea were only a prelude to the hazards of inland China. Without Church or organisation behind them, or any human promise of financial support; without precedent or experience of penetrating beyond the treaty ports, except by a few individuals, they were putting themselves into the hands of God, deliberately, confidently – and cheerfully. The Coborn Street family sorted, sewed and packed to the sound of singing.

The team complete   *May 1866*

So far the experiment of mixing Methodists and Baptists, Presbyterians and Brethren, Anglicans and Congregationalists, artisans and middle-class men and women was working well.[2] Shared beliefs, motivation and fellowship in spiritual experience were common ground. Essential priorities overrode points of difference in creating harmony. No one who lacked this spirit would be suitable for the new mission. Qualification to be a missionary in China involved far more. Physical and mental health went without saying, but a recurrent problem was, Who was to determine the suitability of applicants, and how? Appearances were misleading and medical men often mistaken. Even exemplary conduct could be maintained for months during a period of testing, only to prove unequal to the temptations and stresses of life abroad. Spiritual qualifications came first. Anthony Norris Groves had said, 'By keeping a man at home who ought to be seeking the Lord's glory abroad, you as much weaken the Church at home, as by sending abroad one who ought to stay.'[3] Hudson Taylor looked for the man and woman who clearly had been called by God to leave home and go. If God had indeed called them, shortcomings were secondary, and could be mastered. 'Simple obedience to Christ alone; recognition of Christ alone in my brother . . . unreserved devotion to Christ alone', was the standard Groves set and Hudson Taylor followed.[4] In judging the fitness of one who offered to join him, Hudson Taylor looked for, 'a strong, genuine experience of Christ's power to save and satisfy in the individual life of the applicant; (and) zeal and courage in winning souls'.

In his book he had said that men 'full of faith and the Holy Ghost' need not fear educational disadvantages. Henry Venn was looking for ordained men for the CMS, preferably from the universities, or at least of the type who could be ordained after being trained in a clergy school, such as Islington College.[5] The LMS and WMMS also laid emphasis on ordination following academic training, until after this period in their history. So Hudson Taylor was deliberately avoiding action which might draw away such men from their own church societies. He wanted intelligent, educated men *and* women, but believed that intelligence was found independently of social origins or standing, and that the best, most effective type of missionary was the true man or woman of God, whether educated or not. 'The fear of the Lord is the beginning of wisdom.' Looking at the apostles Peter and Paul as historical counterparts, he valued both types. Eversden mechanic and Dublin student, evangelist and Sinologue. In *China: Its Spiritual Need and Claims* he called for those 'whose superior education will enable them to occupy spheres of usefulness into which others could not enter'. All were welcome, and in time all would be well represented in his mission.[6]

In William Rudland he had a good example of those with social and educational disadvantages whose love for Christ and zeal in pointing others to him made him a good missionary wherever he was. Decades later Rudland was to be known for the strong church he had planted and nurtured, for his translation of Scripture into the dialect of Taizhou, for the products of his printing press, and for faithfulness in the face of danger, suffering and discouragement in many forms. At many points his life touched Hudson Taylor's. The thread of this history returns to him again and again.[7]

To the three Scotsmen, Duncan, Nicol and Williamson, and Nicol's bride Eliza (Calder), was added Jane McLean, a 'Bible-woman' from Inverness attending William Pennefather's training school; and to the Londoners Josiah Jackson, Emily Blatchley and Jane Faulding, another teacher Mary Bowyer, also from Penne-father's fold, and a Romford, Essex, man named John Robert Sell. Information about these new members at this stage is scanty. William Collingwood's governess, Louise Desgraz of Switzerland, James Meadows' fiancée Elizabeth Rose of Barnsley, Susan Barnes of Limerick, Mary Bell of Malvern (the Taylors' nurse but no less a missionary), and Mary Bausum completed the party. One other was uncertain, probably the other Swiss governess Miss Gruber, the only girl listed with the rest who did not sail. When her mother fell ill she decided to stay and take up nursing.

Grace Ciggie's improved health led Hudson Taylor to say she could step into the gap. It was too late. Though she longed to go, she had committed herself heart and soul to taking the gospel into Glasgow's Salt Market. 'I had to say "I can't go," even though it almost broke my heart.'[8] John McCarthy stood by his wife's reluct-ance to face the sea voyage with a new-born babe and three other children, and deferred their sailing until October. The accountant, James Vigeon, and his family had at last accepted the adamant refusal of his employers and her parents to release them, and again had to be left behind. Hudson Taylor felt his loss keenly, having hoped so much of him. After this they faded from the records, though remembered to this day through their inclusion in the photographic 'group of twelve' in September 1865. Why he did not share the load assumed by William Berger has never been ex-plained. The team was complete. The passage money was in hand.

Preparations were advanced and no satisfactory ship had yet been found.

The chairman overruled　　　　　　　　　　　　　　*May 1866*

Two leading Methodists were watching Hudson Taylor. William Arthur, a one-time missionary in India, had been on the General Committee of the Chinese Evangelization Society and was secretary of the WMMS when Hudson Taylor was urging the societies to undertake the evangelisation of inland China. In 1866 he was president of the Wesleyan Conference. The other, Alexander McAulay, also a missionary, succeeded him as secretary at the Wesleyan Mission House in the East End in 1866, and then as president of conference. On August 29, 1876, he recalled at the home of the temperance editor T B Smithies, when bidding farewell to William Rudland on his second departure to China,

> I watched very closely the manner and the spirit of the people who were about to proceed to China ten years ago (1866). I was highly delighted to find that the spirit of self-sacrifice was very deep in every one of them, so far as I could discern. They were all, as far as I could see, given to prayer, and they had all the elements about them that were likely to make them successful missionaries in any land where God might call them.[9]

Another ex-member of the CES General Committee was a Baptist named Robert Lush, recently knighted and made Lord Justice. As members of William Landels' congregation at the Regent's Park Chapel, he and Lady Lush were interested in Jennie Faulding and Emily Blatchley, and in Hudson Taylor's venture. On April 8 the great chapel was filled for the Baptist Union meeting, with more than fifty ministers present. Among them were Charles Haddon Spurgeon and William Garrett Lewis of Westbourne Grove, co-founder with Landels of the London Baptist Association. Jennie wrote to Maria,

> Thanks dear Mrs Taylor for your letter. I shall be so glad to have you both back again . . . The claim of foreign missions was the subject for consideration. Mr Landels spoke beautifully . . . and so kindly of dear Mr Taylor's work and of us. (Working parties at the chapel are making up the outfits) and a good many have taken work home. Everybody is kind to me . . . I am feeling very much what a trial it will

be to leave England; but I long to be in China . . . Oh that we may all
be filled with the Spirit! Goodbye, my own dear Sister in Jesus,
   Yours with warmest love,
                      Jennie Faulding.
. . . Lady Lush has just sent me such a nice parcel of thin dresses for
the Mission.

Packing and crating all the necessities of a large party was
time-consuming, even with so many highly practical men in the
team. Unable to imagine the extreme heat and humidity of the
tropics, how ink and jam would swell and burst their containers, or
the need to keep sea-water out of tin boxes by soldering all cracks,
or the possibility of cabins and saloon being awash in storms, they
needed personal direction in all kinds of detail. At the same time
valedictory meetings and lectures had been arranged in fifteen
locations, involving Hudson Taylor and some of the party almost
daily. Co-ordination of all these activities was important, and only
Hudson Taylor could do it. Everything must be shipshape and
loaded aboard before the sailing date, whenever that might be.
Every day mattered.

On May 1 a philanthropist who had contributed twenty-five
pounds in December, Francis H Mackenzie of Dingwall, Ross and
Cromarty, put into Hudson Taylor's hands one hundred and fifty-
three pounds. Fifty pounds were for current expenses, but the rest
was to provide another fount of type and inks for the printing
presses, and medicines and instruments for his medical work.
Hudson Taylor had accepted an invitation to lecture at the village of
Totteridge near Barnet and on the 2nd went out to Whetstone,
north of London, as the guest of Colonel John Henry Puget who was
to be his chairman, a brother of Dowager Lady Radstock. As usual
he had stipulated that handbills announcing the lecture should state
'No Collection'.

Colonel Puget had protested. He had never had that condition
imposed before. It was most unusual. But he accepted it, and the
handbills were distributed. That evening, using his large map of
China, Hudson Taylor described 'something of the extent and
population and deep spiritual need of China'. Seeing as the lecture
ended that 'many were evidently impressed', Colonel Puget rose
and declared that although at the speaker's request the announcement of the meeting had carried the words 'No Collection', he felt
many present would be distressed if they could not contribute

towards the work in China. Hudson Taylor's account of what then happened, ran:

> He trusted that as the proposition emanated entirely from himself (the colonel) and expressed, he felt sure, the feelings of many in the audience, I should not object to it. I begged, however, that the condition agreed to might be carried out; pointing out among other reasons for making no collection, that the very reason adduced by our kind chairman was, to my mind, one of the strongest for not making it. My wish was, not that those present should be relieved of making such contribution as might there and then be convenient, under the influence of a present emotion; but that each one should go home burdened with the deep need of China, and ask God what He would have them to do. If, after thought and prayer, they were satisfied that a pecuniary contribution was what He wanted of them, it could be given to any Missionary Society having agents in China; or it might be posted to our London office! but that perhaps in many cases what God wanted was *not* a money contribution, but personal consecration to His service abroad; or the giving up of a son or daughter – more precious than silver or gold – to His service. I added that I thought the tendency of a collection was to leave the impression that the all-important thing was *money*, whereas no amount of money could convert a single soul; that what was needed was that men and women filled with the Holy Ghost should give *themselves* to the work: for the support of such there would never be a lack of funds. As my wish was evidently very strong, the chairman kindly yielded to it, and closed the meeting.[10]

At his home, Colonel Puget told Hudson Taylor over supper that he thought him mistaken. A few people had handed him some small contributions, but a good opportunity had been lost.

When Hudson Taylor came down to breakfast the next morning, he was greeted by a letter from Captain Killick. A ship called the *Lammermuir* had come in and would be sailing again soon after May 20. Her accommodation was right for his party; he could have the whole of it. Would he inspect it at once? Colonel Puget came down late, looking tired, and admitted he had not had a good night.

> After breakfast he asked me to his study and giving me the contributions handed to him the night before, said 'I thought last night, Mr Taylor, that you were in the wrong about a collection; I am now convinced you were quite right. As I thought in the night of that stream of souls in China ever passing onward into the dark, I could only cry as you suggested, 'Lord, what wilt Thou have *me* to do?' I

think I have obtained the guidance I sought, and here it is.' He handed me a cheque for £500, adding that if there had been a collection he would have given a few pounds to it.[11]

At Colonel Puget's request this cheque (for what we may now regard as ten thousand pounds) was entered in the accounts as from 'a Friend'.

The 'Lammermuir' taken   May 1866

Hudson Taylor's firmness in not allowing a collection at Totteridge went back to his boyhood training and his father's inflexible, almost obsessive integrity. The outcome strengthened Hudson Taylor's conviction that it was always best to carry out exactly any undertakings once they had been given. 'A little thing is a little thing,' he often said, in his typically simple phrasing, 'but *faithfulness* in little things is a great thing.'[12] His surprise and delight were none the less, for this gift was over and above the ample funds he had already received. He went straight back to London, down to the East India docks, approved of the *Lammermuir*, returned to Killick, Martin and Company, and put down a deposit of £382 10s 0d on the entire accommodation, half the fare for eighteen adults at £42 10s each. There at the shipping office he wrote briefly to his parents, holding his breath.

> 8 South Street, Finsbury
> 3/5/66
>
> Dr. Mother,
>   I have *taken* our passages in the 'Lammermuir'. Heavy luggage on board on the eighteenth, light on the twenty-second when she leaves dock – not going to sea before twenty-fourth or twenty-fifth. Get two prs. of boots for Jas Meadows, to come by Eliz Rose, who should be in London by the 12th Inst. Much love dr. mother and father – pray for me. J H Taylor.

In intention, the floating of his mission a year ago had been the biggest thing in his life. In practical terms this step was the greatest, his largest single outlay of money and the commitment of his immediate family and the largest party of missionaries of any society ever to embark for China together, not only to face the hazards of the sea but the notoriously high risks from disease and violence. Eight of them were single girls in their twenties! Nowhere has any

SPECIAL DAILY PRAYER

is requested for the fellowing Brethren and Sisters in Christ, during their Voyage to Shanghai, in the Lammermuir, which is expected to sail on the 25th May, 1866.

~~~~~~~~~~~~~~

J. H. TAYLOR, Wife and Four Children.

LEWIS NICOL and Wife, Arbroath.

GEORGE DUNCAN, Banffshire.

JOSIAH JACKSON, Kingsland.

WILLIAM RUDLAND, Eversden.

JOHN R. SELL, Romford.

JAMES WILLIAMSON, Arbroath.

SUSAN BARNES, Limerick.

MARY BAUSUM, Walthamstow.

EMILY BLATCHLEY, London.

MARY BELL, Epping.

MARY BOWYER, London.

LOUISE DESGRAZ, Liverpool.

JANE FAULDING, London

JANE McLEAN, Inverness.

ELIZABETH ROSE, Barnsley.

-- ◆ --

"Brethren pray for us."

THE *LAMMERMUIR* PARTY COMPLETE

evidence been found that any of his friends had undertaken to give more than occasional donations, nor that any had conferred or agreed to send regular support. No congregation had adopted any member of the team, as Bryanston Hall had undertaken to provide for Stephan Barchet. Nor was anyone authorised to 'raise funds' for them. When someone asked whether Hudson Taylor would be staying behind to keep reminding Christian people to support those who went, and expressed surprise that he was sailing too, he answered,

> We are taking our four little children, and I never need anyone to remind me that they need their breakfast . . . dinner . . . supper. And I cannot imagine that our heavenly Father is less able or less willing to remember His children's needs, when He sends them forth to the end of the earth about His business.

Their dependence was on God, trusting him 'to move men', his human stewards, in answer to prayer alone. Even to Hudson Taylor, so convinced of its rightness, the plunge was breathtaking. He believed no less now than in June, 1865, that all the responsibility was God's.

The tempo of life at Coborn Street immediately quickened. At a meeting of the team and friends Hudson Taylor announced the news. They were to sail within three weeks. They ran off a prayer card on the hand press, listing their names and expected date of sailing, with the words 'Brethren pray for us'. His hoped-for visit to his grandmother at Nottingham again had to be deferred. He saw Louise Desgraz off from Euston to Birkenhead to say goodbye to the Collingwoods, and took Maria down to Saint Hill for their last visit, to confer with the Bergers while they could.

From there she wrote to his mother: Would she get his tailor to make him another frock coat, waistcoat and trousers, and ask Mrs Birkenshaw to re-style her own brown dress of Chinese silk. If well enough Maria would make a quick visit to the relatives at Barnsley, Hull and Nottingham, but she hoped his parents would come down to London to see them off. They would have 'to rough it . . . as we shall be in the midst of packing'.

He himself wrote on their return to Coborn Street the next day. It seems that an anguished reply had come from Barnsley to his note from Killick's office. Maria hadn't the strength to travel, even if he could spare her, he said, and he himself could not get away for a fortnight at least. He would try to catch a late Saturday train to Nottingham, arriving after midnight, and return by the six a m train, presumably on Monday. It would get him back to London by nine forty for work. But, 'could *you* come up with E Rose on Friday 11th and stay till we leave? – we so much need help . . . Jas Meadows' clothes and boots may be packed away for the voyage in E Rose's box. Please settle all accounts. Dear Mother, live to-day for to-day. Tomorrow may never come; if it does, it will bring grace for its own burdens.' Mrs Taylor did come, and stayed until the *Lammermuir* sailed.

Then followed the succession of farewell meetings at which he spoke almost every night after strenuous days of packing and settling affairs: at St Andrew's Church of England; at Dowager Lady Radstock's in Portland Place; at Brook Street, Tottenham, after his hectic visit to Nottingham; afternoon and evening on the 15th at the old Chapel Royal in Queen Anne's Gate, by invitation of Robert Baxter the parliamentary lawyer. (Ten days later Baxter sent one hundred pounds to Mr Berger.) On May 16 the farewell to Jennie Faulding and Emily Blatchley was at Regent's Park Chapel; then Welbeck Street; J M Denniston's church at Hackney; W G Lewis' chapel at Westbourne Grove; and Bryanston Hall.

All through these days his engagement diary noted other events. The historic photograph of the *Lammermuir* party was taken in the garden at the back of the house. George Duncan stands almost head and shoulders above the rest. James Williamson and John Sell mature and strong, Rudland posed awkwardly but unselfconsciously among the girls, the Nicols seated and relaxed, Jackson in profile, Mary Bausum beside him holding Mary Bowyer's hand, Jennie Faulding seated with little Grace Taylor leaning against her knee, Hudson and Maria Taylor with the two older boys on their laps, Emily Blatchley behind them, and buxom Mary Bell quelling a fractious Samuel. Elizabeth Rose has arrived in time, and Louise Desgraz is back from Liverpool. Individual photographs were also taken as reminders to pray, and advertised on the back of the *Occasional Paper* at sixpence a card.

Five days before sailing Hudson Taylor drafted a farewell letter for the second issue of the *Occasional Paper*, saying of the team, 'If you keep a list of them and read it before the Lord, prefixing a petition for blessing to each name, very little time will be occupied, while *very much* blessing will be secured . . .'

Gifts continued to come in: twenty pounds from Birmingham and the same amount from Kendal, with seventeen travelling rugs; and a hundred pounds from Henry Bewley of Dublin. Farewell letters too, apologies for not seeing them off, and expressions of *bon voyage*. The pressure of correspondence never ceased.

> The rapid growth of the work has been of such magnitude, that I have been absolutely unable to keep pace with it . . . Some kind friends may have been pained by the answer to their letters being delayed, or by my deputing others to write to them for me. This has been a *dernier ressort*. Often I have tried by sitting up till one, two, three, four o'clock, and occasionally by giving up the whole night to correspondence, to avoid this alternative . . . To all the kind donors . . . to the ladies who have sent worn linen (for use on the ship), or have helped in preparing the outfit . . . my heartfelt thanks . . . May the God of all grace ever supply all *your* need . . .

Remittances to the team in Ningbo were not forgotten. Then it was time to start getting the heavy baggage to the *Lammermuir*.

Countdown   May 1866

Bills of lading acknowledged each load as it reached the docks: on May 17, thirty-two packages; May 18, ten, then two more heavy cases, then thirty-three, then twenty-one; May 19, thirty-seven; May 21, forty-five; May 22, fifty-six; May 23, thirty-two. All were labelled, numbered and assigned to the hold or for access at sea. Some of it was furniture. Apart from the light luggage, that was all. Now there was more space in the Coborn Street houses, but one by one they were to be vacated and the travellers to move into the homes of friends for the last few nights. May 25 was still the sailing date. Tom Barnardo took lodgings near the London Hospital. They spent May 20 as a quiet Sunday together, addressing themselves to the voyage. Hudson Taylor spoke frankly. Elizabeth Rose recalled his saying at this or a similar moment, 'It was necessary between the comforts of home and the privations of China to have a sea voyage to break us in.' And another, 'Some said, "Suppose Mr Taylor does wrong, who could we appeal to?" "To nobody except God," replied Mr Berger. "If you cannot trust Mr Taylor, don't go!" I felt strongly that that was right,' commented Charles Judd, a friend of Barnardo's not yet in touch with the CIM.[13]

The 21st was Hudson Taylor's thirty-fourth birthday, and at a farewell meeting at his church in Westbourne Grove, W G Lewis told them, 'It is your duty and your responsibility to preach, to preach faithfully the gospel. It is God's work to convert.' Over everything hung the thought, expressed by John Houghton in a note to Hudson Taylor, 'Should we never meet on earth again, I trust through rich Grace we shall meet in Glory.' The anguish of impending parting from Jennie frequently reduced Mrs Faulding to tears, but Jennie's own excitement and happiness were shared by her matter-of-fact father, her two brothers and 'Nellie' her sister. Hoping his own father would come down from Yorkshire and take his mother home, Hudson Taylor was not surprised when a characteristic note of apology arrived. James Taylor was too painfully shy to face it. 'I can't mix with strangers – I shall ever pray for you.' Highly respected among his peers in Barnsley with whom he felt at home he still shrank from unfamiliar social encounters. A member of the board of guardians and respected as the founder-manager of the Barnsley Bulding Society, he resolutely resisted pressure to allow his nomination for councillor. As a local preacher and evangelist he was loved and valued. Hudson Taylor knew him as a constant man of prayer and prized this strength most highly. That he could rarely be induced to write letters no longer troubled his son. That he had welcomed his grandchildren to disrupt his quiet life for so many weeks while Maria was ill was proof enough of where his heart lay. But for James Taylor to expose himself to meeting so many people at a time of strain was too much to attempt.

When the last thirty-two cases had been put aboard on Wednesday, May 23, the travellers and their close friends all met again at Henry Lance's George Street chapel near Berger's Starch Works. A leisurely hour over tea, then a final hour of singing, prayer and communion, and they separated to meet again at the *Lammermuir*, now to sail on Saturday, May 26. Before they parted, Frederick Gough presented Hudson Taylor with a slim New Testament in the best calf-skin binding by Baxter, with an affectionate inscription, symbol of their five years of taxing work together on the Ningbo vernacular version and of their unimpaired friendship. This marked the end of the Ningbo coterie in London. After Gough and Mary Jones were married, and before they returned to China, they consulted Hudson Taylor about joining the CIM, but in the end returned as missionaries of the CMS. Meanwhile they continued the weekly meeting to pray for China in their home at Montague Terrace, Bow, and the Bergers held another at Saint Hill, headquarters of the Mission in the United Kingdom.[14]

On Thursday even the harmonium was taken from Coborn Street to the *Lammermuir*. Hudson Taylor paid Killick and Martin the balance due on the fares, £425 at £42 10s each, reckoning the four children as one adult fare, and attended his last meeting of the FES Committee to bid farewell.[15] A loving note from Mary Berger brought a white leather-bound notebook with a lock for Hudson Taylor's use as a travelling journal, with the assurance '(*The Lord*) will go with you . . . In His strength you will accomplish far beyond all our petty thoughts. Go! and be blessed!' Two typical notes came from Lord Radstock, militarily to the point, accompanying donations from friends. And a strong letter from Henry Grattan Guinness. After a period of ill-favour with the Presbyterians of Ulster, he was preaching again to packed audiences in the North.

> How I wish I could fulfil my intention of going over to London to see you all before your departure . . . Nothing but absolute necessity would keep me from packing my portmanteau and going to London this evening or tomorrow. But I cannot, dare not leave the work here at this juncture . . . This peace-making may lead to exceedingly important results, opening my way for preaching the Gospel to thousands more in this country. I have met with many of the principal ministers already, and all are cordial . . . Daily . . . my prayers ascend for you . . . I expect that when you more deeply *need* our prayers – on the ocean or in China – in peril or in want – those prayers will intensify and increase. I believe the Lord is with you, and therefore am one soul with you in the work, and look for its success.

The gospel would always come first in his thinking, but since reading Hudson Taylor's book and hearing him speak, the thought of 'a million a month dying without Christ' would not leave him. Poetic and expansive as he was by nature, he expressed his strong feelings in the rhetoric of Victorian verse, entitled *The Voice of thy Brother's Blood*. Florid and perhaps for that reason popular at the time, it was effective, making a mark in its day.

> Over the dark blue sea, over the trackless flood . . .
> They have heard from the far off East
> The voice of the heathen's blood;
> 'A million a month in China are dying without God.'
>
> Oh! church of the living God, awake from thy sinful sleep!
> Dost thou not hear yon awful cry still sounding o'er the deep? . . .

Canst thou shut thine ear to the awful sound, the voice of
thy brother's blood?
'A million a month in China are dying without God.'

Four hundred millions! Lo, I see the long procession pass;
It takes full three and twenty years . . .

– on and on for fourteen six-line stanzas, each ending with the same
refrain. But it caught the spirit of concern stirred up by Hudson
Taylor's writing, lectures and addresses. 'What a power the going
out of the *Lammermuir* party was in the Christian world at the
time,' C H Judd recalled. 'Many of course said it was madness.'
Others said, 'You will be forgotten!' But Grattan Guinness drove
Hudson Taylor's message home, and Charles Judd's commitment to
China was one direct result, after the *Lammermuir* had sailed. Over
a century later his children's children play a leading part in the
Mission.

One day remained. All Hudson Taylor's accounts were audited
and formally handed over to William Berger as the sole responsible
director of the CIM at home. As *Occasional Paper* No 1 had carried
the audited statements as far as December 30, 1865, so *Occasional
Paper* No 2 was to include his final statement embracing January 1 to
May 28, 1866. In these five months, receipts of over four thousand
pounds had covered all expenses, including remittances to China,
and left William Berger with a balance of over two thousand pounds
with which to begin his tenure of office. Again, if these figures are
loosely translated into late twentieth century equivalents, their
significance can be appreciated.

Finally, all the remaining crockery, bedding and miscellaneous
bundles were taken to the *Lammermuir* in 'twenty packages', and
everyone who had not gone already scattered to their overnight
quarters. Joseph Merry had come from Eversden to see Rudland
off, and spent the night with him and James Williamson at Annie
Macpherson's. Rudland assumed that Maria and Hudson Taylor
would go to Amelia's in Bayswater where their mother and Mary
Bell and the children (probably) were, but he was wrong. Emily
Blatchley and Jennie Faulding went home. Tom Barnardo had his
lodgings near the London Hospital. Others were put up by the
Lances of Berger Hall. John McCarthy had come over from Ireland,
and wrote: 'One could not but be struck, with the care he (Hudson
Taylor) took that all the other members of the party should have
comfortable quarters while, in the interests of others, he and his

wife remained in the deserted house, until on the last night or two they slept on straw in one of the empty rooms.' It was no hardship to them, nor anything new. Soon they would be back in China, often rolling out their bedding bundles on slat-beds or boat decks without even the indulgence of straw.

'*Cheer up, Ma!*'[16]   *May 1866*

Typically it was Jennie who noticed that May 26 'dawned a lovely day'. From all directions the travellers and their friends and families converged on the East India Dock and went on board. The *Lammermuir*, 1054 tons, spick and span, was ready to sail, John 'White Hat' Willis her owner with his long white beard, and Captain Bell and his crew waiting full of curiosity to receive them. (*See* Appendix 2.) The public stern cabin and saloon on to which the cabins opened were piled high with luggage, leaving little room to move. A dining-steward and under-steward or cabin boy would wait on them at table. Everything else they would have to do for themselves. Hudson Taylor had inspected the accommodation on the 19th, and with conventional propriety allocated the team to appropriate cabins, the men down one side and the girls the other, with the saloon table between them. Sizing up the situation, someone (presumably he as leader of the expedition) directed that the bed-frames or bunks in all cabins should be removed, and each passenger's trunks be arranged as beds. The men turned to and order was created. 'We were all so busy . . . everything was in the greatest confusion – so we had the less time to think about the partings.'

A large and representative group of well-wishers had come to see them off: the Bergers, the Howards, and Mr John van Sommer (James' brother), T D Marshall and J M Denniston, the Merrys and Miss Annie Macpherson, two ladies from Hackney, the Fauldings with Jennie's brother William, Hudson Taylor's mother and sister, Amelia and Benjamin, two of Mr Berger's factory managers including Mr Mears, Grace Ciggie, James Vigeon, a Miss Helen Pillans Smith and Mary Parsons, John McCarthy and two medical students from Dublin, and others, were there.

As the time approached for the ship to leave the dock, all came together in the saloon and stern cabin. Only the two rooms could contain them. 'All hearts seemed too full for many words,' Mr Berger wrote in the next *Occasional Paper*, but in such a company the travellers were 'repeatedly commended to God in prayer' before those going ashore had to withdraw. Then as the *Lammermuir* was towed through the dock gates, to the crew's amazement someone started singing 'Yes, we part, but not for ever,' and from the dock and deck others joined in. 'The sailors thought we were a strange set.' Mr Brunton, the first officer, a violent and ill-tempered man as they soon learned, was appalled. According to one of the party he complained to his wife, 'It was a pretty go, they were going to have a whole shipload of missionaries psalm-singing all day long, he wished he was out of it!'

Most of the male visitors stayed on board as far as Gravesend and returned with Captain Willis in his 'steamer'. Tom Barnardo (until recently a wine merchant's apprentice) appeared at Gravesend with a supply of wine and groceries, returning 'in his own boat', and so was one of the last to say goodbye. Not so Mr Faulding, who spent an uncomfortable night aboard before leaving with the Thames pilot at Deal on the North Sea coast of Kent. As William Berger shook hands with Rudland he said prophetically in the words of Scripture, 'See that ye fall not out by the way' – a reference not to falling overboard but to the disharmony that could wreck the Mission!

The weather had changed and as the *Lammermuir* lay at anchor off Deal, her motion reduced 'many' of the party, as Jennie put it, to giddiness, headache or seasickness. By then they had had time to unpack essentials and make up beds on their boxes. His father had done all he could for her. 'My cabin is so comfortable I wish you could see it,' Jennie wrote, untouched by seasickness. 'Everyone thinks it a model.' But the memory of her mother in tears led her on, 'I hope you will cheer up. I am very happy and only anxious about you.' The day was soon to come when her mother's pleas for her to come home from growing dangers in China moved Jennie to an indecorous 'Cheer up, Ma! – I am more anxious for you than for myself!' Even if querulous by nature, her mother was realistic. Two of these adults and two of the children would never come home again, and two more of the party would soon come back to die.

The first day had been enough for Maria. At eleven p m she tried to write to Hudson's mother, beginning, 'I am so tired and sleepy that I can scarcely keep my eyes open.' But it had taken two corrections to achieve as much, so 'Please excuse more. For I hardly know whether I am writing.' Two days later when she tried again, she explained, 'If I roused up at the commencement of a word I was asleep before I got to the end of it.' She wished Mrs Taylor could 'see how happy we all are. God ever keep us so.' Hudson, she said, was feeling as well as he ever had in his life. It was exhilarating to see his hopes and plans transmuted into men and women, lapping waves and creaking timbers. He was happy at sea and looking forward to the voyage. At the same time Jennie Faulding was hurrying to send her note ashore by the Channel pilot. 'Through the Captain's glass I watched Father till he landed at Deal and disappeared behind houses, then I went into my cabin and . . . cried myself to sleep.' When she woke again she found to her delight that her father had signed his name on the back of the cabin door.

Most of Sunday they rocked at anchor waiting for adverse winds to change, and feeling wretched. With Captain Bell's approval they managed to get through two services of worship in the stern cabin among themselves. He was friendly, saying they would get more sailors attending in the saloon than in full view on deck. If they would like to mix freely with the crew at suitable times, that was all right too. They stacked all the baggage along the walls of the stern cabin, making it secure. Then, at four a m on Monday Jennie Faulding was woken, 'by the singing of the sailors and a noise overhead as if all our baggage were being dragged from one end of the poop to the other – it really seemed as if they would come through. (Now) the sails are all set and the sailors have put the ship in order, so that it is very pleasant.' Every sight, sound and smell was new and exciting. They were turning westwards into the Channel. 'I don't think anything could make me more comfortable than I am . . . The Captain and mate [first officer] are both extremely agreeable . . . [Jennie had yet to see Brunton under stress.] The cliffs [of Dover and Folkestone] look so beautiful this morning . . . Though I can't tell you how I feel leaving you I am overjoyed at the thought that I am really on my way to China . . . [Better still] we are not troubled with rats or mice or anything' – not even cockroaches. Near Dungeness the pilot left them, taking the last bundle of twenty-four letters with him. Before them lay the open Channel and the Atlantic.

Tuesday revealed more of what they were in for – a 'meat breakfast' at nine, and two more large meals at three and nine p m. 'The men keep (the ship) beautifully clean . . . We have pigs and sheep on board and . . . always have three dishes to choose from, and often have five courses at dinner . . . Rest assured I shall not starve.'

Hudson Taylor set everyone to work, giving them their first Chinese lesson of the voyage. Day by day he was to teach in the mornings and Maria each afternoon. But on this day they 'worked at' their cabins, putting up shelves and securing everything, none too soon. On Wednesday, May 30, they left Devon behind and met rough seas. 'The sailors had neglected to secure the hawse-pipes and the sea broke (into the forecastle) with great violence, destroyed the lee bunks, washing some of the chests aft, and taking the clothes of some of the sailors overboard. A large number of our fowls were drowned.' The passenger casualties were of a different order. With half of them seasick and Duncan and Rudland quite helpless, Hudson Taylor and the others were kept busy attending to them. For most of the voyage Rudland failed to find his sea-legs and could do little language learning. John Sell and Eliza Nicol fared little better. So weakened that towards the end he found it difficult to cross the deck, Rudland was unready for the final storms, yet played his full part in them.

Berger, Judd, Barnardo, and Ciggie[17] June–December 1866

As soon as the *Lammermuir* had sailed, William Berger wrote an editorial to accompany Hudson Taylor's farewell letter to supporters in the second *Occasional Paper*, and reported developments. Aware of the dangers, with 'preservation' and 'spiritual prosperity' he first of all linked 'harmony' as the key themes for which prayer was needed. No hint is found in the records that disharmony had existed at Coborn Street, but he had a shrewd impression of each member's personality. He knew well the strain of living at close quarters on board ship for so long, and many precedents existed for the *Cutty Sark*'s 'hell-ship' eastern run on which the mate killed a seaman, the captain killed himself and Charles Sankey, an apprentice, was the only competent navigator left aboard.

Scrupulous accounting for all monies received was Mr Berger's principle as well as Hudson Taylor's. Explaining the audited statement at the end of the *Occasional Paper*, he showed that Mary Bausum's mother had paid Mary's fare, and 'a special contribution' had met the costs of all the Taylor family and Mary Bell the children's nurse. (He himself had been the unnamed contributor.) Unless clearly specified as being intended for the Taylors or any of the team personally, all donations would be applied to the Mission's general fund.[18]

Berger, the successful manufacturer, was satisfied with Hudson Taylor's accounting. As a boy Hudson Taylor had worked for a few months in a bank and for five years had assisted his father, who ran his own business and a building society, but otherwise he had no formal knowledge of book-keeping. Integrity to the last fraction and meticulous habits helped him to be efficient and accurate, using simple methods to record essentials. As they co-operated by sea-mail during the coming years, William Berger had few questions to raise and in fact proposed even simpler systems, to ease the burden on Hudson Taylor as his responsibilities grew heavier. These accounts for 1866 have been used to support serious but mistaken deductions and flippant essays such as the one which described Hudson Taylor as 'a man of practical sense and great persuasion; he sought money where it existed and the pocket books of the rich simply fell open at his coming.'[19]

In this first editorial letter as director of the Mission in Britain, William Berger promised to give all the help in his power to any local church or combination of churches sending out and supporting their own members as missionaries, 'whom they will know and love, and correspond with, and minister to in part or in whole'. 'The advantages of such a mode are incalculable.' There were many young men and women, he said, already asking God to confirm to them his will that they should go to China. He had the funds in hand for even ten more missionaries' fares, as the financial statement showed.

Then, finally, he referred to his own 'insufficiency' to do the work God had led him into 'step by step'. Far from false modesty, this was recognition of the fact he had observed, that while he himself was the efficient manufacturer widely known for his firm's products, and had ample capital for his own and the Mission's current needs, these were fringe factors in the prospects of the CIM. Money certainly mattered. That many more Christians should care for China and the Mission enough to pray' and therefore to contribute mattered far more. Hudson Taylor's charisma, as well as the compelling power of his message about China's spiritual need and claims, undoubtedly brought results from those he influenced. William Berger knew that he himself was a very different person. In communicating with the public he was pedestrian, too formal to inspire, too stilted for easy reading. And by agreement with Hudson Taylor he was 'alone' in bearing the responsibility in Britain. He did well. *Occasional Paper No 2*, largely prepared in advance by Hudson Taylor, contained

William Burns' letter of January 5 from Peking, and pages of good narrative from James Meadows, the Crombies, Stevensons, and George Stott, Stephan Barchet and Mrs Lord. No 3 contained *The Voice of thy Brother's Blood* by Grattan Guinness, and more news hot from China. By the fourth *Occasional Paper* long accounts of the *Lammermuir*'s eventful voyage had arrived, to be followed by adventures of a different sort. Mr Berger need not have feared.

Here Charles H Judd, a strong man with a great future, must come more fully into the story, although his links with the Bergers began a few weeks later. Judd was a student at the Church Missionary Training College in Islington, preparing to join the CMS but troubled about infant baptism, and feeling more at home with Christians who shared his own understanding of Scripture. He had attended meetings at Welbeck Street and knew Frederick Gough of the CMS, but had never met Hudson Taylor. After the *Lammermuir* had sailed, Arthur Elwin, a fellow-student at Islington, brought him 'a paper' which Judd remembered as being by Grattan Guinness, entitled '*A Million a Month in China are dying without God*'. Unless it was a separate copy of the poem, it seems likely that Elwin's paper was *Occasional Paper* No 3 in which the poem was reproduced in full. When Elwin read it to him, Judd said, 'Stop, I can't listen to that!' and explained, 'It so stirred me up.' He began going to the Saturday prayer meetings at Gough's home in Bow where he met Tom Barnardo, and Barnardo began coming to the Islington College to pray with him in his room.

One day 'in the lunch room' of the college, Judd picked up an issue of *The Illustrated Missionary News* containing extracts from Hudson Taylor's *China: Its Spiritual Need and Claims*. A table of provinces and their population without missionaries caught his attention. 'When I came to Anhui province and the statement that it had a population of forty millions and no missionary I could not understand it and thought, "(Is) it possible that a place on God's earth with forty millions (has) nobody to tell them of the Lord Jesus?" I dropped the paper on the table, went straight to my bedroom, knelt down and said "Lord send me."'

Both Elwin and Judd eventually withdrew from the college. 'Scruples about part of the prayer book grew on me,' Judd wrote. 'I saw I could not go with the Church Missionary Society because of (this), and then I wrote to Mr Berger.' Invited to Saint Hill, he lived with the Bergers for about a year as a tutor in English, geography and a little Greek to the other missionary candidates, and joined in evangelism in the country villages. In October 1867 he was married there, about a month before sailing to China.

Judd's verbatim recollections of the Bergers give the best pictures we have of them.[20]

> He was one of the finest men I have ever met in my life – unquestionably. He was a man that God had clearly raised up for the work . . . 'Berger's Rice Starch' was well known all over England . . . At one time he gave up his business and retired but later took (it) up again simply that he might support missionary work. (He was tall and thin) decisive and sharp in manner. Quick, a little bit inclined to be severe, but very loving; at the bottom of his heart there was intense love, and his wife was as good as he was . . . A little wiry, thin body . . . a loving, bright energetic little body, but she did everything so quietly that you seldom knew she had done it – so efficient and yet so much out of sight. She prayed incessantly. (And her husband) a godly prayerful man who really walked with God (and) loved his Bible . . . He had been the means of the conversion of a number of people in the neighbourhood (but) the nearest church (was) East Grinstead, three miles away, and he consequently built a little (chapel) on his estate . . . He used to minister there.

At Saint Hill, the official office of the Mission in Great Britain, William Berger's private secretary, Mr Aveline, the ex-missionary from Demarara, did much of the daily pen-pushing and errands. But most of the preserved ledgers and personal letters are in Berger's own hand. As it transpired, he and Mary Berger (both born in 1815, so only fifty-one years old in 1866) had embarked on such relentless work and such heavy responsibilities that their health was to fail under it. Into their home they took a succession of men and women to judge with them whether or not they should go to China. With some there was no problem, while with others the faults of personality and spirituality, observed or even directed against them, provided the answer at some cost to the patient Bergers. As they gave themselves more and more to serving China and the CIM, William Berger gave up his hobby of managing his own farm, and sold off the agricultural part of his estate in order to give more time and attention to what had become his primary occupation.

Tom Barnardo returned from Gravesend to carve out a life of his own in London, as exceptional as it was inspired. Unable to register at the London Hospital Medical College until his pre-medical examinations were behind him, he first got down to study. But no academic aims could undermine his zeal as an evangelist. With his eyes on China, however far off in time or distance, he kept in close touch with the Bergers and Frederick Gough. To this we shall return.

Grace Ciggie was another who watched the *Lammermuir* slip downstream, and with a heavy heart made her way to (unnamed) friends of the Mission. She had promised to spend that Saturday, May 26, with another girl. To do so involved a step of faith. 'The friend who had been as a mother to me after my grandmother's death had died during my stay in London. I had, therefore, no home to return to (in Glasgow). I had paid all my incidental personal expenses (while at Coborn Street), and never having referred to money matters, friends must have supposed I had plenty, but in fact I only had enough to take me by rail to Glasgow.'

In order to save four shillings and sixpence, about two days' wage in her previous employment, she had intended to travel by sea. To keep her word, meet the girl, and go by night train, would mean arriving in Glasgow with no money and nowhere to go. She was heading for China trusting God, not Hudson Taylor or the Bergers. She decided to leave this problem with God. At the end of the day as they parted the girl handed her a small package. It contained four shillings and sixpence. 'It seemed as if God had said, "Do not doubt; I will care for you."' She was on her way to Glasgow as a missionary to the red light quarter. 'I had learned to use my needle well, and thought I might help to support myself that way.' Every day she went from ten to two p m,

visiting my poor degraded outcastes of Salt Market district. (I had all my life had a hatred of sin and sinners. A bad person filled me with disgust . . .) I soon learned why God had sent me in this way, for almost the first questions fiercely asked were: 'What Church has sent you here?' 'No Church.' 'Who has sent you?' 'No one.' 'Then why do you come?' 'Because I love you; I have been saved myself and I want you to be saved too.' And when they found that I was not only willing to read with and pray for them, but to nurse poor sick ones, kindle a fire, make beef tea, or sweep a hearth . . . besides nursing their babies, both hearts and homes were open to me at once. [The Church elders were appalled and warned her of the risks] but I felt that that was God's business. He had sent me and He was responsible, and never during the three and a half years . . . did I receive the least insult or hear unbecoming language if they knew I was present.[21]

After three months the elders offered her a small weekly sum of money, which she accepted on condition that her actions would be no less free from control. They agreed and helped her, but never interfered. From one source and another all her needs were met.

> It was not till I was sent down there among the utterly lost, that I began to (distinguish) between the sin and the sinner . . . (I) never lost the consciousness that my life's work lay in China, and I had but to wait God's time.

A shop-assistant with (at that time) little more than primary education, Grace Ciggie was in character and spirituality the superior of many who would have passed her over as unsuitable. Thirty years later, Hudson Taylor was to compliment her on a well-written book. This was the kind of person he and William and Mary Berger were praying and looking for, no less than the Vigeons, Stevensons, Judds and McCarthys. Both kinds were to flock to them after the first stormy years were over.

CHAPTER FIVE

THE CLIPPER *LAMMERMUIR*
1866

Ship's company   *June 1866*

Crew and passengers of the *Lammermuir* were to be thrown together, almost literally, on what was surely one of the most extraordinary voyages in the history of the sea, in a way few ships' companies had experienced since Saint Paul's shipwreck on Malta. In Hudson Taylor's detailed journal and the letters he and others wrote, we have a graphic record, vivid as it reached its climax.

It did not take long for the party to pick up the essentials of life on board ship, already familiar to the Taylors. Captain Bell had a motley crew of thirty-four men and boys from Sweden, Germany, the West Indies and South Sea Islands as well as Britain. (*See* Appendix 3.) J Brunton, his first officer or 'mate', a brutal, violent man, ruled by fear. W Tosh, the second officer, and four officer apprentices (loosely called 'midshipmen' by the travellers) shared deckhouse quarters amidships, and twenty-one seamen or 'foremast hands' crowded the forecastle (fo'c'sle). The boatswain (bos'n), carpenter, joiner and sailmaker, shared seniority with the cook and steward. George Hartley, the cabin boy, and one other disclosed that they were Christians. William Carron, an older, fatherly figure, contrasted strongly in approachableness with Robert Kane, 'one of the worst' of the 'rough set' – a few men who showed antagonism to the missionaries from the start.

Penned on the well-deck near the fo'c'sle was a menagerie of dogs, sheep, pigs, geese, ducks and chickens. Aft of the second mate's centrally placed deckhouse, an entrance on each side of the main mast led past Captain Bell's cabin on the starboard side and First Officer Brunton's on the other, through a second pair of doors into the saloon. Between the two short passages was the steward's pantry, serving meals from the cook's galley 'between decks', below. Each of the five cabins along both sides of the saloon had its porthole, and over the long saloon table and seats chained firmly to

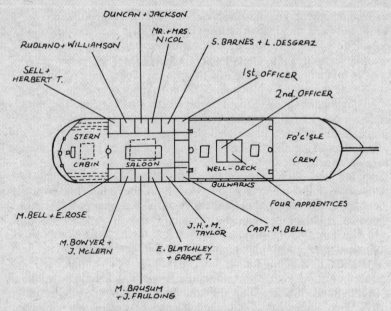

DUNCAN + JACKSON
MR. + MRS. NICOL
S. BARNES + L. DESGRAZ
RUDLAND + WILLIAMSON
1st. OFFICER
SELL + HERBERT T.
2nd. OFFICER
STERN
CABIN
SALOON
FO'C'SLE
CREW
WELL - DECK
BULWARKS
FOUR APPRENTICES
M. BELL + E. ROSE
J. H. + M. TAYLOR
CAPT. M. BELL
M. BOWYER + J. McLEAN
E. BLATCHLEY + GRACE T.
M. BAUSUM + J. FAULDING

DECK PLAN OF THE *LAMMERMUIR*

the floor, a skylight from the poopdeck lit the saloon, unless
battened down in rough weather. At the stern, behind the mizzenmast where it passed through the saloon, the broad stern cabin with
three stern portholes was just large enough to be a common room,
even with both ends tightly stacked with baggage and furniture.
Central to everything in the stern cabin stood Hudson Taylor's
hard-worked harmonium.

Maria and Hudson Taylor had the cabin next to the Captain's,
and Emily Blatchley the next one with Grace Taylor. Jennie
Faulding and Mary Bausum shared the centre cabin, then Mary
Bowyer and Jane McLean, and lastly Elizabeth Rose and Mary
Bell. On the opposite, port, side Louise Desgraz's and Susan
Barnes' cabin lay between the first officer's and the Nicols', and
beyond them were Duncan and Jackson, then Rudland and Wil-
liamson, and finally John Sell with Herbert Taylor. (Howard, called
Freddie, is thought to have been with his lifelong friend Louise
Desgraz, and Samuel with Mary Bell.) So cooped up together for
four difficult months, such a mixed bunch of people could be

expected to get on each other's nerves. That more trouble did not erupt between them is surprising. How Hudson Taylor controlled team life on board, and these contretemps in particular, forms another window on his personality as their leader. If a sea voyage was 'to break them in', it was also to show them what stuff he himself was made of, and how much autocracy to expect from him.

In fair weather life was lived largely on deck where it was light and fresh, a relief from the all-pervading smells of paint and tar and limited ventilation. Captain Bell gave them the freedom of the ship and they used it carefully, learning to make themselves scarce when orders were barked and the crew sprang to action, bracing or changing sails. Hours spent below the billowing canvas, chatting with officers and men, taught them the vocabulary of life at sea, using 'bow' and 'stern', 'fore' and 'aft', 'port' and 'starboard', as the men did, and the more specialised terms that were to represent life and death to them before long. In view of all that happened in the *Lammermuir*, and of its repercussions, the story of this voyage needs to be told in some detail.

Foremast, mainmast and mizzenmast, impressively huge, were extended upwards by topmasts, and above that by topgallant and royal masts. Climbing to such heights looked alarmingly precarious in fair winds, but dangerous in the extreme on rough seas. As they watched the men out on the foot-ropes, looped below the horizontal 'yards', reefing and lashing them tightly on the yard itself, they marvelled at the courage and skill of these 'unsophisticated but highly skilled acrobats, directed by men of resource and ability'.

Each spar and attached sail had its corresponding name, and as the captain at the head of the saloon table talked with Hudson Taylor, long since at home with the terminology, the others picked it up. By the time it mattered to them to know what was happening, the intricate and at first confusing mass of canvas had taken shape as a simple pattern in their minds. That the primary sails were 'square-rigged' at right angles to the keel and others 'fore-and-aft' in line with the keel was obvious. And it took little attention to the mates' shouted orders to see that each mast carried its mainsail or 'course', above that a lower and upper topsail, then a topgallant and a royal, distinguished by the names of the mast as fore royal, main royal, mizzen royal, and so on for each sail. Extending each 'yard' outwards from its end called the 'yard-arm', were spars carrying 'studding' or 'stun' sails to increase the width of the central canvas. High above all, the main mast boasted a graceful skysail or 'moon-

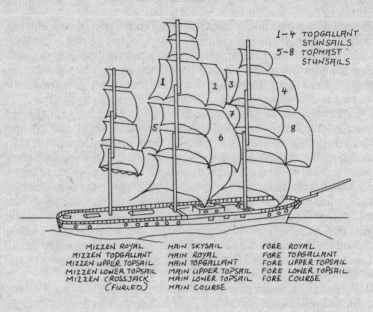

| | 1~4 | TOPGALLANT STUNSAILS |
| | 5~8 | TOPMAST STUNSAILS |

MIZZEN ROYAL
MIZZEN TOPGALLANT
MIZZEN UPPER TOPSAIL
MIZZEN LOWER TOPSAIL
MIZZEN CROSSJACK
  (FURLED)

MAIN SKYSAIL
MAIN ROYAL
MAIN TOPGALLANT
MAIN UPPER TOPSAIL
MAIN LOWER TOPSAIL
MAIN COURSE

FORE ROYAL
FORE TOPGALLANT
FORE UPPER TOPSAIL
FORE LOWER TOPSAIL
FORE COURSE

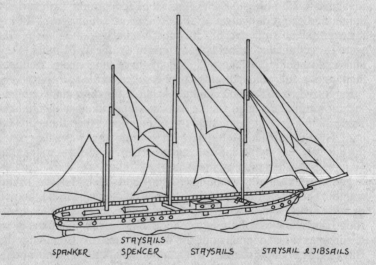

SPANKER   STAYSAILS
            SPENCER   STAYSAILS   STAYSAIL & JIBSAILS

THE SAILS OF A CLIPPER SHIP

raker'. The fore-and-aft sails, essential to the square-rigged ship, completed its beauty.

Projecting from the ship's bow above her figure-head, the massive bowsprit was extended by spars called inner and outer jib booms and a flying jib boom, held fast by stays above, below and on each side. Their corresponding sails, the inner, outer and flying jibs swept gracefully upward to the foremast. Tense drama was to be enacted one stormy night on this cat's-cradle of booms and stays as the voyage proceeded. It seemed a long time to Hudson Taylor since, as the sole passenger on the ill-fated *Dumfries* twelve years ago, he had worked with the crew in the rigging, sat with the Christian carpenter out on the bowsprit under the stars talking about the Lord, and climbed the 'ratlines' to perch on the topgallant or royal yard and sing exultantly at the top of his voice. Not content with half measures on the *Lammermuir*, after they had passed close to Cape Finisterre and were sailing down the coast of Portugal, Hudson Taylor entered in his journal: 'From the top of main sky-sail mast counted 10 ships in sight.'

In line with the jibs was the triangular 'fore topmast stay-sail' and both main and mizzen masts supported their own topmast, topgallant and royal staysails, while above the poopdeck where they sunbathed, exercised and did Chinese language study, were the big spencer and spanker trysails. Storm staysails of very strong canvas were the only sails that could be spread in a full gale. Blissful in the sunshine under fair skies, and in effect a yacht put to work, a clipper ship under full sail had no equal for beauty. All looked very different when storms raged, waves swept the decks and rags and tatters whiplashed from the flailing wreckage of masts, yards and rigging.

Devon to the Cape[1]   *June–July 1866*

By June 1 they were 'making good progress', but Hudson Taylor wrote, 'The whole day seems to be taken up with caring for the sick or taking our own meals.' Accustomed to passengers with time on their hands, Captain Bell, at the head of the table, made meals so leisurely as to last over an hour and sometimes nearly two. After the Bay of Biscay and in calmer water 'dinner took up the afternoon'. But waste of time was not Hudson Taylor's sole concern.

The only fault of the fare [he told his mother] is that it is *too liberal*, and that meals take up too much time. I trust, however, that by God's blessing we may not be spoiled – this is the great danger . . . We began (to-day's dinner) with hare soup and chicken soup. Then preserved mutton, minced hare, chicken and ham, with potatoes, and turnips followed. Next plum pudding, (bottled) apple pie, (bottled) damson pie, (preserved) black-currant tart, (preserved) rhubarb tart. Then biscuits and cheese. Lastly dessert: nuts, almonds, malaya raisins, figs. Time occupied at table, one and ¾ hours. *Of course these details will not be printed* [How else could misunderstanding be avoided? Some readers might not realise that such luxury was not of their seeking]; but you should know them, that you may pray that those who have been accustomed to hard work and homely diet may not be seriously injured by this style of living. There is, Thank God, much unity and love amongst us now. May it continue to increase.

And not only among themselves. 'The good feeling between our party and the crew increases.' 'Mary Bell . . . gets access to the sailors best.'

Almost becalmed from the 5th to the 7th they picked up the north-east trade wind toward the end of the week and 'rolling very heavily' pressed on southward to pass Madeira in the distance on the 10th and the Canary Islands during Tuesday night, June 12. A homebound ship saw them 'in full sail and with a fine wind in her favour', Mr Berger reported in the *Occasional Paper*. One day a capricious wave dashed unexpectedly against the port side cabins when the portholes were open, and 'bucketsful of water' saturated beds, bedding and the boxes below them. 'This for some time suspended all other work,' and it was the 16th before John Sell's cabin was 'once more to rights'. By the 18th they were past the Cape Verde Islands off the coast of Senegal, and sailing south-westwards on the north equatorial current towards Brazil, to benefit from the south-flowing Brazil current. As they approached the equator and the humid atmosphere became more and more oppressive, drenching rain fell, forcing them to close all portholes and endure the stifling heat of the ill-ventilated saloon and cabins. Louise Desgraz discovered that her boxes were standing in water, and they had to be unpacked. Fresh water was too precious to lose, and on the decks everything possible was done with canvas containers to collect and store it.

They crossed the equator on the night of June 25, but most of the

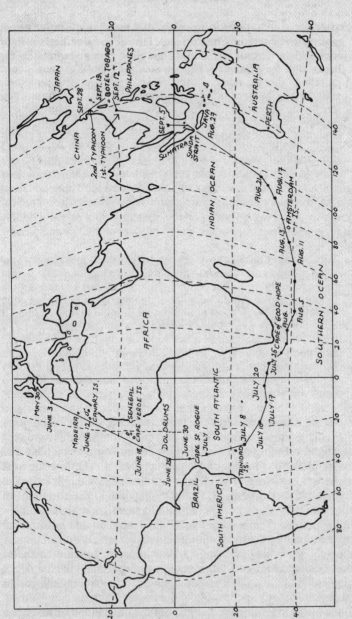

THE VOYAGE OF THE LAMMERMUIR

week sweltered in the doldrums with little movement under winds too light for their needs. Only on the 29th, at five degrees south of the line, Hudson Taylor noted, did enough of a breeze spring up for the stunsails to be spread. A French ship homeward bound promised to report seeing them, and in August William Berger heard from the 'ship-brokers', the '*Lammermuir* was spoken' by megaphone between the two ships on June 30, about five hundred miles off Brazil's Cape St Roque and two thousand from Africa. After that, in spite of light winds, they moved slowly southwards with the Brazilian island of Trinidad in sight all through July 5. For the next two days it blew a gale and after a lull for a few more days became 'almost too heavy' as they approached the Cape of Good Hope. After that strong following winds gave them a good run of two hundred and twenty miles on the 30th and more on the 31st. By then in spite of drawbacks they were revelling in their ocean cruise.

> We almost live on deck [Jennie wrote]. Oh, I have enjoyed today! the sea is so lovely and the air so beautiful . . . the captain makes great pets of the children. The sunsets are so lovely and I never saw the moon so bright. I threaded a very small needle and can read quite small print on deck . . . I never thought it would be so enjoyable. I can't work very hard, I lose so much time watching the waves . . . There is no unpleasantness with anyone on board . . . and the young men don't trouble me in the least . . . Emily and I have nice walks and talks together . . . Mr Taylor has a (tin) bath and an apparatus by means of which we can get the water in at our cabin windows so I enjoy a sea-bath sometimes . . .

From the beginning Hudson Taylor had made sure that everyone had plenty to do. He had fixed up bookshelves for Jennie and himself and all worked to make their cabins more homelike. For Hudson Taylor this meant unpacking more books. During the next week he was reading Winer's *Greek Grammar of the New Testament* and Bishop Wordsworth on *Leviticus*. Rudland described him as 'young and active, quite one with the young men of the party'. Maria was 'quieter, in some ways perhaps more mature – such rare judgement; calm sweetness about her face always; most restful . . . she gave a good deal of time to the children', reading to them . . . Chinese language lessons continued even in rough weather, on deck in the daytime and in the 'cuddy', a little 'tweendeck cabin amidships at night. 'Spent most of the day at Chinese' was Hudson Taylor's entry for Tuesday, June 5, but the day before he had been fishing for 'bonito' (tunny-fish or tuna) over the stern, and watching porpoises and a shark. He got out his microscope and examined sea 'polyps'. We can see him sharing these pleasures with the others.

From the start of the voyage the captain and first officer had attended the Sunday morning service in the stern cabin, and on June 10 all four apprentices joined in. This time, as an innovation, another service was held 'forward' for the crew. Every day the team met before breakfast to pray for their families and friends at home and in China, and for the crew and themselves. And each Saturday afternoon the inviolable weekly hour of prayer for China was maintained, however rough the weather. Long before the *Lammermuir* was engaged, the whole Coborn Street family had begun praying together that the crew of the ship they found might be open to the gospel.

Different members of the party were striking up friendships with members of the crew, and on the 17th John Sell led a service in the fo'c'sle itself. In the doldrums near the equator when they were becalmed one of the apprentices caught a small shark, a change in the fo'c'sle diet, and Hudson Taylor gave them a 'lecture' demonstration on the anatomy of the eye. When a pig was killed he taught them about the heart and circulation, and on other occasions lectured on the alimentary tract and 'digestion', and 'to our party', on 'malaria, its nature, habits and results' and the best ways to avoid it. Even while they sweltered they 'spent the day in Chinese studies', working chapter by chapter through *St John's Gospel*. When she was not looking after the children, Mary Bell hobnobbed with the sailors and found some who welcomed the Bible class she offered to start for them. Hudson Taylor talked with the officers and on the 23rd wrote, 'Mr Tosh, the 2nd mate, has found peace.' Soon he (Taylor) was reading with the cook in his galley. On Sunday, June 24, 'the young men' together ran a service in the fo'c'sle, and the next day Mary Bell came back from her class reporting 'one or two of the anxious men to be rejoicing in Jesus'. By Tuesday Hudson Taylor agreed that 'some of the sailors' were sincerely believing. On Wednesday it was Mr Saunders, one of the apprentices, who had 'found Jesus'. 'But there is opposition springing up.'

To discover early on that Captain Bell, who shortly before sailing had replaced the previous captain, had been converted only two years previously and was fully in sympathy with them, was good news. For almost a month they had been going carefully, making friends with the crew but not forcing their piety on any. Some men were Roman Catholics. All were told they could attend the saloon services, and a few had come. But in Riviera weather all lived an open-air life on deck. The harmonium was brought out and any who wanted to, joined in the singing. To their amazement the hard-swearing, brutal Mr Brunton revealed that he was 'decidedly anxious' about his own unpleasant character.

On the last day of June, just south of the equator, Hudson Taylor's journal read, 'When returning from lancing the cook's foot, I saw Mrs Taylor thrown (by a sudden lurch of the ship). She was much hurt, and unable to get unaided to her bed.' And one of the girls added that she was 'very bruised'. It was the beginning of troubles. She was pregnant again, and for weeks suffered the threat of miscarriage as well as her usual toxaemia with vomiting. From time to time Hudson Taylor was being called upon as surgeon to treat officers and crew. During the gale on July 9 in the south Atlantic he recorded, 'In the evening a man fell from some height on the deck, but fortunately was not dangerously hurt' and a few days later, 'Lanced George's foot and the Swede's finger.' And again, 'Lanced the New Zealander's armpit.' Emily Blatchley had been suffering from neuralgia for days on end and on the 11th it was 'so intense' that she collapsed in a dead faint. At last Hudson Taylor detected and removed an offending tooth, which gave relief. 'I feared she would not reach China; now she is recovering.'

He was not the only one making himself useful. Nicol, the Scottish blacksmith, 'forged some things for the ship'; Louise Desgraz was reading with the four Swedes, and Mary Bausum with the cook; Susan Barnes, the Irish teacher, started a school for the crew, Mary Bowyer began teaching the South Sea Islander to read, and Jennie Faulding the German. When the pumps gave trouble, it was Rudland the mechanic with Nicol and James Williamson the carpenter who put them right. Most of the crew were coming to respect these unusual psalm-singers with such varied ability and interests. On the day that the black cat fell overboard and much of the excess baggage was found space in the hold (giving room in the stern cabin for more crew at the services), Hudson Taylor 'saw the four satellites of Jupiter through the captain's binoculars'.

Near the end of June some 'germs of ill-feeling and division among our party' showed themselves. A few were making better progress in Chinese than the others. Jennie was already learning to read Chinese ideograms while the rest still used the romanised form. Elizabeth Rose, a Yorkshire girl with little education, and

Jennie were being held back by those whose slower progress made them jealous. In the sultry weather off Brazil the patience of some wore thin and July 5 was 'a day of sorrow'. But 'Elizabeth . . . will be a treasure to dear Jas Meadows,' Hudson Taylor noted. So the party had to be divided into separate study classes, making added work for him and Maria.

Less than a week later more disaffection came to the surface in a way that shocked him. If he was going to be autocratic this was the occasion for it. Josiah Jackson invited him into the stern cabin to talk with Duncan, Nicol and himself,

> and desired to know whether they had got all their outfits. I told them that they had, as far as I knew, except the stockings – about which I feared there had been some mistake. Mr Duncan then said that they had not been supplied as Mr and Mrs Berger had told them they would be. I asked in what respect they were deficient, and requested each to give me a list of what they had received, which they promised to do. Mr Jackson said he had seen a list of the articles supplied to the Presbyterian missionaries, which contained a very different outfit from theirs. I told them that we did not intend to take them as our pattern. That they were persons of different position in society; and that moreover they were to wear these things when in China, which we should not do. [As all the CIM party had agreed to wear Chinese dress, their foreign clothing was mostly for the voyage.] I told them that we had done what we could to get them comfortable outfits; that I regretted that I had been unable to get them some light clothes, and that there was some mistake about the stockings; but that there was notwithstanding a good useful outfit, for which we ought to be thankful.

He knew how 'light' and airy clothes had to be if they were to be comfortable in the great heat and had searched in vain for Indian materials flimsy enough. He himself had been so overworked during the last days in London that he 'forgot all about getting cool clothing for himself, and consequently (felt) the heat a good deal'.

It would all have been too petty for mention if it had ended there, but the seeds of deep dissension had been sown. Bulk buying had been the practice for the sake of discounts and to avoid the waste of time if each should go shopping for his own things. Writing to Mrs Berger Maria explained what had gone wrong. Emily Blatchley had told Maria that the men's outfits were complete, meaning the parts she had been asked to provide. Maria took this to mean their whole outfits, 'concluding that Mr Taylor had purchased what could not be made'. Hudson Taylor thought she must have bought them. 'So after we got to sea we found they had been omitted.' Some stockings of Hudson Taylor's which had almost been left behind as super-fluous were divided among them; he accepted responsibility for the administrative failure, they accepted the explanation, and that was that. Maria was less easily consoled. 'I felt so sorry about it: again and again I have dreamed that we were obliged to turn back to England for something and I was so glad.'

The following day he 'had some private conversation with Mr Nicol about the present state of matters', and was joined by Sell and Williamson, two who had not complained. 'We concluded on holding a special prayer-meeting for confession and prayer for increase of the spirit of love and unity. Spoke to most of them privately, and affectionately urged on them the need of a better spirit. We met in the evening and the Lord was with us indeed. I trust that He gave a real desire to be united in love to all present.'

But a day later he wrote again in his journal that mutual confes-sions when they all met together to put things right had exposed more pettinesses, small in themselves but damaging to their oneness and spiritual health. 'The feeling among us appears to have been worse than I could have formed any conception of. One was jealous because another had too many new dresses, another because some-one else had more attention. Some were wounded because of unkind controversial discussions, and so on. Thank God for bring-ing it out, and removing it.'

As a result Sunday was 'a most blessed day' with a communion service. Nicol preached in the fo'c'sle, the sailors coming for more Bible-reading in the evening, and Mr Brunton asked John Sell into his cabin to pray for him! Some meetings were being held in the steward's room and Russell, the steward, although not a believer began attending the passengers' own prayer meetings through curiosity. Even the newly converted 'fo'c'sle hands' began to pray aloud, Robert Dummelow and William Carron, the older man, among them. On Sunday, July 2, Mr Fickling, an apprentice, dared to pray in their presence. More and more of the men were coming to the meetings in the stern cabin, but opposition from the diehards to fo'c'sle meetings continued.

Brunton's choice *July–August 1866*

From the moment when the *Lammermuir* had moved out of the East India Dock and on wharf and deck they had begun singing a hymn, the first mate had wished himself 'out of it'. These people were for ever singing. Their enjoyment of life was transparent. His trouble was his conscience: nominally a Roman Catholic, he knew his religion had little to do with his life and less with his beliefs. To keep up appearances he had been affable at saloon meals, had attended Sunday worship with Captain Bell, and controlled his temper when the passengers were around. At other times his men lived in terror of his fists. Hudson Taylor in his journal made no reference to the fact until August 2, after they had passed the Cape, but Rudland reminiscing said, 'Mr B, the first mate, was such a bully, all the men feared him; nothing and nobody pleased him . . . a very violent man (he) seemed at times almost devil possessed. For the sailors he made the ship a hell for days at a time. He was especially violent at night when we were out of sight.'

Mary Bausum, although only fifteen, was astute. She tailored her table-talk to suit his moods. Writing to Amelia, Hudson Taylor's sister, she said,

> He was so discontented and miserable. Miss Barnes used to talk so often and so long with him; but to argue and dispute seemed to be all he could do . . . It used to make me quite wretched to see him. I sit [*sic*] by him at meals, and I got to know so well how he felt, by his looks. It seemed . . . as if I could read his thoughts. Then Mr T used to go and read with him in his room, and Miss Barnes went too; but he wouldn't consent to her going unless someone else came too . . . Miss Bowyer or me. Well, I always used to go and sit . . . while she talked and read to him. At last he became so wretched that some of us feared he would do himself some harm.

After some men had been converted in the last week of June and 'decided opposition' had broken out, Brunton softened. Then on Sunday, July 8, after the happy day when most if not all the petty jealousies and differences in the team had been sorted out and mutually forgiven with Hudson Taylor's help, Mr Brunton had 'begged' John Sell to pray with him. Two days later Hudson Taylor 'spoke to Mr Brunton about his soul', and read the first three chapters of *Romans* with him, about God's anger and judgment against sin, and acceptance of Christ's death in place of the sinner's as the ground for reconciliation. Brunton was impressed. All mixed up with journal entries about carpentering and medical lectures and minor operations came the note two days later, 'read *Romans* 4 and 5 with Mr Brunton', about access to God and peace with God. By trusting in Jesus, alive after death, he could become 'reconciled by his death and saved through his life'. Brunton understood and even agreed, but could not apply it to himself.

The strong gales in the second half of July were putting captain, mates and crew under great strain, and on August 2 Mr Brunton 'who had a terrible fit of passion this morning and who was swearing terribly . . . seemed almost in despair' when Hudson Taylor talked with him again. The evil in him seemed too strong for him to overcome, but that was exactly the point of *Romans* chapter 7: 'Wretched man that I am! who shall deliver me from this body of death? Thanks be to God – through Jesus Christ our Lord!' His hope revived. The next day the missionaries met to pray for him, and William Tosh the converted second mate, apprentices and members of the crew prayed together in the steward's room.

Hudson Taylor had been unwell for ten days or so but carried on giving Chinese lessons, reading the history of *Christianity in China* with the team, and teaching Greek to Jennie Faulding and Mary Bausum. 'I began to try the plan of speaking only in Chinese, but after a few days had to relax considerably, or jealousy would have possibly resulted.' After explaining to Captain Bell 'the sacrament' of communion, Hudson Taylor 'could not retire without seeing Mr Brunton. Read to him part of Mackintosh on *Exodus* (chapter) 12 at 12.30 a m when he came from his midnight watch.'

Exodus 12, the story of the 'Passover' in Egypt before the great exodus of the Israelite people, told how the blood of a sacrificed lamb was daubed on the lintel and doorposts of the Israelites' homes. After two hours of reading and explanation, God's message, 'when I see the blood I will pass over you' and not slay anyone so protected, suddenly made sense to Mr Brunton of the passages in *Romans*. He called out, 'I see, I see, how blind I've been!' His release was dramatic. Soon he began thanking God and praying 'not only for himself but for the crew and Captain Bell' for his wife and children and for the Mission.

When Hudson Taylor left him at two thirty a m he first told Maria and Emily who had stayed awake to pray, and then woke Williamson and Sell 'who rose and joined with me in praise and thanksgiving. Oh how glad our hearts were.' Elizabeth Rose was asleep in her cabin. '(John Sell) came and awoke me, and at 3 o'clock in the morning we rejoiced together. It is impossible to describe the joy of that day.' Mary Bausum agreed: 'The next day [Saturday] there was not much done. We all seemed as if we couldn't settle to anything. There was such a change in him. His face didn't look the same. I went to the breakfast table on purpose to see him; but I had to come away before very long' – seasick. They were entering the Indian Ocean on huge 'rollers'. Hudson Taylor wrote, 'Mr Brunton feels his burden quite gone, and all the party are overjoyed.'

Brunton 'called out his watch', Rudland recalled, confessed to them his unreasonableness – (saying) he had been on the wrong side – and completely confessed Christ. The effect on the men was that they said to one another, 'If the mate is converted then there is some chance for us.' Hudson Taylor preached about the Passover on Sunday, and made the communion service 'public'. The steward watched 'anxiously' and was 'much affected', still unable to see his own way through to the same experience. Some of the crew had laughed together at the start of the voyage, saying, 'I wonder what it feels like to be converted!'

The end of opposition   August 1866

That stormy Sunday night the drama in the bows took place. The ship was tossing and plunging through the waves but a sailor named McDougall was out on the jib boom foot-rope when she rolled far over. Combining two accounts by Hudson Taylor, what happened is clear.

> The bowsprit . . . has four sets of rope supporting it. Some go up to the foremast, some out on each side, some down under it to what is called the martingale. The ship was lying over when he fell from the jib boom. Instead of falling into the sea, providentially he fell on to one of the ropes which run out horizontally on each side of the booms, but which from the ship's lying over was much lower than the man was. From this rope he was thrown inwards and had another almost miraculous escape, falling astride one of the martingale stays. Stunned and now insensible he would have fallen into the water, but (Henry Elliot) one of the (newly) converted sailors (cried 'Man overboard!' and) at the risk of his life, was down with the quickness of thought (on the plunging stays), holding him on. Then (Mr Tosh) the second mate (also converted), at the same risk got a rope round (McDougall), and he was drawn up . . . The unconverted sailors looked on, petrified, but not daring to help.

During the next day another hand, Charles Pryor, was 'brought to the Lord', and that midnight Hudson Taylor was talking with another. Tuesday was also 'a day not to be forgotten'. Russell the steward at last 'found peace', and Mr Brunton, on duty with one of the apprentices, Carter, told him what had happened to himself and 'invited him to come to Jesus'. He said he was thinking it over. In the stern cabin Hudson Taylor and some of the party were praying for them, when word came that Dixon, the West Indian, 'was rejoicing' as Brunton had, and he came in to join them. Brunton and Carter were due to end their watch at midnight, so all waited for them. 'And what a meeting it *was* when they came; and then what a parting! [Elizabeth Rose wrote home]. There was such a shaking of hands and such a recognition of each other as brethren and sisters in Jesus.'

Lewis, the senior apprentice, was the next. Personalities were being changed before the eyes of the crew, and one and another was

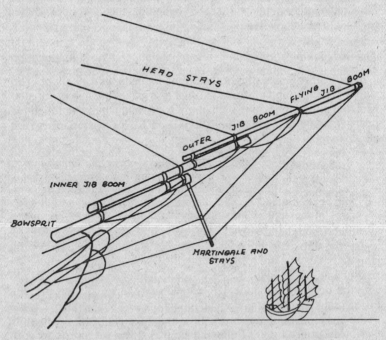

MCDOUGALL'S RESCUE: BOWSPRIT AND JIBS

thinking hard. Naturally the children, caught up in what was happening, asked questions and Jennie Faulding told Maria she thought Grace was believing intelligently. But life went on from day to day, unaltered by these spiritual upheavals except in the morale of the crew. In spite of the storm still raging Hudson Taylor made no mention of it in his journal. 'Making perceptible progress at our Chinese lessons' was his entry for Wednesday, August 8. 'McDougall, who fell overboard, decidedly worse; in great pain and delirious at times. Complains of great pain over precordial area. Applied mustard plaster . . .' But he was better the next day – the day they covered 288 miles and reached 'Long. 54°19'. Lat. 40°53''', far south toward the Southern Ocean, taking advantage of the earth's curvature and shorter east-west distances.

The jib boom with the flying jib boom broke off close to the bowsprit, and for two more days and nights there was a 'terrible sea on. Taking water over in very large quantities.' Sleep was almost impossible by day or night. The kindly captain had already taken pity on Emily Blatchley and had a 'cot' made to keep her from being thrown off her bed of boxes. As for the crew, 'the poor men had very little rest last night and were all wet through with the rain and the seas which swept over (the ship).' Undeterred, the missionaries 'had the China prayer meeting' as usual, for it was Saturday again.

Sunday, August 12, was quieter, but before breakfast on Monday,

> the port Stunsail Boom came down from the Fore-mast Yard, severely bruised poor Wm Carron, hurting his back and (crushing) his body, and tearing open his fore-arm. Benjamin (Buchan) also received a scalp wound. They thought Wm was killed and ran for me. We got him to bed . . . Mr Sell dressed Benj's head after I had examined it. In Chinese began (*John's Gospel* ch. 10). Most of the young men helping to repair the loss of the bowsprit.

Williamson and Jackson as carpenters probably worked with Stewart, the ship's carpenter, while Nicol and Rudland as blacksmiths forged bands (we are told) to bind the new jib booms together.

Buchan's scalp (with the periosteum) had been torn back, exposing the unfractured skull. He 'cursed and swore' at the time, but after realising his narrow escape began reading the Bible. Carron 'who has given us so much joy since his conversion, was much more seriously injured. . . . Believing he was dying his words were of Jesus, and of thanks and praise.' 'A nice middle-aged man, a favourite with them all since his conversion' was Jennie's description of him to her parents.

The new jib boom was put in place on Tuesday and Wednesday while they were passing Amsterdam Island, midway between the tips of South Africa and Australia, and watching 'a water-spout', a tornado. With the sails set again they ran well, making 276 miles. In ten or twelve days' time they should be at Anjer, the provisioning point on the Sunda Strait between Java and Sumatra. From Anjer to Shanghai could take only three weeks, 'this ship sails so well'. On August 15 Hudson Taylor wrote to William Berger that, apart from language study progress and conversions among the crew, the voyage had been very uneventful, 'but being very fully occupied, the time has *flown* away'. To everyone's amazement Carron appeared at a meeting. Mary Bausum told Amelia, 'He said, "He told me to take up my bed and walk, so what could I do?" though he didn't bring his bed with him! . . . He is quite a father to them all . . . While he was ill, Mr Brunton used to go three or four times a day to see him, and he used to kneel on the bunk below while William (Carron) prayed with him.'

'Johnson', one of the Swedes, believed he had been mastered by Satan and thought, 'I must try and get out of his hands,' with the result that the next day he too 'found Jesus'. 'Robert Kane is deeply impressed,' Hudson Taylor noted. Kane was 'one of the worst men on board' in Mary Bausum's view, and in Jennie Faulding's, 'the ruler of everything in the forecastle, outspoken and fiery, scorning anything mean, unable to read, rough and ready to fight in a moment, with a thoroughly pugilistic countenance, using awful language and keeping the whole crew in awe . . . Miss Barnes noticed him one day and said to me, "Look what a countenance that man has, I'll try and talk to him," so she asked him to come to the meeting, almost expecting to get knocked down . . .'

Kane's opposition had put the fo'c'sle out of bounds for any meetings with the crew, but the steward's room could no longer hold all who wanted to attend. Twenty-seven or eight had managed to get in. Then on Sunday, August 19, Susan Barnes saw Kane 'in the deepest distress, and led him to Jesus. Oh! how glad we all were! In the evening at the communion Wm Carron, Robt Dummelow, and Mr Fickling, joined with us in commemorating Jesus' dying love. Others were present among them, Kane full of joy.' 'The change in him had great weight with the others.' Of the fifty-two adults on board, thirty-six were present.

From then on for the rest of the voyage, every night from eight to nine the meetings were in the fo'c'sle. 'Eleven of them . . . told how they were brought to see themselves sinners and led to the Saviour.' As there was no room for everyone, the missionaries took it in turns to be present. 'All the opposition party had come over to the Lord's side, and the men themselves proposed removing to the forecastle . . . Some men were seated on their sea-chests, some on planks, some on chairs which we had taken forward, some on various parts of the ship's fittings, while (some) more than half ashamed to be seen . . . were hiding behind the capstan or hanging about the doors. . . . [Again on the 22nd] the first mate, Mr B, and three of the men joined in prayer, and the joy was so great that it was with difficulty that I [Hudson Taylor] was able to get the meeting concluded half an hour after the time for doing so had come. . . Our minds were kept in peace as to the future. Were we never to reach China at all, we should all rejoice in the work God has done in the *Lammermuir*.'

Jennie told her father, 'Instead of four professing Christians (in the crew) there are twenty-four.' Wisely she recognised that the onus was on them when they 'professed' to believe. Whether they had the heart of the matter was another question. For long after this voyage Mr Brunton kept in touch with 'the *Lammermuir* party', visiting them in China when he could, and calling on the Bergers when at his home port. If some of the crew were insincere or even play-acting to keep in with the officers, relapsing to their former ways as seamen when ashore, others continued true to their profession of faith. In August they were far from the end of their strange experiences in the company of these unusual passengers.

North to the China Seas   *August 1866*

On August 20 Hudson Taylor began his journal entry with 'Got the trades. Noon long. 97°24′ E, lat. 30°27′ S.' Three thousand miles from South Africa and a thousand from Perth, Australia, they changed course and turned northwards, exceeding two hundred miles a day. On the 23rd it was 'very warm now, 78°F' and the prospect of landing, if only for a day, excited them all as they wrote letters to post at Anjer. Language study continued unrelentingly, though Maria was 'in a very poor state of health'.

Mary Bausum's long letters to Amelia illuminated features of the voyage taken for granted by others, especially 'the flying fish run' over sunny seas to Java. She enjoyed,

> the steady everyday walk we get on deck – so far and no farther . . . This has been such a happy voyage altogether . . . I seem always to be laughing. I actually have a kind of dread of landing, it is so pleasant here, that the battle seems to be all in front . . . *Any* one can speak to the crew, so that the ladies think nothing of going in and out of the forecastle now, though there may be some of the men in their bunks . . . (Mr Brunton) is so anxious for the salvation of all on board. He wants us all, crew and all to be able to sit down to one table and commemorate our Saviour's dying love before we leave the ship . . . Last night Mr Brunton came (to the forecastle), which was very nice, as the Mates are generally so frightened of making themselves equal with the men.

Having lived so much with Amelia since her mother returned to China, she signed herself 'your own loving child, Mary Bausum'.

Elizabeth Rose described how Mr Brunton prayed 'in a manner that melted one to tears, praying that God would bless Mr Taylor and each of us'. A week later Jennie, on the same theme, told her parents,

> He was very much disliked among the crew . . . but they all say he's not the same now. [And of the fo'c'sle meetings] the men look forward to them all the day through . . . They are so fond of Mr Taylor, his medical skill has been of great use, both cook and the cabin boy ran nails into their feet and were laid up . . . Mr and Mrs Taylor are so kind to me and I'm so thoroughly at home with them. . . . Captain Bell has done everything in his power to please us . . . the whole party of us are thoroughly happy together . . . The days slip away so fast I don't get through half I want to.

So much euphoria in a shipload of young men and women could not but have its romantic side. In the height of the South Atlantic gale, Emily Blatchley had written the date beside the words in the *Song of Solomon* (2.7) 'I charge you . . . that ye stir not up nor awake my love, till he please.' After they reached the South China Sea, Hudson Taylor noted in his journal, 'Mary Bell, thro' Mr Sell, told me of the mutual attachment between herself and Mr Tosh. Advised her, sympathetically, to strive to get nearer to Jesus.' Was her vocation to preach the gospel in China to be exchanged for a sailor? The reminder was all she needed. And Duncan needed a word in his ear about Susan Barnes who was feeling 'sorely tried'.

It could not all be roses without thorns. Hudson Taylor found his cabin awash and had to unpack soaked possessions, make a false floor to the cabin, and sleep in the stern cabin until it was finished. For days he was not only ill with conjunctivitis but doctoring six seamen, one with a serious abdominal emergency, and the captain 'very shaky' with malaria. Maria seems to have moved cabins, probably sharing with Emily Blatchley for they were both ill most of the time.

At last on August 27 they 'shortened sail at 1 a.m. and went on under Top-sails until daybreak. The Java-head was in sight and we made more sail, passing through the straits of Sunda all day.' At the entrance of the Sunda Strait they passed Krakatau volcano, then a large island. In 1883 it was to undergo the greatest eruption in recorded history and virtually to disappear into the sea.[2] 'We cast anchor close to the fairy hills of Java . . . mountainous and beautifully wooded,' Jennie said. William Rudland remembered a huge banyan tree covering a large area not far from the beach on the mainland. When Krakatau erupted and sank into the sea the banyan was carried five miles inland by the tidal wave.

The excitement over anchoring, buying fresh fruit, going ashore in two boats, collecting and posting their mail at the immense cost of £3 5s, buying curios in Chinese shops, watching and joining a Muslim procession, nearly treading on 'a serpent', eating fresh coconuts and sitting with the apprentices in a breeze near the beach while they read their mail – all this and more filled their journals and letters home. 'We went to the boats tired out after a long, happy day,' and boarded the *Lammermuir* at ten thirty p m. Many of the crew had bought 'monkeys, Java sparrows and other birds'. The next day they 'were all too tired to do anything'. They could not forget that nowhere among the charming people of Anjer was there any Christian presence, though farther away in Java there was a Church. And scattered through the islands were one hundred and fifty thousand Fujian-speaking Chinese. Hudson Taylor had tried to make himself understood at Anjer in the Shantou dialect, without much success.

Baptisms at Anjer   *August 1866*

For the past two weeks they had been preparing for a baptismal service, but not for the crew. As the only references to it were in a letter by Jennie and in Hudson Taylor's journal, it is hard to know exactly what happened. On August 16 Mary Bausum had had a conversation with Hudson Taylor about baptism. Her Anglican mother had married the Baptist E C Lord in Ningbo, and Mary was going to join in their work. Two days later Elizabeth Rose, a Methodist, had spent most of the Saturday morning with him on the same subject. Her fiancé, James Meadows, although a Methodist, had been baptised by Mr Lord and was preaching 'believer's baptism' in the Bridge Street church. On the 21st Hudson Taylor wrote in his journal, 'Miss Maclean, Miss Bowyer and Miss Rose desire to be baptized at Anjer, D.V. May the Lord guide us aright.' As both Mary Bowyer and Jane McLean had been students in William Pennefather's training school, it has been assumed that they were Anglicans, but the Inverness girl Jane, at least, was not definitely so. Then on Sunday 26th, he added, 'had a meeting in the afternoon with the candidates for baptism.'

Hudson Taylor had made it clear in Britain that in his view the mode of baptism should not be an issue between Christians. As for re-baptism, after a brief period under the influence of Andrew Jukes in Hull (Book 2, p 42), he did not mention the subject again. He neither advocated nor practised the re-baptism of baptised Christians, yet he was willing to meet the wishes of these three. If they had been baptised previously, he was providing a rod for his own back. As Jennie told her father, 'Mr. Taylor baptized Miss Bowyer, Miss McLean and Eliz Rose who without the subject having been named asked him to baptize them; he was afraid that in China some of the paedo-baptists might take offence, so did not wait to get there.'

While some Christians denounce re-baptism as a theological absurdity, impossible in theory, others regard baptism without faith as null and void, on the theological ground that neither an unbeliever nor his child could be incorporated into Christ's Church solely by an act of baptism. Hudson Taylor appears to have shared this view. If the girls were converts of the 'Evangelical Awakening' they might have come from non-churchgoing families and never have been baptised. Or if they had been christened but had had unbelieving parents, they might have seen the rite as a mere religious or social formality – such as the fourth-century writer Jerome referred to in saying, 'They that receive not baptism with perfect faith receive the water, but the Holy Spirit they receive not.'[3] We are not told. Incorporation into the Church-visible without that faith would not have been enough for them.

Conjecture helps us little. All we really know is that Hudson Taylor baptised them at their request, after consultation with them. His critics could be shadow-boxing. He must have accepted the girls' belief that they had never before received true baptism. Maria and the Presbyterian young men, who were satisfied with their own infant baptism, raised no objections. So out of consideration for others and to preserve harmony among the missionaries they were to join in China, it had become a question of when and where, rather than whether the three should be baptised.

Instead of waiting until they all reached China and letting E C Lord or someone else officiate, (foolishly, some say) Hudson Taylor did it himself. He grasped the nettle, and the sting was surprisingly sharp. His own note simply read, 'We . . . found a place (a stream) suitable for baptisms . . . where, after a short service, I baptized Misses Bowyer, McLean and Rose.' Eight of the CIM party were present, and Mr Brunton who had met them on their way. Although a Roman Catholic he wished to be baptised with them and was displeased that they had not told him of the plan. To have included any of the ship's company would have raised more problems. John Sell, who was present, summed up the whole time ashore as 'a glorious day at Anjer'.

CHAPTER SIX

TYPHOON!
1866

'Last lap to China'[1]   *September 1866*

Sailing due north from Anjer and 'passing with a fair breeze the beautiful islands of the Java sea' they made for the Gaspar Strait between Bangka and Belitong islands, arriving two days later, and anchored for the night at the entrance. Daylight was essential for passing through the rock-strewn narrows. There were no lightships, lighthouses or buoys.

The Gaspar Strait was the doorway to a new life. Two or three weeks' good sailing could bring the *Lammermuir* to Shanghai. When day dawned, however, the first hint of trouble was revealed. In the darkness before dropping anchor they had run within five hundred yards of disaster – the Fairlie Rocks lay 'just below the water'. To spread sail and get away without being carried on to it by the current taxed Captain Bell's skill. Not far off, on the Amherst Rock, lay the remains of the first *Lammermuir*, wrecked only three years before, and they could see several other wrecks. Named from the vessels on them, like most of the submerged or half-hidden rocks and reefs abounding in these Malaysian, Indonesian and Bornean waters, the Fairlie and Amherst Rocks were only two among many on the charts. Others were uncharted.

They safely passed Gaspar Island, entered the China Sea and on September 1 crossed the equator off Pontianak, scene of W H Medhurst's early pioneering.[2] 'The weather is increasingly oppressive,' Hudson Taylor wrote, and his journal entries became brief and even more to the point. On September 5 it was 97°F in the shade. Crew and passengers were paying the price of their day ashore. The first mate had 'intermittent fever'. Louise Desgraz was 'very ill with dysentery', and various others including Mr Brunton, and Hudson Taylor himself, had it more or less severely. Soon all were better but light breezes meant slow progress and they longed to be cool again. The iron parts of the ship radiated heat. Safely

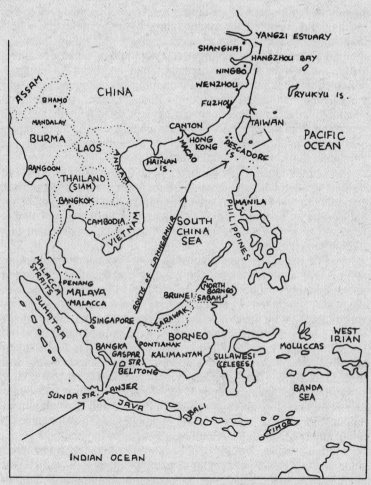

THE SOUTH-EASTERN APPROACHES TO CHINA

through another archipelago of tropical islands, they 'passed under the Sun about 2 p.m. so hope for cooler weather and more wind'.

Laid up with abdominal pain Hudson Taylor was 'thinking over our position and prospects; felt we ought to lose no time in waiting on God for guidance as to our future movements, by prayer and fasting'. His first task on reaching China would be to deliver

Elizabeth Rose and Mary Bausum safely to Ningbo, Mary to her mother and Elizabeth to marry James Meadows. But the whole nightmare of arrival at the scene of spiritual warfare in China had loomed up before him. Idolatry and evil would be all around them. Antagonism from secular Shanghai could be taken for granted. When they knew he had young women in his party and that they were to live among the Chinese in Chinese clothes, the scorn and censure in the newspapers would be less painful than the same reception from some missionaries. He asked the whole team to join him for a day of 'waiting on God' in subjection to his will and guidance, that they might make no false move.

The whole of Friday 7th was taken up with doctoring the sick, but he had a word with the captain about their arrival at Shanghai, possibly in a week's time. True to his nature, Captain Bell said they could all stay on board for five or six days until Hudson Taylor returned from Ningbo. Harris, the sailmaker, was converted that day. 'Thanks be to God!'

Most of the team spent Saturday, September 8, in prayer and fasting. All were present at the meetings in the stern cabin, but unaccountably the Nicols, Duncan and Jackson neither prayed with the others nor fasted. They were free to please themselves, but this was unusual. Why should disharmony rear its head again at such a time? 'Almost all the party are deploring the want of more unity and love. May God make bare His arm on our behalf,' Hudson Taylor confided to his journal, for this was no social rift. God's power was needed to counter the Adversary's intrusion.

Sunday's services, attended by the crew, were treated as farewells, and Hudson Taylor spoke of Paul's farewell to the church leaders at Ephesus. This was also the day he talked with Mary Bell about the second mate's attentions. Twelve of the crew came to a communion service, but Mr Brunton stayed away, deeply disturbed since being denied baptism at Anjer. The ominous sunset that evening was so peculiar that remembering Piddington's *Law of Storms* and his experience of the typhoon at Shantou (Swatow) (Book 2, p 343) Hudson Taylor remarked that it 'was like those preceding a typhoon'. Emily Blatchley's accounts of the next few days are amongst the best, quoted at length by Hudson Taylor in his reports: 'a strange unearthly tone; a dark, conscious-seeming frown over the whole sky'. No one familiar with typhoons could forget it.

The first typhoon[3]   *September 10–14, 1866*

Monday, September 10, was squally but the crew were busy cleaning and painting the poop, to look its best on arrival at Shanghai. The ship was running well, northward toward the lowering skies. But 'the glass was steadily falling', and the sea quickly became rough. Because of the painting some of the deck gear had been cast loose and was soon being tossed about out of control. The men were hard put to to restore order and lash it firmly without injury to themselves. 'At the short prayer meeting in the forecastle, we asked God to preserve the sailors' lives and limbs.' All through the Monday night and Tuesday 11th it was

> fearfully rough, with a wild sea, and the rain descending as if the clouds were coming down bodily; while the raging of the wind made it exceedingly difficult to pass orders. More than once the whole of the watch were very nearly washed overboard by the heavy seas that swept our deck. [Immense quantities of water were shipped, but no

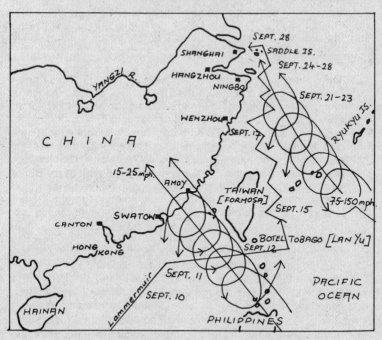

THE *LAMMERMUIR*'S COURSE IN THE TYPHOONS

one was hurt.] In the darkness very little could be done: we could only watch and commend ourselves, and more especially the crew, to God's keeping . . . But we were beginning to hope, from the direction of the wind, that we were on the outer edge of the typhoon's orbit. (*See* Appendix 4)

Writing on the 12th, Jennie's unquenchable spirit rose to the occasion.

Almost all the sails had to be furled and the things washed about the main deck in utter confusion; dogs, sheep, geese and fowls all got drenched continually and narrowly escaped with their lives. It poured in torrents and the sea came over the poop and got into the saloon till there was hardly a dry place anywhere . . . It was impossible to sleep in bed . . . until this morning; we . . . thought it not at all impossible that the vessel might be lost, the largest boat was washed away, the ship was put before the wind . . . the sea was very grand but I have no desire to be in another typhoon . . . I didn't feel frightened but my head ached and it was so thoroughly uncomfortable.

And she had toothache. All Hudson Taylor entered for Wednesday, September 12, in his journal was,

The typhoon has passed away. Made land passing the South Cape of Formosa about 6 p.m. and Botel Tobago [Lan Yu Island] about 10 p.m. [After a fine night] the wind left us for a time and then a North Wind set in with violence. We had to run nearly E.

[Emily Blatchley:] On Wednesday . . . we were safe – (and) sighted Formosa, having been helped on our course, rather than hindered, by the typhoon. But all Thursday a strong gale blew right ahead, with a tremendous sea on, so that we were driven due east, whereas our course lay almost directly north. This gale continued all Friday; moreover, we were now among shoals and breakers; heavy seas were continually sweeping our decks, and loosening things from their lashings; the sailors were many of them ill; the storm we had had already, had weakened the ship, and made her very unprepared for weathering another gale; we were all feeling worn out with want of rest, the perpetual tossing, and our wet clothes; and were longing to reach our desired haven. We were indeed within a couple of days' good run of it; but the wind continued adverse, and we were constantly tacking . . .

Both Emily and Jennie lost count of the days. Day after day seemed the same, so rough as to be barely tolerable. Normally they would have sailed due north between mainland China and Taiwan. Unable in the face of the head wind to do that, they had passed between Taiwan and the Philippines into the Pacific where there was more room for manoeuvre. Even there it was with difficulty that they had turned north again.

Hudson Taylor was reading to the fo'c'sle hands, and learned from them that the first mate, Brunton, under great strain, was being 'very unhappy and stern in his manner to the sailors, several of whom privately threatened to strike him'. Feeling 'very sad', Hudson Taylor called his team together in the saloon to pray about it. Then another incident occurred:

> The weather was very rough, shipping much water. The sail-maker passing on the lee side of the ship was thrown down and a large number of things were torn loose from their moorings and washed to leeward by an immense sea. Had he got on to the spars (as he intended and was only hindered by falling down) he would have been washed overboard. And had he fallen six inches or less either side of where he did fall, either he would have been killed on the spot or would have had his legs broken. So God preserves His children.

False respite[4] *September 15–20, 1866*

On Saturday, September 15, the weather eased at last, and they 'were able to make about 30 miles of northing', heading through the channel between the north point of Taiwan and 'Loochoo', the Ryukyu Islands. Conditions were not bad enough to prevent their weekly hour of prayer for China. After it, at Jennie's request Hudson Taylor extracted her painful tooth – without anaesthesia. Sunday was fine and they held morning service with Hudson Taylor preaching. Then he managed to take Mr Brunton aside and talk with him. He was contrite and wanted to join his men and the missionaries 'at the Lord's table' in the afternoon. Suddenly, 'just before breaking of bread', to the distress of many, Jackson and Duncan stood up and walked out, in protest, as it later emerged, against the first mate and one of the seamen being allowed to take part.

> *Monday 17th.* After much prayer and at the desire of all our party, called a special meeting, and desired Messrs Jackson and Duncan to give us their reasons for acting as they had done on the previous

evening. They did so: asserted that Jas (Byolds) and Mr Brunton were not converted, and gave us their judgement about and against many persons and things. Through God's goodness, all the others who were present, and took part, felt and urged with me the great mistake they made in setting themselves as censors and judges – and all present (unless Mr and Mrs Nicol, who took no part, differed) were satisfied as to their conversion and rejoiced in their communing. Afterwards had some private conversation with Mr Duncan, principally about Miss Barnes.

That was not the only reason why Susan Barnes had been so 'sorely tried' for some time past. She had begun siding with the dissident ones.

Progress had been fairly good over the weekend, and at noon on Tuesday, September 18, they were 'not far from Weng-tsiu Bay [ie Wenzhou]. Then the wind became less favourable.'

Had some conversation with Mr Nicol who I found to be in a truly deplorable condition. This one and that one had shamefully treated him or his wife; but when I got them face to face, these things proved to be pure fancies or the most trifling of trivialities. In the afternoon and evening all were explained, and through God's goodness, ill feelings were removed.

'The accuser of the brethren', Satan, had been busy, but they were almost there, less than three hundred miles from the Yangzi estuary and Shanghai. Hudson Taylor gave the fo'c'sle men a talk about China and a copy each of the *Occasional Paper* No 1 with the address in London of Mr Lomax of Berger Hall near the docks, who would befriend them. Then, as they 'might be called out to 'bout ship (he) held a very short meeting'. The weather was worsening and they re-lashed everything in the stern cabin. 'We were losing ground, owing to the heavy sea.' He was feeling ill, but he 'had a conversation with Miss Barnes, Jackson and Duncan'. On Thursday, September 20, the weather was worse. 'Another hard day of beating to windward. Heavy seas were striking us and flooding the decks. (Conducted) a conversation between Mr Sell and Messrs Jackson, Nicol, and Duncan. Then held a meeting in the saloon on the basis of re-established harmony and union.' His ability as a leader had been tested and his quiet pastoral emphasis on restoration was reaping its reward while the seas rose. Emily Blatchley recalled,

Those old familiar hymns had an intensified meaning for us now. While the winds raged we sang, 'Jesus, lover, (of my soul),' 'Rock of ages,' 'Oh God, our help in ages past,' and others. We could not always get our voices to rise above the storm; but at least they mingled with it, and they and it both praised God.

In the night, especially, we had prayer, because the darkness prevented much from being done or attempted about the ship. Of course *rest* was out of the question, when the tempests were upon us, and we were being tossed up and down by the billows, as if our great ship were nothing; – now on the crest of a wave, now in a deep valley; now lying on her port, now on her starboard side, almost dipping her yard-ends into the sea; now plunging forward with her forecastle right under water.

Writing to Mr Berger afterwards, Maria said she had been 'quite laid up' for five or six weeks and was not nearly as strong as when she left England. 'There has been a cause for this however, and one which we hope will check the weakness in my chest.' On the contrary, pregnancy had a detrimental effect on pulmonary tuberculosis, and toxaemia of pregnancy could not help. Her baby was due to be born in late January or February. Emily, she said, 'has suffered very much and for a long time', and Hudson was not well and not getting the rest he had hoped for on the voyage. Uncomplaining, Emily and William Rudland had endured their constant seasickness patiently.

The second typhoon[5]   *September 21–23, 1866*

By Friday, September 21, they knew they were in for another typhoon. It was 'very rough, both wind and sea increasing'. 'A stiffer gale than any we had yet had . . . also the captain was seriously ill.' He had been exposed to the storm for days and nights on end. Half his face was paralysed. 'While the ship was being put round, (the) main tack' or fastening of Hudson Taylor's cabin porthole broke and would have let in dangerous floods of water if another had not been fitted at once.

[Hudson Taylor:] We had prayer together from time to time during the afternoon and night. The decks were swept over by the sea in a manner such as I have never seen before. [Again Emily filled in the story:] That Friday night we shall not soon forget. We had been carrying a good deal of sail. Now, the wind was reefing our sails for

us, after its own fashion; and in the darkness we could do nothing.
Our starboard bulwarks were washed away, leaving a wide and free
entrée for the waves, which thenceforth kept up a continual surging
sea on our main deck.

Early on Saturday morning, September 22, the jibs and fore
staysails gave way.

[Hudson Taylor:] So fearful was the sea that the men refused to go
out and secure them. Capt. Bell and Mr Brunton went on the
forecastle; and Mr B. going out [on the jib booms] himself the men
followed; but soon all had to be recalled as the vessel was diving into
the sea. Soon after this the lee upper bulwarks began to give way and
soon all this side was washed overboard. Next, the jib boom and
flying jib boom gave way, followed immediately by the fore top and
top-gallant masts, and the main top-gallant mast. They hung by the
wire shrouds; swinging about most fearfully, owing to the heavy
rolling of the ship. [Emily: threatening every minute to fall and stave
in the deck or side of the vessel] Its appearance was now truly
terrific. The decks, full of water, which poured over both sides as she
rolled, were full of floating spars, tubs, buckets, casks, etc. Besides
the danger of being washed overboard, there was no small risk of
having one's limbs broken by the moving timbers, which had torn
away from their moorings.

He was writing after the event, from memory and such notes as he
managed somehow to scribble in odd moments. That phrase 'one's
limbs' was his first indication of the part he and his team were
playing. Soon he had more to say. Rudland, Jennie and Emily
supplied some of what he omitted.

[Jennie:] The captain said we had not room to run before the
wind – and so felt it much more. It seemed impossible that we should
weather it. I am glad to say we were all kept calm and ready for life or
death . . . I did feel so thankful that you did not know, for I had the
strongest conviction that our lives would not be lost.
    [Hudson Taylor's account continues:] Prayer to God was our only
recourse: the sailors paralysed gave up work: the probability seemed
to be that our hours if not minutes were numbered. I kissed the dear
children, and, with the rest of our party, went out, to work ourselves,
and to encourage and stimulate others to do the same. We commended ourselves to God, and began to secure the floating things,
while others helped to cut away the wreck. By encouragement and example we got some of the crew to assist us. Many of the smaller

A – B FRIDAY NIGHT, SEPT. 21 ~ BULWARKS LOST

C ~ D SATURDAY ~ JIB BOOMS

E – F SATURDAY ~ FORE-TOP & TOP GALLANT MASTS

G ~ H SATURDAY ~ MAIN TOPGALLANT MAST

J ~ K SATURDAY NIGHT ~ MIZZEN TOPGALLANT
                               & ROYAL MAST

~L SATURDAY NIGHT ~ MIZZEN TOPMAST FOLLOWED

G – M SUNDAY 23rd. ~ MAIN TOPMAST DOWN,
                  BRINGING SKYSAIL YARD H TO DECK.

BEFORE THE WORST

things washed overboard, and the larger we secured from time to time; for the fury of the waves was such that no lashings would stand long. The water casks having been washed away, there was no fresh water procurable, as we dare not open the tanks in the gale. Cooking was out of the question, and we had to eat a little biscuit and cheese or butter from time to time.

Through God's blessing the wreck of the foremasts and jib boom was safely got over the side. The main-mast was swinging fearfully and large quantities of water were going down into the hold by the foot of the mast, and by the anchor-pipes, the covers of which had washed away. These places were now secured, and as the afternoon was far advanced, no more could be attempted. The appearance of the wreck was very sad. Rolling fearfully, the masts and yards hanging down were tearing our only sail – the main lower top-sail – and were battering like a ram against the main yard. The deck, from the forecastle to the poop was one scarcely broken sea. The roar of the water on the decks, the clang of the chains, the tearing of the dangling mast and yards, the sharp smacking of the torn sails, made it almost impossible to hear the sound of any orders which might be given.

[Rudland supplied the missing facts:] Mr Taylor was perfectly calm. When it was almost at its height the men refused to work any longer. The captain (came into the saloon and) advised them all to put on their lifebelts (saying), 'She can scarcely hold together two hours more.' [Together they sang 'Rock of ages'.] At this juncture the captain went towards the forecastle where the men were hiding in despair, with his life-preserver [a club or bludgeon used for self defence]. Mr Taylor went up to him saying, 'Don't use force till everything else is tried,' then he [himself] went in quietly and talked to the men, [according to the master of the *Cutty Sark* there was no way between decks, so he would have had to cross the surging well deck] saying to them he believed God would bring them through it alright, but that of course their safety depended upon the greatest care in navigating the ship, in other words, upon the men themselves. 'We will all help,' he added. 'Our lives are in jeopardy just as much as yours.' The chief danger just then was from the broken spars, especially two iron ones which were hanging over the side of the ship and in danger of ramming in the woodwork. The men were completely won over by his quiet demeanour and friendly reasoning, and officers and midshipmen and all went to work in earnest at the wreckage and got in before long the two great iron spars . . . By this time the boats had all gone overboard. . . . The men began to take courage again.

[Jennie again:] Mr Taylor and all our young men worked with all their might, the sea often washing them down, constantly they were knee-deep in water yet they managed to haul ropes, lash spars, pump, etc. It was such a Sunday, the vessel looked a perfect wreck. [Another ship,] the *Assyrian* came out of course to offer us assistance, but there was nothing they could do for us . . . (On Saturday) I put on the waterproof cloak you got me, and went on the poop; it was an awful sight, the vessel was knocked about like a shuttlecock, and rolled and quivered and plunged as you could hardly imagine; the flapping of the torn sails added to the wildness of the scene.

The worst of the typhoon had moved away, but such winds and seas could not abate for many hours to come. Under less lowering skies their danger was still extreme.

[Hudson Taylor:] Providentially, the moon was bright, and the night light; nevertheless there was little sleeping, though we were all tired out. About ten p.m. the mizzen top-gallant and royal mast gave way and with the royal yard hung swinging about. The rain and spray beat about piteously, and the force of the wind was such that it was difficult to stand on the poop – at times impossible, without holding on to ropes or stays. Captain Bell kept moving about though so unwell.

All hands to the pumps[6]   *September 23–24, 1866*

The danger now was that they might founder.

[Hudson Taylor:] *Sunday 23rd.* Very weary in body we commenced work at six a.m. There was now much of the wreck of the main mast hanging down almost as low as the bulwarks of the ship. Ropes and blocks were procured and fixed to the more heavy spars, and the ropes and wire stays were gradually removed, and the wreck got down on board. The pumps were got to work, and ropes being carried into the cabin, the ladies helped us in pumping. The main top-mast staysail, and upper main top-sail reefed, were set: by this time the lower main top-sail was all torn and blown to pieces. We were somewhat steadier when this sail was set, and the glass continued rising; but the rolling continued to be very heavy, at times the decks were one sheet of water rolling about and foaming and roaring in a way sufficient to appal the stoutest heart. [Maria:] . . . those who were outside on (deck) were often washed off their feet, and carried about by the force of the water; indeed, it was a wonder that no lives were lost or limbs smashed. [Hudson Taylor:] The ship began to labour very heavily, and led us to think that she was making water, but of this we could get no certainty. Worn out, after a hard day's work, we could not keep awake for any service, but lay down for a little rest. This was often disturbed by unusually heavy seas or rolls, at which times we seemed as if we were going down at once. But after a time she would get more quiet and the moonlight and lessening wind gave rise to hope.

[Emily:] I stood at the saloon door. It was awful to see the raging, heavy seas go over the deck – for the moment burying all – not knowing who might be missing when they had swept away in their thundering course. And Mr T was there. I held my breath each time the waters rose, roared, rushed over us and subsided. . . . But for Mr Brunton and Mr T there would be nothing done. Into every most dangerous position they are the first to go.

For the first time since we left home, the rest of our sabbath was broken. All were busily engaged in getting the vessel into sailing condition, which was very difficult to do with a heavy sea on. We found ourselves to be in a worse condition even than we had supposed. We had shipped a great deal of water, and were doing so still; we had suspicions that somewhere the side of the vessel was sprung. The pumps would not work; and Monday, though the storm may be said to have passed, was the most anxious time of all. We were so thoroughly tired. The pumps which we had managed to work a little while – ladies and all helping – were again out of order, and the question was at last seriously raised, as to whether a boat could live. In such a sea it was impossible.

Captain Bell was near the end of his tether, still in command but scarcely able to think or to take decisions. He had been deaf and unwell since August 23, for more than a month. The men knew that another gale would leave no hope of survival and had lost confidence in him. Hudson Taylor had to intervene again.

I believe there would have been mutiny and the ship taken out of Capt Bell's hands, but for our influence. The water was now increasing [again] in the hold, probably four feet were in her and all three pumps were useless, and out of order (Nicol, Sell and Rudland, and Jackson and Williamson got them put to rights); and the crew weary and dispirited saw no preparations for running into port. I went to Capt Bell and spoke to him about the state of matters. He saw no danger and did not believe she was making water. He however soon after wore ship and made more sail. On the other tack we headed well and took less water on deck; but we made no progress, or next to none.

Shanghai at last[7]   *September 25–30, 1866*

The typhoon was over, but the problem had become how to spread enough sail on the fractured skeletons of masts to make any headway toward Shanghai. Maria, writing to Mrs Berger, looked back saying,

For three days, Saturday, Sunday and Monday, Sep. 22nd, 23rd and 24th, we were in imminent danger, not knowing for the greater part of the time that we had another hour to live; and by Monday evening I felt constrained to ask the Lord to move His stroke from us, and to deliver us out of painful suspense. Still it was sweet to rejoice in the Lord and His past proofs of love . . . and I realized Habakkuk's song as I had never done before. ('Although the fig tree shall not blossom, neither shall fruit be in the vines . . . and there shall be no herd in the stalls: yet I will rejoice in the Lord, I will joy in the God of my salvation.' *Hab*. 3.17, 18) Our danger was enhanced by various causes [including mutiny] and I believe that in all human probability had not we and our party been on board, the Lammermuir would not have reached port. This we should not like to be generally known; but the moral influence of the *passengers* (ladies not excepted) working to save the ship was I believe the means of inducing the men to do their duty instead of giving way to despair.

Tuesday, September 25, dawned another fine day. The sun shone brightly and the sea was quieter. The fixed rigging of the main mast, the complex of stays so loosened that the huge mast had been swaying dangerously, was tightened. The hold was opened and new sails, 'all wet and containing water in their folds', were hauled out and 'a new lower main top-sail was set. The pumps were worked and the water got down to 22 inches.' Constantly tacking through still turbulent water, at last they began 'making good progress towards Shanghai' through the 'fine moonlight night'. 'Wednesday 26th. Another fine day, sea quiet, wind fair, and more of it. The young men were at work helping the crew, and pumping. Got the water down to 10½ inches.'

But Hudson Taylor was too ill to work. He seldom gave an explanation. He was so accustomed to his old colitis relapsing when he was run down and his diet upset. For the 27th a pencilled jotting reads: 'Jury fore-mast. Poorly.' And for the 28th, 'made Ragged Isles, rounded Saddle and got pilot.' Emily said, 'On Friday, the 28th, we passed the Saddle Islands' [between Hangzhou Bay and the Yangzi estuary]. They had had enough.

[Emily:] The same evening a pilot came to us; but he did not dare to take us in before Sunday morning, when a tug steamer came and took us up to Shanghai. Our broken and dismantled condition made us the general object of curiosity; but we in our hearts thanked God for the great deliverance He had wrought for us, in sparing the lives of all on board through such unusual perils – perils arising not only from the over-sweeping waters themselves, but also from the frequent falling of splintered yards, etc. Though some of the crew met with severe bruises and such like hurts, not one life was lost, and not one limb broken. There were, indeed, very many narrow escapes. A vessel came in soon after us which had been in the same typhoon that we were, with only six lives remaining out of twenty-two; sixteen were drowned. It was well that we got in on the day we did, for they had some terribly stiff gales outside, which our disabled vessel could not have weathered.

The irrepressible Jennie, continuing her serial letter to her father, wrote of 'another exciting Sunday tho' the circumstances were so altered'.

God grant that having been brought to the gates of eternity and then spared for a while our lives may be entirely devoted to Him, and the work before us. Through it all I never felt the least regret or indeed anything but joy at the thought that I had come. *Oct. 1st.* Yesterday we cast anchor and here we are safe and sound off Shanghai . . . We are really in China . . . I am ready to sing for joy all day . . . The captain has invited us to stay on board as long as we like.

Officers and men felt understandably indebted to passengers with that spirit.

CHAPTER SEVEN

JOURNEY'S END
1866

Gamble's go-down[1]   *October 1866*

Survival had been all that mattered for the past ten days or more. For three weeks the *Lammermuir* had battled with one typhoon and then another. From the ominous sunset on September 9 to dropping anchor in the Yangzi estuary on the 29th anxiety, injuries, hot tempers and a 'deplorable condition' of mind in some on board had dominated Hudson Taylor's thoughts. The last weekend, with Monday, 24th, 'the most anxious day of all', had been most fatiguing. With only the troubled sleep of exhaustion, 'wet to the skin' for three days and nights, foundering and 'all but lost' even after the skies cleared, and helpless with a flare-up of colitis, Hudson Taylor could give little thought to the rush of responsibilities and work ahead of him.

The arrival of a pilot with world news and the talk of Shanghai changed all that. Bismarck's 'blood and iron' policy had brought short, sharp war to Austria and Italy, and treaties of peace. France, threatened in the north, was withdrawing her protecting troops from Rome and the Vatican. The Muslim rebellion in the far north-west of China and her central Asian dependencies had plunged the Manchu government into new tribulations, not two years since the end of the Taiping rebellion. Shanghai was half empty, no longer the haven of a million fugitives from war. Rid of danger and restrictions, the foreign community had turned to sport and social diversions as never before. The editorial of the *North China Herald*, hot from the press that morning, greeted the latest anti-foreign outpourings with typical cynicism:

> The doom of foreign residents in China is evidently sealed. A *jehad* has been proclaimed against them in Hunan and they are to be swept from the face of the Flowery Land . . . Against missionaries and the iconoclastic religion they teach, are the thunders of the proclamation principally directed . . . Mixing with the people, acquainting them-

selves intimately with their customs and prejudices, the Catholics
have succeeded in obtaining a certain hold, facilitated by the extreme
similarity in the outward practices of the two priesthoods (Buddhist
and Roman). With altars, incense, gorgeous robes and images, the
uneducated Chinese hardly knows whether he is in a Buddhist temple
or a Catholic cathedral . . . We are evidently indebted in great
measure to iconoclastic missionary teaching for the sweeping denunciations in the proclamation, and the exhortations to indiscriminate
massacre which it conveys.

The Hunan proclamation followed the usual lines of lurid provocation and threat – about baptism with oil from the melted corpses of
priests, for example – ludicrous to the discerning, but calculated to
inflame the superstitious majority of the people.

As soon as visibility permitted, the *Lammermuir* made her way
up the Yangzi to the mouth of the Huangpu river at Wusong,
Hudson Taylor's so familiar stamping-ground, and waited for the
tide and a tug. At last, on Sunday evening, 30th, at five p m they
dropped anchor in the muddy brown river below Shanghai and the
journey was over. During the voyage Hudson Taylor had been
talking with his party about what to expect on arrival. The Ningbo
missionaries, the Lords and the CIM's eight members, knew of
their sailing. His good friend, William Gamble, manager of the
American Presbyterian Mission press and an admirer of Maria's
father, Samuel Dyer, had moved the press to Shanghai in 1860. He
also knew they were coming. But Hudson Taylor did not know what
arrangements, if any, had been made to receive them. If there were
none, he knew what he would do. Until he opened a business centre
at Shanghai a few years later, his custom was to take rooms in a
Chinese inn, or to hire houseboats, especially if a journey by canal
was planned.

Five or six days for discharging her cargo and reloading would
have been the extent of Captain Bell's hospitality – but for the
typhoons. A month or more of repairs and refitting would instead be
needed to make his ship seaworthy again. Without question all his
passengers could stay aboard for as long as they wished. He could
not forget his indebtedness to them. With most if not all of their
possessions in cabin and hold soaked with sea water, they would
need two weeks at least to unpack, wash and dry all they could.
Hudson Taylor's problem was partly solved, but not entirely. For
the overland journey by canal to Hangzhou or Ningbo, he would

have to lay in provisions for his big party, soon to be enlarged by the addition of Chinese companions. The solution was not long in coming.

> Besides the private effects of each individual, we had brought with us stores which former experience in China had taught us would be useful; printing and lithographic presses, with type and other accessories; and a large supply of medicines, with the requisite apparatus for commencing a hospital and dispensary. All these things had to be stored somewhere, before we could be free for proceeding into the interior. During the voyage we had made it a special subject of prayer that God would help us in this matter; and we had hardly cast anchor when He answered our prayers, and met all our need. On the very evening of our arrival we were visited by W Gamble, Esquire, of the American Presbyterian Mission Press, who generously offered us, for an indefinite period, the use of his 'go-down' (a large warehouse), which amply accommodated all our luggage; and he himself entertained our whole party during our stay in Shanghai.

The timeliness of William Gamble's appearance at the *Lammermuir* impressed Hudson Taylor in such a way that a year later he overlooked Captain Bell's offer. Writing to William Berger on September 30, 1867, he said, 'A year ago, about five o'clock p.m., we anchored in Shanghai, not knowing what we were to do, where we were to go. That very evening dear Mr Gamble found us out . . .' Hudson Taylor knew the captain, officers and crew had their own quarters and possessions to dry out. A forest of masts, spars and rigging had to be replaced or repaired, as well as bulwarks, deck gear, boats and sails. Every inch of space would be needed. Genuine as Captain Bell's offer was, to be in his way was unthinkable.

Hudson Taylor went ashore with William Gamble the same evening and saw the empty 'go-down' and living space he had talked about. He could wish for nothing better. As Maria told Hudson's mother, 'That any one missionary should be able to accommodate all our party seemed an impossibility, and here God has raised up one who not only can accommodate us all, but whose views concerning missionary work and missionary agents coincide in great measure with Hudson's.'

Before they could get away from Shanghai there were formalities to be gone through. Each one would have to be registered with the consul, and passports for travelling inland would have to be negotiated with the mandarins. The international missionary community and Chinese Christians would wish to meet the young men and women whom Hudson Taylor proposed to take up-country in Chinese clothes. That clothing had to be bought or made and the men's heads shaved and fitted with a *bianzi* or queue. Not least, the whole team of novices would have to be introduced, in the Chinese city, to Chinese courtesies, the correct ways of walking, eating and performing their ablutions. But before he could embark on any of those tasks he must escort Mary Bausum and Elizabeth Rose to Ningbo.

On Monday morning, October 1, the *Lammermuir* was towed upstream, nearer to William Gamble's home in the French concession and close to the Chinese city. In the afternoon they embarked for Ningbo. One of the great changes in the six years since he had left China was that steamships now plied twice daily between Shanghai and Ningbo. But courage was needed to go out to sea again, even for two hundred miles. Writing to Mrs Berger about the *Lammermuir* adventure, Elizabeth wrote, 'The feeling of our hearts when the storm subsided was that we had been brought back from the verge of the grave that we might devote ourselves afresh to God . . . May we live as those who are alive from the dead.'

Gales were not the only hazard. The first issue of the *North China Herald* after their arrival carried reports of piracies, if anything more daring than before and against steamers as well as sailing ships. Letters of tribute to the Captain of the P & O S.S. *Nepaul* and a column on the loss in the typhoon of (ironically) the *Cyclone*, by her surviving second mate, accompanied the particulars of the '*Lammermuir*, 1054 tons, Capt Bell' and her passenger list, without comment.

They reached Ningbo early the next morning, Mary Bausum to rejoin her mother and stepfather E C Lord, and Elizabeth to meet her fiancé James Meadows after four years apart. Hudson Taylor had a few hours with them, with his Chinese friends whom he had expected never to see again, and with 'the Ningbo five' whom he had sent out; and made good use of his time by concluding an arrangement for five Chinese to travel and work with the *Lammermuir* party.

> I have engaged a native preacher, (Mr) Tsiu, to go up the country with us. He was, I think, the third person Mr Jones and I baptized, after we commenced our permanent work in Ningbo, and has been

employed since 1860 by Mr Lord. I have also engaged three male and one female servants, all natives in Ningpo, for the double purpose of acting as teachers of the language, and of assisting us in their own departments.

It must have been planned in advance, for he boarded the coaster again in the afternoon with Mr Tsiu, a young man and an amah 'to cook and wash and teach us to talk fluently' as Jennie put it. They were back at Shanghai on Wednesday morning, October 3.

Ningbo revisited   *October 1866*

Little had changed in Ningbo since the 'chequered news' received in London before the *Lammermuir* sailed. Large mission buildings towered in unseemly prominence over their surrounding Chinese neighbours. The missionaries had built as they would at home. The CMS were still undermanned with only the Moule brothers and J D Valentine remaining. The American Presbyterians were little better placed since the Greens had moved to Hangzhou in 1865. Dr D B McCartee, a veteran of over twenty years' residence in Ningbo, was matched by E C Lord who had been there since 1847. Neither moved far from Ningbo in pursuing their work. Lord's consular and pastoral duties took up his time, but Mrs Lord (Jemima Bausum) made up for that ten times over. The Knowltons, American Baptists, had twelve years' service to their credit and travelled deep into the countryside. The rest had come since the Hudson Taylors' departure in June 1860, no less than twelve of them sent by him.[2]

James Meadows, with only four years' experience but a good grasp of the local dialect, was the most established. Much could be expected of him and Elizabeth Rose, his bride to be. Stephan Barchet, by living with a Chinese evangelist in his 'house' of mats at the town of Ninggongqiao, was rapidly becoming fluent. Isolation from fellow foreigners was ideal for learning the language. And supervision by the Lords supplied what other training he needed. Not surprisingly Mary Bausum and Stephan, already friends when in London, were in love before she was seventeen.

The Crombies and George Stott were installed at Fenghua, thirty miles south of Ningbo. Exorbitant demands had made it impossible to rent premises, and Stott observed, 'Before they will be influenced by us, they must trust us, and prove that we are trustworthy; and before they can trust us, they must know us . . .' But with persist-

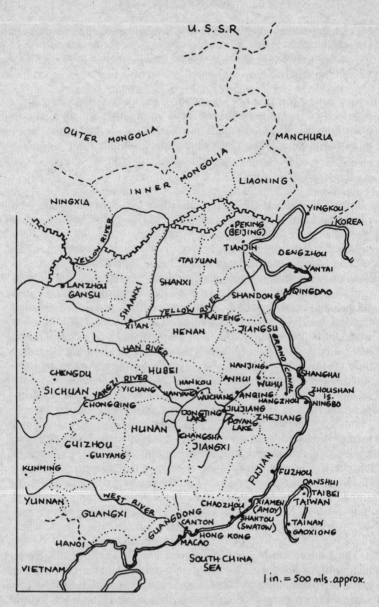

CHINA'S MAIN CITIES AND WATERWAYS

ence they had found three rooms as a foothold and begun to make friends.

In May John Stevenson, James Meadows and Feng Nenggui had visited the city of Shaoxing, ninety miles west of Ningbo, and from lodgings in a temple succeeded in renting a house at a busy crossroads. John Burdon had preached there in 1862, until driven out by the Taiping rebels. But no preacher had attempted to re-occupy this 'Venice in China', with its population of two hundred and fifty thousand, since the Taipings were expelled in March 1863 (Book 3, p 315). On September 9, 1866, a Chinese preacher had begun work, and on the day the *Lammermuir* anchored in the Yangzi estuary, John and Annie moved in. Downstairs they had seating for seventy or eighty people, and upstairs a room for themselves and their baby, another for cooking and eating in, and a third for receiving callers and doing language study, all as bare and utilitarian as could be.[3]

With Ningbo, Fenghua and Shaoxing occupied, the China Inland Mission already had three centres, only one of which was a treaty port. Since John Jones and Hudson Taylor began work in 1857, over a hundred people had been baptised. Though death and defections had left the church with only fifty-nine members, a high proportion were active Christians. Young Tsiu, the teacher, and his wife and mother (the 'man-hunter': Book 3, p 315) were outstanding, but not unique. Feng Nenggui, the basket-maker, and his wife were missionaries in the village of Kongpu near Fenghua, where nine people were already Christians. Nenggui's first convert in Ningbo, no less than the Taylors' friend Wang Lae-djün, was working with William Fuller the Free Methodist. Fan Qiseng and his wife were two more. From this small church all the expansion of the China Inland Mission's early pioneering was to spring. It stood as a model of the Mission's aims, to preach the gospel, to bind believers together in thriving congregations, and to show them how to repeat the process among their own people.

The opening cage   *1860–66*

The *Lammermuir* party reached China at a crucial time in the history of foreign missions. The coastal treaty ports were still a cage confining the missionary body. Since the first historic deployment of a handful of waiting pioneers, after the unequal treaties of 1842–4, missionaries had been restricted to those ports, unless they took risks. The notable few were the exception to the rule. For seventeen years, from 1843–60, at an immense price in lives and health, the majority had studied China and the Chinese, translated the Scriptures and books of science and law, conducted their schools and preached their hearts out, with scant results in terms of converts and churches. Disappointment was not for lack of zeal or prayer. Tenacity gave what success there was. The CMS began work in Fujian in 1850 and ten years later reported seeing no interest being shown in the message, 'no visible results, no converts to the truth, no baptisms'.[4] Soon afterwards two believed in Fuzhou and were baptised. By 1866 there were twenty. At this rate the evangelisation of China 'would take a millenium'.

Small wonder then, that when the Peking Convention of 1860 opened the gates to widespread penetration of the empire, few missionaries were able or ready to hand over their responsibilities to others, foreign or Chinese, and to launch out. Institutions and established local churches tied the missionaries to the cities. Such as could, moved from the five old treaty ports to the nine new ones. This second deployment was only possible by a slow process of division. Where one left the old work to take up the new, his experienced colleague carried twice his former load, or novices succeeded the veterans, sometimes with sad consequences. Here and there the old work was abandoned. Where Chinese Christians were mature and trained they took over, but they were few.

In the whole of Zhejiang there were fewer than four hundred Protestant Christians and less than a score of Chinese preachers; in Jiangsu and Fujian fewer still.[5] Missionaries of other societies often helped to preserve what could have disintegrated. At other times the work of two societies was merged. When the American Episcopal missionaries had to leave Shanghai, the CMS nurtured their congregation. And when no CMS staff were left, after W H Collins joined Burdon in Peking,[6] the Episcopalians obliged. Both were of the Anglican communion. Differing denominations co-operated no less faithfully. E C Lord had nursed Hudson Taylor's Ningbo Mission church for five years, preserving its identity.

Conspicuous in the reports and reviews of the *Chinese Recorder* was the inability of society after society in place after place to report activities under the title of 'itinerancy' or 'itineration'. Few attempted anything resembling the extensive travels of Burdon, Muirhead, Griffith John, William Aitchison, William Burns, Hudson Taylor and others. The Bible Society representatives and colporteurs were outstanding in their achievement, following the pattern set by Alexander Wylie in 1863. Most mission stations were static, looking to local growth for future expansion throughout China.

Progress by this method was painfully slow. William Muirhead advocated a strong base in a secure treaty port, with adventurous expeditions from it. Exactly this had been done since 1843 and was still favoured by some besides Muirhead. It had been Hudson Taylor's policy and practice from 1854–57, and his policy while he built up the Bridge Street congregation in Ningbo from 1857–60. Now, on his return with the *Lammermuir* party, Ningbo was to be the springboard but not his base. His policy was to live and work at increasing distances away in the interior. Then his base would be wherever he himself was up-country.

Muirhead travelled more than four hundred miles from Shanghai. Because tall and fair, he was called a 'real devil' while the dark little Welshman, Griffith John, was a 'devil in disguise'. Muirhead's penetrating voice could reach the farthest in a crowd of two thousand with perfect ease. With his 'great command of language and perfect self-control, he had no difficulty in commanding his audiences, however . . . rude and turbulent.' He was often seized and savagely beaten to yells of 'Kill the barbarian!' Once he had been rescued at the last moment from being dragged on board a pirate junk to certain torture and death. On another occasion officials saved him from a murderous rabble. W H Medhurst's daughter recalled watching her mother wash the blood from Muirhead's battered ankles after he had been stoned. Like Hudson Taylor he loved and was loved by children. Twenty years later, in 1886, a CIM missionary became his second wife. In 1866, the year of the *Lammermuir*, he joined Joseph Edkins on a journey into Mongolia, crossing the border two hundred miles north of Peking.

Griffith John of the LMS went in 1861 to Hankou, the new treaty port in central China far up the Yangzi river. There he built up a strong church as the nucleus of an aggressive and extensive missionary penetration into the surrounding provinces. Josiah Cox of the Wesleyan Methodist Missionary Society came from Canton to Hankou in 1862 and two years later penetrated up the Yangzi into Sichuan, and to Changsha in Hunan. He was the first Protestant to attempt the evangelisation of this most antagonistic province, the last to be opened to the gospel. A medical missionary, Dr Porter Smith, joined him at Hankou in 1864 and the saintly David Hill the following year.[7]

In June 1865 Dr James Maxwell of the English Presbyterian Mission went from Amoy as the first pioneer to Taiwan, at Tainan, one of the two open ports on the island.[8] He was in for trouble. Driven out by a mob he took refuge at Dagao (now Gaoxiong), there to become the focus of a major international incident in 1868.

Deployment to treaty ports, nominally safe, did not mean immunity from difficulty or danger. At Yantai (commonly called Chefoo) in Shandong, the toll of missionaries was particularly heavy.[9] Joseph Edkins, the first to move there from Shanghai, was followed by O Rao of the Paris Protestant Mission. Both went on to Tianjin in 1861, but Rao returned to Yantai with a Mr and Mrs Bonhoure. When she died both returned to Europe. J L Holmes, the American Southern Baptist, and H M Parker of the American Protestant Episcopal Church were killed at Yantai in October 1861. The wife of Parker's colleague, D D Smith, died in 1862 and he returned to the States. D B McCartee spent three years in Yantai for his health before returning to Ningbo. Yantai and Shandong province also became the grave of the first missionaries in China of the (English) Baptist Missionary Society, Hudson Taylor's friends C J Hall, R F Laughton and others.

Alexander Williamson, Griffith John's LMS contemporary, made Yantai his base after joining the National Bible Society of Scotland, and travelled far and wide. In 1864 he traversed eastern Mongolia, four years before the famous James Gilmour began his life's work there. 1866 saw him travelling overland from Peking through Shandong to Yantai. He reported finding many Muslim mosques between Tianjin and Linqing on the Grand Canal. Some cities had three or four. In 1866 he was travelling with considerable courage through Shanxi, Shaanxi and Henan provinces with Jonathan Lees of the LMS, provinces the China Inland Mission would not touch until 1875–6. A colleague of Williamson's was to be killed on a similar journey. Williamson himself penetrated 'repeatedly through all parts of Shantung province . . . north, south and central Manchuria . . . and portions of . . . Hupeh, Hunan and Szechwan'.[10]

Tianjin drew more missionaries from the south. When the Allied invasion to enforce the Treaty of Tientsin sailed north in 1860, the health of Henry Blodget of the American Board was so poor that he sent his wife home to the States, and himself joined an expeditionary supply ship to seek healing in the 'champagne air' of the North China Sea. No Protestant had been as a missionary to Tianjin since

Charles Gutzlaff in 1831. Blodget preached in the streets and settled there, at first in British troop barracks. All seemed as blind to the obvious political implications as Gutzlaff and others had been before and during the First Opium War. In May 1861 he succeeded in renting a house in the Chinese city and opened a chapel. The Methodists, John Innocent and W N Hall, followed him in April 1861 and Edkins in May. Justus Doolittle of the American Board exchanged Fujian for Tianjin in 1862.[11]

By then Peking was becoming accessible. The very tentative beginning made in late 1861 by William Lockhart (LMS) and John Burdon (CMS) as surgeon and chaplain to the British legation opened the way for others. Joseph Edkins (LMS) arrived in May 1863 and W H Collins MRCS (CMS) the same year. William Burns came from Shantou (Swatow) in the autumn of 1863 and John Dudgeon MD relieved Lockhart to return home in March 1864. Another notable arrival in Peking was Miss Elizabeth Smith of the CMS, one of the very few single women among foreigners in China.

W A P Martin, the American Presbyterian of Ningbo, had been in Tianjin in 1858 as an interpreter-negotiator with William Reed, the United States Commissioner, and again in May 1859 with his successor the Hon John E Ward. From January 1860 until midsummer 1862 he was in the States, but was back in Shanghai when Dr Culbertson, the veteran American Presbyterian, died suddenly of cholera. Martin stayed long enough to reinvigorate the stagnating work in Shanghai before returning to Tianjin, this time as a missionary.[12] Peking, he said characteristically, was 'swarming with Jesuits' while the residence of Protestants, let alone any overt work, was still restricted.

With the help of Samuel Wells Williams and the new US minister, Anson Burlingame, Martin managed to find a toehold in a temple three miles outside the west gate of Peking and soon afterwards in the city, near the Zongli (Tsungli) Yamen, the Foreign Office. Chinese officials with whom he had had dealings over the treaties even welcomed him. Set on preaching the gospel, he wisely lay low rather than risk being evicted. John Burdon gave him the welcome news that Martin's *Evidences of Christianity* in Chinese had reached the Imperial household.[13] But when William Burns arrived the two of them opened a small chapel in which they preached. A high Manchu official asked Martin to warn the other missionaries to be very careful, but even after this he rented another building as a preaching chapel on a main street near one of the city gates.

Martin was also a daring traveller. In February and March 1866 he travelled overland from Peking to Shanghai, taking sufficient interest in his route to lecture on March 29 to the China branch of the Royal Asiatic Society, on his forty-day journey, including the imperial road south from Peking; the present condition of the Jews in Henan; the navigation of the Yellow River; and the central section of the Grand Canal.

Before going to Peking, W A P Martin had begun translating Wheaton's *Elements of International Law*, to help influential Chinese to understand Western attitudes in international relations.[14] His good friend from Ningbo, Robert Hart, was by then in the exalted position of Inspector-General of the Imperial Maritime Customs though only twenty-eight. When the Grand Secretary, Wen Xiang, asked the American envoy, Anson Burlingame, for advice in China's frequent confrontations with the French, Burlingame arranged for members of the Zongli Yamen to meet Martin. Robert Hart had already acquainted them with his unfinished translation. So on September 10, 1863, he discussed his Wheaton book with members of the Yamen, to the chagrin of the French chargé d'affaires. Chinese ignorance of international law suited France better than an informed government.[15] The Yamen seconded four literary experts, including a member of the Hanlin Academy, to advise Martin and promised five hundred taels towards publication costs. This was the beginning of increasing approval and honours. Meanwhile his translation of Wheaton was reprinted in Japan in 1865. An evangelist at heart, Martin was pioneering a new approach for the gospel to the heart of the Chinese nation.

A passing reference to a few other stalwarts of the faith is all that can be made, to set the arrival of the *Lammermuir* party in perspective.[16] A P Happer and Issacher J Roberts were still at Canton, where they had been since 1844 with a few enforced absences. The Methodist George Piercy was there again. James Legge was still at Hong Kong. Based there, but usually on the mainland, were the dogged continental veterans Rudolf Lechler and Ph Winnes of the Basel Mission, and August Hanspach of the Chinese Evangelization Society of Berlin. The English Presbyterians and American Baptists were at Shantou (Swatow), Alexander and John Stronach of LMS, doyens of 1838 vintage, at Xiamen (Amoy), joined by Carstairs Douglas. In Shanghai a new star had risen in 1860, in the person of Young J Allen of the American

Methodist Episcopal Church. Much was to be heard of him as he gained in influence. With William Gamble was another young American Presbyterian, J M W Farnham, who became as good a friend of the CIM. J T Gulick of the American Board had settled in Kalgan, outside the Great Wall of China, sixty miles north of Peking and the gateway to Mongolia. Elijah Bridgman, Robert Morrison's colleague, had died in 1861, but his indomitable widow, in China since 1845, was among the Peking pioneers at the heart of the empire in 1864. Joseph Schereschewsky ('Sherry') of the American Protestant Episcopal Church had arrived at Shanghai in 1862 and gone on to Peking. William Burns was still there, preparing to move up to Newchang (now Yingkou).[17] As for the wider missionary scene of East Asia, there were only five male Protestant missionaries in Japan and the wives of three; and in Thailand only William Dean, with his wife and daughter, as always taking the gospel to the Chinese, and nine missionary couples and one single lady among the Thai.[18]

Apart from the *Lammermuir* party, two hundred and four missionaries in China or absent on furlough, with two hundred and six Chinese colleagues, was the full tally almost sixty years after Morrison first landed at Canton. A year earlier only ninety-one had been actually in China, by Hudson Taylor's calculation. The total Chinese Church membership of three thousand one hundred and forty-two included twelve ordained ministers. Preaching Christ to China's millions had scarcely begun. Even with treaties of toleration it was to be an uphill grind and would continue so for many years to come.[19] The *Lammermuir* party was only a small addition to a painfully inadequate force.

The 'pigtail mission'[20]   *October 1866*

Forty hours after leaving Shanghai to go to Ningbo, Hudson Taylor was back again with 28-year-old Mr Tsiu, another Christian man and the 'Ningpo amah'. To the missionary newcomers' amazement, Mr Tsiu had grown his finger nails a full inch and a half beyond his finger-tips, the true sign of a teacher who never put his hand to manual work. He moved in to live with the team and introduce them to Chinese life. Aboard the *Lammermuir* everyone had been busy preparing to disembark, drying their clothes and bedding in the now perfect weather, packing up and making their first sallies into the Chinese city with Maria or William Gamble as guides. They collected their mail from the little building that still served as a consulate beside the Suzhou river and 'St Catherine's' toll-bridge, and wrote their descriptions of the experiences they had passed through.

To read those letters is to see the confusion of their thoughts. While Jennie Faulding wrote in one breath of being 'ready to sing for joy all day', enlarging on the sights and sounds of China and things Chinese, in the next she was homesick and anxious about her family in London's worst cholera epidemic. John Sell, sick for so much of the long voyage, confessed to being reduced to tears by the turmoil of his emotions. 'I cried bitterly and could not help it.' Rudland visited a temple and saw idols, to him the embodiment of evil, 'two on one side and two on the other; and in the centre a figure of Satan himself, seated above the rest. I thought of the (typhoon) and . . . felt I could put up with anything, could I but tell (the Chinese) of a Saviour's love.' Saved from the fury of the sea, they knew they had survived for one thing only, to do what they had come to do. The bond uniting them was all the stronger.

Shanghai was a strange mixture of the familiar and the exotic. 'There is so much English mixed with what is foreign,' wrote Jennie, betraying her unadapted viewpoint – though sooner than most she was to see and feel the foreignness of everything Western imposed upon the natural rightness in China of everything Chinese. Chinese houses looked 'prison-like' with their high walls enclosing the courtyard. The shops were 'large and fine', open to the very narrow streets and displaying so many wares. 'I heard the gong of evening idol-worship, but we got back in time for Christian Chinese worship in a nice chapel under Mr Gamble's house . . . I could understand a good deal.'

Chinese courtesy impressed Duncan. 'They are very quiet and polite with us; far more than many of our countrymen would be with them . . . We hope to go up the country as soon as we can, away from Europeans. I believe with you, that the only way of reaching the Chinese is to become Christian Chinese, and live like them as far as is right . . . We must show them that we are come to seek their good and not oppose their customs.'

For Louise Desgraz it was watching a Chinese funeral that was most stirring. Fire-crackers 'to frighten away the evil spirits', counterfeit paper money being burned for the dead man's use in the other world, lanterns to light his way; 'what with the noise and the glare of the fire, it was an awful sight . . . I was glad to go away.' To her it was a lurid demonstration of the enslavement by Satan of those who were 'without God and without hope'.

Along the Huangpu waterfront embankment the international (Anglo-American) Settlement boasted a metalled road called by the Hindi word, the Bund, between the leading merchant houses and the mud bank down to the water. All other so-called roads were still mud tracks and footpaths, slowly receiving clinkers and hard core to make them all-weather. The British consul owned a horse-carriage and the Commissioner of Customs another. Everyone else walked, rode on horseback or hired a sedan chair or wheelbarrow. When John Stevenson had reached Shanghai in January, besides Chinese junks there were only five clipper ships at anchor, and very few steamships and tugs, but when the *Lammermuir* arrived in the early autumn the river was busy. Rudland saw a hundred sailing vessels.

By Saturday, October 6, most of their possessions were ready to be transferred from the *Lammermuir* to the warehouse near the East Gate of the Chinese city – that gate outside which Hudson Taylor was chatting with two Chinese in 1854 when cannonfire began and he ran for cover, to find afterwards that the Chinese had been hit and mortally wounded (Book 2, pp 142–3). Gamble's house was semi-foreign and spacious, alongside his printing works. Unmarried, he had room for the Taylors, John Sell, the seven remaining girls and the children. The Nicols were to have camped in the warehouse with the single men, had not Hudson Taylor seen to it that Maria and he took their place. Rudland's recollection was that all stayed aboard the *Lammermuir* until the 6th, and Captain Bell would accept no remuneration for feeding twenty young people through that week. But Jennie wrote home on that day saying, 'We have been a good deal at the ship this week packing up, the last of our (personal) things have come away today. They are all so kind to us on board and so loathe to part with us. Mr Brunton says "It's like parting with those that are dearest to me," and it's the same with them all more or less.' It looks as if the women and children moved early to William Gamble's house, while Rudland and the other young men stayed on board a little longer.

The immense 'go-down' had been built as a Chinese theatre, broad and long, ideal for printer's stock but not yet put to use, with an upper floor or gallery at one end reached by a stepladder. With the baggage all deposited below, they divided the gallery with sheets into three rooms and a passageway, for Duncan and Jackson,

Rudland and Williamson, Hudson Taylor and Maria. Intending to be there for no more than a week, they were two weeks without better privacy before they could exchange those quarters for the even closer confinement of houseboats for the journey to Hangzhou. All meals were at Mr Gamble's house, except when some stayed at the warehouse to save time. 'There was room enough for all the baggage (in the go-down), without piling the boxes at all,' Louise Desgraz told the Bergers. '(Your letters) found me very busy looking after the washing, which was not a small one after our long voyage, and for so many persons . . . We had the two stoves put up, the washing machine, the mangle, and the ironing stove; so there was plenty of work going on at the same time . . . It looked like a beehive. We often wished our friends at home could have had a peep at us, and see how happy we all were.'

The rest of the Ningbo employees seem to have arrived, as four or five Chinese were helping. 'My part has been folding for several hours every day,' Jennie added. Unpacking everything revealed that most had suffered more or less but nothing very seriously, not even the harmonium or Maria's sewing machine, a gift from Mrs Berger. Only the heavy baggage remained to be unloaded, when the go-down was less festooned with laundry – the printing presses, medical supplies, furniture and perhaps Colonel Gordon's magnetic electric machine'.

The crew had had their ups and downs since reaching Shanghai. The unconverted ones could be expected to follow their normal behaviour on making port, but that some of those who said they had turned to Christ should go with them had been a bitter disappointment to the rest. Hudson Taylor was careful how he spoke of them. 'Several of the men, who professed to receive Christ, have fallen through drink; but their deep contrition gives us good hope that they are indeed children of God.'[21] Mr Brunton himself knew only too well from his ill temper that genuine spiritual conversion did not mean an instant transformation of character. New sap in the veins took its time to replace old leaves with new. And as in Christ's own parable of the sower, stony ground, thorns and the wild birds of temptation could be expected to take their toll even of good seed. When Brunton reached Britain again and called on the Bergers, he confirmed that while some of the crew continued to stand firm, others went back on their decisions taken during the voyage.

Contrition and affection for their passengers were plain to see, and 'the kindness of Captain Bell and his officers could not have been exceeded'. On Sunday, October 7, after attending a Chinese service the missionaries all visited the *Lammermuir* again. Captain Bell's invitation to spend the day on board included what was meant to be a farewell service. They expected to be away from Shanghai within the week. After it they 'were obliged to stay to a beautiful lunch'. At the Settlement service in the evening, held in the new Union chapel, 'one might have fancied oneself in England'. For people intending to adapt as far as they could to China and the Chinese that had its drawbacks. Far from home, human nature cried out for links with the familiar, and bits of Britain on Chinese soil weakened resolve. Again Jennie recognised it. 'I'm glad we are not going to stay in Shanghai – the Chinese here are money-loving . . . and the English are so worldly and stylish, everyone knows everyone's business. I suppose we are pretty well talked about.' She was putting it mildly.

William Muirhead of the LMS, 'always a warm friend' of Hudson Taylor and the CIM, did not get back to Shanghai in time to see them. Alexander Wylie, now of the Bible Society and often away, was on his travels. As an old friend and travelling companion he would have been among the first to hail Hudson Taylor's return. William Gamble's young colleague, J M W Farnham, although living near the South Gate, on the far side of the city, came over on most days to see how they were getting on. In fact, the Americans were more friendly than the British. 'Mr Gamble's kindness was wonderful.' As Hudson Taylor was to learn before long, a Mr Howell of Dent and Company and a Mr Petrie of Jardine, Matheson were both well disposed, but he did not meet them at this time.

The small missionary community (of twenty-two when none were absent) were invited to come and meet the team at Gamble's home on October 17. The ten who came 'all expressed very kind feeling for us' and prayed warmly for the party about to set off for 'the interior'. But not all were as approving, especially when on the following day all the CIM men had the front part of their heads shaved, false *bianzi* (queues) attached to the back, and donned full Chinese dress. Maria also dressed as a Chinese lady, but the girls' outfits were not ready. They would have to be completed at Songjiang, the first big city on the way to Hangzhou. This was Maria's first experience of living in Chinese dress and, according to Stephan Barchet, 'a very real trial for her' at first from its unfamiliarity.

To have arrived with so much of their Western clothing wet and spoiled was embarrassment enough. To measure up to the social standards of Shanghai was impossible. Not that they wished it. None had shown any inclination to exchange the status they had known at home for that of new friends they had made either in Britain or China. The time was to come when a few would succumb to the pressure and conform to the foreign circle, to their personal advantage, but not yet. In *The British in the Far East*, Dr George Woodcock, no partisan, wrote of earlier days but equally of this period,

> The curious combination of faith and reasonableness in Hudson Taylor led him immediately to see (what) was wrong with the missions of the China coast. His missionary colleagues dressed and behaved like European clergymen. They belonged, visibly, to the same world as the merchants and the administrators and the soldiers whom the Chinese collectively classed 'red-haired foreign devils'. The first step was obviously to get out of devildom by looking and behaving as much like a Chinese as possible and thus approaching one's potential converts on their own terms . . . He could travel into the country districts without being conspicuous. He could approach the peasants and the inhabitants of inland towns without their distrust having been aroused beforehand by an outlandish European garb.[22]

In 1890 the CIM was to hold a reception in Shanghai. According to Montagu Beauchamp who was present, 'the oldest resident missionary' in Shanghai said in a speech,

> We remember how twenty-five years ago Mr Taylor arrived with his first party. We gave him no warm welcome; the Shanghai papers ridiculed the 'pigtail mission' and dubbed him a fool or a knave, but he answered not a word . . . I for one feel ashamed of my attitude towards Mr Taylor in those early days.[23]

William Rudland's recollection of those weeks in October 1866 was that 'most of the other missionaries either ignored us or opposed', and another note read, 'Mr Gamble had to suffer a good deal . . . The *Consular Gazette* and *North China Herald* put in strong things about Mr Taylor's policy, especially bringing single ladies to China . . . enlarging upon the injustice and cruelty of it.' For bringing young women with him in the *Lammermuir* Hudson Taylor was indeed castigated as '(he is) either a fool or a knave, and we have reason to believe that Mr Taylor is not a fool'.[24] He made no reply. It was no crime to be unconventional, and he had been subjected to similar abuse in 1855 when he first dressed like a Chinese. Rudland commented, 'So characteristic of Mr Taylor, he said nothing about it, no reference to any unfriendliness . . . just let them drop.'

Unhampered by the necessity to convince conservative advisers at home, Hudson Taylor had acted on his own convictions, guided he believed by the Spirit of God. Half a dozen young women were to put his policy to the test. They could gain free access to Chinese women and girls and into homes from which men would be barred. Prejudice among foreigners was based on fear for their safety, and on ignorance. There were only six unmarried Western women in Hong Kong, two in Fuzhou, one in Peking, one in each of the ports of Canton, Xiamen (Amoy), Ningbo and Yantai, and not one in Shanghai.[25] So bold an innovation as to take his party inland was unacceptable. That did not deter him. He trusted God to protect and the Chinese to respect them.

Goodbye to Shanghai[26]   *October 1866*

Apart from drying out their possessions and looking respectable again, the main reason for the delay in Shanghai – 'sorely against my will', Hudson Taylor said – was the difficulties encountered in procuring consular passports to travel beyond the treaty ports and live in the 'interior'. Consular hesitation over the wisdom of so large a party arriving even in Hangzhou, the provincial capital of Zhejiang, was exceeded by the inaction of the Chinese authorities charged with counter-signing the permits. It looked as if Hangzhou would have to be abandoned as the Mission's forward base, and Ningbo used instead. This would have badly undermined Hudson Taylor's plans. No Ningbo missionaries were wearing Chinese clothes. Even the Stevensons at Shaoxing were in foreign dress. The *Lammermuir* party would find it difficult to become Chinese to the Chinese with others following a foreign life style alongside them. For quick adaptation and quick acquisition of the language, to dress, eat and live like the Chinese was in Hudson Taylor's experience and conviction the best beginning. The Chinese were very tolerant, but foreign clothing was most strange to them.

Stephan Barchet had described how he visited a country village with Mrs Lord. 'We were the first foreigners who visited the place. Their fright and astonishment were not small at first beholding us; but after they felt somewhat assured that we were harmless creatures, and finding that we spoke their language, they paid good attention to the gospel. They could not believe that Mrs Lord was a lady.' Why add such obstacles to an already difficult task? Even at Hangzhou there were British and American missionaries living much as they would in their homelands, but no more than two or three young couples. For the *Lammermuir* party to live there like Chinese should be possible, where the tide of opinion might be too strong in a treaty port. The treaties were clear enough. They provided for Westerners to reside anywhere in the empire, and the authorities were obliged to provide documents identifying each traveller who wished to do so.

At last the formalities were completed, three weeks after the party had set foot on Chinese soil. By then, as Maria told Mrs Berger, 'The reasons for our leaving Shanghai without further delay seemed so important that it was better to defer the girls' transformation.' Hudson Taylor hired four canal junks, houseboats, for the journey up the Huangpu river and then by branch canal to join the Grand Canal at Jiaxing; one for the women, one for the men, a third for the Chinese employees as a kitchen and laundry – and a small boat for John Sell whose 'bronchitis' and coughing were so troublesome as to prevent others sleeping. 'The boats are very superior as to accommodation, and very moderate as to price,' Hudson Taylor wrote.

On Saturday, October 20, the time had come to say goodbye to the men of the *Lammermuir*. Susan Barnes described the scene.

> We all went up in the boats to say farewell, and have a parting hymn in the moonlight. It was most solemn to see strong rough men bowed down and weeping bitterly; then just as we moved off, they began the verse 'Pilgrims, may we travel with you?' then climbed the ropes, and shouted 'Hurrah' as long as we could hear them. [Jennie wrote home:] We had a short farewell service and sang together on the deck 'Yes, we part but not for ever.' It was a sad evening. We all went into our cabins to take a last look. Nearly all the men were in tears . . . As we left the sailors started up a verse 'Whither pilgrims' and then cheered us until we were out of sight . . . Mr Brunton came with us . . . He didn't know how to say goodbye last night, he took your address . . .

Sadly, Captain Bell was still a very sick man. When he reached London again by early May, he was carried to Guy's Hospital paralysed and unconscious. Mr Berger spoke of meeting him later but made no reference to his health.

The work in Shanghai had not been completed. The plan was to go only seven miles, after dark to avoid being conspicuous, and to anchor in the countryside near the Longhua pagoda (Book 2, p 206). It was high time to relieve William Gamble of their prolonged invasion of his home and warehouse. A few of the party would return to Shanghai after the weekend to clear up, arrange for the heavy freight to be stored, and inspect the contents of the packing cases for damage. Mr Brunton was baptised that Sunday, and on Monday Maria, Louise Desgraz, Hudson Taylor and some of the men went back to Shanghai. Two nights and a day of boat life had shown that 'this and that would be needed'.

Left with Mr Tsiu to speak for them but with no way of communicating with him apart from signs and simple phrases, the rest of the party began routine language study. The girls were in a 'fine large Mandarin's boat with three rooms in it for us – it is such (a) romantic gypsy kind of life,' Jennie said.

They expected to be travelling for a month. Hudson Taylor was introducing them gently to houseboat life. Instead of leaky matting protection he had given them solid wooden cabins with decoratively carved lattices and not even shell window lights but glass. Jennie observed that the soft-spoken Maria raised her voice when speaking Chinese as if their hearing was defective, and this had drawn Jennie's attention to the way most Chinese spoke, 'in such a tone and so loud; they have a good deal of action too'.

On the Wednesday Hudson Taylor went to visit Longhua again to see how they were. 'I have great comfort in all our party,' he told his mother. He would get himself and Maria photographed in Chinese costume, 'for you to admire our civilized appearance'. Jennie thought Chinese dress improved the appearance of the young men, 'except Mr Taylor'. Two years later Maria revealed that he had given the men the first choice of the Chinese clothing available to them and took for himself what was left. William Rudland told the Bergers, 'When we were in Shanghai, every dog was barking at us; but no sooner had we put on the Chinese costume, than the dogs left off . . . I did not like the dress much at first, but I like it better now . . . and hope to be spared to wear it for many years to come.' Jackson was frank, 'It was not a little trial to us . . . especially the shaving of the head.' And a month later he confessed, 'At the first I could not see the necessity of wearing the costume; but I can quite see it now.' Nicol's reaction is more significant in view of his subsequent change of mind, 'The Chinese costume . . . has been a trial to me; but when I think it is for God and not man, it eases my mind; and that I also vowed to my God when at home, if He sent me to China, by His grace I was to count nothing dear to me but the glory of God and the salvation of souls; and by His grace I hope to spend and be spent for Him.'

Maria's concern was deeper. As a girl of fifteen she had lived, worked and played with Chinese girls and could see things more from a Chinese point of view.

> I feel there is considerably more danger of our offending Chinese prejudice in the native costume than in our own. Things which are tolerated in us as *foreigners* in *foreign* dress could not be allowed for one moment in (Chinese) ladies. I do not at all mean to imply by this a doubt as to the desirability of the change. But the nearer we come to (the Chinese) in outward appearance, the more severely will any breach of their notions of propriety be criticized. Henceforth I must never be guilty, for instance, of taking my husband's arm in the street. And in fifty or a hundred other ways we may most inadvertently shock the Chinese by our grossly immodest and unfeminine conduct.

By Friday, October 26, the working party had finished and were ready to leave Shanghai. Little serious damage had been found inside the crates of medical and printing equipment. When William Gamble had come aboard the dismasted *Lammermuir* on her arrival and welcomed the whole party to make his home their own, Hudson Taylor had accepted with the proviso that Gamble should allow him to refund all expenses. When he asked before leaving the house what sum he owed, Gamble answered, 'Let it stand at a hundred dollars.' Hudson Taylor handed him the money, a cylinder of silver coins. They went together to the riverside. The others had gone ahead, leaving Hudson Taylor and Rudland to settle up. A small boat was waiting for them and Gamble joined them on it. Farewells over, 'he was going ashore again when he turned back, placed the roll of dollars on the nearest seat and was gone.' 'I don't suppose he is well off,' said Jennie when she heard of it.

They were ready to launch out into what foreigners still called with a touch of awe, 'the interior', always unpredictable and potentially dangerous. Even Maria had little experience of it. From now on all the responsibility of leading the team, managing the boatmen and deciding when to travel and where to stop, would rest on Hudson Taylor. All had confidence in him and he could say, 'Most of the places on the way to Hangzhou will be familiar to me, as I have often visited them and preached in them.' So Hangzhou was their destination, unless they found another city open to some of them. But to have his wife and four little children with him, John Sell 'very unwell' with 'bronchitis', and fourteen complete strangers to the language and the life they were facing, was a different matter.

He felt the strain when he gave the word to start. 'Mr Taylor does manage so nicely for us,' Jennie told her parents, glad to be away at last from the unnatural atmosphere of Shanghai. 'He thoroughly understands how to go about everything. We have missionary life under most favourable circumstances. I wish the missionaries of Shanghai didn't live so little among the people, they mix a good deal with English society [the merchant community] and have very few sacrifices to make.' Things had changed little since at the same captious age he himself had arrived in 1854 – except that this time he was leader of twenty-eight men and women who shared his aims, and three more already on the high seas coming to join them.

Reaction to stress   *October 1866*

For the first time in the history of Christian missions in China, unmarried women were to leave the treaty ports far behind as they penetrated the territory between Shanghai and Ningbo. Hangzhou, their destination, was a hundred miles as the crow flies from both ports, but two or three times farther on meandering rivers and canals. In terms of the empire's vast distances a mere step over the door sill, the venture was still daring and its outcome uncertain. Twenty years had passed since the Sisters of St Paul had arrived at Hong Kong, in 1846. A year or two later twelve representatives of the Daughters of Charity had followed from France, with a sister of the Lazarist martyr, Perboyre, among them.[27] After a period at Macao some had proceeded to Ningbo, and in 1863 to Shanghai. As far as the records appear to state, none, and no unmarried Protestant women, had travelled inland. Even the teachers and nurses of the Berlin Ladies Society (1851) and the Society for Promoting Female Education in the East were confined to Hong Kong. If the

Lammermuir party knew this they failed to mention it in such letters and journals as have been preserved.[28]

Travelling steadily, the journey to Hangzhou could have been over in three or four days at most. That was not the plan. A gentle but more thorough introduction to the Chinese people and their ways would be good preparation before they settled among them in a city. The transition from foreign food and table manners to Chinese food with bowl and chopsticks was not to be forced on them. Even completing the women's Chinese clothing would need a few days' delay at Songjiang. The boat had been hired for a month. With an opium-smoking *laoban*, the foreman or 'captain', complete with his family and a crew of twenty men and boys to pay, the expense was greater than renting premises anywhere, but worthwhile. In the end they travelled for all or part of only eight days and spent the rest at towns and cities en route or preaching at smaller places, 'prepared to enter any door (to occupy any town or city) that God might open to us on the way'. Cooped up together, the forbearance of every one of them would be tested, in a way even the storms at sea had not done.

The interlude at Longhua with its country walks and views from the top of the pagoda between language study sessions was over. As soon as the Shanghai working party arrived back on October 22, sails were set and they travelled up-river on the tide, joined the canal system, and covered the twenty or more miles to the prefectural city of Songjiang before nightfall. 'Captain Bell heard we could not get butter and sent us two pots,' Jennie wrote to her mother, 'besides a jar of treacle, a cooked ham, a joint of beef cooked and a cheese. We gave him a nice Bible, and a very pretty travelling rug.' Already she felt at home among the Chinese. 'Everywhere the people are civil and goodnatured.' That morning she had gone ashore and gathered a crowd of children around her, as delighted as they that she could talk a little with them. She had found the *laoban*'s wife friendly and receptive and began teaching her to read the romanised script.

Sunday they spent quietly on the boats. On Monday, October 29, Hudson Taylor went ashore to preach and to buy essentials. To his dismay, since he had last been there Songjiang had been devastated far more in the Taiping war than he had realised. 'Once populous suburbs are now heaps of ruins, covered with weeds and brushwood. I was told that three-fourths of the people had perished from the sword, famine, or pestilence. I had a few opportunities of preaching the gospel . . . and one or two inquirers came to Mr Ts'iu; but my time was almost wholly occupied by . . . secular affairs.'[29]

He could not buy the supplies he wanted. With the winter approaching, wadded gowns, Chinese bed rolls (*pugai*) and fire baskets would be needed as well as basic Chinese clothing. He would have to try again at Jiaxing, forty miles on. But Maria, now in her seventh month of pregnancy, was ill and unfit to travel. They stayed at Songjiang a whole week, chose Chinese names for each person and dressed all the girls in Chinese clothes with Chinese hair styles.[30] Wide blue trousers, a silk pair for best occasions and cotton for everyday wear, with a black apron wrapped over itself at the back, was Jennie's description before confessing her reaction. 'It has some advantages but it feels clumsy . . . I very gladly wear it . . . but I shall never like it.' She soon thought no more about it. The Taylor children were also dressed as Chinese children.

Some of them walked out to a temple outside the city, 'the whole of the way . . . treading on overgrown ruins, everywhere in this province we meet with devastation.' But these were the highlights. Life on board followed a disciplined routine: all up at six a m, breakfast at eight, then English and Chinese family prayers, Chinese language study from nine thirty to twelve thirty, 'dinner' at one, Chinese again from two until five, each one spending an hour reading aloud with a Chinese, tea at six and prayers again before bed at ten. 'All lights are expected to be out by 11.00.' Exercise on shore was limited to the intervals.

During the week William Gamble arrived from Shanghai with an English-speaking Chinese from Malaya. Educated in a mission school at Penang, he had lived in Singapore and travelled widely over south-east Asia, China and Japan. On his way back from Japan Mr Wu had been caught in the same typhoon as the *Lammermuir*. Faced with death he thought about the gospel he had known as a schoolboy, and at last acted on it, committing himself to Christ. When he reached Shanghai safely he looked for a missionary to talk with, and found William Gamble. Gamble became convinced of his sincerity and brought him to Songjiang in the hope that, impressed by the young missionaries' concern for China, he would take the spiritual needs of his own people to heart instead of continuing in commerce.

After a few days, Hudson Taylor preached from the poopdeck of the largest junk until a crowd of very attentive Chinese had gathered on the canal bank, and then with the *Lammermuir* party watching from their boats, he baptised Mr Wu. They travelled on together as far as Jiaxing before Mr Wu returned to Shanghai. In itself this incident was encouraging. But the outcome after he reached Shanghai was remarkable. They knew nothing of it until letters from Gamble reached them in Hangzhou.

All was not well. Already one or two were chafing under the cramped conditions. Meals were served on the ladies' large boat, and the main room was also used as a classroom. Privacy was limited. When the sensitive Louise Desgraz tried to escape and be alone on shore from time to time, half a dozen spectators would be sure to follow her and stare. When the Chinese clothes were all made and on November 2 they put them on, she did so with '*mauvaise grâce*', she confessed to Mrs Berger. Crowds jostled them whenever they showed themselves. When Hudson Taylor took Emily Blatchley and Jennie Faulding for a walk with his daughter Grace, Jennie reported, 'We had at least 150 men, women and children after us.' And a few days later, 'What we should do if we had not on the Chinese dress I cannot imagine, for as it is about a hundred people stand on shore to watch us all day long; and if we go for a walk we are as much run after as the Queen would be; but at the same time the people are not rude . . . I long to get to work among them.'[31]

Such annoyances were intolerable for some, and Louise, a first-rate missionary in the making, was at odds with Emily and Jennie for a few days. Their friction was nothing in comparison with the men's. Jackson and Duncan had shared a cabin on the *Lammermuir* and now were crowded in with Hudson Taylor and the other men. The sharp-tongued London shop-assistant and the big, rough Banffshire stone-mason had seen more of each other than their self-control could stomach. The rest of the journey was made wretched for everyone by their bickering. 'Let the unhappiness of this journey, reaching a climax toward the close, go unrecorded,' Emily's journal reads. Early separation of the men was clearly desirable, earlier than planned. With the help of a Chinese Christian, two who got on well together should be able to lie low in a city along this route. They could make themselves understood, and by reading Scripture to people would even do something worthwhile. Hudson Taylor could easily visit them from Hangzhou from time to time. The plan was premature but had much to commend it.

No house to be had[32]   *November 1866*

On November 3 the boats moved on, heading for Jiaxing. Finding a fellow-sportsman in John Sell whose 'bronchitis' was better, Hudson Taylor dug out the shotgun William Berger had given him and they enjoyed a day's shooting from Sell's small boat. Wildfowl were plentiful and no game laws or ideas of conservation existed to deter them. Sell brought down 'three geese with one charge'. Every few miles they came to another village, town or city, and Mr Tsiu or Hudson Taylor or both together would go ashore to preach the gospel. Each place cried out to them, it seemed, to stay and work there. On Monday 5th, after the Sunday at Fengqing, they set off 'long before daylight', reached Jiashan by seven and were away again after breakfast. The devastation from the civil war seemed endless. Writing to the Bergers, Hudson Taylor showed how his mind was working. The thousands upon thousands of people they were passing by would need missionaries in great numbers. China would need thousands, not hundreds, of missionaries, preferably Chinese, but foreign also until enough Chinese Christians existed to do the work.

> This and the last town, even now, number some twenty to twenty-five thousand souls each, but have *no witness for Christ*, so far as I have been able to learn.
>
> About 7 a.m. we reached (Jiashan) a large city, alike destitute of the gospel. It would make an excellent missionary station, if the Lord provided the house and the missionary. Oh! it makes one's heart bleed to think of the spiritual need of this people . . . Leaving (Jiashan) immediately after breakfast, we have been making all day towards (Jiaxing), and have not yet reached the part of the suburbs at which I propose to moor our boats. Miles of suburbs we have passed through without a single house remaining: desolation seems to reign all around. But we are kept in peace, and the Lord will still lead us on . . .

Another town of fifty thousand inhabitants 'wholly neglected, a good place for a mission' impressed Jennie in the same way.

They stayed at Jiaxing another full week, preaching as Hudson Taylor had done years before, and looking for premises to rent. Lewis Nicol wanted to go no further. Hudson Taylor himself was prepared to make Jiaxing his base, if the indications for doing so were strong enough. Hangzhou had three missions already, and the work of CIM could be co-ordinated and extended from Jiaxing, strategically situated on the Grand Canal, as freely as from the provincial capital. Mr Tsiu could open a school and preach while Lewis and Eliza Nicol made friends and progressed with the language. In his *Brief Account* Hudson Taylor said,

> This place, a city of palaces when the writer left China in 1860, is now the greater part of it in ruins; of all its former glory we could see only the debris of lordly mansions, once the abodes of wealth and pleasure, now the habitations of desolation and silence. And its condition fairly represents that of many of the cities and towns which we have seen since our return to this land. Among the ruins of (Jiaxing) there are now some thousands of inhabitants, and the number is rapidly increasing. For several days we tarried here, endeavouring to get a house, in which we might leave some of our party, with a (Chinese) teacher, to open a school, as a beginning for wider work; but all our efforts failed. This part of the country is very unsettled at present, and the people are afraid to let their houses – the few habitable ones that were vacant – to foreigners. (*See* Book 3, p 292, map showing extent of Taiping scourge.)

Jiaxing was close to the border between Jiangsu and Zhejiang provinces with their different jurisdictions. Such districts were always relatively unsettled. One side provided a safe refuge after a felony committed on the other. For many destitute people banditry was their only recourse. Neither Hudson Taylor nor Nicol was deterred. Nicol added,

> I went through the city of (Jiaxing) along with one of our servants, in search of our messenger, who had been sent to Shanghai for our letters. We entered at the East Gate and came out at the North Gate, and all the way between these two was one mass of ruins: for oh! how the Lord has been dealing with this people, and showing them there is no help for them in their idols. This city is laid very heavily on my heart; and I am inquiring of the Lord if it is His will that I may go and unfurl the blood-stained banner of King Jesus in their midst, as they have no one to tell them of the way of salvation. Oh, may the Lord soon enable me to enter fairly into the field, and help me by His grace to be a good soldier of the cross of Christ.

Jennie told her parents, 'We could not get (a house) then, but hope to do so some time . . . They are building as fast as they can, and before long it will be a very important place again . . . Very

THE FIRST DEPLOYMENT AREA OF THE CHINA INLAND
MISSION, 1865–70

soon it is likely to have 5 or 6 hundred thousand inhabitants, and there is no missionary there.'

A brief scare on the 7th when five-year-old Bertie (Herbert Taylor) fell overboard, then final disappointment over housing, and on November 13 they were all on their way again. The next day they passed Shimenwan and the following day Shimenxian, the scenes of Hudson Taylor's robbery and befriending by unknown boatmen when he was at his last gasp in 1856. (Book 2, pp 354, 357–8) 'They too are large places needing missionaries.' Perhaps he wanted to see the scene of his adventure, and think, for he spent the first day on deck with the shotgun – unless it was simply to restock the larder. Then they were at Tangqi, still on the Grand Canal and only twenty or so miles from Hangzhou. Jennie was a good letter-writer and her family kept all she sent. Surely here they would succeed. 'We are going to leave Mr Jackson and Mr Rudland; they cannot speak much, but we must make a beginning, and they can read the Gospels to the people,' she said. 'In none of the cities, towns and villages that we have passed since we left Shanghai is there one (Chinese) or foreign missionary.'

While Mr Tsiu went house-hunting they all took the day off and climbed the pilgrim way up good stone steps to the temples on top of a hill. 'We got such pretty views of Hangchou Bay and the canals (like beautiful rivers) that cut up the land in every direction,' Jennie went on. 'We had our Saturday prayer meeting and ate some cakes on another peak.' She would have liked to invite her parents to a meal in the boat with them, if only there were space, 'besides which you barbarians would not know how to behave'. Mr Tsiu and Hudson Taylor had chosen a Chinese surname for her, but she quickly became known as Fu Guniang, appropriately meaning 'Miss Happiness'. The name 'Emily' reminded Hudson Taylor of the young man from Nanjing who talked with him about home and always spoke of his 'loved sister' as his '*ai mei*'. So Emily Blatchley became 'Aimei' to the others.

Adaptation to Chinese customs was proceeding faster than expected. All along they had been having some Chinese meals but still used knife, fork and spoon much of the time. Lately, however, so many plates, cups and saucers had been stolen or broken when spectators became excited and made a rush at them, that almost all meals were Chinese by this stage in the journey. Why be different and provocative? But Mary Bowyer told Mrs Berger,

Though I do not admire it, (the Chinese costume) is comfortable, and it seems quite natural to go out without either hat or bonnet, and many other things we have been accustomed to wear. To my mind it is most decidedly the right thing to do. We . . . have adopted the Chinese basins and chopsticks. I thought I should never be able to eat with them at first, but soon became quite expert . . . Our principal food now is rice, and indeed we do eat a quantity of it. It is much nicer than rice in England, and I prefer it to almost anything else.

Again at Tangqi Mr Tsiu failed to find anyone willing to let a house to foreigners. Negotiations would progress and a contract be agreed, only to be revoked. Jennie wrote, 'The arrangements for letting us a nice house were all but completed, when the landlord drew back because we were foreigners.' The landlords were under pressure from outside. Would Hangzhou be any better? Or were they to be faced with staying on the boats at whatever cost the boatmen chose to charge? Or to eat humble pie and seek sanctuary with the other missions until they could arrange to travel on to Ningbo? Such thoughts would have passed through Hudson Taylor's mind. If he was apprehensive what he wrote to his mother was,

Our party is so large, and most of them so uninstructed as to Chinese ideas, that the difficulty of arranging for them is not small. But He to whom *all power* in heaven and on earth is committed, is with us; He holds the key of David; He opens and no man shuts; He shuts and no man can open. At the right time and in the right place, He will help us to get quarters; until then we must be content to wait. Hope deferred makes one feel disheartened at times. Just now, our teacher has come in to tell me that once more we are foiled in our attempts, so we must move on tomorrow morning to Hangchou. [He described the devastation in every place visited.] But oh! the tens of thousands and hundreds of thousands still remaining in village, town, or city, utterly destitute of the Gospel . . . I cannot tell you how it grieves me to leave them without any witness for Christ . . . I hope (Mr Berger) will send us some more helpers soon . . .

Ever since leaving Shanghai they had been enjoying wonderful weather. Rain would have made their close quarters in the canal junks unbearable. But as the week of house-hunting in Tangqi ended in disappointment it turned very cold. The servants were 'dissatisfied with the insufficient shelter of a boat', and the boatmen pointed out that their contract was expiring. They needed to return home and complete the autumn's work on their smallholdings before the winter set in. Dysentery had struck several of the party, not severely but distressingly in such accommodation. And ill feeling persisted among the men. Morale was low. Less than a month ago Hudson Taylor had been able to say 'I have great comfort in all our party.' How things had changed! How would they shape up to greater testing?

They left Tangqi on Wednesday afternoon, November 21, and quickly covered the twenty miles to the great city of Hangzhou. 'We knew that we were being led,' Emily told Mrs Guinness, 'by the same hand which had prepared for us at Shanghai a hospitable roof and storage for all our goods – and so we prayed and moved forward, nothing doubting.' The seeming setback of water too shallow for their big boats forced them to tie up beyond the outer suburbs, some miles from the city walls. They soon saw the advantage. Instead of a large party of foreigners arriving conspicuously, they had time to plan the next move.

> But how [Hudson Taylor wrote], judging from the experience we had already had of the difficulty of renting houses, should we obtain lodging, especially for so large a party, and where the unsettled state of the country made every stranger an object of suspicion? We felt how helpless we were; but we . . . trusted that God would magnify His strength in our weakness.

Foreign and Chinese missionaries met to pray. Mr Tsiu was intrigued to see what would happen next.

Emily Blatchley observed how deeply Hudson Taylor was feeling the strain, even when exercising faith. Like others he had dysentery, but not badly enough to account for her phrase, 'seeming nearly worn out'. It was evening and they all stayed where they were. In the morning he and Tsiu hired a one-oar *sanban* to take them into the city, 'to seek a house or temple that might afford us temporary shelter'.

When they had gone, Maria called the party together again in the big boat to pray, and read *Psalm* 108:

> Oh God, my heart is fixed; I will sing and give praise . . . I will praise Thee, O Lord, among the people: and I will sing praises unto Thee among the nations . . . Who will bring me into the strong city? . . . Wilt not Thou, O God . . . ? Give us help from trouble: for vain is the help of man. Through God we shall do valiantly . . .

Emily wrote, 'Nov. 21, 1866' beside it in her Bible. Years later William Rudland reminisced about Maria's 'quiet, steady faith with no wavering in anything'. Then they waited, for four or five hours.

'Into the strong city'   *November–December 1866*

The turreted walls of Hangzhou stretched for twelve miles round the ancient city, two miles wide, like the beautiful West Lake on whose shore it stood. Not far from the South Gate the wide Qiantang (Ch'ien-t'ang) tidal river flowed into the estuary and Hangzhou Bay. Forested hills with tier upon tier of mist-shrouded peaks flanked the lake on the other three sides, with here and there a pagoda, a temple or ancient tomb showing above the trees. Little islands and thousands of wildfowl dotted the lake surface. Magnolias, azaleas and camellias grew prolifically everywhere, and in times of peace mulberry groves had supported a thriving silk industry since the seventh century.

A city had been there for over two thousand years. When this section of the Grand Canal was dug in AD 605–10, linking the north with Hangzhou Bay and the southern provinces, by the Qiantang river, its importance was assured. Sea-walls were built, and when the Song emperors were driven south by the Mongol conquerors, Hangzhou became the fabulous capital of the Southern Song dynasty. The population swelled to a million, palaces of the rich and influential multiplied, and poets and painters made it their home. 'The gardens of the imperial palace were decorated with flowers made of silk' through the winter months.[33] Then the Mongols conquered the south, and became masters of all China. After Marco Polo visited Hangzhou on the orders of Kublai Khan in the thirteenth century he devoted two chapters of his *Travels* to describing the glories of 'Kinsay' (the capital). Before the Taiping rebellion the population was said to be one and a half million, but three times during the holocaust the city had been besieged, stormed and partly sacked. The Qian Long emperors' palace, gardens and libraries went up in flames, with most of the ancient city and its treasures. When the *Lammermuir* party arrived, great areas within the walls were derelict, littered with the debris of ruined buildings. Other parts were under cultivation while waiting to be built over. A Manchu garrison filled the quarter near the West Gate. Restored mansions housed the provincial governor and his mandarins. And a long north–south road through the busy renovated central section

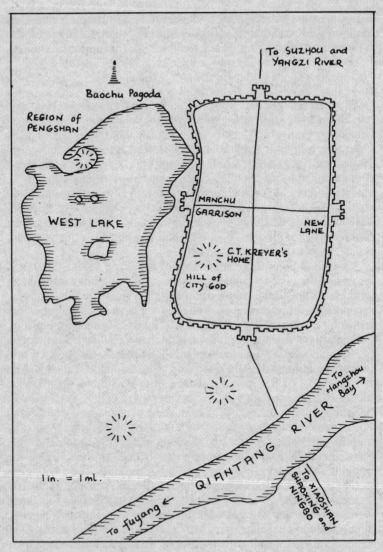

HANGZHOU LAKE AND CITY

led to the south-west corner. There a beautiful little hill dedicated to city gods lay within the walls. Before the Mongol conquest the walled city had enclosed twice the area, now forming the suburbs Hudson Taylor and Mr Tsiu were crossing to reach the city.[34]

Hudson Taylor knew that the Nestorians and Franciscans had been there centuries ago, that Charles Gutzlaff had advised the CMS (on October 13, 1835) to make Hangzhou their station, and that John and Helen Nevius and John Burdon had pioneered Hangzhou in 1859 when Mr Tsiu was newly a Christian. He also knew that after the Taipings were forced to leave Hangzhou, two members of the CMS church had pleaded with George Moule to strike while the iron was hot, not to lose the opportunity to establish a mission there. One of the two, a Mr Dzang, had gone himself, rented premises and opened a preaching room on a thoroughfare nearby. Moule had visited him occasionally during 1864–5, and moved in with his own wife and children that autumn, leaving his brother Arthur with the Ningbo church.

But Hangzhou was a large city, larger than Ningbo, with scope for several missions. As a temporary base it had much to commend it. In January 1865 D D Green of William Gamble's American Presbyterian Mission had moved in to pastor church members who had returned there. Both George Moule and Green had arrived in China shortly before the Taylors left in 1860, Moule in 1858 and Green in 1859. They were already acquainted. Finally, a few months before the *Lammermuir* party reached China, the American Baptist Carl Kreyer had rented a house on a busy street at the foot of the Hill of the City God.[35] Leaving his wife and new-born child in Ningbo he had used it until satisfied that it was safe for them to join him. He it was who, passing to and fro through Shaoxing, roughly sixty miles from Hangzhou and ninety from Ningbo, had persuaded John Stevenson to occupy it. Kreyer knew of Hudson Taylor's plan to travel overland to Hangzhou, and saw his chance to repay a debt of kindness by Anne Stevenson to his wife and babe.

So on that Thursday, November 22, when Hudson Taylor and Mr Tsiu called first on Green for information and advice about current rentals and down payments, to their surprise he had a message for them. Carl Kreyer had gone to Ningbo, to bring his wife back with him the coming Wednesday. If the CIM party arrived in his absence, 'his house was to be put at our disposal'.[36] Their prayers were answered. 'Mr Tsiu's delight knew no bounds,' Rudland recalled. It may be assumed that they went at once to the south

A BUSY CITY STREET

quarter to see where Kreyer lived, if only to plan an inconspicuous
arrival by so many foreigners and to decide how to fit them all in.
Then back to the boats where the news brought everyone together
again, this time 'to praise the Lord'. Instead of having to house-hunt
from the boats, they had a toehold and could satisfy the boatmen
and their own Chinese helpers. 'The very fact of there being a house
ready for our temporary occupation,' Maria told Mrs Berger, 'made
one think that God was perhaps going to establish us at Hangchou.'

Most of the baggage was being held in Shanghai until they had a
home for it, but including the five Chinese in the party, twenty-one
adults and four children with their bedding and immediate possessions could create a disturbance if seen arriving in Hangzhou
together. They must land secretly. Shallow-draught *sanbans* with

grass-mat awnings would hide them as far as the canals made it possible. The last few hundred yards would then be through the streets. They would have to do it after dark, and in two operations. The first ten or twelve to go packed up and roped their bedding rolls the same afternoon. Late in the evening when most townsfolk were indoors and shopkeepers had boarded up their premises, they lay low as the *sanbans* slipped through the walls by a water gate and crossed the city (*see* Book 3, pp 295, 310, water gate and canals). First through the devastated wasteland, then the built-up regions, and finally in the darkness they landed and walked in twos and threes through the silent streets to the Kreyers' Chinese house alongside a crowded tea shop – the equivalent of a pub. All went well. Friday night brought the second group again unchallenged and without drawing an excited crowd, and on Saturday the last of their effects arrived from the houseboats.[37]

By then the Greens and Moules were being 'exceedingly kind' to them, while Hudson Taylor and Mr Tsiu were busy looking for a large house to rent. Chinese homes were seldom more than two storeys high, though during the Song dynasty Hangzhou had been noted for its high buildings, all now destroyed. Single-storey rooms surrounded open courtyards, one leading into the other. Farthest in from the street the main buildings usually boasted a staircase and upstairs rooms. With malaria still blamed on miasms at ground level, foreigners considered airy upstairs bedrooms essential for health. For the work Hudson Taylor contemplated, requiring a preaching hall for an audience of a hundred or more, a dispensary, doctor's consulting room, space for the printing press, and reception rooms for Chinese visitors, as well as domestic quarters, extensive premises would be needed. Such places in good repair had long since been occupied. A foothold firmly their own was what they were looking for. Its state of repair mattered little.

A week of lengthy negotiations in both Jiaxing and Tangqi, involving much tea, much talk and much manoeuvring ('exceedingly prolix', Emily Blatchley told Miss Waldegrave) had led to nothing. The last moment before signing an agreement was as precarious as any. Long after John Stevenson was safely installed in his hired house in Shaoxing and on good terms with his landlord, neighbours and the mandarins, he had discovered that every name except his own on his contract was fictitious – a last ditch escape route, should letting to a foreigner turn out to be dangerous for the landlord and middlemen. The Kreyers were due home in five days' time and one of those days was Sunday, the Lord's day when Hudson Taylor would not work, even for 'an ox in a pit'. There was no time to lose.

No 1 New Lane   *November 1866*

Almost at once they found just the place. Out on the edge of the residential sector among old houses which had suffered too much in the rebellion to be wanted by merchants or mandarins, they were shown an old mansion of about thirty rooms, capable of being made into twice that number. Next door stood another large house in a better state but not available. Only a mile from Kreyer's place, and quietly isolated among acres of ruins near the east wall, it was still near shopping streets. The main entrance at the corner of two high whitewashed walls led into a large pavilion ideal for a preaching chapel. Round a large courtyard, partly roofed, stood a dozen useful rooms. The upper storey in two separate sections was reached by different stairways admirably adapted for the men in one and the rest of the party in the other. The large airy ground-floor rooms allowed of a clinic being right beside the preaching hall. Patients and their relatives could listen to the gospel until called to see the doctor. Farther in, reception and dining rooms, office and printing room, boxrooms and separate men's and women servants' quarters would all be provided for. Within high surrounding walls a 'good large' secluded rock-garden provided for relaxation. Only these walls and the west side of the house were of stone and brick. The rest, like most in Hangzhou, were wooden panels or lath and plaster. They would be within earshot of each other and have no room to spare. After six months of close confinement since leaving Britain and the friction on the journey just ended, this mattered little at the moment, but would be one more indication that some of the party should move out before too long.

Two more shortcomings could be made the most of in negotiating the rental of this place. Five or six families were in occupation and could not be compelled to move within a month;[38] and with winter upon them, doors and windows were almost entirely lacking and there were no upstairs ceilings, only bare tiles. Heat from fires would pass straight through the roof; wind and snow would blow in. All this made bargaining easier but the 'shabby gentility' of the place held promise of an ideal base once it was repaired.

Giving no hint of eagerness to reach agreement, Hudson Taylor

and Mr Tsiu asked what rental the owner had in mind. The
exorbitant figure he named made bargaining simple. Twenty dollars
a month and 'key money' of two hundred dollars might be appropriate for a mansion in good repair but not for this shell. After long
courtesies and protestations that they were wasting his time and
must look elsewhere, they took their leave and went to see less
suitable premises. The 25th was Sunday. If they were to be out of

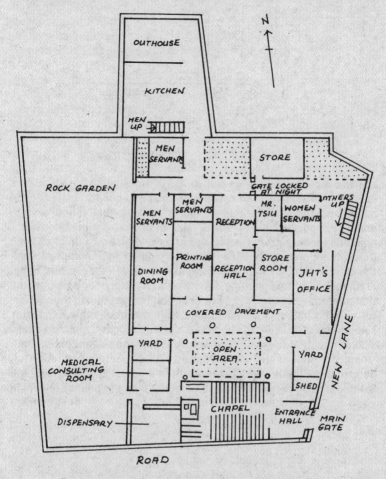

NO 1 NEW LANE: GROUND FLOOR PLAN

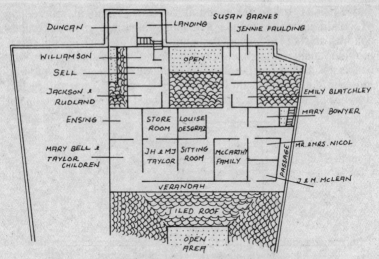

NO 1 NEW LANE: UPPER STOREY

the Kreyers' house by his return on Wednesday, little short of a miracle was needed. To be imposed upon and pay too high a rental would seal their fate in that or any other deals they might have to make. Worse still, it would affect the other missions in Hangzhou.

Sunday was spent in fasting and prayer. Hudson Taylor had been thinking for weeks about the fifteenth chapter of *St John's Gospel*, the True Vine. On October 14 he had preached in the Union Chapel at Shanghai on this passage. 'I am the vine, ye are the branches: he that abideth in me and I in him, the same bringeth forth much fruit: for without me ye can do nothing.' In her journal Emily Blatchley had commented then that he preached 'with more power than ever'. This time when they all met to pray together he again expounded '*John* fifteen' – as the secret of fruitfulness resulting from faithful, determined clinging to Christ and drawing the sap of spiritual life from him. Deeper insights were to come to him two years later. He also read the twentieth psalm, and Emily was moved, as she wrote,

> 'The Lord hear thee in the day of trouble . . . send thee help from the sanctuary, and strengthen thee . . . Grant thee according to (the desires of) thy heart . . . Some trust in chariots and some in horses: but we will remember the name of the Lord our God.' Then his prayer – such as *lift* me. Others also caught his spirit and prayed – truly.

On Monday morning he went to see another house. The landlord of Saturday's house in *Xin Kai Long* (New Lane) had spent an anxious day wondering all through Sunday whether he had lost a reliable tenant. By asking too much had he driven him away? When he found on Monday morning that the foreigner was on the track of something better, he came to find him, a sure sign of capitulation. Even so it was hours before the matter was settled and a deposit paid. On Tuesday the agreement was signed, with the right of immediate occupation, and the all-important counter-signature of the mandarins secured. The landlord had agreed on fourteen dollars monthly and only eighty-four dollars down payment. No 1 New Lane was theirs. Emily's long letter to Miss Waldegrave went on,

> Before daylight on Wednesday morning, we passed quickly and noiselessly through the city, and established ourselves in it. Here then for a time, Mr Taylor intends us to remain (with God's protecting permission), as quietly, and as little seen as possible; the study of the language affording sufficient occupation. By the time that any of this party are ready for missionary work among the people, it will have become a well known fact that a party of foreigners are dwelling in the city, and that no disturbance or mischief has resulted therefrom, and we shall thus get among them with less difficulty, and excite less suspicion than might otherwise be . . . We have it very cheaply, and it is very large, having evidently been . . . the mansion of some wealthy family of mandarins; but . . . in its present dilapidated condition . . . resembling most a number of barns or outhouses . . . There is a great superabundance of both dust and of ventilation, and it comes far short of its full complement of doors and windows; but we have temporarily supplied the latter deficiency with old sheets . . . Before us is one wide wilderness of ruins – very fairly representative of all this part of China . . . But they are coming back, such of them as escaped the fire and sword; they are rebuilding their walls and their temples, and moulding new idols, and regilding old ones, and worshipping them. And yet they do not believe them . . . not having the truth they set up a lie.[39]

The Kreyers arrived the same day to find their house swept and ready as if no invasion had taken place.

Descending so suddenly upon the families in occupation of No 1 could cause trouble, so a policy of patience and friendliness was adopted. The newcomers would fit in where they could and inconvenience the old tenants as little as possible. It paid handsome dividends, for they responded in kind. Within five days one family had moved out and another was about to go. Some of the missing doors had been in use as beds. The other families stayed the full month, a mission field which Jennie seized upon. As they were all on the ground floor busily making paper money to be burned at funerals, the upper floor became home to the missionaries, relatively secure from prying eyes.

Hudson Taylor amplified Emily's account, saying they hoped that, 'remaining as quiet and unobserved as possible (would) win the confidence of the people, as the first step towards admission and welcome into their homes. This was most important, as the work among the women which we contemplated must of necessity be based upon such confidence.'[40]

Being in the premises with more time to look round they decided they could start a small school in addition to the medical work and printing. 'To do this we have, of course, to be ourselves content with the smallest amount of accommodation; but for that a voyage is a good preparation.' Now, however, most of them had the prospect of a room each and space for exercise. 'We can get a short walk in any direction without being seen,' Jennie told her parents. 'At the same time we can soon be in the heart of the city if we wish.'

There they were, ideally established in the capital city of Zhejiang province, about a hundred and fifty travelling miles from Ningbo and sixty from the Stevensons at Shaoxing, when on the last day of November James Meadows and George Crombie suddenly arrived. The link-up had been made. The CIM was a unit of twenty-four, eight deployed in four southern cities and the rest about to start work. The very next day Hudson Taylor and the two from Ningbo were out preaching the gospel together.

CHAPTER EIGHT

FROWNING SKY
1866

Settling in[1]   *December 1866*

A roof over their heads could be shelter and security for a day, a week or a month. There was no knowing how the authorities would view the sudden swelling of the foreign community in Hangzhou from six to twenty-six, or whether the common people would protest. The part played by foreigners in the defeat of the Taipings was well known, but three years had passed since Hangzhou was freed and memories are short. So far no indication of disapproval had appeared.

Acting as if all would be well, Hudson Taylor bought timber, nails and loads of stout grass-paper. The carpenters and handymen of the team fell to and made frames and partitions, of planking for deficiencies in the outer walls and of paper for inner walls and ceilings. 'There is a deficiency in the wall of my own bedroom 6 feet by 9, closed by a sheet,' Hudson Taylor told his mother. Trestle tables and benches, shelves and rough cupboards quickly turned barns into dwellings of a sort, and draughty expanses with 'roofs like churches' into something more like rooms. A little furniture was bought, a few essential chairs and tables for the reception room in case important callers came. Brass pans in which a bed of charcoal was kept burning gave some warmth to sit by, but all fuel was expensive. Fortunately it was a mild winter. To work was the best way to keep warm.

It was 'all confusion' to Jennie even when writing home on December 13, 'but getting on'. By then they (including the girls) were papering the walls with more grass-paper because they were of 'three eights of an inch larch planking, and let in plenty of wind' and as a luxury four shillings' worth of reed mats adorned the bedroom floors. A large downstairs room which, when they moved in, had not one complete wall became their dining and sitting room. A large window of white paper (after the Chinese custom) let in light while excluding draughts. Their home was becoming wind-proof if not cold-proof. Letter-writing with frozen fingers and toes was difficult. In Shanghai a supply of window glass was ready for them, but the heavy freight and making of strong windows would have to wait until the first essentials had been completed. Hudson Taylor planned to go to Shanghai as soon as he could be spared from Hangzhou. By the end of the month a few pictures had appeared on the walls and a tablecloth recognisable as an old dress made the place even feel homelike! Maria's confinement near the end of January would at least be in a house of their own. With the new year the next stage began. Plasterers came in to replace sheets and paper with thick lath and plaster.

So much for material comfort. James Meadows, living very simply in Ningbo, felt sorry for the *Lammermuir* party, not for wearing Chinese clothes (though in the treaty port he himself did not), 'for *that* he heartily concurs in . . . for persons located any distance from a foreign settlement', but for the conditions they would have to adapt to. He was wasting his sympathy. Morale was high. Hudson Taylor's letter to his mother went on,

> We heed these things very little; around us are poor dark heathen. Large cities without any missionary; populous towns . . . villages without number, all destitute of the means of grace surround us; and I do not envy the feelings of those who would forget these, or leave them, for fear of a little external discomfort. May God make us faithful to Him and to our work. At present nearly everything depends on me, so that I have no time for correspondence.
>
> [And in his next letter,] So many look to me, and on so many points, that did I not *believe* and feel *assured* that God has put me where I am, and that He will be with me in all the details of His own service, I should tremble for the result. I am very happy in the service, however, and have the sympathy and prayers of those with me; and in time some of our preliminary difficulties will be got through and room be made for others of some different kind.
>
> [Josiah Jackson told the Bergers,] At the first, I could not see the necessity of wearing the (Chinese) costume; but I can quite see it now. And the further we go into the interior, the more we shall find it so . . . I can speak a little, such as to ask for what I want at meal-times, and in making purchases at the shops . . . I don't feel at all discouraged; instead of becoming a task it now becomes very interesting. We are already able to do something for the Lord, by reading the Scriptures to the Chinese, and putting a few Gospel sentences together.

But almost his only experience was with the five Chinese of their party, within the walls of the house, though the men sometimes ventured outside.

Lewis Nicol was still hoping on December 1 to return to Jiaxing, but Hudson Taylor had discovered that Carl Kreyer's mission, the American Baptists, had plans to do the same. 'Missionary life is no romance,' Susan Barnes reflected. 'I would have *all* count the cost.' And Jane McLean, 'I have never been tempted to doubt that (the Lord) has led me hither. And so far am I from regretting taking the step, that (He) will use me here, I shall never wish to return (home) again.' On December 3 William Rudland could write, 'I attribute a great deal of the quiet which we have had, to our wearing (Chinese) dress; we go about and are taken but little notice of.' Duncan too, before the repairs had been properly started, in the sheet and paper state of affairs,

> If you were to . . . see us now, you would think we were very comfortable although you would have much to do to recognize some of us . . . [He had been in Hangzhou a fortnight and had little experience to go on, but continued] I don't think that there are many outward trials in China . . . I like the (Chinese) costume very well. I could not see it necessary, at home, to wear it, but I soon experienced that by wearing the English dress I should (be followed everywhere), whilst I can now go freely among the (people) . . . Mr Taylor, as you know, labours very hard for us all, and I am sorry that we can help him so little. I think we will be able to get on much faster with the language, when we are scattered a little.

'Outward trials' as he called them, were not difficult to accept when unexpected bonuses like 'venison as cheap as mutton and very nice' as well as plentiful game were available.

With her cheerful extrovert personality and strong family circle, Jennie had no lack of friends or home letters – twenty-one since leaving Britain. Emily Blatchley, sensitive, introverted and from a non-Christian home tended to be lonely and to have a smaller share of the incoming mail than most. 'Always give me news for her,' Jennie told her parents, while she shared her own letters with Emily. The Taylors treated them both as sisters. They had promised Jennie's parents that they would. She could say, 'I feel more and more glad to be here . . .'

The friction on the canal boats had apparently ended when they wrote at the beginning of the month. When the Bergers with good insight had seen difficulties from one or two of the thornier personalities in the party before they left London, they had spoken to some and urged others to help in keeping the peace. The disharmony on the *Lammermuir* had been no surprise to them. At Anjer Jennie had a letter from Mrs Berger written before news of trouble reached England,

> I remember hearing Mr Geo. Müller say to my dear husband about 25 years ago 'I never expect much from man, so that I am never very greatly disappointed' . . . I cannot but think you are all most highly favor'd in having such dear experienced Christians to look up to as dear Mr and Mrs Taylor. May all yield to them their proper place! Theirs will be a much more difficult part than that of the rest.

In September William Berger wrote, 'The claims upon my time have been almost inconceivable. And now a visit to Ireland and Scotland seems imperative . . . There are still about 40 persons desirous of coming forward for China, but until I hear from Mr Taylor I feel it wisest to move cautiously.' Mrs Berger was in London helping to outfit John McCarthy's family and Jane McLean's sister, Margaret. By the time his letter arrived they were half-way to China.

A change of circumstances and plenty to do had been good for morale. Hudson Taylor hinted to Grattan Guinness on December 17, however, that all was not well: 'Strive to stir up the Lord's dear people to earnest prayer for China, and for us . . . The difficulties of the work, intrinsic and extrinsic, are so great, that apart from the mighty power of God, we should indeed have a hopeless task before us.' As late as New Year's Day, 1867, he clarified one point in a letter to his mother, 'We are still principally occupied in arranging our new house, and in various secular matters connected therewith. As yet, no difficulties have been placed in our way by the authorities, and we trust that we shall be permitted to remain here in peace.' The pressure of purely business matters was heavy, but he was troubled about personal relationships in his team.

A place for Nicol[2]   *December 1866*

When James Meadows and George Crombie arrived from Ningbo on November 30, they had just passed through the 'large and important city' of Xiaoshan (Hsiaoshan), the county town on the south side of the Qiantang river, ten miles from Hangzhou and fifty from Shaoxing and the Stevensons. Hearing about the journey from Shanghai and disappointments at Jiaxing and Tangqi, they urged the claims of Xiaoshan as a strategic alternative for the Nicols to occupy, and the next day went back with Hudson Taylor to prospect. Even after preaching to city audiences they were successful in renting a small house 'which, with a little repairing, could be made habitable'.

> The landlord being informed by (me) that, though foreigners, those who were to reside there had adopted the Chinese dress, etc, agreed to let it to us, and the requisite documents were forthwith drawn up. Some members of his family making trouble about it, however, [a familiar ploy] he came over to Hang-chau and requested us to give it up, offering to help us to rent another house. We agreed to this, and made inquiries, which resulted in our finding a house; but a deposit of $60 was required; and the necessary ten percentage to the agent would bring it to $66 (about £15). As our initial expenses had already been very heavy, and the subscriptions since we left home but few, we were questioning whether we ought to make this expenditure immediately, and were laying our difficulties before God, when a letter from Shanghai came to hand, telling us of a subscription of 50 taels, which would equal $66.75.

The first landlord's introduction meant that the same terms applied to the second, and the occupants would avoid provocation in Xiaoshan by wearing Chinese clothes and observing Chinese courtesies. So far so good. It remained for Lewis Nicol to comply. There might be anti-foreign elements in the city, but other Chinese, although strangers, considered obtrusive foreignness to be the only potential objection to his residence there.

News from Shanghai had been mixed. One of the converted sailors on the *Lammermuir* (unnamed) had collapsed and died while walking on deck. 'Mr Taylor got a very nice letter from Mr Brunton,' Jennie wrote, 'enclosing a cheque for $126, about £30, a subscription for our mission from the officers and crew of the *Lammermuir*, 29 people, poor sailors; it was a freewill offering begun by the crew' – by the fo'c'sle men themselves. And in a letter of thanks from Mr Wu for so much kindness during his stay with them on the canal boats, he told them to expect an interesting letter from Mr Gamble about a Mr Alfred Howell, Dent and Company's agent at Hakodate, Japan.

'About a fortnight ago I went to the commercial Bank to see a Chinese friend (a Christian) and show him (my) Certificate of Baptism and the picture of (your) party. It happened . . . that Mr Howell was standing beside my friend.' On seeing the certificate and photograph, Mr Howell had asked who these foreigners in Chinese clothes could be. Wu explained. They not only dressed as Chinese but ate like Chinese, enjoying food cooked in the Chinese way. 'He seemed to take (an) interest in your party at once and wanted to see your friends in Shanghai . . . I referred him to Mr Petrie.'

Howell called on David Petrie, the Jardine, Matheson agent in Shanghai, and told him 'how he had just happened to fall in with a Singapore China man who spoke very good English' and who described these foreigners who 'went in and out among the people, just as Chinese did themselves'. When he had learnt a little more about the CIM he asked Petrie to forward a subscription for him. Describing this 'pleasant little incident', Petrie told Gamble,

> From what he heard, he considered the self-denial and self-renunciation carried to such an extent . . . was something so noble in itself, that it was impossible sufficiently to admire it . . . and he did not care to what denomination they belonged (whether Blue Baptist or White Baptist) or what they were, but he would be happy to be . . . a subscriber of 50 or 100 taels a year . . . and he gave me an order . . . for 50 taels to begin with [the exact amount needed to cover the deposit on the Xiaoshan house]. I have the more pleasure in relating this . . . to you, that in the Singapore Chinaman I recognize the friend whom I met at your house, and whom you have so lately been the means of guiding into the fold of Christ.

Jennie's niche[3]   December 1866

Maria was away from Hangzhou almost all of December. From the age of fifteen until she left in 1860 at twenty-three, Ningbo had been her home. When Meadows and Crombie returned there she went with them, to see old friends and enlist more Chinese Christians for Hangzhou. She arrived back on the 17th with two women and several men, but the very next day heard that the pagan husband of the amah who had joined her in Shanghai was spreading malicious rumours about his wife. To silence him Maria, now less than two months from her confinement, started back to Ningbo with her, taking Jane McLean for the experience. Christmas came and

went and it was December 29 before she reached home again, this
time escorted by Stephan Barchet and John Stevenson – bringing
some of Jennie's possessions which had been packed inside a piano
for Ningbo.

To teach Jennie the vocabulary and money values, Maria had left
her in charge of checking the domestic accounts with the cook, who
did the daily buying in town. Her grasp of Chinese improved daily.
In Shanghai Jennie had changed five pounds sterling for twenty-one
dollars, and found that one dollar was worth one thousand and
twenty brass cash, a heavy load. 'If one wants anything worth a
shilling or two they have hundreds of cash to carry to the shop.'

Morning and evening, Hudson Taylor or Mr Tsiu conducted
'family prayers' for the Chinese staff, and the families of 'lodgers'
began attending. And on Sundays they held services to which
people from the neighbourhood began to come. 'They feel much
more at home with us, seeing that we eat rice and dress like
themselves,' Jennie thought.

On December 6 she visited two of the 'lodger' families in their
rooms.

> It seems something like beginning missionary work. The woman
> A-lo-sao seems very pleased. I found I was intelligible to her (though
> unless they talk slowly I cannot understand them very well).
>
> [And a few days later] I am so glad for them to have been here . . . I
> could not have visited out of doors . . . but I go and read and talk to
> these women every day . . . [Alosao] I have great hopes of; she has
> given up burning incense and says that since we came she has begun
> to pray to God . . . As I read they often take up their [tobacco] pipes
> and have a few whiffs almost choking me with the smoke.

By her innate, outgoing friendliness she had found her role. By
December 17 besides all the 'lodgers' and the Chinese on the team,
ten neighbours were attending the service, complete with pipes and
teapots. Alosao had brought them. A week later Jennie was writing
that she had not yet moved more than a few hundred yards from the
house or been shopping. It was wise to lie low. Christmas was on
them and she thought, 'Oh dear, the shops will be shut tomorrow!'
Then, how absurd! No one in Hangzhou even knew of Christmas!
But more of the women were inviting her to their rooms to read to
them. They were illiterate and she had seized her opportunity by
asking Maria to bring from Ningbo all the Christian books in
romanised colloquial that she could. Scarcely a month since arriv-

ing, her time was full with missionary work. And so much time spent with the women was quickly giving her a grasp of the colloquial.

On New Year's Day Hudson Taylor wrote to his mother that on Sunday, December 30, he had held two meetings for the Chinese household and two public ones with audiences of fifty or sixty. 'The attention and apparent interest have been cheering; and one or two persons have come repeatedly to inquire further into the truth.'

Plan of campaign   *December 1866*

Back in Shanghai from his visit to north China and Manchuria, William Muirhead learned that Hudson Taylor and his party had come and gone. On December 3 this prince of missionaries wrote,

> My dear Brother,
> I was sorry that I missed seeing you and your colleagues, thro' my absence in the north. Only I wish you and them every blessing . . .
> I have been requested to communicate with you by some friends in Shanghai, as to the nature and exigencies of your mission . . . They are desirous of aiding the China Inland Mission, and I want to know how it is supported, and in what way it is to be carried on. [They already had copies of *China's Need* and the *Occasional Paper*.]
> I am rejoiced at your having such a number of devoted women along with you, who are entering into the interior for the sake of preaching the gospel, and I have no doubt that if the work is done faithfully and well, you will have abundant support. Of course you will meet with ample difficulties in the way, but you calculated on this, and will not be cast down when they actually occur . . .[4]

This letter reached Hudson Taylor on the 18th. On December 27 he replied that he had been so pressed for time that an adequate answer had had to be deferred from day to day. To William Muirhead he could be frank and businesslike. He used the term 'agents' for 'missionaries' as Muirhead would. It had been a disappointment on reaching China to find his old friends Wylie and Muirhead both away, he began,

> I had calculated on obtaining much valuable information from you, especially with regard to the circulation of the O and N Tests, and the eligibility of the ports up the (Yangzi) for points of departure into the Interior. (But he hoped to visit Shanghai soon.)
> At present (the CIM consists of five married and fourteen unmar-

ried agents in China, and one married and one unmarried missionaries on the way [*sic*!] . . . and due in January or February) ['married' implied the presence of a wife as well]. With the exception of Mr and Mrs Meadows in Ningpo, they are all residing away from the free ports; and, so far *as we can*, we shall avoid residing in free ports or stations already occupied by missionaries of other societies, our object being rather to carry the gospel to those who are wholly beyond its reach. We desire, and shall, D.V. endeavour to place at least two missionaries with the same number of (Chinese) helpers in each unoccupied province of China proper; and likewise, if the work is not taken up by others, to plant missions in Chinese Tartary and Thibet, – and possibly Corea. But of course some years must elapse before this can be effected, and in the course of that time our plans may be considerably modified. At present I am seeking stations in the adjoining cities for those with me, where they may work under less disadvantageous circumstances than they would meet with in more remote provinces, until they have become acclimatized, and in some measure acquainted with the language, manners, resources and other (characteristics) of the Chinese. By the time that they are ready to move, there may be others to fill their places, or (Chinese) assistants competent to do so.[5]

Of special interest (in addition to his policy of not overlapping with other missions except in the ports and, if necessary, in an administrative base), was his emphasis on working new missionaries in; training them and Chinese Christians for deployment farther afield on their own. He continued,

Those already with me represent all the leading denominations of our native land – Episcopal, Presbyterian, Congregational, Methodist, – Baptist and paedo-Baptist. Besides these, two are or have been connected with the 'Brethren' so-called. It is intended that those whose views of discipline correspond shall work together, and thus all difficulty from that score will be avoided. Each one is perfectly at liberty to teach his own views on these minor points to his own converts; the one great object we have in view being to bring heathens from darkness to light, from the power of Satan to God. We all hold alike the great fundamentals of our faith; and in the presence of *heathenism*, can leave the discussion of discipline while together, and act as before God when in separate stations.

As to support, we have none guaranteed, nor have we, to my knowledge, more than three or four stated subscribers. At home we had on the 24th Oct. about £1,000 in hand, most of which would be expended, on the maintenance and training, outfits and passage money of those who follow us – some ten or twelve of whom may sail in the spring and summer of next year. And we have now in hand in China somewhere about 900 Taels which will be expended in rent and deposits on houses and chapels, together with alterations that cannot possibly be dispensed with; in salaries and expenses of (Chinese) assistants; and in the maintenance of the agents now at work. For our future support we rest on the faithfulness of Him who has sent us to do *His* work – not *ours* – and we fully believe with you that 'if the work is done faithfully and well we shall have abundant support.' But of this at least we are resolved, that by God's grace we will make the attempt to carry the Gospel to many who have never heard it; and so far we have been helped beyond our expectations . . .

I am at present unable to form any definite estimate of our probable expenses. If any desire, as you kindly intimate, to aid in our work, any sums can be paid into the 'Oriental Banking Corporation' to the credit of the China Inland Mission. Our accounts will be placed, not less frequently than twice in the year, in the hands of those who contribute towards our funds.

After the inefficiency of the Chinese Evangelization Society of which he had been a defenceless member, this last statement was as necessary as it was careful. As for Hangzhou, Hudson Taylor was to say a few years later,

Experience proved how desirable it was that the new missionaries, after having acquired the language to some extent, should have further training and development by labouring first in cities comparatively easy of access, and at distances which would allow of some measure of mutual support, before attempting to carry out our primary purpose (of spreading the gospel).[6]

From the beginning the strategy was 'both systematic and methodical. There was no aimless wandering' – the tag with which uncomprehending critics were to label the planned probing into the surrounding country. The policy was to turn men, women and children from Satan to God, by carrying the gospel to the whole Chinese empire as speedily as possible, rather than to win converts by concentrating on the few in static work.

As the apostle Paul sought to establish churches in the great strategic centres of the Roman Empire (p 70), so Hudson Taylor recognised the importance of gaining a footing, if practicable, in the provincial capitals, though these were the most difficult places in which to found churches. With the provincial capitals opened, the next step was to open stations in the chief prefectures, and thus downwards to the smaller towns and villages. The capitals, it was recognised, were the key to the smaller cities, since the subordinate officials were generally guided by their superiors, and so, though a larger number of converts might have been gained through work in some country centres, the slower but more far-sighted policy was adopted in preference to that which would have brought quick returns. Without a recognition of this plan of action no just estimate of the Mission's work can be obtained.[7]

This summary echoes what Emily Blatchley as Hudson Taylor's secretary wrote to Miss Waldegrave on December 3, 'We trust also to find an advantage in coming direct to the *capital* of the province; because having gained a footing here will in part pave our way into any lesser town.' Zhejiang province was administered by the governor in Hangzhou through eleven prefectures in four circuits, each under a *daotai* or prefect, controlling the many *xian* (hsien) magistrates, the county and district mandarins.[8] Of the eleven prefectures only two, Ningbo and Hangzhou, had been occupied by other missions. Jiaxing had resisted strenuous attempts to rent premises.

As Hudson Taylor considered the remaining seven, he was laying plans to prospect and then to locate missionaries in each of them as soon as his young men showed sufficient progress to be entrusted with the task. Unfortunately, it was not only adaptation to the culture or mastery of the language that fitted them for it, but innate discretion and above all Christlike spiritual maturity. It remained to be seen how they would shape in circumstances akin to those that had proved Hudson Taylor's own mettle between 1854 and 1860.

South of Hangzhou the prefectures of Yanzhou (near Tonglu), Qu Xian (Kiuchow), Jinhua (Kinhua), Taizhou (now Linhai), Chuzhou (now Lishui) and Wenzhou two hundred miles distant, beckoned him by virtue of their 20 million inhabitants. Fifty miles to the north, close to the Great Lake (Tai Hu), yet another, Huzhou (now Wuxing), lay in the area he had visited with William Burns when they challenged the immoral drama festivals. Within a year he and his men were to be driven out of one and rioted out of another. In two more, and other smaller cities, churches were to take root and grow, persecuted but uncowed.

To look far ahead, in the Wenzhou area alone, when the 'open century' ended and the anti-Christian pressures of Mao Zedong and the cultural revolution had had their day and were relaxed in 1980, visitors from Hong Kong found fifty thousand zealous Christians 'who had not bowed their knee to Baal'. The task was huge in the one province of Zhejiang, yet eleven provinces, with populations as vast but no Protestant missionaries at all, were his objective, and four more in which the handful of missionaries were almost exclusively in the ports.

Smoke and fire[9]   December 1866

Hudson Taylor knew China and human nature too well to expect plain sailing. He least expected some of his worst experiences to come from a member of his own team and from a colleague in a sister mission. In the early stages he said nothing, even to the Bergers, except as in his reference to 'intrinsic difficulties' when writing to Grattan Guinness. And he mentioned no names. Maria thought the Bergers should know more but he asked her not to send the letter she was writing: when it blew over they might wish they had been more patient. In any case, he maintained, nothing should be sent which was not first shown to the individuals concerned, so that they could give their version of it.

For an understanding of Hudson Taylor, the facts of the matter need to be stated, for they throw light on his character and leadership. The pact between them all was under challenge, and with it the principles he had been at pains to establish. Piecing together the evidence in various private records the truth emerges. In her personal journey Emily Blatchley wrote on December 30,

> The smouldering fire showing a flame now. The young men met in Nicol's room and Mrs N came to me to ask me to request Mr Taylor to join them. She said a good deal about Mr Taylor being changed, the young men feeling hurt, etc.

Lewis Nicol was 'a powerful man' in every sense, whom the others tended to follow in disaffection. Eliza, his wife, though quiet and friendly to all, was loyal to him and his views. What began with grumbles and grew in complexity and seriousness for two years is difficult to condense. Pages of letters, memoranda and journals contained statements denied in reply and pettiness unworthy of repetition.

The other individual to take a leading role in what would have been a mere storm in a teacup, if it had not escalated to serious proportions, was George Moule, a young man of about Hudson

Taylor's age (*see* Book 3, Index). In London Hudson Taylor had enjoyed a friendly correspondence with his father, the Rev Henry Moule, about the romanised Ningbo vernacular, after drawing up a vocabulary for Arthur Moule to learn on his voyage to China. An Anglican clergyman, Henry Moule was well enough endowed to send his sons to Cambridge, and George, Arthur and Handley (the future Bishop of Durham) followed him into the Church. Hudson Taylor's good friend, Frederick Gough, had been George's Greek tutor at Caius College, and both Gough and Hudson Taylor were in Ningbo in 1858 when George and his wife, Adelaide, arrived. No one could have been kinder to James and Martha Meadows when they followed Arthur to China as the first of Hudson Taylor's 'Ningbo five', or to their child when Martha died. The Moules' warm welcome to the *Lammermuir* party also promised good co-operation in their work. Suddenly it all turned sour.

The reasons are not hard to understand. George Moule's background in the established Church of England with all the convictions of his upbringing had been reinforced by an apprenticeship under W A Russell at Ningbo. A traditional Anglican church, even to the quasi-Gothic architecture of the building and the surplices of the clergy (*see* illustration, Book 3, p 171), provided a continuation of the ways he had known at home. Three American missions and three other British societies in Ningbo were the limit of their experience of differing viewpoints on mission to the Chinese – the United Methodist Free Church under William Fuller and John Mara, after 1864; the Church of Scotland under Dr John Parker; and the CIM with James Meadows, the Crombies and Stephan Barchet. (By the time Stott and the Stevensons arrived, George Moule was already in Hangzhou.) All in Ningbo dressed and lived largely as Westerners, the members of the CIM more simply than the rest.

As pioneers of Hangzhou the Moules and Greens of the American Presbyterian Mission continued their Western style of living, as did Carl Kreyer when he arrived. Here again George Moule's policy was to build up a congregation of Ningbo Christians and new converts before extending into the countryside. Ten years later he reported in the *Chinese Recorder* that his movements were limited to within a twenty-mile radius from Hangzhou. His chapel and outstation took all his time. So his policies for missionary work in China had little in common with Hudson Taylor's. Friendly though he was at first, the sight of all these young men and women in

Chinese clothes, living, eating and behaving as nearly as they could as Chinese people disturbed him. Then he learned that two of them were from William Pennefather's training school at Mildmay and had come with no introduction to him as the ordained minister, and no intention of maintaining their Anglican connections in China.

He had not accommodated himself to this surprise when a worse shock struck him. Someone (unnamed) in the *Lammermuir* party told the approving Carl Kreyer about the baptisms at Anjer. Kreyer, unwisely but probably in all innocence, mentioned to George Moule that two of those baptised were Pennefather's students! Carl Kreyer said he 'noticed his countenance change the moment he mentioned this'. Perhaps because differences of theology and conscience between the denominations were scrupulously avoided in conversation, George Moule did not challenge Hudson Taylor on the subject or raise it subsequently, if its absence from the remaining records may be so interpreted. Instead he acted on what he possibly thought were stronger grounds. To the Taylors' surprise their whole policy and practice came under strong criticism.

Unknown to Moule, as indeed to Hudson Taylor or others at the time, Lewis Nicol had let his imagination run away with him in conversation with the Moules. Petty resentments harboured since the voyage he now transmuted into distortions of the truth, exposing a fatal flaw in his own personality. Not until too late were those affected able to identify it. His imagination ran riot until he himself believed the fictions he was fabricating, and George Moule accepted them at face value. Slurs against the Taylors and others in the party looked more and more serious as Moule thought about them. Visiting New Lane he thought his own observations supported his worst fears – that all these unmarried men and women were housed together and the familiarity of their supposed chaperone, Hudson Taylor, with them was dangerously intimate.

Before facing Hudson Taylor with protests, George and Adelaide Moule began to have the young men and women over to meals, beginning with the Nicols' closest friends, and learned what they could from them. At a time of difficult adaptation to a new way of life, discontent found ready listeners in the Moules, whose misconceptions fed on thoughtless grumbling.

Within three months George Moule came to the conclusion that neither Hudson Taylor's policy nor his personal integrity could bear scrutiny. If damage to the missionary cause was to be averted, the responsibility for taking action rested upon him, George Moule.

Henry Venn had recalled him to Britain to recuperate. He was to leave in the spring. He must as far as possible put things right in Hangzhou, and bring the state of affairs to the notice of influential people in Britain. At first his aim was the reform of the CIM. Later, only its dissolution would satisfy him. As in the South China Sea before the typhoon, dark clouds were gathering.

During December, life at No 1 New Lane took on a regular routine. While Maria and Jennie Faulding were making friends among the 'lodgers' and Hudson Taylor prepared to open his clinic and invite neighbours to chapel services, the 'smouldering fire' was being fanned by real and imagined wrongs. The simple issue of Chinese clothes was the first to be raised. When the Greens, Kreyers or Moules left their premises they did so as gentlemen and ladies in their own or hired sedan chairs, receiving the deference foreigners in foreign dress had come to expect. Foreigners mixing with the Chinese, on foot and in Chinese clothes, were introducing a completely new relationship. When the two types met, the subject could not but be discussed. When Nicol, Sell and Jackson visited his home, George Moule made no bones of his objections and found them sympathetic. If that had been all, no more need be said, but it was not.

Business as usual[10]   *December 1866*

Early in December George Moule remonstrated for the first time with Hudson Taylor about his team and policies and told Nicol about it. Sensing the coming storm Hudson Taylor wrote to his mother on the 16th that but for his certainty that God had put him in the position he was in he would 'tremble for the result'. His letter to Grattan Guinness was written the next day. But to the household he said nothing. Maria arrived from Ningbo on the 17th and left again on the 19th.

Christmas came, and for a treat they changed into European clothes and used plates, knives, forks and spoons. 'It was quite delightful to be once more in our barbarian dress,' Jennie wrote. 'Mr Taylor thought it rather condescending for a Celestial [himself] to consent to sit down at table with such barbarians as we had made ourselves . . . The pressure of work and of different matters he has to attend to all at the same time, seem sometimes too much for him.'

The big rooms upstairs had been partitioned at last, and on Christmas Eve Jennie Faulding had papered the walls of her own private cubicle, in time for a 'happy Xmas day'. Emily Blatchley and Susan Barnes had the others. 'I feel quite cosy, like a queen in a castle when I come in and shut my door . . . Mr Taylor has contrived it all so nicely.' As for Christmas dinner, 'Emily and I thought we might as well be English altogether while we were about it, so I did my hair in my old way . . . and she put on my black silk dress and I the mauve one and we turned out collars and brooches and made ourselves presentable to English eyes once more . . . Even our Ah-mas cannot but exclaim that our dress is *very* pretty.' Annie Stevenson had sent a supply of real bread and the *Illustrated London News*, and for the Christmas meal Hudson Taylor had ordered 'many surprises' including two pheasants, two haunches of venison (all cheap and plentiful), a very good plum pudding and two fruit pies.

The last day of the year was to be kept as always as a day of fasting and prayer for China and the Mission. Maria arrived back on the 29th with John Stevenson, Stephan Barchet and Jane McLean, to find the household working hard to complete the papering and cleaning before the year ended. Until late in life John Stevenson remembered the vivid impression he received when first introduced to the *Lammermuir* party. Their zest and cheerfulness as they worked, and even more, 'their prayers impressed me immensely. I felt that the mission *must* succeed with such an amount of real waiting upon God.' The respect was mutual. Tall, broad and upright, with Scottish reserve, he carried his Chinese costume with natural Confucian grace, 'with an ease and dignity which stirred the Chinese to involuntary compliment as he moved among them. Yet he was obviously free from all self-consciousness . . .', a 'superior man', as could be seen at a glance.

Sunday saw 'large and remarkably attentive congregations' at the Chinese services and all the team were looking forward to ending the year in a day of good fellowship on Monday. Yet it was at this point that 'the smouldering fire' showed its flame. Eliza asked Emily to invite Hudson Taylor to meet the men (without Stevenson or Barchet) in the Nicols' room. He went. What was said to Hudson Taylor is not known, though complaints about his allocation of funds (little more than pocket money, for he was providing almost everything they needed communally) and his attitude to some of them, seem from later references to have been among the topics. Perhaps he revealed a little of what they had not known, for on January 1 John Sell wrote, 'We were startled by learning that some of the petty officers of the City wall have written to the city authorities stating that we foreigners go in twos upon and under the city walls and into all the quiet places we can find, our intention being to see where the weakest places are, and where best to make and lay mines ready for an attack upon the city at some subsequent day. In fact (they) believed we were spies of some rebellious army, not yet heard of.' Hudson Taylor was carrying greater worries than they had realised.

Whatever happened, Monday was 'a day never to be forgotten' and the watchnight service at nine thirty p m went on until one a m with more and more prayer and hymns. In his diary Hudson Taylor noted, 'God graciously drew us together and answered prayer in reuniting our party in love and peace,' while to his mother he wrote,

> It was a time of confession of sin and failure before God, and of mutual confession one to another. God was with us indeed; may we live more for Him and with Him during this year . . . It is an easy thing to *sing*, 'I *all* on earth forsake'; it is not very difficult to think, and honestly, tho' very ignorantly, to say 'I give up *all* to Thee and for Thee.' But God sometimes teaches one that that little word 'all' is terribly comprehensive. Thank God, He has left me much, very much – and above all, *He* never leaves us. But you will think me gloomy; I suppose I am a little so; my liver is a little out of order . . . let me assure you that I am not wearied of, though wearied in the service of God and China.

Writing intimately to 'my very dear Mamma' Jennie said,

> It *is* a joy to feel that God can and will supply all our need individually and as a mission; that He will overrule all things so that His own glory may be promoted, that with Him on our side we need nothing else. I never realized so much before the fullness of blessing that there is in Christ for each one of us. There is, and I believe there always will be very much of trial, now from one source and now from another in this work – very much need of self-crucifixion – and yet because it leads one to lean only upon God and because I believe He will be glorified by us and in us, I am full of adoring thankfulness that I am here. There is nothing that I would rather do, nowhere that I would rather be – indeed no-thing, no place that I would like half as well as this . . . Here we are in the midst of Satan's kingdom seeking to overthrow it and is it likely he will not try to baffle us? . . . Dangers are on *every* hand, but God has delivered us from them and He will deliver . . . If He were not working for us we could not stand secure a single

day . . . Mr Sell shot two pigeons one day and a report got abroad
that he had shot two men; we have sometimes wandered among the
ruins and they say we are wanting to undermine the city walls . . .
looking out for the best places of attack.

Her feet were firmly on the ground. This paragraph followed the
inquiry, 'Did you see the Royal Academy pictures this year?' And
before long she was asking them to send fashion notes. 'Has the
crinoline gone out? . . . I should like to be able to form a little idea
of how you are dressing.' She had just turned twenty-three.

PART 3

THE PACT REBORN

1867

CHAPTER NINE

FOOL OR KNAVE?
1867

Taking stock[1]   *January 1867*

The eventful year of 1866 had ended. A more eventful year was beginning. And of each year until 1871 the same could be said. A crescendo of distresses lay ahead. Already it seemed as much as Hudson Taylor could bear that those men of the *Lammermuir* party he had counted on appeared to be broken reeds. Only James Williamson seemed unshakeably loyal to him. At least his earlier recruits, Meadows, Barchet, Crombie, Stott and Stevenson, were of a finer mould.

The city mandarins did not share the suspicions of the guards on the walls. A military mandarin to whom Hudson Taylor had lent a Gospel and the *Acts* returned them with the comment, 'What a contrast between Judas and Paul – disciple turned traitor and persecutor turned apostle!' His interest and friendliness augured well. Rumours at the national level were more disturbing. During 1866 inflammatory anti-foreign propaganda had been circulating. The literati were restive. To quote from *The Jubilee Story of the China Inland Mission*,

> The long-standing enmity of the literati of China to all things foreign must be remembered as well as the fact that the Chinese people were at that period 'in the point of superstition very much where we were in the sixteenth century.' Should the literati stir up the passions of the people by playing upon their superstitious fears, few officials had the moral courage as well as the ability to keep the peace for long, for their tenure of office was largely dependent upon the goodwill of the scholarly class.
>
> Du Halde tells of a book dated as early as 1624 which circulated the base and foolish charges of the foreigners kidnapping children, extracting their eyes, heart, and liver, etc, for medicine, and the Roman Catholic practice of extreme unction, and the habit of closing the eyes of the dead, may have given some basis for part of

A MILITARY MANDARIN

such a belief. In 1862 a book entitled *Death-blow to Corrupt Doctrine* . . . brought forward similar charges. In 1866 Mr S R Grundy, the *Times* correspondent in China, called attention to a proclamation extensively circulated in Hunan and the adjacent provinces. Clause vii of this Proclamation read: When a (Chinese) member of their religion (Roman Catholic) is on his deathbed, several of his coreligionists come and exclude his relatives while they offer prayers for his salvation. The fact is, while the breath is still in his body they scoop out his eyes and cut out his heart; which they use in their country in the manufacture of false silver.[2]

How safe was it to deploy the young men while they were so new to China? The plan had been to scatter them as soon as they showed enough understanding of Chinese ways. Their restlessness pointed strongly to the need to act sooner rather than later. But did it also show that they were unfit to be on their own? Before John Stevenson left Hangzhou on January 1 he agreed to take Jackson and Rudland for a time at Shaoxing. Williamson agreed to join the Nicols at Xiaoshan when a house was ready. They were fellow-Scots from Aberdeenshire. Stephan Barchet stayed on at Hangzhou with George Duncan and John Sell, to support Maria and supervise repairs while Hudson Taylor was away visiting the older members of the Mission in their cities and going on to Shanghai for the freight.

As the plasterers moved in on January 2 to repair the walls and make permanent ceilings, Stephan and Lewis Nicol travelled the ten miles to Xiaoshan, called on the landlord, clinched the rental of the house he had found for them, for an outlay of the amount Mr Howell had donated (p 256), signed the deeds and returned on the 4th. On the 7th they set off again with a Chinese companion and their belongings and took possession. Eliza joined them when they were safely established. Hudson Taylor took Jackson to Shaoxing – to be welcomed by none other than Tianxi, 'Heaven's Delight', the once destitute boy he had adopted from his dying father in the ruins of Shanghai in 1857 (Book 3, p 63). Now a young man, he was to teach Chinese to the newcomers.

After midnight Hudson Taylor pressed on to Ningbo. He had been invited to explain his involvement in the revision of the Ningbo vernacular New Testament. The bitter cold was tolerable in the fur-lined travelling gown he bought for the journey, and a hood to go with it. Delay at all the locks, where buffaloes had to haul his boat over the slippery banks between river and canal, prevented his arriving until the day of the conference at Dr McCartee's. In his notebook he simply wrote, 'All spoke in favour of Rom. Col. (romanised colloquial) Versions and most thought they should be extended.' James Meadows on the other hand said bluntly that Hudson Taylor was called to defend himself against accusations that he had acted improperly in undertaking the revision and securing its publication by the Bible Society. 'All this Mr Taylor was charged with doing without having first consulted his missionary brethren in Ningpo.' Thirty-six years later Meadows recalled his 'wonderful power of disarming criticism . . .' on this occasion.

He did it in such a modest and gentle, yet withal so convincing a manner, as to disarm all criticism of the brethren present, and which really called forth admiration of the good man, who, they perceived, knew as much about Greek exegesis and the principles and laws of translation as they themselves did. And they were surprised at his grasp of the subject . . . Mr Taylor being careful at the same time to let them know that the colleague he had with him in London was a Ningpo missionary of the CMS, who was once (George Moule's) Greek tutor at Cambridge University (F F Gough). So instead of a vote of censure, admiration . . . and they thanked him for his work.[3]

From Ningbo he went on to the Crombies at Fenghua; from there to George Stott at Kongpu and then back to Ningbo for the week-end of January 13 (map, p 237). In an interview with the consul, R J Forrest, probably about the technicalities of registering properties and establishing more foreigners in Chinese cities, he learned that the consul saw danger ahead and wished to be told of any complications. It was his duty to see that the terms of the Treaty of Tientsin (1858) and Peking Convention (1860) were observed by the mandarins. So they discussed what action should be taken if anti-foreign demonstrations took place.

Hudson Taylor was still at Ningbo when news came that Maria had fallen down the ladder-stairway at Hangzhou. He finished his business, arranged for James Meadows to go to Shanghai and bring the printing press, medical supplies, window glass and some furniture by canal to Hangzhou, and hurried home. The men's staircase, more a ladder, to their bedroom, now divided into cubicles, led out of the kitchen behind the men servants' rooms, so that all their comings and goings were observed (diagram, p 247). The Taylor family, the Nicols when there, and the single girls went past Mr Tsiu's room, through a gate, locked at night, past the women servants' room and climbed another steep stairway without banisters to the upper storey. Maria's baby was expected in less than a month and she used the stairs with care. On January 9 as she descended in the semi-darkness she trod on the cat lying three or four steps from the top, lost her balance, fell heavily two or three times on the way down and finally over the unrailed side to land on her head. Her only serious injury was a sprained wrist. The fear that she might go into labour while her husband, the only available person with any training, was away, soon faded.

On his brief tour of the southern outposts of the Mission Hudson Taylor had renewed contacts with many of his old Chinese friends and made new ones, men and women converted since he was last in China. Writing to the Mission's supporters he said,

We hope to have the press in immediate operation, and have been able to secure the services of a (Chinese) who has learned to print at the American Mission Press, and who has since been in the employ of Mr Valentine, of the Church Missionary Society, Ningpo. Through the aid of the Romanized Colloquial, some of our party are already able to commence work. The extension of this system to the dialects of localities in which we may labour, will be one object ever before us . . . Might we request special prayer to God for the raising up and thrusting forth of more native evangelists? This is one of the greatest wants of the church in China at the present time . . . Mr Meadows desires to labour in the interior; but at present his services cannot be spared from Ningpo.

Hudson Taylor returned from Ningbo disappointed by one thing – not one of the married couples was willing to have single girls attached to them while they gained experience of life in China. All were comparatively newly wed, and valued their privacy. Maria and he had seen advantages for the missionary wives in having the companionship of another woman when visiting Chinese homes, and for the newcomers in scattering rather than having to share the limited work being built up at Hangzhou. At New Lane Maria could train and find work for only one or two at a time. The rest would have to find their own work as Mary Bowyer and Jennie were already doing. The clinic could draw men and women to the premises, but the girls would have to show what stuff they were made of. But what could be done as more and more missionaries came out from Britain? How many were the Bergers about to send? On January 16 Hudson Taylor wrote asking them not to send any more until further notice, but before the letter could arrive some might be on the way. Mr Berger at once published the news in the *Occasional Paper*. 'We fear disappointment may be felt by several' who were hoping to sail soon.

The big hall inside the front gate of No 1 was ready by mid-January to be opened as a preaching chapel. Seats for the women on one side and men the other were separated by the customary partition for the sake of decorum. By sitting among the audience, the newcomers could strike up conversations in the intervals. Hangzhou was noted for the intelligence, education and good looks of its women, Jennie told her father. On the 28th one invited her into her home. 'I had about thirty for a congregation . . . The woman gave me tea and cakes, and begged me to come often; in fact, they all seem pleased . . . the woman next to me said, with an air of satisfaction, "Your clothes are like mine." I am very glad to wear it, though most missionaries are unwilling to give it a trial; it is certainly an advantage. If I had on English clothes, the women would at first be afraid of me and if I succeeded in winning their confidence, my dress would be the one subject of their thoughts . . . to those who have never seen any costume but their own, what guys foreigners must look.'

One day Jennie was reading *Luke*'s account of the crucifixion to the 'Hangchow Ah-ma' while she did her hair in the Chinese style,

changing it, with her help, from the Ningpo colloquial into that of Hangzhou . . . Today she got so interested in the story that she only

INTELLIGENT, EDUCATED AND GOOD-LOOKING

listened, and forgot all about giving me Hangchow expressions; I saw how it was, and went on reading, till she having finished, I was going to close the book, having reached the verse where it says, 'And they all forsook Him and fled,' but she said, 'Did they take him then?' and I couldn't but go on to the end of the Gospel, she all the while putting in remarks as I went on, and when I stopped she said, 'We ought to believe in Jesus.' She is a nice old woman . . . and I believe she would do anything for me. She has a great deal of taunting to endure from her relations for 'eating foreign rice' as they call it.

By February 18 she and another were wanting to be baptised, and by March 6 Jennie was telling her father of four men and one woman who 'publicly confessed Christ and asked for church membership. The sacrifices they will have to make will test their sincerity. One would have to renounce his share in property which he held on condition of offering ancestral worship. Two others had no other livelihood than the making of paper money for idolatrous purposes.'

'The Xiaoshan outrage'[4]   January 1867

With little of the language, Lewis Nicol and James Williamson had used their time in converting a ground-floor room at Xiaoshan into a guest hall in which to receive visitors. When this 'chapel' was ready to be opened to the passers-by, Nicol returned to Hangzhou on January 25 to ask that Mr Tsiu might come and inaugurate it. To the amazement of all at New Lane, Nicol was in foreign dress. He had been wearing it for a week. Though he knew that in renting his house, the promise had been made that the occupants would dress as Chinese, he had broken it. In disregarding Hudson Taylor's wishes he had gone back on the agreement reached in London, the pact of loyalty Mr Berger had believed would bind more strongly than a written code. Nicol knew also that Mr Howell, their benefactor, had been told they would be living like Chinese.

Taken aback and seeing that Nicol's attitude was defiant, Hudson Taylor did not challenge him. In the heat of the moment he could make the wrong move. He decided to speak or write later. The self-sufficiency and arrogance of Nicol pained Maria. 'I felt God's blessing could not rest upon a work commenced in the spirit in which *it seemed to me* Mr Nicol was commencing his.' The following day Nicol returned to Xiaoshan with Mr Tsiu.

On Sunday the 'chapel' doors were opened and both morning and afternoon 'many came and listened attentively.' On Monday they went out on the city streets and Mr Tsiu preached again, with Nicol in his foreign suit beside him. That night trouble suddenly erupted. Tsiu was flogged and they were all driven out of Xiaoshan by the city magistrate. Leaving at daybreak, Mr Tsiu went ahead with a servant and reached New Lane first, disfigured by a hundred lashes to his face. Speaking with difficulty he described what had happened. Nicol came next, late in the morning, leaving his wife and James Williamson in the boat with such possessions as they had been able to bring with them. Unabashed, he spoke as if it was his own affair but asked, Should he go straight to Ningbo and lay the matter before the consul?

This was the kind of disturbance the consul had referred to. It should be reported at once. Hudson Taylor replied that it was for him as superintendent of the Mission to write. But 'he felt that before he involved himself in this capacity and consequently the whole Mission with him in Mr Nicol's matters he must know whether Mr Nicol was prepared to acknowledge him as *his* leader and director.' Did he consider himself a member of the Mission, 'a fundamental principle of which was that Mr Taylor should be, in all matters not affecting the conscience, the guide and director'? Why had he discarded his Chinese clothes without consulting him, in disregard of Mr Howell's grounds for making his donation? It involved such serious complications for the Mission that, although at this moment he would prefer to show only sympathy, he must have Nicol's answer before he could report to the consul. Who were the victims of the outrage, individuals or the Mission?

Nicol's answer was lame. He acknowledged Hudson Taylor's right to direct, but he had been away in Ningbo; he had so much on his mind; so Nicol had used his own judgment. Had he been fluent in Chinese, he said, he would have stayed in Chinese clothes. He would wear them again when he could speak freely. But he felt insecure. Foreign clothes gave him 'protection and respect'.

They brought Eliza and the baggage up to the house and Hudson Taylor waited for Nicol's 'own good feeling' to lead him to change back into Chinese dress like the rest of the household. When each described the events of the previous evening, to Hudson Taylor's concern it became evident that when Lewis Nicol embellished a statement he seemed to become convinced that whatever he said had indeed happened. His word could not be trusted. When the facts had been established, Hudson Taylor wrote to Consul Forrest (using dialect place names here replaced).

Hangchou,
January 29th, 1867

To R J Forrest, Esqre
HBM Consul, Ningpo

Sir,

I regret to be compelled to inform you that your prediction of difficulties arising in this quarter have met with an early fulfilment. The outrage of which I have to complain is so peculiar and aggravated, that in accordance with your own kind suggestion, I am obliged to make you acquainted with the facts of the case, and to beg the favour of your interference for its redress.

As you are aware (Xiaoshan) the nearest city within the jurisdiction of (Shaoxing) is only ten miles from here. Finding the people there kindly disposed towards us, we secured temporary accommodation (now given up) in a small house . . . subdivided into four rooms. In the upper part of this house, one of our missionaries, Mr L Nicol, and his wife stayed for three weeks, and were intending to pass the winter. One of the rooms downstairs was temporarily used as a small chapel. The landlord having seen from Mr Nicol's passport, that he was at liberty to travel in this province, expressed his satisfaction at the arrangement.

On Saturday the 26th inst, my (Chinese) assistant, Mr Tsiu, went over to (Xiaoshan) to preach there on the following day and return on Monday. Mr J Williamson . . . was intending to return to Hangchou on Tuesday morning. Mr Tsiu was therefore detained to return with him . . .

On Monday the 28th inst, about 8.30 p.m., Mr and Mrs Nicol and Mr Williamson were upstairs writing, and (Mr Tsiu) and a servant were downstairs. The door had been opened and suddenly Mr Tsiu saw the street full of men with lanterns, and the (magistrate's) sedan chair being set down before the door. He at once went upstairs to inform Mr Nicol, who, coming down, found the (magistrate) standing at the foot of the stairs, while about fifty of his retainers filled the chapel. Mr Nicol bowed to the (magistrate) who immediately seized him by the shoulders and very roughly turned him round. Mr Nicol indignantly turned back again and faced the (magistrate) upon which he became more polite and seated himself, (motioning) Mr Nicol to sit down also.

Mr Nicol called for tea, but the (magistrate) said, 'I don't want it! Do you think I will drink (foreign devils') tea?' He then . . . called for Mr Williamson who came bringing his passport, but the (magistrate) refused to look at it. Mr Nicol sent for his own passport which was brought to him; but the (magistrate) twice refused to look at it, or recognize it, pushing it away from him with an exclamation of contempt . . . for a time he would be very polite, and then without any apparent cause would become boisterous and rude. His own retainer said he was intoxicated . . . He insisted with loud threats that Mrs Nicol should appear before him, and Mr Nicol thought it prudent to bring her. The (magistrate) stared at her very rudely, and made some coarse remarks about her. He then asked to see over the house and was shown into every room.

In moving about he had to be assisted by his retainers, being too much intoxicated to move steadily alone. Upstairs he seated himself, and made many inquiries about England as to its direction, distance, etc.

At this juncture the landlord came in, evidently much alarmed, and presented a (petition) and endeavoured to exculpate himself. The (magistrate) however, took little notice of him. On coming downstairs again, the (magistrate) commanded Mr Tsiu, who had acted in some measure as interpreter, to kneel down, and ordered him to be beaten. This was without any charge being brought against him – not even his name had been asked.

Nicol provided more detail. 'Two took hold of him, one by the (*bianzi*) and another by the feet, and held him down; and two men then began their brutal work of beating him on the thighs whilst lying on his face on the ground, and they gave him six hundred lashes on his bare skin, which was very hard indeed for me to see; but he was a Chinese subject, and I dared not interfere. This done, he then received a hundred lashes on the sides of his (face), fifty on each, with a thing like the sole of a shoe, made of leather.' Hudson Taylor's letter continued,

He then commanded (Mr Tsiu) to ask Messrs Nicol and Williamson whether they would leave the place on the morrow. I had previously advised them, after my interview with you in Ningpo, in any case of ill treatment to place the whole matter in the hands of the Consul, and not to attempt to interfere with the local authorities. Notwithstanding his brutal conduct, they had, therefore, not interposed as they might otherwise have done on behalf of the native teacher. When the beating was suspended to see whether they would promise to leave, they concluded that the best course was to do so, to prevent the further ill treatment of Mr Tsiu, determining to refer the matter to you for redress. On receiving their promise to leave early

DISPENSING 'JUSTICE' AT THE *YAMEN*

the next morning, the (magistrate) seemed satisfied and went away, reviling them, and distinctly threatening Mr and Mrs Nicol, Mr Williamson, Mr Tsiu and the native servant, that all and any of them who should remain after the following morning should be summarily beheaded. This was in the presence of upward of a hundred persons.

About 10 p.m. some messengers from the (magistrate) came again, and insisted that Mr Tsiu should accompany them to the *yamen*. Mr Nicol went along with him, not daring to trust him alone in their hands . . . When the (magistrate) found that Mr Nicol had come with Mr Tsiu, he did not see him, but sent out word that they must not remain till morning – that they must leave immediately. This, however, Mr Nicol positively refused to do, though again promising to leave in the morning . . .

Finally, they left (Xiaoshan) in the morning to fulfil their promise, though unable to remove all their effects. Having been so publicly disgraced, it was with great difficulty and increased expense that they were able to engage a boat for themselves and part of their goods. And I feel assured, that however great the need, no inn-keeper or boatman in (Xiaoshan) will venture to allow a foreigner to pass the night in his inn or boat within the limits of the city and suburbs, unless some public redress is afforded . . .

I think you will agree with me that we have just cause to complain . . , Perhaps I should further add that the landlord has also been severely beaten by the mandarin. I would fain hope that you may see it right to vindicate the honour of our country, and our rights under the treaty of Tientsin, by requiring such a proclamation to be put out, as shall cause our persons and our passports to be respected, and shall give the natives confidence in rendering us their legitimate services.

I find I have . . . neglected to mention that the (magistrate) on being informed that Mr Nicol's object in (Xiaoshan) was the propagation of Christianity, denounced it as a depraved and prohibited religion. This, I believe, is not only contrary to one of the Articles of our Treaty, but is directly opposed to proclamations that have been issued in Hangchau (Shaoxing) and elsewhere, by the (Chinese) authorities themselves.

Regretting the necessity for thus troubling you,
I have the honour to remain,
   Your obedient servant,
      (signed) J Hudson Taylor,
         Superintendent of the China Inland Mission[5]

By the standards he later set himself, it was the immature letter of a harassed man with no precedents from working under the new treaty conditions. With experience in more riotous circumstances, Hudson Taylor was quickly to reach a balance of co-operation with the well-meaning consular authorities and the mandarins in the best interests of the Mission, its members and the cause they existed to promote. The vindication of national and religious rights ceased to concern him.[6]

Tsiu and Nicol[7]   *February 1867*

After the news of Mr Tsiu's flogging reached Britain, several friends of the CIM wrote letters of sympathy, and he himself replied in the customary idiom,

Your younger brother [meaning himself] sends many thanks; these words he will remember as if engraven on his bones, and written in his heart. For he feels that although many hills and seas may intervene, and though personally unknown by sight, yet in very truth we are as the hands and feet of the selfsame body . . .

When formerly your younger brother, at the direction of Mr Taylor, went to Mr Nicol and Mr Williamson, at the city of

(Xiaoshan) in the prefecture of (Shaoxing) to preach the doctrine of truth, and, unexpectedly, was ill-treated by the Mayor of (Xiaoshan), and punished with beating, he thought this truly is not real disgrace: though deeply painful, there is joy in it. For he remembered the words of the Holy Writ spoken by Jesus, 'Blessed are they who are persecuted for righteousness sake, for theirs is the kingdom of heaven'; and likewise the Scripture, 'Behold, happy is the man whom God correcteth; therefore, despise not thou the chastening of the Almighty: for He maketh sore, and bindeth up; He woundeth, and His hands make whole.' These passages made him feel that, though weak, he must bear all with patience . . .

Such a spirit threw into contrast Lewis Nicol's attitude which the Mission family bore with until Saturday, February 2, when Hudson Taylor asked him to change into Chinese clothes again. He could have pointed out that James Williamson, dressed as a Chinese, had gone unmolested, while Nicol had been man handled. Instead he reminded Nicol that the reasons he had given for wearing foreign clothes in Xiaoshan did not apply in Hangzhou. Nicol answered, 'No, I won't. I will not be bound neck and heel to any man.' And when told 'that his wearing the foreign dress was likely to prove injurious and possibly dangerous to the Mission,' he said, 'Then I suppose I had better make my way at once to one of the free ports.' 'I'm not sure but what that may prove to be the best course,' Hudson Taylor replied.

After a few days of illness Nicol continued to go about the house and city as a foreigner, 'trying to behave as though nothing were amiss'. Then one day Maria said to a Chinese helper 'that I thought so many people coming to be cured was a proof' that they did not believe that foreigners wanted to take out their eyes. Her friend replied that a woman who had come to the clinic was so frightened by the sight of Nicol that she went away without being attended to. The issue was important. It was right to insist on the agreed policy being observed. But John Sell sided with Nicol and took to Western clothing, and Jane McLean sympathised with them. Jennie told her parents, 'Mr Landels' prophecy that the typhoons were the precursors of other and different storms is likely to be fulfilled.'

It was May of the following year, 1868, when William Berger disclosed that Nicol had been writing 'disgraceful' letters to him. 'It is a grave question whether a brother who avows he has no confidence in you and desires never more to write to me in times of trouble, etc, should continue connected with the Mission . . .

Should you decide to send (him) home you are at liberty to do so at my expense.' He enclosed a copy of Nicol's latest, written from Xiaoshan, full of complaints about life on the *Lammermuir* and in Shanghai nearly two years previously. An example read,

> For the want of (stockings) . . . the skin was all off my feet . . . I went to Mr Taylor and the only comfort he gave me was to ask me to go without, and showed me his feet, that he had none . . . Are you aware that we had only old dirty Chinese cast-offs in which we were such figures that it tempted more than Mr Taylor to call us Coolies? . . . You at home can have no idea of what Chinese cast-off clothes are . . . It is . . . common to see the Chinese day by day take off their clothes and pick the vermin (*lice*) off them . . .

Maria replied to the Bergers,

> I hardly dare trust myself to speak of Mr Nicol's letter, for the downright *falsehood* about his Chinese outfit. Neither Mr Nicol nor any other of the brethren had a single article in his Chinese outfit but what was quite new and *clean* . . . (What he says) about vermin . . . is as false as disgusting . . . They were dressed as *gentlemen*.

Down to work   *February 1867*

When James Meadows arrived on January 30, two days after the 'outrage', with the freight from Shanghai, Hudson Taylor set up his dispensary and started seeing patients. Within a few days the chapel was in full use as a medical waiting room, and a hundred or so patients daily sat listening to Mr Tsiu preach the gospel until their turn came to be seen by the doctor. Several came constantly, simply to listen. Soon Hudson Taylor was seeing more than two hundred patients daily, morning and afternoon, and from time to time would emerge from his room to relieve Mr Tsiu and address them himself. Outside in the lane stood sedan chairs waiting to be hired, and vendors of food and drinks. New Lane had come alive. The work he had come to do was in full swing, and Hudson Taylor (Jennie wrote) was 'so busy he hardly ever has time to get a meal comfortably'.

With Maria's confinement approaching, Louise Desgraz had taken over the housekeeping. Emily Blatchley was busy as secretary and teaching the older Taylor children, Grace, Herbert and Howard. Never really well, she found rice tasteless and trying as a basic diet, but did not complain. Mary Bell, the nurse, was helped by a girl called Ensing whom Maria had 'adopted' in Ningbo years before. Mary slept in the nursery with the children, and Ensing in a room leading from it. With little time of her own, Mary still found ways of being a missionary to the Chinese whom she met in the course of her work, as William Rudland noticed approvingly after his return from Shaoxing. Jennie Faulding and Mary Bowyer had their hands full. Both were in demand by friendly Chinese women.

George Duncan, a linguist by nature, could not wait to be able to speak to the patients and their relatives.

> I feel very sad that I am not able to say more to them . . . I teach others to read what I do know . . . I think Satan has a peculiar power here in tempting, for truly it is his seat as the prince of the power of the air, and he is sorry to lose any of his captives. But by the help of God we shall triumph . . . If we are to learn, we must go to school; and if we are to wear a crown we must fight for it . . . The people are very patient in listening to hear what I have to say. Some of them wonder to hear a foreigner speak their language at all. They do not laugh at mistakes, as persons do at home. They are a wonderful people in many things . . . It is encouraging, too, that we have the favour of this people so much.

As the atmosphere soured with Lewis Nicol's return to Hang-zhou, Duncan wished to have no more to do with his complaints. His true nature prevailed and from this time he quickly developed the pioneer skills for which he became well known. Rising above the circumstances, those who were not of Nicol's faction, all but five, gave themselves to the language and the Chinese people and soon saw results. James Williamson found the language difficult to acquire, but spent hours with the cook, the laundryman and the printers, reading to them from the romanised colloquial books and listening to them talk. Perceptibly his understanding and ability to imitate them increased. When Hudson Taylor and Mr Tsiu for any reason were away, to their own surprise but no one else's, Duncan and Williamson shared with Maria the daily devotional meetings and Bible-teaching of the Chinese staff.

Accounts of the life they led during the first half of 1867 are long and colourful. As soon as word spread through the city and country-side that a Western doctor was not only treating but healing people, any thought of being inconspicuous had to be abandoned. The crowds that thronged Hudson Taylor became too great. At times there was no standing room in the guest-hall-chapel and some had to spill out into the yard. Only he had any knowledge of medicine, so after he had seen a few patients he would himself make up their prescriptions and instruct his Chinese assistants. They would then pass on his directions to the patients and their relatives. From time to time he opened abscesses, removed small tumours and operated on eyes and eyelids. When he removed cataracts and the old man or woman could see again, the pressure of work increased. A stream of totally blind adults and children began to come, too late for cure. On every day except Sundays and when he had to be away, the gates were flung open and work would begin. Domestic life continued against this background. On Sunday evening, February 3, Maria was moving about until a quarter of an hour before her baby Maria was born and she consigned her duties and accounts to Jennie.

On the same day John McCarthy and his family reached Shanghai with Margaret McLean, Jane's twin sister, to be received by James Meadows and William Gamble, introduced to Chinese dress and Chinese life, and brought to Hangzhou by canal boat. The Chinese New Year holiday had swollen the clinic crowds on the day they arrived. Hudson Taylor, in his enthusiasm for preaching the gospel above all other work, had taken to playing his harmonium and singing, to the people's delight, and addressing them, 'as quiet as an English audience', before his afternoon surgeries. Maria lay in bed listening. When the McCarthys came in from the road, the first sight to catch their eyes was Hudson Taylor standing on a table (before a platform was made) addressing a 'full house'. The mental picture stayed with John McCarthy all his life. A wave of his hand and 'a word of welcome was all that could be given as we passed into the house.' At last Hudson Taylor had a colleague with some basic medical skills.

In a very short time I found myself in the dispensary weighing out the medicines . . . Here for months . . . Mr Taylor saw on the average 150–160 persons each day . . . Some successful operations for cataracts . . . seemed little short of miraculous to people who were so ignorant of foreign medicine and surgery . . . Only those who were nearest (to him) could at all estimate the amount of self-denial involved in giving up (his own part in evangelism) in order to be free to help others in a more widespread evangelization of the country.[8]

In her home letter that Saturday evening Jennie said,

> Mr Taylor preaches I think almost entirely impromptu, indeed he has no time for (preparation), and yet his illustrations are so varied and good and his words seem to come with a power which would be astonishing did we not know how many are praying that God's blessing may rest on our work; that the people should come again and again and pay such attention is also very remarkable. I believe our influence is widely felt in Hangchow even now . . . We are praying that the ruler may not think we want to steal away the hearts of the people for any bad purpose.

Her own work among the Chinese women was expanding steadily, and the 'Hangchow Ah-ma' and another were wanting to be baptised. 'One woman heard of us from her neighbours, and came three miles to the service.' All the indications were favourable. This work was going to be a success and very soon a wholly Chinese congregation would be established in Hangzhou. Hudson Taylor began to think of asking Wang Lae-djün to come and take charge, as soon as William Fuller and John Mara no longer needed him in Ningbo.

Accusations[9] *February–March 1867*

Concurrently with all the progress at Hangzhou, cheered on by a letter and cheque from George Müller himself, Hudson Taylor was facing more serious accusations by Nicol, taken up, with the best intentions, by George Moule. After Nicol's refusal to wear Chinese clothes with the rest of the team, Hudson Taylor called them all together. Outlining what he had said in London about his principles and plan of campaign, no less than the terms on which they had offered him their services to achieve his vision for China, he asked each one to say what he had understood to be their agreement with him and Mr Berger. Nicol answered, 'Until we had got the language we should wear the English dress for our own protection . . .' Williamson disagreed, saying to Hudson Taylor, 'I understood according to the views you have expressed,' about financial arrangements and Chinese dress. Rudland supported him, saying, 'Mr T would be the director of (the) mission and have the direction of funds.' Duncan confessed inarticulately to having 'always some darkness in my mind. I understood that when I came to China I was

unintelligent and in these things was under your direction.' From
then on all but Nicol and Sell began to support Hudson Taylor. But
Emily Blatchley wrote in her private journal on February 18 (before
McCarthy's arrival), '(Williamson) is the only one of all the brothers
who still stands fast by him in *all* things.'

On the 15th George Moule came to New Lane to see Nicol, and
handed him a letter for Hudson Taylor to reinforce 'two long
conversations on the subject (of) my serious view of your present
missionary establishment'. It revealed that he had already written to
the Taylors' friends in London.

> My main objection, – and which I felt it necessary, after our last
> conversation, to communicate directly to Mr Berger and indirectly to
> Mr Gough and Mr Pennefather – is (quoting that letter) 'that by
> domiciling in (your) own house so many unmarried females' you are
> 'doing that which if I am not mistaken would be viewed with mistrust
> and disapproval even in England; and which among the Chinese
> gives a reasonable handle to the worst of imputations upon the
> morality of European Christians' . . . I felt obliged . . . to draw the
> attention of your friends at home to the subject, *in the interest of the
> 'sisters'*, whose present situation, every Christian but yourself with
> whom I have conversed on the subject feels to be an altogether
> improper one. [So he had already made his own views public.]
>
> I write these lines to you that I may urge upon you a consideration
> of *the hazard your own soul runs* in the connection that exists
> between you and the single 'sisters' of the Mission.
>
> Living as you all do in very confined premises, having some of the
> restraints of social etiquette relaxed (as you may conceive) by your
> relation to these ladies as their physician, and some by the position
> you have assumed as their spiritual pastor, having them, further, to
> so large an extent dependent upon you as their only easily accessible
> friend and adviser of experience in China, since you have removed
> them from the neighbourhood of the bulk of missionary society, –
> *you would be more than human if you were not capable of being
> tempted to lay aside* in some measure the reserve with which for their
> sakes and your own they ought to be treated.
>
> You are conscious that you are not more than human and therefore
> as one who has known something during more than twenty years of
> the single 'plague of his own heart'; and something of the infirmities
> of other Christians, and who is, in respect of age and missionary
> experience, not younger than yourself, I have taken upon myself
> most solemnly to urge you . . . *to consult, in all reasonable self-
> diffidence*, with those of the other missionaries whom you can trust
> for their piety and wisdom, as to the best method of putting a speedy

end to the present organization of your mission, so that imminent perils (as I conceive them to be) may be averted . . . I would solemnly warn you not to undervalue my remonstrances . . .

I have . . . done nothing by word or deed to prejudice against you those of your party whom I have intercourse with.[10]

He had criticised the domestic arrangements at New Lane, if no more. A year later he was to hint darkly about kissing and 'nocturnal visits'. What had Nicol been saying? When Adelaide Moule wrote in the same strain to Maria she replied indignantly,

Both you and (your husband) appear to ignore me entirely . . . I do not desire to bring *myself* or *my* work before public notice, but it seems so strange that you should write to *me* of 'the establishment of unmarried sisters which *Mr Taylor* has thought it right to have in *his own* house,' – as though his house were not my house, and his work, at least as far as our dear Sisters are concerned, my work . . .

I am aware that (your husband) has received . . . serious misrepresentations – to call them nothing worse. Would it not have been the right course, before allowing these to affect his *conduct*, to have endeavoured to ascertain the other side of the question? 'Against an elder' – and such my dear Husband surely is to the rest of our party – 'receive not an accusation but before two or three witnesses.' I am more intimately acquainted than anyone else with the whole tenor of my beloved Husband's private and social walk, and . . . that walk is in all *meekness* and *forbearance*, in all *purity*, in all *sincerity of purpose*, in all *singleness of eye*.'

Hudson Taylor's preoccupation with his patients and incessant work meant that he waited before doing anything more than to show the accusing letter to James Williamson, Emily Blatchley and Jennie Faulding. On the 15th he had been busy with an operation under chloroform. On Sunday the chapel had been so packed, although the clinic was not open, that Emily could not get in. He asked her to write to his mother as he could find no time, to say how Maria was getting on since her confinement. The disjointedness of Emily's letter betrayed her turbulent emotions.

Dear as beloved Brother and Sister they have been to me a long time; but now that I have heard of the death of my own dearest loved, passionately loved, *almost* idolized Sister, they are doubly so . . . Be assured that all a sister can do, may do, for them, my love will ever eagerly seek to do it . . . (Mr Taylor) is somewhat overworked, – but what a *blessed* life is his! . . . Dear Mrs Hudson Taylor sends her love.

– probably the first recorded use of his names in the combination soon to be customary. In her diary that night the sensitive Emily said,

> *In re* Mr Taylor and us ladies – full of unreasonableness and absurdity, caused of course from reports taken to him from *some* of our young men. So this great grief is added to dear Mr and Mrs Taylor: for me – I cannot but feel that tho' innocently enough, it is I who have been the immediate cause. I don't know whether I felt most of grief or surprise or indignation in reading that letter . . . I am so lonely, so utterly alone; and now my intercourse with them must be straitened even yet more. But why should I cling so? Oh! Christ, take hold of my hands.

To all intents Jennie and she had been part of the Taylor family long before any of the others joined them. Group photographs often showed Hudson Taylor holding a child, but no less frequently the adults beside him have a hand on his shoulder. One, of 1865, shows John Stevenson doing this. In another it is George Stott. In the photograph of the *Lammermuir* party issued to supporters of the Mission and later published in *The Jubilee Story*, his son Herbert is on his lap and Howard on Maria's at his knee. Emily has a hand on Hudson Taylor's left shoulder and Jennie appears to be holding his right arm. A goodnight kiss from them would have been only natural. Affection was vital to Emily as her own family died one by one of phthisis.

Having read Moule's letter Hudson Taylor insisted on face-to-face clarification of the issues and asked James Williamson to go with him. But the interview was futile. After midnight Emily turned to her journal again and poured out her woes:

> *Feb 18. Monday* Mr Taylor (asked) Mr Williamson . . . to receive from each of us ladies individually a statement as to Mr Taylor's bearing towards us being nothing but that of a *Christian* and a *gentleman*. I rebelled, revolted at his having to stoop so, – as if his character were even on an impeachable level; but he thinks it *better* to condescend to unquestionable proof, for the mission's sake: and so it was settled, and from each of us Mr Williamson received the required testimony; – for me, I did try to keep a quiet meek spirit, – but it was

in vain, my indignation *would* have the rule, and I couldn't help saying a little – very little – of what I felt.

In the evening they went . . . and to the surprise of us all Mr Taylor returned shortly. (Asked) if he had come on business, Mr Taylor (had) said Yes, and referred to the letter . . . He replied he had nothing . . . more to say, if Mr Taylor adhered to his plan of work . . . Mr Taylor then gave his other ground for coming . . . namely to demand of (him) an explanation of his impeachment of Mr Taylor's private moral character . . . (at which he said) 'I deny it: I *have not* impeached your private moral character' . . . and so he bowed them out with frigid politeness . . . Mr Taylor's words are that his behaviour has been the most consummate piece of 'priestly presumption he has ever heard of'.

Mr Duncan said he wished to have a few words in private with Mr Taylor; and they went down into the chapel. Mr Taylor did not come up again till past 12 o'clock, and all had left the sitting-room but Miss Desgraz, Jennie, Mr Williamson, and myself . . .

Notes of Mr Taylor's statements: Mr Moule has been trying to disaffect several of our number and to prejudice them against Mr Taylor. He advised Mr Duncan to leave the Mission: he has told him Mr Taylor is a hypocrite: calls this establishment scandalous, – worse than a Romish convent. In fact, he has determined to overthrow the Mission, and for that end will leave nothing unattempted . . .

And now Mr Taylor says, that such a wave is coming down upon us as shall sweep away from us every false and cold adherent . . . Matters are in a crisis: now God shall pick out most signally whom He has elected to the work.

Mr Moule has written to missionaries in China, and Mr Taylor expects the next thing will be that we shall receive letters of dissuasion from every missionary in Ningpo, Shanghai and Hong Kong . . .

Mr Taylor is seriously considering the advisability of convoking an assembly of the *whole* Mission. Are we, he asks, prepared to stand firm in the cause we have undertaken at *all* risks? – thro' suffering, slander, persecutions, forsakings, to characters blackened and believed to be black, even by those who have hitherto been friends?

Maria had dutifully refrained from telling Mrs Berger, until Hudson Taylor agreed that the time had come to let them know everything. On March 18 she therefore wrote,

With all this encouragement we have some sore trials. Perhaps the sorest is that disaffection exists in our own party, tho' we hope it is confined to two or three . . . I think gross misrepresentations must have been made to (Mr Moule) before he could go so far as to say Mr T was a hypocrite, our work a sham, and our profession of faith in God a delusion to (the Christian) public . . . (and that Mr T must) break up our establishment . . .

Jennie had also written, probably earlier in the day,

We have been in trouble the last day or two . . . Mr Moule . . . thinks we ought to be organized as other societies are . . . and he wishes that we should either alter our plans or that the Mission should be broken up. He has advised most of the young men to leave the Mission and is trying to hinder us in every possible way . . . But our mission is of God and I don't believe that he or anyone else can destroy it.

In her next letter she returned to the subject after mentioning 'Mr Landels' prophecy' (p 283), 'I think he would like us all sent back to England, but God brought us here and "if He be for us who can be against us?"'

The Moules were to leave for Ningbo on the 19th, en route to Europe, and in saying goodbye to Louise Desgraz he said he hoped to see her in foreign clothes on his return. He intended visiting the Stevensons and Jackson on the way through Shaoxing. When Hudson Taylor learned of this he asked Duncan to go ahead and tell them what had been going on. From Shaoxing Duncan wrote, 'All sympathize with you.' Jackson, he added, had heard Lewis Nicol saying a good deal more.

Calling a spade a spade   *February–March 1867*

The arrival of the McCarthys and Margaret McLean at Hangzhou on February 23 was like the sun breaking through cloud. An older, maturer man of about thirty, John McCarthy fitted in cheerfully and energetically from the start, wearing Chinese clothes, making rapid progress in the language and restoring a healthy sanity at No 1. He politely brushed off Nicol's attempts to influence him, and his sense of responsibility and quick understanding allowed Hudson Taylor to feel less isolated in the direction of affairs. Margaret McLean was staggered, she told Maria, to find that some of the party had stopped wearing Chinese dress. But she was immediately swept up by the Nicols, John Sell and her sister Jane, and saw little more of Maria. A month later 'she was prepared to do anything to win the confidence of the Chinese. She had seen enough to form her own opinions.' But while they all feasted on the letters, newspapers and presents the newcomers had brought from the Bergers and friends at home, and revelled in hard work, Lewis Nicol was brooding over supposed wrongs. When he persuaded John Sell and Jane to boycott the Chinese services, the others found it hard not to protest. Emily wrote,

I do wish . . . friends in England could see . . . that crowd of faces changing gradually from their expression of mere curiosity and wonder to that of interest – even earnestness in one or two, as Mr Taylor, mounted on a chair in order to throw his voice further, first explains to them the nature of our meeting and of our worship, how that there is no visible form to bow to, no incense, no silver paper, no candles; but the great invisible God Himself present, seeing and hearing all that we do, and say and think. Then . . . Mr Taylor explains and illustrates bringing each point in it home *to them* with peculiar adaptedness . . . I think *only* next to the privilege of preaching Christ to them, is the privilege of standing by the preacher's side and pleading (in prayer) for them while he speaks . . . The place could hardly seem more solemn ground, did one of its doors open upon hell and the other into heaven. [And the next weekend:] Yesterday a man who attends the services, told Mr Tsiu that he believes in our Christ; and today another man asserted his belief and desired to enter the church: we cannot yet vouch for the genuineness of these cases. Also our servant Teng-miao, though he has not . . . openly avowed belief in the truth, seems nevertheless to be sincerely believing in Christ, from the earnest zeal with which he talks to the patients, exhorting them to receive Jesus for their Saviour . . .

Sunday, March 3 . . . After the service a man came to (Mr T) and said he believed; he wished to be baptized. This and the interest manifested by some of the patients, made Mr Taylor so glad and joyful that he seemed quite lifted above the clouding of the manifold troubles . . . Some of (the audience) have such sorrowfully touching stories. One tells how she has lost every relation – all slain by the rebels. Another poor old blind woman, with cataract in both eyes, says how it is much weeping that has made them so, for her husband was beheaded before her eyes, and her son dragged away to be made a soldier, and she was left desolate. One of our in-patients . . . was in a dying state when he came in from the street, where he would have lain and died: he had been turned out of house, lest he should die there and his ghost annoy the other inmates. . . . The woman upon whom Mr Taylor operated for cataract is doing well; and *can see*.[11]

But on February 27, a week after the Moules had left and calm of a sort returned, Lewis Nicol although in the same house wrote Hudson Taylor a note, complaining that he was misunderstood. Hudson Taylor replied,

> My dear Brother,
>   I am glad you have written to me . . . a mode of communication the least likely to be 'misunderstood and misconstrued' . . . Any breaches which may exist I heartily desire to see healed. But they need healing and not plastering over: their cause needs to be discovered, and, if possible, removed. Now to do this we must be *definite* and open . . . (I) therefore must beg you candidly and in a friendly spirit . . . to write to me again and inform me of what you have to complain . . . for it is only in this candid way of dealing with difficulties that there can be any real healing of breaches, or reestablishment of confidence among us.
>   Believe me, sincerely,
>   Your Brother and well-wisher . . .

Nicol's three foolscap pages suffered in clarity from his scanty education, but the drift in his arguments was clear.[12] They were mostly about clothes. He avoided the burning question of disloyalty and innuendoes. But when in conversation he used the phrase 'nocturnal visits', Jennie jumped on it and answered with some very plain speaking. Her long friendship with Hudson Taylor was not to be slandered, nor was Emily's position in the family to be maligned. Both were beyond reproach. The sisterly freedom the two girls enjoyed with the Taylors had to stop, however, to the grief of both.

If they had known the contents of George Moule's letter to William Berger they might have been more outspoken. It had to reach London before a copy could be sent back to Hudson Taylor, a delay of four months. It has not survived, but quotations from remarks made after he reached Britain say enough. Captain Fishbourne was told 'that the *Lammermuir* party were quarrelling all the way out.' Captain Bell, Dennis the cook and Mr Brunton on the other hand separately told Mr Berger 'that as far as they could judge the missionaries lived in the greatest harmony on board,' and the Bergers recognised the shadow of Lewis Nicol behind the story. That was tolerable. But Captain Fishbourne's impressions were of gross improprieties at Hangzhou. He had been told, Mr Berger wrote,

Some of the Sisters came to Mrs Moule claiming her protection; they said Mr Taylor was in the habit of kissing them all and they objected to it. Mr T defended this practice to Mr M (who complained of) the sleeping accommodation being so bad in the (Hangzhou) house; of Mr T being a Pastor, Doctor, Paymaster, and the term Confessor was used on the paper Mr G P (George Pearse) gave me . . . I am at a loss to comprehend it as I have a copy of a paper signed by all the sisters except Mrs Nicol and J McL, the first a married woman and the other engaged to Mr Sell . . .[13]

Eliza Nicol or perhaps Jane had said something which all the others disowned, and the phrase 'claiming her protection' was a gloss. 'Confessor' referred to his practice of clearing the spiritual air by an honest setting to rights on days of united fasting and prayer, and bringing complaints into the open. 'Pastor, Doctor and Paymaster' implied improper relationships and pressure such as George Moule had suggested in his letter and had been denied from the outset. Scandal died hard. When these reports reached China indignation was renewed, but in March 1867 they already had enough to refute.

Word had come that before going on to Shanghai George Moule was drawing the Ningbo community into the upheaval. This was too much. The 'Sisters' of the *Lammermuir* party with the exception of Eliza Nicol and Jane McLean met together and drew up the declaration referred to, intending it for the Bergers and any others open to the truth. The moderation of their language masked the indignation they were feeling. Nicol they could cope with, within the Mission family, but attacks outside could only be answered publicly.

March 7/67

We, the members of the China Inland Mission, at Hangchau, – being aware that a missionary of this city has thought fit to write a letter, or letters, attacking the character and position of certain members of our Mission, and knowing that he has also intimated his intention, from a sense of duty, of following up this course by other and more public acts, – we desire to place on record our entire disapproval of such conduct, founded as it must be upon mistaken information, from whatever source obtained. The principles and distinctive features of our Mission were clearly defined in Mr Taylor's Pamphlet, and are clearly understood by most of our personal friends, and the friends of the Mission generally, both at home and in China. Our household arrangements are far more strict, and 'the restraint of social etiquette' more rigidly observed, than they would be at home; and in Mrs Taylor, (whose presence amongst us seems to have been ignored,) the lady members of our Mission have one to whom they can at all times look for sympathy and counsel . . .

Those steps having been taken professedly in our interests, more especially in that of the ladies, we feel called upon to state, that we have no sympathy with any movements made to assail Mr Taylor's character, which has ever been, throughout our intercourse with him, that of a gentleman, a Christian, and pre-eminently a Christian missionary. He has ever manifested a kind and considerate regard for our *best* interests, and our prayer to our Heavenly Father is, that we may be enabled to follow the example he has set, of a holy, consistent life, self-denying devotion, and untiring zeal in his Master's cause.
Signed
[*the copy on record lacks the names*][14]

The Mission's friends in Ningbo needed to know the background of the tales they were hearing. The damage done must be repaired if possible. Enclosing a copy of Moule's letter to Hudson Taylor, Emily wrote for him to E C Lord and his wife, the 'Mrs Bausum' who had stood so loyally by Hudson and Maria in attempts to prevent their marriage. Those experiences could now be seen as preparation for this fiercer onslaught.

Having learned [she said] that he had been strongly spoken against . . . to certain members of our own party, (Mr Taylor) with Mr Williamson, the senior member of the Mission [in Hangzhou] had an interview with each one of our number (except Messrs Rudland and Jackson who are away from Hangchau); and all, including Mr and Mrs Nicol and Mr Sell, positively affirmed that they knew of nothing in Mr. Taylor's conduct, either towards themselves or toward others, which was inconsistent with the character of a *gentleman*, a *Christian*, and a *minister* of the Gospel. [But Mr Moule had also said] that you (Mr. Lord) had expressed your entire disapproval of Mr Taylor's conduct in residing in the same house with so many unmarried ladies. . . . Mr Taylor (has) been informed by certain of the members themselves that Mr Moule *has* denounced him to them as 'a hypocrite', his faith 'a sham', his work 'a delusion', and this establishment 'scandalous'; and has advised some of our missionaries, both of the *Lammermuir* party and of those previously in China, to leave the Mission . . . It is painfully evident . . . that in taking his stand so decidedly by Mr. Taylor in the present difficulties, (Mr McCarthy) is incurring the dislike and jealousy of the disaffected . . .[15]

A few nights later Hudson Taylor himself wrote to Mr Lord, a letter ending, 'Please excuse all errors etc; it is 3.30 a.m. and I am very sleepy.' All around him and upstairs, as he wrote by the guttering light of an oil lamp, the household, Chinese and foreign, were asleep.

> (Mr Moule) stated that unless I was prepared to give up this (establishment itself) he would have no further communication with me on any matter whatsoever . . . He 'solemnly' urges me to consult with friends (on) 'the best method of putting a *speedy end* to the present organization' of 'my mission' . . . My work is a very peculiar [unique] one; in many respects it has, and *can have* no precedent. It may be called an experiment; to a certain extent it is so. And by God's help it shall be, as it is being, *faithfully* made. My work is the expression of public feeling too, to a considerable extent. God *has* greatly blessed it, and, I feel, assured, *will* do so. I have, as it were, to my friends and supporters pledged myself to a considerable extent to a certain course. Details may require modifying, and doubtless will be modified; but on the whole I am more satisfied than ever that *for our work* we are right in the main.

He emphasised the fact that he had no thought of prescribing Chinese clothes or women's work for other missions. This was his own and his Mission's experiment, proving successful so far. The progress being made by Jennie Faulding and some of the young women was promising.

> I have the testimony of large numbers of (Chinese) that our work appears *here* to the people unobjectionable . . . Officials and private citizens of this city have urged missionaries in English dress to imitate our example, and this in our absence.

E C Lord replied immediately, denying what had been said about him.

> The matter of your 'residing in the same house with so many unmarried ladies' had never been a subject of correspondence or conversation betwixt me and anyone . . . I knew the fact of course, but I had never thought of it in the light in which it is presented by Mr Moule.[16]

With twenty years' experience in China Mr Lord's reassurance encouraged Hudson Taylor.

More plain speaking[17]   *March 1867*

Nearer home, at Hangzhou, Lewis Nicol had not finished. Another note brought the complaint that his wife had received five dollars less than the other women when they reached China! On March 13 Hudson Taylor replied at length, still accepting Nicol's animosity without demanding a halt or his resignation. For nearly two years he was to work for his reformation. Groping for Nicol's meaning he dealt with point after point in a letter as revealing of his own personality as the matters in hand.

> And now you wish me to let you know of what I have to complain. It is a task which gives me no pleasure . . . I have to complain of your want of truthfulness, – often I believe unintentional . . . but yet, untruthfulness . . . persisted in after you have been corrected. I have to complain of your want of honest, open, straightforwardness, – of your jealous, proud self-confident spirit, which makes you a torment to yourself, and a source of sorrow to those around you; – of your perpetual fault-finding and grumbling about almost every one and everything . . . And finally of that spirit of insubordination which leads you to persist in your own way . . . Your difficulties are in yourself and not in your surroundings. These traits of character have caused troubles in Scotland, in England, on the *Lammermuir*, and here . . . I told you expressly and explicitly, in the presence of Mr Berger . . . that I should only feel bound to assist you so far as you acted in accordance with my directions . . . if you still wish me to feel myself *responsible* for affording you all assistance of every kind, I must in view of all that has passed, request you to give me in writing a statement of your intention to recognize me as placed by God at the head of this mission and to submit to my direction in its affairs . . .

If he must lead a team of novices he must have their loyalty. If he could save Lewis Nicol from himself and make a good missionary of him, he would. No one was bound to follow his direction unless of his own volition. As free agents they could go or stay. But if they stayed it must be to pull together. In this mission the leader lived as servant of the led, not as a dictator.

Repugnant as these administrative problems were, the end of March brought an emergency more harrowing to overcome.

CHAPTER TEN

PACT, NOT CONTRACT
1867

Skeleton in the cupboard[1]   *March 1867*

The consul at Ningbo, R J Forrest, had been doing all in his power towards a peaceful resolution of 'the Xiaoshan outrage'. The magistrate's superiors had been co-operative and the return of the Nicols to Xiaoshan was in sight. Even the drunken magistrate was to continue in office if he compensated Mr Tsiu, reinstated the missionaries and put out a proclamation in their favour. First, however, the consul wished to meet the Nicols, James Williamson and Mr Tsiu. On March 14 they set off for Ningbo, and on the 20th Hudson Taylor sent John Sell after them as he too insisted on wearing foreign clothes. Working with Stephan Barchet near the treaty port he could wear what he liked. His marriage to Jane McLean was planned for May 25, to take place at Ningbo.

Rumours of all kinds were commonplace, even at the most peaceful times, but recently anti-foreign rumours had intensified. Jennie's parents knew from the newspapers as much as or more about them than she did, and asked anxiously after her safety. 'On arriving we heard about (an inflammatory proclamation),' she replied, 'but I have never heard it mentioned since, so I suppose no one is any the worse for it.' A sure barometer of danger told Hudson Taylor that Hangzhou was caught up in the tension when attendance at his clinics dropped dramatically. Word had been put around that the city's druggists and practitioners of Chinese medicine were incensed by the foreign doctor's success, depriving them of trade.

With 'only 160-odd patients' on March 19, Hudson Taylor finished early, felt as if he were on holiday and took Maria for a walk up the hill of the city god, her first since they arrived. It had to be a Chinese walk, with Maria and an old serving woman following a few paces behind him and a manservant. What she saw was 'ruin, ruin, ruin,' and then the built-up part of the city, so vast and teeming with people that her heart sank. 'It was hopeless to expect to make a perceptible impression on Hangchow.' But they 'heard of a man living 24 miles from Ningpo, who some ten years ago received from a missionary part of the Bible and who without having any communication with missionaries or any Christian fellowship, has been setting apart a room in his house and there worshipping God with his children.' Hope revived.

In 1866 Ningbo and countryside had been agitated by rumours of kidnapping for the 'coolie trade'. Agents of foreign ships were said to prowl after dark 'with sacks which they suddenly threw over the heads of unsuspecting passers-by; the sack was drawn tight, the man gagged and carried perforce . . . to the sea. The rumour . . . extended with alarming rapidity. Foreigners were to be exterminated . . .'[2] On the insistence of the consuls, proclamations by the mandarins restored calm.

Now in Hangzhou each of the missions found that wild stories were being circulated about them. Kidnapping was again the theme of some. The Greens had had a rainwater tank built for them. They were said to have enticed women into their premises and drowned them in the tank. A man created a disturbance in their chapel. 'On Monday things began to look serious,' Jennie wrote to her father. 'Everyone was hearing that if they came here they would be poisoned by our medicine . . . It was said . . . that children were missing . . .' In Hudson Taylor's words,

> On Tuesday, 26th inst a (Chinese) friend, a subordinate in the (prefect's) *yamen*, came and told me that he believed these rumours were got up at the instigation of the Siaoshan (magistrate), in the hope that the (mandarins) finding very much trouble arising from the presence of foreigners in Hangchau, might be led to sympathize with him, and to admit that after all the Siaoshan (magistrate) was not so far wrong in endeavouring to get rid of foreigners. He assured me that unless prompt measures were taken some very serious outrage would occur . . .
>
> Very suddenly, a number of reports . . . as absurd as they are false were sedulously put into circulation, and gave rise to great excitement . . . A soldier . . . in a state of real or feigned intoxication, created a disturbance in front of (our) chapel and dispensary [at New Lane] throwing stones at and slightly wounding several poor people . . . and also throwing stones after my children, who were out with attendants . . .
>
> It was likewise reported, that at my own house we had cut out the kidneys of a girl, causing her death, at which the mother not being pleased [!] we soothed her spirit with a present of $20 and a feast. It

was also reported that we were poisoning patients at the dispensary. Against Mr Valentine [p 98] it was affirmed that on the 25th inst, he had killed and salted down seven children, whose bodies were to be found on his premises. Mr Green [pp 98, 213] was stated to have forced a woman upstairs into his house, and to have opened her bosom with a large knife, and sucked her blood out, 'after which she died' [!] and he buried her at the back of his house . . . The people declared that unless the authorities took vigorous action at once, they would take matters into their own hands. (Some) are reported to have banded themselves together, determined to kill at least one foreigner, in the hope of frightening the rest away.[3]

To his horror Hudson Taylor suddenly realised that in his baggage brought from Shanghai was a crate of anatomical specimens, human bones and demonstration models. He had brought them from London hoping to teach others as he had taught Wang Lae-djün at Coborn Street. Left with William Gamble until such time as it was safe to use them, the box had mistakenly been brought with the rest of the medical equipment and not sent back. This was dynamite. 'A mandarin might come at any time and with perfect right make minute search . . . to see if he could find any remains of the salted children or women of whom medicine was made for the foreign market. These human remains once seen, it would have been utterly useless to attempt explanation.'

Losing no time, Hudson Taylor asked Rudland and Duncan if they would take the box by boat to the safety of Ningbo. To be intercepted and made to open it could put them in grave danger. To keep it at Hangzhou or to be seen throwing it into the river or burying it could precipitate a murderous attack on all foreigners and Christians in the city. They agreed and set out.

But 'suspicion might be raised at our sending a large case away and reports about it go against us; it might be stopped at the city gate . . . At the same time that they left with the box, Mr Taylor in his dress of ceremony set off in a chair to go with Mr Green and Mr Valentine to call upon one of the higher mandarins. The very fact of showing that we were not afraid to go to the magistrates would go a long way to prove our innocence in the eyes of the people.'

Still the tension persisted. For part of the way a mandarin's underling travelled on Duncan's boat – but did not ask what his box contained.

A proclamation[4]   *April 1867*

Hudson Taylor had already called on his friend Jarvis Valentine of the CMS, replacing George Moule in Hangzhou, and on Mr Green. Carl Kreyer was away. Together they had agreed not to appeal to the mandarins unless the danger increased. But during the night the outer gate of No 1 was stoned, more stones came over the walls, and 'greater violence was used against (the Kreyers') house'. Friendly Chinese urged that they go at once to the city prefect and ask him to intervene before rioting began. So each with his Chinese 'teacher' went in a sedan to the official residence, the *yamen*. Valentine and Green were in foreign dress, but Hudson Taylor 'completed his attire as a Chinese gentleman in official costume', and rehearsed with Mr Tsiu the correct depth of bow and formal behaviour necessary in the official's presence. He wore 'a long blue silk robe, confined by a girdle round the waist, and over this, a short jacket of dark brown satin; black satin boots, and a cap with a very broad brim, red tassel, and a gilt button (the 'mark of literary distinction').

At the *yamen* the great man's subordinates kept them waiting for an hour, saying he was away, and then that he was too busy to see them. Not to gain an interview would quickly be known through the city. Such a snub would be taken as a signal to the agitators to do as they liked. So at last Mr Green said to Hudson Taylor deliberately in their hearing that they might as well go home, though it would be a pity to have to conduct their business so circuitously as through their consuls. That was enough. The mandarin was told and a message quickly came that he awaited them.

Instead of being taken to the formal judgment hall where only the mandarin would be seated and petitions were presented, they found themselves received by the prefect himself with full courtesies as guests. When they moved correctly towards the least honourable position on the right of the reception hall, he motioned them to the superior position on the left and himself took the lower place as host. With his retainers standing behind him and the missionaries' teachers behind them, he took his seat. For a moment there was silence. The foreigners were trying to remember what rank their host's blue cap button indicated. Was he in fact the prefect or the intendant, a *daotai*? (*See* Appendix 5) At that moment a waiter brought Hudson Taylor a ceremonial cup of tea and he asked surreptitiously, Is that the prefect? He was, a senior prefect.

Reassured, they presented their case, the danger to themselves, the women and children occasioned by the rumours. 'Pay no attention to those *xu-yan*, empty words!' the prefect said. 'Not *xu-yan* but *yao-yan*, provocative agitation,' they submitted. And they invited him to send representatives to inspect their premises and see what they were doing. He inquired about the clinic, approved of its being without charge to the poor, smiled at Mr Valentine's love of exercise on a horse and Green's preference for walking, advised them only to go by sedan chair after dark, and promised a proclamation in their favour. Then he personally escorted them to the courtyard where their sedan chairs were waiting – proof to the whole city that they were innocent, or they would have been afraid to meet him, and that they had his protection.

Nothing better could have been desired. The proclamation when it was made might have been more generous, but effectively silenced the rumour-mongers. Hudson Taylor informed the consul in some detail, saying all was well again, and the matter was left at that.[5] When people saw that danger had receded they began to talk, divulging the origins of the agitation. Four months later Jennie's home letter carried a postscript. By then the Muslim provincial governor, Ma Xinyi himself, had intervened.

> A proclamation has been issued for the whole of this province recognizing Christianity as one of the religions of the land, and forbidding rulers or people to persecute native Christians . . . The mandarin in Ningpo – or some say really the (Xiaoshan) mandarin – has sent Mr Nicol a very handsome present consisting of a silk umbrella, two ivory fans, twenty-two handkerchiefs, glasses, coffee cups and saucers, a teapot, cigars, etc; the mandarin of (Xiaoshan) has also sent some fruit as a peace offering . . .[6]

Consul Forrest replied to Hudson Taylor at length in a letter which must have influenced his thinking when greater violence occurred in other places in the coming months. Drawing important lessons from an incident in which James Meadows and George Crombie had intervened on behalf of a Christian arrested by a magistrate, the consul commented on the Hangzhou affair at some length.

Her Brittanic Majesty's Consulate,
Ningpo,
April 4, 1867

Sir,

. . . Your action in claiming the protection of the Hangchowfoo (prefect) was the correct course to pursue. Foreigners travelling in the interior have a perfect and legal right to claim legitimate local protection. In all cases where troubles arise recourse should be had at once to the mandarins as with them the ultimate responsibility in cases of disturbances rests, and if they are unacquainted with particulars they have always a loophole whereby to escape such responsibility. But it cannot be too strongly borne in mind that such local protection should only be demanded in real emergencies . . . Foreigners, especially missionaries, should always most carefully abstain from interfering between natives and their own authorities. . . . So that while claiming protection for themselves foreigners should never attempt to stand between a native and the authority of the Chinese officials . . .

With regard to the annoyances and rumours alluded to by you the best course is to treat them with indifference. For so long as we English live in China so long shall we have to bear the insults you complain of, and a rowdy Chinaman has his feelings doubly gratified when he finds that not only does he insult the foreigner but that the foreigner is hurt by the insults . . . Similar rumours to those mentioned by you have afforded me amusement for the last eight years. But a short time ago it was currently reported that we were all going to be killed at Ningpo, and that the 'braves' then actually in the city had been sent down to do the slaughtering. But few people were in the slightest degree disturbed by this report, and yet we are still alive! Such stories have always been, and always will be current; in your case I think the Prefect's proclamation will be sufficient protection . . . The further you go into China, the greater will be your difficulties, and it will be injurious to your enterprise if at starting you get involved with Mandarins. They are people whose existence you should as much as possible ignore, unless you have some good grievance. It will be better to endure ten years of rumours and pebbles thrown against your outer gates than to get a name with them as the giver of trouble.

I trust you will take it in good part, that the adoption by yourself and Mission of the Chinese dress is far more likely to be the cause of trouble than the source of advantage. The foreign dress is of itself a passport in China, and I shall never be astonished that both Mandarins and people view with suspicion persons who while assuming all the outward signs of Chinese citizenship still claim to belong to foreign countries . . .

I shall forward copy of this correspondence to Her Majesty's Minister . . .

P.S. Now that much alarm seems to be felt at Hangchow about the Nienfei my remarks about national costume deserve especial attention.[7]

Consul Forrest was entitled to his personal opinion, but was speaking out of turn about personal dress. He was writing from the point of view of most foreigners, from the standpoint of armed conquest and of confrontation with the Chinese instead of alignment with them, as preferred by the CIM. As for the main issue, the Hangzhou missionaries had appealed to the Chinese civil authorities for civil rights to which under the treaty of amity they were as entitled as any Chinese citizen. This, and Hudson Taylor's *report* to the consul, was a totally different situation from his earlier appeal to the consul after the 'Xiaoshan outrage'. It mattered little, for Consul Forrest was replaced not long afterwards.

On the day after the interview with the prefect, his private secretary visited New Lane 'unofficially' and Hudson Taylor showed him round, demonstrating the printing presses, the laundry mangle and a thermometer. They wished they had had Colonel Gordon's 'magnetic electric machine' or a 'galvanic battery' in Hangzhou, to display the wonders of modern science. The next day saw Nicol and Williamson back from Ningbo, and at the consul's request Nicol went straight to Xiaoshan to resume work. Peace was restored.

Jennie enclosed plans of the New Lane premises in her home letter, to set her parents' minds at rest about insinuations (p 247). And Maria wrote to Mrs Berger, 'What turn (Mr Nicol's) matters will take I cannot think . . . One thing I know, (the Lord) will not forsake us. One is tempted to ask "Why was Mr N permitted to come out?" Perhaps it was that our Mission might be thoroughly established on a right basis early in its history.' To his mother Hudson Taylor also enclosed a plan of the house. It would speak for itself. He closed the clinic for a fortnight, while the confidence of the people returned, and went with Williamson for two days' holiday in the hills.

Jennie wrote home cheerfully enough, 'The man who would have to give up his business if he became a Christian has determined to do so, and notwithstanding all our troubles, others have applied for membership so that now there are twelve on the list.' But an unnatural segregation from each other at New Lane had descended on their happy family life. For weeks she and Emily had seen as little as possible of Hudson Taylor and less than usual of Maria. The sensitive Emily wrote in her journal that she had been trying to cheer Jennie up 'in this hard time of restraint' but added, 'my own heart aching so unspeakably from the same cause'. At least she and Jennie had each other's friendship unchallenged.[8] With April and the departure of their critics they could at last relax and be more natural again. Except that at the height of the excitement word had come from Ningbo that Stephan Barchet had smallpox.

'This "onward and inward" mission'   April–June 1867

Eugene Stock, the remarkable historian of the Church Missionary Society, completed his encyclopaedic and highly readable volumes in 1899. As Editorial Secretary from December 1875 to December 1906 he had handled the records and reported events for thirty years. He wrote of great men and small, great movements and minor incidents as if an eye-witness of them all, as he was of many. At D L Moody's great meeting in the Agricultural Hall one evening in 1875 when fourteen thousand seats were filled, he said, 'I myself gave Mr Gladstone a seat.'[9] As an admirer of Hudson Taylor he returned again and again in his chronologically arranged history to this contemporary of his who became so influential. His chapter on 'China: New Missions and Old' (1862–72)[10] began with China 'bleeding at every pore' at the end of the Taiping rebellion, and continued as we have seen.

> The whole country was now open to missionary enterprise as never before . . . but the opportunity was not availed of. Certainly not by the . . . Church of England. 'Onward and inward' was the motto suggested by Mr (W A) Russell; and some little advance was made . . . But the Church at this time . . . totally neglected its duty to China . . . What did the CMS do? . . . at the end of 1872 it had fifteen men and (one) lady (in China) . . . But the period was not one of marked advance in the missions of the other leading societies. The American Missions were crippled by the terrible civil war in the United States in the earlier 'sixties; and the English Non-conformist Societies were feeling the general decadence of missionary zeal at home . . . The LMS, however, and the American Presbyterians and Methodists, did advance up the Yangtze to Hankow, Wuchang and Chinkiang, and also northward to Chefoo, Tientsin, and Peking. Yet

. . . of the eighteen great provinces of the empire, there were mission stations in only seven . . . [Outlining the origins of the China Inland Mission, Stock continued:] The occupation of the eleven then un-occupied provinces proved, of course, a task involving much faith and patience . . . But gradually, as more labourers appeared, nine of the provinces, including the remote western and north-western ones, were successfully entered; and many of the societies have since followed the example of this 'onward and inward' mission.[11]

In 1867 success was still years away. Both faith and patience were being taxed to their limits. Hudson Taylor's own evangelism and medical work were yielding results in spite of the obstruction and adversity he was encountering. A few of his colleagues were having comparable success but not to the same degree. The Bridge Street church under James Meadows' pastoral care was hardly growing in numbers, but in active spreading of the gospel and the training of evangelists it was laying a strong foundation for expansion in the years ahead – a fact of salient importance. The Crombies at Fenghua were plodding on, enjoying the fruits of the indefati-gable efforts of their outstanding Chinese colleagues, Fan Qiseng and his wife, rather than their own. The baptism of their first convert had been their great excitement in December 1866. Before that Anne Crombie could only report, 'We have nothing good to tell you of (Fenghua). We labour on from day to day, but it is like Gideon's fleece, unwatered still and dry.' Stephan Barchet at Ninggongqiao had a few Christians around him and was co-operating closely with the E C Lords. George Stott with stolid tenacity was disregarding his disability as if having only one leg made no difference. During the summer he wrote, in passing on to his real news,

I had a rather severe fall from my horse, which broke my collar-bone and gave me some internal injury. By the good hand of God upon me I am now almost recovered, but my arm is still weak, I cannot raise it to my head yet . . . [and continued] Some word I have been enabled to drop, has been blessed to a fine young man I have with me for servant. Rather more than a month ago, perhaps nearly two, I asked him quietly if he believed the doctrine of Jesus. At once he said, very emphatically, 'Yes, I do believe it' . . . After I was hurt, it was about a week before I enjoyed much sleep, and for three days and nights I was subject to fits of severe sickness; and all the time that poor fellow stood by me and watched me as tenderly as could be; at night he took his mat and lay down on the floor by the bedside. I had only to call his name and he was up at once. By his daily conduct, I am confirmed that his heart has undergone a change.[12]

John Stevenson at Shaoxing still had little to report. It took time to become known and trusted, let alone to make a strange doctrine intelligible and convincing enough to change the whole course of people's lives. Hudson Taylor was careful not to impose his leadership on any of these older missionaries, and certainly not his authority. He left them to work in their own way, following their own sense of God's guidance until they welcomed his help. Nor did he ask them to adopt Chinese dress. He preferred them to see its advantages and make their own decision. The members of his own *Lammermuir* team were different. They had agreed to come out to help him in his work and in his way, especially while they were little more than learners.

Lewis Nicol at Xiaoshan insisted on having the last word and had an uphill slog before him. If that was his attitude, he too could have his head. He returned to Xiaoshan defiantly as a foreigner to plough a lonely furrow. His foreignness and the consul's intervention to support him made him no new friends.

Hangzhou was the Mission's only other centre. Popularity had suffered a setback while the macabre rumours did their damage, but with time and patience all that would be forgotten and the crowds would return. The team all needed a holiday and made the most of the opportunity while visitors were few. A day on the lake with his shotgun far away from the crowds gave Hudson Taylor the change he liked best.

John McCarthy walked into the foothills north of the city and came home with news of a secluded derelict temple on a forested hill, high enough to be cooler and greener than the plains. A few habitable rooms remained in the care of a handful of priests. Only six miles away, it was the kind of retreat they needed. Hudson Taylor went out to see it, stayed over Sunday, found the accommodation ideal for a makeshift camping holiday and came back for half the household. 'Pengshan' became their holiday resort among the rhododendrons and camellias – with tragic memories. James Williamson, Mary Bowyer, Susan Barnes and the McLean sisters, Maria and the children, all embarked with their bedding and other essentials in canal boats, and Hudson Taylor took them to Pengshan and saw them established. Living and eating in Chinese style at home made adaptation simple.

Leaving Emily and Jennie in Hangzhou was part of an attempt to mollify those who resented their longer and closer friendship with the Taylors. Jennie's account read, '(They have) gone gipsying to what (we) call a fairy spot . . . in the midst of hills and flowers, where they can roam about at will . . . no small luxury in China.' Maria could be alone with Hudson and carry the game he bagged, free for a change from the obligatory presence of an attendant servant woman. To their delight they discovered at Pengshan a Christian tract pasted outside a cottage door. An old woman had been to their clinic, heard the gospel, believed and returned home to practise her faith alone. She had given up idol worship and told all her neighbours what she had learned.

But five locations in one province, worked by a few novices apart from Meadows and himself, was a far cry from the evangelisation of the whole empire. The goal of the puny CIM was no less than that. With a handful of Christian Chinese in four of them, and a congregation of any size (about sixty) only to be seen at Bridge Street, Ningbo, even the evangelisation of their own province of Zhejiang looked impossible within a lifetime. As for eighteen provinces and hundreds of millions of inhabitants, the concept was irrational. No wonder Jarvis Valentine had heard Hudson Taylor's detractor speak of him 'as being a person of no judgment whatever'.

Criticism and differences of opinion had to be expected. In a few years' time his team of beginners would be maturer men and women of experience, and trained Chinese Christians would, in the goodness of God, exceed them in numbers and effectiveness. He need look no further than five years ahead with the eyes of faith to see a geometric progression of believer upon believer carrying the gospel far afield. Beside them would go the Mission. But why five years? Nicol, Jackson and Sell might be losing out by wanting their own way, with Susan Barnes and the McLean sisters who shared their disaffection, but the rest were in marked contrast already.

One of the Chinese engaged by Maria as a laundryman, Jiang Aliang (Tsiang Ah-liang), had lived 'a wild and reckless life vitiated on board a French man-of-war'. Among the vices he had picked up was the ability to curse and blaspheme in French. When he gave vent to his feelings he was surprised to be rebuked by Louise Desgraz, and thought, 'There must be foreigners *and* foreigners! These people are different from any I have met before.' George Duncan had discovered that Aliang could read the Ningbo romanised vernacular and spent hours beside his washtub and ironing board trying to make himself understood while Aliang corrected his mistakes. Aliang was impressed. Why should this giant foreigner take so much trouble to learn the language simply to share his religion with the Chinese? There must be something real about his beliefs. Before long Aliang understood and himself believed. He sent for his brother Liangyong and the two of them in time became evangelists who played a key role in the progress of the CIM.

While the Taylors and Williamson were at Pengshan, and Duncan and Rudland still not back from escorting the 'skeleton' to Ningbo, John McCarthy 'took prayers' for the Chinese of the household. Jennie noted his rapid progress with pride and joy. She herself, in spite of hours spent on accounts and help to Emily and the Taylors, was engrossed in work among the Chinese women. Fu Guniang, 'Miss Happiness', was being invited into more and more homes, including their 'stout old landlord's and even some officials''. Her fluency and knowledge of Chinese customs increased accordingly. Soon mandarins' ladies were sending their sedan chairs for her. 'I have only to . . . pass along the streets, and houses are opened to me,' she wrote.[13] Friendliness was more powerful than any propaganda. Even the 'Hangzhou amah' and others whom she was teaching, and who accompanied her as attendants in the approved way, were catching her enthusiasm for talking about Jesus. Maria wrote to Mrs Berger, 'I believe that twenty sisters could easily find work in Hangchou tomorrow. I feel pretty sure I could find work for ten Miss Fauldings and ten Miss Bowyers . . .' As for Jennie's home letter,

> Oh! it is worth anything. It is such a joy to see the truth dawning on the minds of one after another . . . How shall I thank you enough for letting me come? It is a joy to me every day I am here . . . If only Mr T could be in three or four places at once . . . He is wanting to visit the Fu cities (prefectures) of this province to look out the most eligible places for stations. He and Mr Duncan have been on the point of starting several times . . . here he is just overwhelmed with work . . . yet he goes so quietly and calmly on always, just leaning upon God and living for others, that it is a blessing just to see his life, and Mrs Taylor too is so good . . .

Those excerpts were interspersed with day-to-day matters such as the intolerable itching of her hands and feet (from insect bites) and the nightly visits to her bedroom of two or three rats who had eaten her candles, flowers, stockings and atlas. Only her mosquito curtains deterred them from climbing over her as she slept. The change in the lives of the converted Chinese 'lodgers' was a joy to observe. The one who had given up his source of income from making idolatrous paper money had dug up a silver dollar in the garden. Instead of pocketing it he had handed it in – to be told he could keep it. When a man who had swallowed three times the lethal dose of opium was brought to Hudson Taylor for treatment, Jennie and Emily took turns right through the night, walking him up and down incessantly, giving him stimulants and slapping him to keep him awake and active. When Hudson Taylor urged them to go and get some sleep themselves Jennie would not, as long as he himself had to stay.

Maria had set up an 'Industrial School for Women' with two purposes. While the women worked, mostly at sewing, Maria talked and read to them, with the result that they became familiar with the gospels. Several were among the first to be baptised. When Maria's family commitments took her away, one and another of the team would take her place, reading from the romanised vernacular or simply listening and chatting with the women. They could not but absorb the language. For the women's final hour each day Jennie taught them to read for themselves. Typical of her diary comments was that for May 5, 'nice day with (the) women nearly all the time'.

The men were developing 'tea-shop evangelism', sitting among the Chinese men of leisure and sipping tea while they discussed anything under the sun. It taught them more than they could learn by other means, and opened up opportunities, when answering endless questions, to introduce the gospel. McCarthy and Duncan led the way in this.

Rudland was slower than the others at picking up the language. Seeing him becoming discouraged ('fearing that I was going to be an entire failure', Rudland wrote) Hudson Taylor had asked him as a mechanic to help Dengmiao, a bookbinder they had employed, to assemble the components of the main printing press and put it to work. To his surprise William Rudland found himself using Dengmiao's expressions and before long talking good colloquial Chinese.[14] He took over the supervision of all the printing and continued it successfully for four years. From printing the romanised form of several dialects he also became familiar with their variations, a useful skill when he himself came to render the New Testament into yet another. In order to print Scripture and tracts specifically for Hangzhou, Hudson Taylor, Green and Valentine agreed on a standard orthography and Rudland set to work, initially printing a primer for the CMS. A year later Hudson Taylor reported 'several works are in the press'. For Rudland May ended happily with his engagement to Mary Bell.

May 7 saw the first baptisms at Hangzhou of four men and two women, including Dengmiao the printer and Ling Zhumou, an assistant cook. On June 2 three more men were baptised, none of them employees of the Mission. They had nothing else to gain from association with the foreigners. On July 21 two of Jennie's women and another man brought the number to twelve. Six or eight more were preparing to follow their example. Moreover, each of the baptised ones was 'showing concern to spread the Gospel'. The time had come to bring them together in the form of a local church, independent of the missionaries.

In Ningbo the Taylors' friend Wang Lae-djün had ended his period of service with the United Methodist Free Church. 'Please God, give him back to Mr Taylor,' Emily wrote in her diary. He was once again free to renew the links which had begun with his conversion at Bridge Street and continued through the years 1860 –64 in London at Beaumont Street and Coborn Street. On July 12 he arrived at Hangzhou and was introduced to the new Christians. Then on the 16th he was appointed pastor of their little church. He continued as such for many years.

When the subject was first mooted he had intended leaving his wife at Ningbo 'on account of her irascible temper', and probably started without her. But by the end of the year Hudson Taylor was writing to his mother, 'He gives us much joy – and what is more, his wife works as hard as he does in the Gospel.' This was what Wang Lae-djün had asked William Pennefather's conference at Barnet to pray for, and he recognised the change in her as an answer to those prayers. In Mrs Wang, Maria and Jennie had acquired a colleague and teacher without price. By then they had bought land to build a chapel, as the one in No 1 New Lane was too small for the scores who wished to attend.

All this was happening in Hangzhou during the Nicol rumpus. And as so often, in spite of encouragements Hudson Taylor's health suffered from the emotional strain and extremes of different kinds following one upon the other – accusations, danger, popularity and success. Maria told the Bergers that whenever trials pressed most heavily on him his 'enteritis' tended to cripple him. But he was also trying to advance into the province. After an 'exploratory journey a little way inland' with Duncan late in April, as Maria expressed it, he was planning to go out again in another direction the next week. They had travelled as far as Huzhou, visiting and preaching in two other walled cities and eight unwalled towns and villages. 'We want if we can to begin to plant out,' Maria continued. 'And I'm thankful for any step taken inland. We want to be a China Inland Mission; although I suppose we must for the present be content to take short steps.'[15]

Shocks for the dissidents[16]   *April–May 1867*

Stephan Barchet was recovering from smallpox, but danger lay in the contagion that might be passed on by almost any object he had handled. There had been a good deal of coming and going between Ningbo and Shaoxing where Josiah Jackson and Rudland were at the time with the Stevensons. Both had visited Hangzhou in April and John Sell had travelled with Jackson. At the end of April Sell arrived at Hangzhou with the foreign mail to escort his fiancée Jane McLean and her bridesmaids, Margaret her twin and Susan Barnes, to Ningbo for the wedding. The consul required a month's residence there. The girls stayed with Mrs Lord and Sell with John Mara.

On May 14 Jennie heard that 'Mr Sell has had smallpox . . . very lightly and is getting better.' Stephan Barchet was nursing him. The marriage had had to be deferred. On the 18th Sell was dressing himself although 'still very, very weak', getting ready to move over to Stephan's place. He 'seems to have burst a blood vessel, and in about two hours' time he fell asleep' – dead. A massive haemoptysis (coughing blood) was the end, but it explained his so-called chronic 'bronchitis'. All the time he had had an undetected tuberculous cavity in his lung – another threatened member of the team. Jackson was the next to go down with smallpox. The news reached Hangzhou four days after Sell's funeral. Jackson recovered, but other cases occurred.

John Sell had often taken sides against Hudson Taylor, but on the day Mr Moule left China he had written to Mr Berger, 'I trust every difference between some of our party and Mr Taylor is come to an end now, and that we shall all work in peace and love together.' Hudson Taylor wrote kindly of him, emphasising the good work he had done among the crew of the *Lammermuir*, and ending, 'His end was peace. The providence of God which removed him so soon after his arrival in China, from a sphere where labourers are so much needed, seems mysterious . . . But to us who remain, his death speaks loudly and solemnly, urging us to work while it is day . . .' He was not wasting time on clichés. He had seen too many deaths and meant every word. If he was to lead the way inland the time had come to begin. Wang Lae-djün and John McCarthy could hold the fort at Hangzhou without him. James Meadows had his hands full at Ningbo. He himself must lead the way. He planned to go up the Qiantang river and deep into the south-western area of the province, to assess the possibilities and if possible to occupy two prefectures without more delay.

John Sell's death was not the only major trouble in May. It happened during an episode more painful than any so far in Lewis Nicol's challenge to Hudson Taylor's leadership. On April 19 Hudson Taylor wrote to tell Nicol that he had heard from the consul, who had referred the matter of the 'Xiaoshan outrage' to Sir Rutherford Alcock sending copies of the correspondence. Hudson Taylor had written to Nicol asking for clarification of certain points, had read it to him in Williamson's presence and put it into Nicol's hand. But he had received no reply. 'Further complications at Siaosan might occur at any time, and this renders it the more desirable that you should, as soon as possible, definitely decide on the position you mean to take and should inform me of it without loss of time.' Was he going to resign and withdraw to one of the ports, or remain in the CIM under Hudson Taylor? This time Nicol replied at once, but to say, 'It would take more time than I have to spare' to answer the first letter. On May 3, however, Nicol wrote for advice about the rent and asked 'whether I am to be here permanently or not'. It was impossible to know how long the Mission would continue at Xiaoshan, Hudson Taylor replied. He left it for Nicol to realise that an international incident had developed and his own future was in doubt. But Nicol wrote again asking Hudson Taylor to come to Xiaoshan, 'as I wish to talk with you of some things as well as see about the house'. His new landlord wanted it back – on the ground that his son was soon to be married. Did this mean that he regretted having become involved with the foreigner?

Nicol's letter was rude. What could be done? Hudson Taylor and Maria decided that only a confrontation in the presence of others could have the desired effect. But things could go badly wrong. They told the New Lane family and all agreed to fast and pray together about it the next morning, May 10. Then at eleven a m they met 'for the purpose of humbling ourselves before God and seeking

His blessing'. Hardly had they finished than they learned that Nicol himself had arrived unbidden from Xiaoshan. 'We took this as an answer from God.' Nicol joined them in the living room upstairs and aired his latest grievances. Emily as secretary took notes throughout the interview, a confusion of self-contradictions. In telling Mrs Berger a week later, Maria said: 'What is very sad about him is that when compelled to admit that statements he has made were not true, he manifests no compunction and yet as positively as ever makes other statements which to all around him appear equally incorrect.'

In the presence of his peers who knew what he had said and done in Hudson Taylor's absence, Lewis Nicol was unable to hold his own, and finally agreed to sign a statement embodying the real facts. Again it would all have been too sordid and petty to be given space in the records, if it did not throw light on how Hudson Taylor acted in such circumstances. He had prepared his own statement of the principles they had all accepted before leaving Britain. Those present in Hangzhou on May 10 confirmed its accuracy, and in their presence Hudson Taylor and Lewis Nicol appended their signatures.[17]

Even now they respected William Berger's preference for having no document which all members of the Mission had to sign, believing that no document would bind contumacious or frightened men or women. The new mission must be a 'family', united by love and mutual confidence in all circumstances or it would fail. That the CIM became such a family, and has thrived as one for well over a century, is due to this principle. However, since 1885 the act of signing the *Principles and Practice* has helped waverers to adhere to the agreement they shared on entering the Mission. As the fore-runner of that future *Principles and Practice of the China Inland Mission*, this declaration of May 10, 1867, is historic. (*See* Appendix 6) As a pact between like-minded men and women still in the refiner's fire, it was then the flux that would separate true from false.

Positive matters having been dealt with, it only remained for Nicol to retract in writing the more contentiously false statements he had made to others. He composed it himself a few days later when Hudson Taylor and John McCarthy went to Xiaoshan to see the Nicols' landlord. With the proper courtesies shown to him the gentleman agreed to let Nicol retain the house until a suitable replacement was found.

That was the day John Sell died. Soon afterwards Josiah Jackson fell ill with smallpox. Both Nicol and Jackson were shaken and mellowed by the experience. Jackson wrote to Nicol, 'I have fully made up my mind not to have anything more to do with these unhappy affairs, moreover I believe them to be most wicked and opposed to the teaching of Scripture. I therefore give you clearly to understand that I decline to answer any further communication from you or anyone else . . .' Lewis Nicol replied, 'I want to drop these things. I wish they had never been. Therefore I would say with you, bury them for ever from our sight, and let us live in unity as brethren . . . May God stay His hand now . . .'

For some months they tried to be conciliatory but remained in frock coat and cravat. After her parents had become privy to the allegations, and the difficulties the Bergers faced in answering them without the facts from Hangzhou, Jennie wrote, 'Mr Nicol . . . has been a great trouble to Mr Taylor and done much to injure the Mission, still Mr T thinks he may be useful among the Chinese . . . Mrs Nicol is an earnest, good woman but wholly led by him.' At the end of May she added that the Minister, Sir Rutherford Alcock, was himself coming to Ningbo to look into the Xiaoshan affair.

Early in June an anxious Lewis Nicol came saying Eliza was ill. Hudson Taylor returned to Xiaoshan with him. So began his supervision of her pregnancy, occupying many journeys to and from Xiaoshan, for Maria as well, as if there had been nothing between them. He found another house for them and leased it for ten years on most favourable terms. Reporting this to William Berger, he saw it as a step of faith, that Nicol would reform his ways, and that no opposition would drive him out. Jennie said to her parents in June,

> I am so glad of your sympathy for Mr Taylor. I feel I have known him under all kinds of circumstances . . . If you could see him daily, you would indeed admire his self-forgetfulness, his humility, and quiet, never-flagging earnestness. Very few in his place would have shown the forbearing, loving spirit that he has done . . . No one knows how much he felt our troubles . . . Grace, not natural temperament, supported him.

It was well that this was so. His testing had scarcely begun.

Repercussions in London *April–May 1867*

Contrition in the face of smallpox and death came none too soon. Little did the blacksmith Lewis Nicol know what anvil blows were falling from his mindless lies and insinuations in Hangzhou. Taken at face value they were being passed on from one to another in Ningbo, Shanghai, Hong Kong and Britain. Trivia about socks and vermin mattered little. They were discounted. But the serious allegations were relayed and their echoes reverberated wildly, coming back on the Bergers' and Taylors' heads. Until Maria's factual letter reached them, William and Mary Berger could only answer the criticisms in George Moule's letters, and questions from others he had informed, from their own unshakeable loyalty and faith in Hudson and Maria Taylor, and from the plans of the Hangzhou house which Emily had sent them before trouble erupted. They, the Goughs and William Pennefather, the first to be involved, had been unmoved by overt statements or hints at dark doings in the Taylor camp. George Müller, the Howards, Lord Radstock and his family were equally unshaken. But when accusations reached Henry Venn, the illustrious general secretary of the CMS, Captain Fishbourne and Robert Baxter, the constitutional lawyer, who knew Hudson Taylor less well, they were credited with truth and stirred up such strong feelings that they endangered the existence of the CIM.[18]

William Berger's indignation led him to arrange an interview with George Moule after his arrival in London, and Henry Venn agreed to a meeting in his company at Church Mission House in Salisbury Square with Frederick Gough also present. The plan of the Hangzhou house, the declaration by the women of the CIM (p 295) and many letters had reached Britain a month before. But George Moule's 'strictures' against Hudson Taylor and his refusal to concede the possibility of misunderstanding of the Hangzhou situation, were too much for Mr Berger. By his own admission and in the opinion of the conciliatory Gough he spoke his mind too strongly and Henry Venn abruptly closed the consultation. 'I confess I did feel righteously indignant at such an attack being made upon you,' William Berger wrote.

A year later, however, when the whole truth was known but the old criticisms were still being circulated, Hudson Taylor's staunch friends were able to deny them factually. George Moule himself then came under criticism and appealed to Henry Venn for support.

His vindication came in the only document so far discovered giving his side of the story:

9 April 1868

My dear Mr Moule,

You tell me that Capn Fishbourne and other friends of Chinese Evangelization have heard charges brought against you of prejudice or jealousy in the remonstrances you have made against the proceedings of Mr J H Taylor in China. You add that I am cited as disapproving your conduct in this respect.

I am most happy that you have given me the opportunity of contradicting so false a report of my sentiments on this subject. You mentioned the case to me when you first returned to England. Afterwards you had a long conference with Mr Berger in my presence at the Ch. Miss. House, and I have since from time to time heard from other Chinese friends of Mr Taylor's proceedings in his mission and of your sentiments concerning him.

I have no hesitation in saying that from first to last I have never heard you speak any otherwise than as a Christian brother of a brother missionary – giving Mr Taylor full credit for his zeal for Christ's glory and his self-devotedness to the cause of China's evangelization. But you thought him so injudicious as to run the risk of injuring the cause he desired to advance.

In the interview with Mr Berger I took upon myself to close the conference because I saw that your motives were mistaken and your strictures though made in a most Christian and brotherly spirit were treated as the accusations of an opponent. I stated this conviction in the conference as my apology for abruptly terminating it.

I trust you will make any use of this letter which may counteract the notion that I am one of those who suspect you of unworthy motives or unbecoming conduct towards Mr Taylor.

Believe me
My dear Mr Moule
very sincerely & aff(ectionately) yours
Henry Venn
Secretary[19]

Rev G E Moule

By the time that letter was written more fuel had been added to the flames in a personal report to Robert Baxter by his cousin C R Alford, the new bishop of Victoria, Hong Kong, whose inquiries in China unwittingly resulted in a recognisable repetition of Moule's own statements, almost point by point.

The 'explosion' *May 1867*

In May, 1867, the *North China Daily News* published a despatch from Ningbo alleging that the CIM had 'exploded'. William Gamble in Shanghai responded instantly, and as soon as they received their copies of the paper both D D Green of Hangzhou and Hudson Taylor wrote warmly refuting the charge.

Hangchau,
May 24th 1867

To the Editor of the
North China Daily News.

Sir,

On receiving last night your issue of the 17th Inst., I was much surprised to see a paragraph headed "Ningpo" so utterly untrue that I feel compelled to request you to contradict its statements. The party which came out in the "Lammermuir" has not "exploded", the ladies have "rebelled" against no "edicts". Three ladies, two of whom came out in the "Lammermuir", left Hangchau for Ningpo a little more than three weeks ago, not on account of any change in their plans or purposes, not on account of any "explosion" or dissatisfaction, but simply under the following circumstances. One of them was to have been married in Ningpo on the 25th Inst. to a member of the Mission, who subsequent to their arrival there was taken ill with smallpox, which suddenly terminated fatally on the 18th Inst. The other ladies were accepting an invitation to stay in Ningpo until after the expected marriage should take place.

It is only necessary to add further, that so far from the unfavourable notice of the Chinese having been drawn down on the mission by our wearing the Chinese costume, the very reverse is the case. Not only have numbers of private citizens manifested their appreciation of the course we are adopting but not less than six of the leading Civil and Military Authorities of this city have expressed their appreciation of our mode of procedure.

As your paper is read by not a few of the friends of this Mission, may I beg the insertion of this letter in an early issue?

I remain, Sir,
Your obedient Servant,
J Hudson Taylor,
MRCS, FRGS[20]

Gamble's nudge[21]   *June 1867*

Within a few days Mr Gamble himself arrived, to stay with the Greens of his own American Presbyterian Mission and to visit the *Lammermuir* party. He had written on May 7 to comfort Hudson Taylor but did not mince matters. 'I believe you have many friends in your work . . . among missionaries of other Societies, so you must not be discouraged by the fault-finding in your immediate neighbourhood, and I question whether these would have had scarcely an existence had it not been for the folly and discontent of some of your own people.' On the day of William Gamble's visit, May 30, Hudson Taylor had written to Mr Berger,

> More than a year has elapsed since we parted on the deck of the *Lammermuir* . . . Burdens such as I never before sustained, responsibilities such as I had not hitherto ever incurred, and sorrows compared with which all my past ones were light, have been part of my experience. But I trust I have learned . . . more of the blessed truth that – 'Sufficient is His arm alone, and our defence is sure.' I have long felt that our Mission has a baptism to be baptized with; it may not be passed yet. It may be heavier than we can foresee; but if by grace we are kept faithful, in the end all will be well.

On June 17 Gamble followed his thanks for an enjoyable visit by offering his advice. 'I hope you will not delay any longer to find fields of labour for each of the gentlemen of your party. This is now the most important matter connected with your Mission. Medicine and printing and everything else is of minor importance. I was pleased with Jackson's spirit. I see he is very anxious to find his field . . .' How true. But to those who really knew him, of all men how unready. His grasp of Chinese was still inadequate, and his understanding of the people no better. However, Hudson Taylor had already concluded that Jackson must be given rein and had written to him on June 12 – in the circumstances a remarkable letter, wholly forgiving and treating him as the mature missionary he hoped Jackson would become (p 340).

William Gamble went on to say that he had heard from Mr Berger, 'He says he intends sending out no more ladies for the present, a good thing. I fear those at Ningpo have their heads turned – they won't put on the native dress again at any rate.' He did not know that Hudson Taylor himself had asked the Bergers not to send more women for the present. As for Chinese dress, both

Susan Barnes and Margaret McLean eventually returned to it.

But Gamble had heard from young Chauncey Goodrich, a new colleague of the veteran Mrs Bridgman and Henry Blodget of the American Board in Peking. There in the imperial capital he had taken to wearing formal Chinese dress, and hearing of Hudson Taylor's party had been a cheer to him. 'It is pleasant and gratifying,' he wrote, 'to find that *some* approve . . . Since I made the change (16 mos. ago) I have spent nearly one third of the time travelling and preaching and the dress has certainly been a *comfort*, to say nothing of its use in giving me a nearness of access to the people.'[22] 'This is the spirit,' Gamble continued. 'Go intward [*sic*], keep off the sea coast,' adding that 'Johnston', Alexander Wylie's intrepid colporteur, could give him more information than anyone else about the places he might wish to occupy. (Wylie employed five Europeans as colporteurs. One, referred to in the *Chinese Recorder* as 'Johnson', failed to return from a journey into the interior and was presumed killed. By 1875 only one was left. The rest had been invalided home.)[23]

When Gamble's letter reached Hangzhou, McCarthy, Duncan, Hudson Taylor, Mr Tsiu and two other Chinese companions were already reconnoitring south-westwards and at their first objective, the prefecture of Yanzhou up the Qiantang river.

CHAPTER ELEVEN

DEPLOY!
1867

The Qiantang river[1]   *June–July 1867*

If the complications of life at Hangzhou had not been so many, Hudson Taylor and Mr Tsiu would have been up and away into the surrounding prefectures long ago. Seven months had slipped by and the best travelling season been lost. June and July could be the hottest and wettest months of the year. An exhausting overland journey on foot was out of the question in this season. Travelling by boat was another matter. A minimum of bedding and baggage was needed, and a minimum of exertion.

From Hangzhou as their base they had the choice of six directions (map, p 237). North-eastwards lay the extensive region well reconnoitred by Shanghai missionaries of several missions and by none more than Hudson Taylor himself. (*See* Books 2 and 3) Already Jiaxing and Tangqi had demonstrated the difficulty of renting premises in places often visited by silk and tea merchants and sportsmen from Shanghai. And other missions spoke of occupying them.

Northward, up the Grand Canal lay the great lake, Tai Hu, and its southern city Huzhou (now Wuxing), defiantly anti-foreign. Beckoning the bold, farther north the old battlefields of the Ever-Victorious Army offered city after city still unoccupied by Christians, but more naturally an area of expansion from Shanghai. William Muirhead still had his eyes on Suzhou. Long ago he would have followed up his and Griffith John's reconnaissances if the LMS had been able to send him reinforcements. Colonel Gordon's one-time officer of the Ever-Victorious Army, Charles Schmidt, converted at Ningbo through the zeal of James Meadows, was making Suzhou (where he had fought) his mission field. The mandarins had received him with great respect and honoured him as a former ally. He had formed some links with the American Presbyterian Mission. Beyond Suzhou the Grand Canal led on to the Yangzi, to Zhenjiang (Chinkiang), Nanjing and Yangzhou, gateways to remotest inland China.

South-eastwards towards Ningbo, John Stevenson was already established at Shaoxing. His natural area of influence was eastward to Shangyu and southward to Zhuji, Sheng Xian and Xinchang. The CMS had opened two adjoining outstations at Cixi and Sanbo, and when additions to their team permitted would return to John Burdon's old stamping ground of Yuyao and Shaoxing (see Book 3, Index). In 1867 they had more than enough to do already. The other missions in Ningbo and Hangzhou had no plans to extend beyond their immediate locality. An American Baptist outpost at Jinhua, where a Chinese evangelist had responded to the call of a local 'inquirer', was too remote to be satisfactorily maintained and Hudson Taylor's good friend Miles Knowlton invited him to put missionaries there.

Consequently, south of Ningbo lay the whole of Zhejiang province as virtually virgin territory crying out (to the pioneers' perception) to be explored and occupied. Thirty miles south of Ningbo, the Crombies had been a year at Fenghua. Fifty to a hundred miles still farther south the cities of Ninghai and Tiantai presented the next goals. The route made the difference, for the Tiantai mountains blocked the way. But nearer the coast and more accessible by sea were the cities of Taizhou (now Linhai) and Wenzhou, each with their hinterland of subsidiary cities, towns and myriad villages.

James Meadows agreed to accompany (in effect to take) Josiah Jackson to Taizhou and get him and a Ningbo Christian established there. Meanwhile Hudson Taylor would do the same with John McCarthy and George Duncan in the south-western region, the drainage area of the Qiantang complex of rivers. Then Meadows and Hudson Taylor would together cross the provincial borders into Jiangxi and Anhui to their west, 'to see how the land lies', on an exploratory journey of the type only fluent, experienced men should undertake.

The Qiantang region of rivers, lakes and mountains south-west of Hangzhou was therefore the goal of the reconnaissance begun on June 12, 1867. Hudson Taylor and Mr Tsiu, John McCarthy and George Duncan, Ling Zhumou the recently converted cook and another employee Feng Aseng made up the party. If tolerable accommodation could be found, McCarthy and Duncan, each with a servant companion, would be left in occupation to learn the local dialect and do what spreading of the gospel they could.

No roads fit for wheels existed. Rivers and canals honeycombed the plains and were used extensively. Where none existed, narrow centuries-old tracks paved with granite slabs, ideal for rapid travel on foot and by sedan chair, made light of hill and valley. In the hilly terrain even river travel suffered limitations. Stronger currents hindered the use of sail and sweep. Tracking became necessary – the laborious towing upstream of junks small and large by teams of highly experienced but often opium-besotted men. Rapids were negotiated by the subtle use of back-eddies and split-second timing, by men who knew each rock, contour and water-level from childhood to old age. Such knowledge was available over a score or two of miles but no farther. A boat and crew from Hangzhou could only ply as far as Fuyang. From Fuyang to Tonglu a smaller boat and local men were needed. Higher upstream only men with detailed knowledge of the rapids could survive.

The name Qiantang strictly applies to the broad expanses of river at and below Hangzhou city.[2] Two hundred miles away half a dozen tributaries with individual names led like spokes of a wheel from surrounding mountain ranges to the main stream flowing from Qu Xian to Lanxi (map, p 237). Any city on these waterways was important. Lanxi at the confluence of major streams was naturally the commercial hub. The importance of Qu Xian, Jinhua and Yanzhou was political. All looked to Hangzhou where the provincial governor ruled, second only to the viceroy.

Hudson Taylor's strategy of working from the major cities into the countryside, from the lap of the civil government to the subordinate region, combined two elements. They must prove by experience, first, that the foreign missionaries could move and preach at will in this part of China; and second, that living quietly in the major cities of their choice they could be as safe and welcome as at Hangzhou. That choice was paramount. Unknown factors could not be weighed. They depended on God to guide them. Therefore when all was ready for the journey to begin, all the Hangzhou team met for half a day to submit themselves to God and pray with fasting for receptive minds, before boarding the river boat. Only a year and two weeks ago they had prayed and gone aboard the *Lammermuir* in the London docks.

For the first forty miles, to Fuyang, they had the advantage of the forward area of the regular 'passage boat' or ferry to themselves. A flat-bottomed sailing junk of seventy or eighty tons with a continuous 'deck' of planks roofed over by arched bamboo matting, it glided upstream by night to Fuyang and down again by day. Passengers of every kind packed into it and through long experience bore with discomfort stoically. Before the mast, just enough space for the six missionaries allowed some to sleep while others sat crosslegged, waiting for their turn. All through the night their fellow-travellers, 'some lying, some sitting, some eating, and some smoking', kept up a constant babble of voices. A boat to themselves, hired at far greater cost, would have allowed more comfort, but Duncan and McCarthy needed to learn the ropes of rural travelling.

When day broke the wind had dropped and with first light they saw their team of eight or ten 'trackers' on the towpath, bent almost to the ground, towing them against the current. 'I have seldom had such good accommodation in a passage-boat as we had last night,' Hudson Taylor wrote to the Bergers, 'four out of the six of us having room to lie down at night. I don't know how it is, but the boards seem to me to grow harder than they ever were. However, I can pass a night very contentedly, if not always very comfortably; and if I never fare worse it will be long before I complain of the "hardships of missionary life".' And to his mother,

> The first beginning of any work, anywhere, is more or less difficult. Here it is peculiarly so. But when some of our new stations have become established, when some of the still inexperienced junior members of the mission have made such progress as to enable them not merely to stand alone, needing only general guidance and direction, but also each one to give shelter to one or more young men on their arrival, or soon after such arrival – then our progress will be comparatively rapid. But while so much devolves upon me, we must be content with such an amount of progress as is within our reach.

They sang a hymn together, to the amazement of their fellow-passengers, and having caught their attention Hudson Taylor held it as he preached the gospel to them. Mr Tsiu had travelled with missionaries before, and knew Hudson Taylor's custom. To Aseng, Zhumou, Duncan and McCarthy this demonstration set the pattern for each day of the weeks they were together, and for their own future as evangelists.

At devastated, blackened Fuyang they trekked through the partly rebuilt streets to the anchorage of the next passage-boat to Tonglu, and sat huddled in it, deafened by thunder and torrential rain. Later the boat filled up with passengers but could not leave while the storm lasted. An uncomfortable night at very close quarters with 'some strange bed-fellows', gave John McCarthy grist for his journal. 'Next Mr Duncan lay a poor unfortunate with chains around his legs, who was being conveyed from the province of Honan down to the southern extremity of this province for banishment – it appears he had been an accomplice in a murder, and his sentence of capital punishment had been commuted to banishment. Opposite him were a couple of opium smokers, who, as soon as everyone else had settled down to rest for the night, had their lamps out, and after settling themselves in a comfortable position, indulged their depraved appetite. At the other side, and packed very closely, were five or six mandarins' servants with a few soldiers and other people . . .' In the morning, after a night using books wrapped in clothing as his pillow, Hudson Taylor preached the gospel to them too.

Tonglu was as derelict as Fuyang. Less than five hundred families remained of the five thousand before the Taiping rebellion. The rest had mostly been put to the sword. In that setting of surrounding hills 'magnificent beyond my power of description', 'the vileness of man and their need of Christ' came home to the younger men. They sold Scripture and books in the town and preached at a temple and pagoda. The idols had failed when the people cried to them, their audience agreed. 'What you say is true,' said the priest, 'but if we gave up the false we would not be able to repair our temple.' Someone recognised Hudson Taylor from having heard him preach years ago at Ningbo. Slowly the gospel was permeating the country. Their Chinese companions arranged with a boatman for them to sleep in his boat and go on to Yanzhou the next day, but the heavens opened again, the river rose dangerously, with 'a furious current', and floods swept through the town. Nothing could be done but to sit and wait. They found a crowded tea shop on higher ground to shelter in and 'gossip the gospel' with attentive customers.

One of them, a Nanjing man, found his way to their boat in the evening. He too was making for Yanzhou. Earning his living as a travelling 'doctor', this Mr Yu seemed so affable and informative about the route and cities ahead that they asked him to join them on the boat. And as they went Hudson Taylor invited him to come to Hangzhou as Mandarin language teacher. He seemed ready to agree. When the boat moored somewhere for the trackers to rest and smoke their opium an expedition to buy food broke the monotony. McCarthy described their appearance. 'First came Mr Duncan, with his shaved head protected by a white straw hat of considerable dimensions, covering head and shoulders, in one hand a palm-leaf fan, and in the other a live cock hanging by the legs, which we had secured for dinner. Next came Mr Taylor with other purchases under his arms, and the same head-gear, followed by myself with one thousand cash – the change of a dollar – slung round my neck. Our gowns had once been white, but alas! a week's wear in a boat had changed their colour considerably . . . We have had abundant evidence . . . of the immense advantage of wearing the dress of this people. Not only have we heard repeatedly their own opinions expressed favourably on the subject, but our own observation offers continual proof that . . . its adoption does create, notwithstanding all that may be said to the contrary, a feeling of confidence in the minds of the people.'

At Yanzhou[3] the innkeeper told them that Mr Yu was a local constable. 'That explains why he has kept us such close company,' they thought – his way of keeping them under scrutiny. They were wrong. The landlord merely had a sense of humour. Mr Yu set off for Hangzhou with a letter to Maria. 'Use Mr Yu as a teacher but be on your guard.' In the event Mr Yu stayed with them at Hangzhou for some years.

While Aseng returned to New Lane to see that all was well, they preached and sold books for days on end at Yanzhou to friendly people. A mandarin whose little daughter Hudson Taylor had treated at Hangzhou learned that he was passing through and sent her to him again with an invitation to visit him when he took up a new post as magistrate in another city. A boisterous drunkard tried to provoke a riot but was foiled and later forced by the authorities to apologise. They had left home with whooping cough in the house, a constant anxiety during the month they had been away, and ten days had passed without news of their families. West's *Diseases of Children* was there at No 1 for reference, Hudson Taylor reminded Maria, but medical knowledge was not their refuge. 'I could full well trust you in Mr Berger's care; may I not fully do so in our Father's?' Then Aseng came back with Dengmiao and the news that all was well at home.

Intending to leave John McCarthy and Aseng for a month or more at Yanzhou, they engaged a teacher of the local dialect and rented good rooms in his friend's house. The population of Yanzhou had been so decimated that few native people remained. Almost all were mandarin-speaking immigrants from other provinces. Then Hudson Taylor and the others went on in 'a fine boat with good boatmen' to the busy commercial city of Lanxi, the key to Jinhua and Qu Xian. But there they searched in vain for even a room to stay in.

The five of them were resting in an 'eating-house' – Hudson Taylor, Mr Tsiu, Zhumou and Dengmiao all talking in the Ningbo dialect – when a man came over and greeted them. A Ningbo man himself, far from home, he looked on them as friends. They asked if he knew where they could stay and he left them while they had their meal. Before they had finished he was back. They could use a friend's loft, reached by a ladder. It was all they needed 'but in such a state! Dust lay in royal profusion on every hand, broken bedsteads, old oars of boats, baskets of rags and rubbish, bamboo matting, boat-covers, firewood, charcoal, etc, etc, etc, lay in the most indiscriminate profusion. Such a scene of sweeping and dusting followed; turning out and arranging etc, but at last we got the room into occupyable condition, had our bedding and mosquito curtains arranged, and began to feel in something like order.' Here at Lanxi too they preached, sometimes Mr Tsiu and Hudson Taylor to different audiences at the same time. They had more tracts printed locally, and distributed them widely. Again they were well received.

After five days Hudson Taylor set off with Dengmiao on a quick visit to Hangzhou, leaving Duncan, Zhumou and Mr Tsiu at work. George Duncan saw them to the boat and went back to his garret. They were to start downriver at daybreak. 'On his return,' Duncan wrote, 'we may visit some more cities, and explore the most important ones among them . . . For the first time I am entirely separated from Europeans, and thoroughly among the Chinese. I have been longing for the time when I could be so, that I might know more of their language and customs, and be more capable of dealing with them.' Five years later a postscript to this story appeared in the *Occasional Paper*. The Hangzhou church had by then increased in strength and opened a daughter church at a village they called 'Kongdeo'. One day a man came in from the country wanting to become a member. He had heard the gospel from a foreigner and a Ningbo teacher at Lanxi in 1867, had given up idolatry at once and worshipped 'God who gave His son to die on the cross for the sins of the world'. The foreigner and his friend were Duncan and Mr Tsiu.

If they wanted to cross over into Anhui province they had only to leave the Qiantang for a major tributary and could get there by boat. Hudson Taylor was strongly drawn that way but opted for Qu

Xian and Jinhua first, after the weekend at Hangzhou. His colourful journal went on: '*July 10th, Wednesday*. Awoke soon after 3.00 and sat alone for a time in front of the boat. Then returned to my place and began to talk to the men. One of the passengers went (ashore) and ere long it was discovered that he had stolen 700 cash.' On the strong current they made good time. He dropped in on John McCarthy at Yanzhou and moored the next night within sight of Tonglu. '*11th, Thursday*. Moved off again at 2.30 a.m. . . . The sunrise was very beautiful and reminded me of some at sea. All were asleep except the three men sculling at the stern of the boat, and I was able to enjoy the rare privilege of engaging in audible prayer in the stem of the boat, without fear of any ear save One overhearing my petitions. Spent the morning in writing. At 2.30 reached Fuyang . . .

'In the evening, our boat being lashed to another going the same way, all the passengers of the two boats were collected together, and I preached to them till I was tired, and I supposed that they would be so too. After a short prayer I concluded, but no one moved away. They seemed to want to hear more of this new way. I commenced again, and talked to them for a long time, and again stopped. Still no one moved. A few leading questions were asked me, and again I spoke to them at great length; and at last . . . it was I who had, after urging on them the *immediate* importance of turning to Christ, to remind them of the lateness of the hour . . .'

He went out of his way to visit the Nicols in their new house at Xiaoshan and on Friday morning was home again, intending to start back to Lanxi on Monday, July 15, and go on with Duncan to Qu Xian, the true goal of the expedition. It was not to be. Too much had happened in his absence, demanding his attention; the McCarthy children were ill, and before he could get away again, John McCarthy arrived back, himself unwell. Late in life, when McCarthy reminisced about that experience up the Qiantang river, the primitive living conditions came to mind, but chiefly,

> All the way, either on boat or on shore, in the teashops – in the street or in temples, wherever people congregated, they heard the story of redeeming love . . . It was evident that the real motive power of the life of the Lord's servant [Hudson Taylor] was that the love of God had been shed abroad in his heart, and that there was a real love for the Chinese people and a true appreciation of the many sterling qualities in the Chinese character, which raised them so entirely above the other heathen nations . . .

The lesson was not lost on either McCarthy or Duncan, exceptional pioneers of the future, or on their Chinese companions. Of his contemporaries, Duncan was to penetrate farther west and over greater distances. John McCarthy on the other hand was to make history by an epic journey on foot from the Yangzi to Burma nine years later. Walking two thousand miles, he 'did not meet with a single act of incivility'. After reading a paper at the Royal Geographical Society (in 1879) he was complimented by the chairman who said his success 'had been in great measure due to his having travelled in the native costume'. The chairman was Sir Rutherford Alcock. But much more was to happen before the great man would be heard saying that.[4]

Maria left in charge[5]   *June–July 1867*

From mid-June to mid-July Maria was virtually in charge of the Mission at Hangzhou. Although 'always ailing', Jennie observed, Maria was the one to whom others turned. James Williamson directed the plasterers putting up partitions and ceilings, in stumbling Chinese took the daily meetings and Sunday services, and gave her moral support. Rudland supervised the printing. The girls pressed on with their increasingly productive work for women. But keeping the peace, briefing the Bergers, advising the embryo church, renting a second house, the superior No 2 New Lane, and dealing with emergencies fell to her lot.

Whooping cough spread no further. Lewis Nicol seemed subdued by John Sell's death. Josiah Jackson at Shaoxing received the masterly letter from Hudson Taylor (*see* p 340), written on the day he started up the Qiantang, and agreed to pioneer Taizhou with Meadows. After a week he and Wang Lae-djün brought Susan Barnes and Margaret McLean from Shaoxing to Hangzhou, both dissidents in foreign clothes. Jackson collected his belongings and set out to meet James Meadows at Ningbo. Jane McLean, ill with dysentery, had stayed in Ningbo with Mrs Lord. Susan packed her belongings and returned to work with the patient Stevensons, she in crinolines and they in Chinese dress. The other girls' voluminous skirts and crinolines had become bedspreads and curtains. As soon as possible Hudson Taylor found her a separate house in Shaoxing in which to run a little school with a Chinese teacher.

Most difficult for Maria was her task of writing to the Bergers when, just as her husband was leaving home, two letters of April 24 came from them, enclosing a copy of George Moule's accusing letter, a thunderbolt. They only had time to read them and consult together before Hudson Taylor had to go. At the end of March, in commenting on the seeds of disaffection, and feeling deeply for his friend, William Berger had written, 'You must take and keep your place of Rule!' Fortunately Hudson Taylor's idea of doing so was less authoritarian than Mr Berger seems to have had in mind. Mrs Gainfort of Dublin (p 121) was offering at sixty-one to go out to China and 'shelter' the young women. But her suitability was in doubt. The difficulty of managing the young men was making Mr Berger hesitate to send any more until told specifically that they were wanted. Once the problem ones had scattered, 'you will see it right to take and hold your place of overseer' with new arrivals.

> The difficulties at home are neither few nor slight, but yours are truly mountainous . . . You need our every sympathy and prayer; and be sure, my dear brother, whatever Mr Moule may have penned, you hold the same place in our hearts as ever . . . The many sad letters . . . have so cast us down that were we not sure God has given us this work to do I fear we should be disposed to question whether it was right to continue it.

About a month earlier, Jennie had written to Emily, away for a rest, '(Mr Taylor) seems so low-spirited about these latest inner troubles, and says he seems to feel that if things go on like this the Mission cannot continue.' For the Bergers of all people to waver was even more unsettling. Like the *Lammermuir* the CIM was in danger of foundering. But it could not do so while they could still say, 'That God will supply you and me with increasing wisdom and ability for the work to which He has called us we will neither doubt nor fear.'

Insinuations in a letter to William Pennefather, which 'I feel sure everyone upon reading it would say referred to moral delinquency,' Mr Berger could not allow to pass unchallenged.

> This I shall see it right to clear up. (Even if all the men of the Mission were to be scattered and the women to be) separated still more perfectly from yourself and family, I am not sure that Mr M would be satisfied, but I think it would satisfy most persons. You will I am sure be extra careful to put it out of the power of Mr M to establish any lack of prudence or undue intimacy . . . He intimates having certain information which he holds as a rod, in case I do not act in accordance

with his wishes. I think it may be this that lies at the bottom of his dark hint to Mr Pennefather.

At the time of writing Mr Berger had no more to go on than Lewis Nicol had admitted to saying, so, exhorting him to mend his ways, he had written, 'I believe God has put honour upon dear Mr Taylor as he has upon Mr Müller of Bristol.' This may have contributed to Nicol's becoming more respectful.

Three more men were ready to sail from Britain and could not well be kept back, he told the Taylors. 'You will need to well consider how best you can carry out your intentions in China, informing me whether a superior class (of men) to those you took with you will be desirable.' In any case 'you must maintain the supremacy.' And again, 'act . . . calmly, lovingly but firmly and unflinchingly.' It was not that artisans were unsatisfactory. Meadows, Williamson and others were admirable. Not social superiority but excellence of personality and spiritual maturity were the qualifications the Bergers were looking for. The zeal and ability of some of the *Lammermuir* party were no substitute for such qualities.

The Mission's financial position was satisfactory, he went on. Willing to contribute a thousand pounds, the Bergers themselves had given a hundred because more than enough was coming in from others. He had made 'provision for a time' in his will, but was glad, as he knew his friend would be, that any provision he could make would be temporary, inadequate and no substitute for complete dependence on God himself, not men. This point he had emphasised to Jane McLean. When contemplating marriage she had written (bypassing Hudson Taylor) to ask Mr Berger, 'What does the Mission provide for us?' and he had replied, 'I am compelled to say, "The Mission provides nothing."' This historic statement has ever since expressed the essential principle that each member trusts in God alone and neither asks nor expects from the Mission anything as due or of right.

In answer to his letter of April 24 Maria wrote decorously to Mary Berger on June 14, while Hudson Taylor was back on the Qiantang reconnaissance.

I am satisfied that our Chinese dress gives us a decided advantage. I had a misgiving before leaving England about the *ladies* wearing Chinese dress on this ground: – the Chinese despise their own families, while they respect foreign ladies; will they treat us with as much respect, and shall we have as much weight with them, if we change our dress? But I have found no ground for retaining this misgiving; on the contrary I am satisfied that force of character, education, and Christian principle give us weight with (Chinese) of both sexes, which neither wearing our own dress could give, nor adopting the Chinese costume take away. I, for one, have been treated with quite as much respect in the latter as in the former. I know that those who prefer the foreign dress think that it commands respect. I very strongly disbelieve this – at any rate as far as inland places are concerned, and these are what we want to have to do with. It commands *fear*, not respect; and far be it from us to wish to inspire such fear . . . A mercantile house (or company) erected an iron shed at some place inland for some part of the process of manufacturing silk. The Chinese came and pulled it down, or partially destroyed it, I forget which. (The merchants) appealed to the Consul, and requested him to represent to the native authorities that this shed was necessary for the proper preparation of silk. The authorities eventually allowed the shed on condition that (they) would put up a high wall all round it, and thus *take away its foreign appearance*.

There is one statement in Mr Moule's letter which I most *emphatically* deny. There *is* a *large* opening for the labours of such persons as he considered would be *wasting* their *life and energy* out here . . . *I* have always found that *the* great difficulty in the way of female agency has been *location*. So few married couples are prepared (and I do not wonder at it, or blame any for it) to give up the retirement and privacy which are so pleasant, and to receive comparative strangers into the family . . . But I believe the Lord Himself did lead us, both into this house, and in the general arrangement of it. And so far I have not heard from the Chinese the *slightest* aspersions on the character or position of our dear Sisters. A great deal that we do *must* appear strange to the Chinese. Our coming out here at all is strange. That so many grown-up ladies should be *unmarried* is certainly strange; for an unmarried woman of twenty would probably be hard to find among them . . . Miss Faulding was saying to me this afternoon that she wished she could make herself into a dozen persons and yet keep one, for then all the time might be well spent.[6]

The question of wearing Chinese clothes was still uppermost in Maria's mind when she wrote again on June 29, but by then she knew better what the Bergers were going through.

I believe the entering heartily into the Chinese costume or otherwise depends upon the question, do you wish to throw yourself among the

Chinese or to mix with foreigners, to gain the confidence and friendly feeling of the former, or to approve yourself to the latter . . . We knew that the storms thro' which we had been passing would break over you ere long, and now we can only ask God to sustain you and guide you . . . I am very much struck with the coincidence between Mr Berger's judgement and our own, altho' the only evidence he had was the letters of the (dissenting) brethren themselves. It was very trying at the time to be unable to write, and I am very thankful the constraint (by Hudson) is removed, but I think it well that Mr Berger was able to tell Mr Nicol at that stage that Mr Taylor had not brought a single charge against him.

Two months' wait until her letter reached Saint Hill added to their difficulties. And two more until she even knew it had arrived, so many mails were being lost at sea or going astray.

Lovers apart   *June–July 1867*

Maria and her husband kept writing to each other, letters too cryptic to follow when referring to their troubles, and full of business details interspersed with love. As on June 29 from Hudson, 'My heart yearns after you. I long to hear how the dear babes are . . . I don't know how to break away from you (by ending the letter) . . . Send me $20 or $25 if you can. Wrap them up so that they cannot (jingle) in something that no one would suspect (them to be in).'

She wrapped the silver dollars in an air cushion, the latter 'to soften the boards'. The cow had been ill, she said. Rudland, having been a farm hand, had treated it. Jungeng, the outside servant, had protested. A Chinese cow must not be treated in an English way. '"Very well," I said, "when Jungeng is unwell he must not come to Mr. Taylor for medicine."' She had dreamed that Hudson was asleep beside her and put out her hand to see if it was real or a dream. It was real! But then she woke up.

He was anxious, he confessed, wondering how Meadows and Jackson were getting on at Taizhou, about Sir Rutherford Alcock's visit over the Xiaoshan affair, about Nicol, about Lae-djün. Hot weather and hard work were taking their toll. 'I never felt more my own weakness, and never more fully realized how truly *any* mere human wisdom and foresight would be insufficient for our guidance and help.' McCarthy and Duncan were lapping up the language. 'It would not take long for Mr Duncan to be preaching in the Mandarin,' while he himself and Mr Tsiu were using 'broken Mandarin' interspersed with dialect. He planned to see McCarthy settled at Yanzhou and Duncan at Qu Xian, and himself to alternate between the two cities assessing the situation before deciding on their final location. Maria must be sure to get those spare shirts finished and sent to Duncan as soon as possible.

Mr Yu arrived at Hangzhou and began work. Wang Lae-djün was welcomed by the Hangzhou Christians and promised to come permanently as their pastor. Jane McLean recovered from her dysentery and grief enough to go and convalesce at the Stevensons' hill retreat, a cottage high above the hot plain. Maria sent her children to join them. Suddenly, a new intense anxiety: Bertie (Herbert) Taylor, while there on holiday with them, had received a dog-bite on the cheek. Rabies was endemic. Nothing could be done but to wait and see if it developed. Hudson Taylor stayed on the Qiantang venture to see it through. On and on their letters ran.

The right spirit[7]   *June–July 1867*

Morale was high among the contented, co-operative members of the team. When the magistrate whose daughter Hudson Taylor was treating sent as a thank-offering baskets of peaches, two to three hundred eggs and six packets of cakes, Jennie explained the Chinese custom to her parents, 'We "being now in some degree civilized" knew that it was proper that (most of the gifts) should be returned. To (accept) all would be greedy, to (accept) none would be to insult the sender, so think the Chinese.' A second window, to provide a through-breeze, had been put into her bedroom and *glazed*! 'It was Mr Taylor who suggested (it) . . . In all his multitude of work he is always contriving something or other that will be for our advantage.'

To her parents Jennie lamented the triviality of some articles in a magazine they had sent her, about Chinese food and clothes. The odds they were up against at Hangzhou and the persecution her newly converted Chinese friends were suffering – these were what ought to be published.

> How I wish that burning soul-stirring words could be written, words that would induce wrestling prayer and earnest effort . . . How few are those who live for souls as worldly men live for riches, from year end to year end, first thing in the morning, last thing at night, every

obstacle made to give way by persevering effort . . . People speak of
the progress of truth being slow, and in the half-truth hide the
Church's guilt . . . Must the conversion of souls be such a rare thing,
that if some dozen or two are converted at once, it is thought that they
must be treated with caution, that it is too good news to be true? . . . I
can't believe that God wills the progress of truth to be slow. One
longs for men of strong purpose, whose whole being is wrapt up in
love to Christ and a determination to make the salvation of souls their
life-long end. [And to an unnamed friend] Everywhere hearts seem
prepared for the truth . . . If I could have fifty lives, I would live them
all for poor China in its terrible destitution . . . We look before long
to have stations far and wide in the interior.

She longed for her language teacher to become a Christian and a
preacher.

He (Mr Tso) is a tall pleasing-looking man, the best specimen of a
(Chinese) that I have seen, his politeness does not seem hollow . . .
but instinctive, springing from refined feeling . . . He seems to take a
real interest in us and to be thinking about the truth. He has passed
several examinations and told me the other day that he hoped in two
or three years' time to be a mandarin . . . His prospects are bright
for this world and that makes me wish that Paul-like he might count
them all dross for Christ. We want to be the means of raising up
native preachers, the need of them is so great.
P.S. Excuse grease spots; a rat was just scrambling about and in
taking up my lamp to send him off, some oil dropt out.

With growing fluency, telling everyone about Jesus and encouraging them to do the same had become Jennie's preoccupation.
Her letters sparkled with her enthusiasm. She told of a converted
bricklayer who went outside the city gate (where people converged)
and talked the gospel to four different congregations. 'We heard our
washerman, a superior lad, persuading some people to seek salvation . . . He told Mrs Taylor . . . that when he saw Mr Williamson
so in earnest to preach tho' he could speak so imperfectly, that he
could not help crying that he himself was doing nothing.'

Meetings for the new believers were being held every Wednesday
and Sunday, but they were also meeting on their own, in their own
quarters. She visited the home of a military mandarin (an army
officer) whose sense of guilt for having killed so many gave him no
peace. He wanted to know how much money he would have to pay
for forgiveness, and listened as Jennie told him how to become

reconciled with God, 'without money and without price'. Home after home was pressing her for a visit, and even a Buddhist nunnery.

More rain in torrents, a swollen river and extensive flooding made Hudson Taylor's return to Yanzhou impossible. He had intended taking 'us' (Jennie gave no clue) as far as that. Wang Lae-djün had arrived and on July 16 was appointed pastor of the church of eighteen (of whom fourteen were men), with fifteen more applicants for baptism including six women. Mr Tsiu was named church-evangelist, three others as elders and two on account of their testifying were recognised as 'exhorters'. This, after nine months since reaching China – evangelism consolidated by the organisation of a self-governing church, as a stride towards wider evangelism. Jennie wrote,

> Everything will not be so immediately dependent on Mr Taylor . . . (The) organization and responsibility thrown upon the (Chinese) will be for good . . . We want to see large flourishing churches in this city and . . . (Chinese Christians) to go and proclaim the truth with power . . . in other parts.

The more distressing the assaults on the Mission's integrity became, the more effective it seemed to be. They had come through typhoons for this, and they would come through more. The pact uniting them paled into irrelevance beside the unity of heart and purpose that increasingly bound most of the *Lammermuir* party together. By October, one year since their landing, twenty-five had been baptised and with Ningbo Christians living in Hangzhou, the church membership was only one short of forty. The new and larger chapel site had been bought, and plans to seat five hundred were in hand. In No 2 New Lane a boarding and day school for boys had been opened under Mr Yu, and the printing presses were producing more and more books in several dialects.

In July, when the river subsided and Hudson Taylor intended going up the Qiantang again, he was down with conjunctivitis. With his eyes bandaged or behind dark glasses he dictated to Emily, working hard as his amanuensis. Even introvert, affectionate Emily was cresting the waves, enjoying Chinese life and Chinese food at last. Writing to Mrs Faulding, as always she opened her heart, 'Even Jennie has been looking pale this last week or two . . . I cannot bear to see her with anything the matter . . . I have been used to illness and sorrows; but she has not; and besides she is so good without such discipline . . . My love to Mr Faulding, and tell him . . . he had better write *me* direct instead of sending messages thro' Jennie; for she has only just given me love that came two days ago, – time enough for her to steal ever so much for herself . . . I have four or five hours work (for Mr T) to get thro' before night.'

Emily's journal held many secrets. The joy of having Hudson Taylor back again and sometimes being able to be alone with Maria and him drew this entry, 'A few minutes of the old time returned. But it did not intoxicate me. I did *not* revel in it. I thanked God for it and took it with very quiet joy . . . (yet) I could hardly keep tears from my eyes.'

Proclamations and despatches   *July 1867*

A week before Hudson Taylor's return from the Qiantang, diplomatic activity intensified between the Ningbo consul, now W H Fittack, and high-ranking mandarins. Apart from the 'Xiaoshan outrage' the Ningbo missions had complained to him of several cases of molestation of their church members. The consul had asked Lewis Nicol on June 14 for more particulars of his fracas but had had no reply. Sir Rutherford Alcock arrived and Consul Fittack had to send a special messenger more than a hundred miles each way for an immediate answer. 'Will you kindly point out to me my errors in my reply to the Consul?' Nicol lamely wrote to Hudson Taylor, sending a copy. In turning to him for help when out of his own depth, he at least showed a change of mood.

On July 18 a consular despatch to the English Baptist veteran T H Hudson, Samuel Dodd[8] and other British missionaries gave them the assurance that on his return to Peking, HBM Minister would draw the attention of the Zongli Yamen, the Foreign Office, to these 'various acts of molestation . . . emanating from the local authorities, or perpetrated with their connivance, with a view to the more effectual repression of any covert hostility, whencesoever proceeding, directed against missionaries or their converts in (Zhejiang province).'[9]

A week later another was addressed to Arthur Moule (George's brother) and the other recipients, enclosing copies of a despatch and proclamation by the Ningbo *Daotai* Wen (over three prefects) saying,

From the tone of this despatch, and from information I have received from various sources, as to the treatment of the different missions located in the interior, I am induced to hope that there will be no further cause of complaint of molestation or undue interference on the part of the authorities with your labour. His Excellency the *tao-t'ai* has suggested that it will be advisable whenever any of you takes up your abode in a town or village, that you forward your passport with a card to the chief authority of the place for his information.

Daotai Wen's despatch in spite of customary circumlocution left no doubt of his intentions or, by deduction, his instructions from his superiors. Translated by C Gardner, consular interpreter, it read,

Despatch no 75 of July 7, 1867
Sir,
   In a previous communication I did myself the honour to write to you in reference to the affair of the Rev. Mr. Nicol, at Shaoshan [ie Xiaoshan]. In this communication I enclosed a report I had received from the (magistrate) stating that, as had been agreed, presents should be sent to and *bienveillance* bestowed on the Missionaries, and that the two parties (magistrate and Mr Nicol) would, in future, live in concord . . .
   (To meet the danger that) among the various prefects and magistrates there might be some, probably on account of there being so many treaties, and the consequent difficulty of learning them all, who, not being very well acquainted with the provisions of the said treaties, might through their ignorance cause the occasion of complications . . . I have extracted from the various treaties the clauses which would be most likely to be most continually applicable to the exigencies arising from the intercourse of foreigners with the natives of the interior; and having selected the most important, I have had them printed in the form of a proclamation, which I have forwarded to be posted up at the various *yamens* great and small, for the instruction of officials and non-officials. There is not a place in the province of (Zhejiang) to which I have not sent this proclamation. Hereafter, all classes in China, employees of Government, the common people, and the literati, will be able to see at a glance the effect, and acquaint themselves with the purport, of the treaties, and thus, in future, when your countrymen go into the interior, whether for the object of teaching their religion, for pleasure, or for trade, they will, in all three cases, be secured their peace and quiet, and be free from molestation and hindrance . . .
   I now enclose ten sealed copies of the proclamation in question to

you, and beg you will be so kind as to put them on record, and also to affix one outside your official residence.[10]

The outcome of the Minister's intervention looked wholly satisfactory, and it was natural that Hudson Taylor should base his actions in the next emergencies on this experience. As the CIM advanced into other provinces, to his surprise he encountered a totally different attitude. Instead of this courteous, friendly cooperation by the highest provincial authorities, in the spirit of the treaties of amity, even the viceroy Zeng Guofan was shown to be either in direct connivance with the instigators of riots or turning a blind eye. Unable to anticipate this change, Hudson Taylor was to walk into more than one hornets' nest. He had no other precedents as he probed so strongly into the interior.

For the present all was well and the fact that 'a proclamation (had) been issued for the whole of this province (of Zhejiang), recognising Christianity as one of the religions of the land, and forbidding rulers or people to persecute native Christians,' gave the team at New Lane the fillip they needed to work on without anxiety in the heat of the summer.

Jackson's city   *June–July 1867*

In June, before the proclamation, it was no small matter for Meadows and Jackson to contemplate their journey from Ningbo to Taizhou, a hundred miles farther south than Fenghua and two hundred and eighty from Hangzhou. They could be well received or equally well be driven out or assaulted. Even James Meadows' leading role in getting Jackson started somewhere was muted, so as to let him shoulder the weight of responsibility. Before starting on his own Qiantang journey, Hudson Taylor had tactfully written treating Josiah Jackson as the responsible pioneer and James Meadows as his companion, although Jackson himself was nervous and in no doubt who was the leading figure.

June 12th, 1867

My dear Brother,

I am so glad that you answered Mr Nicol as you did. Now I hope we are once more at peace. May God grant that it may long continue. I am thankful to hear that you have recovered so well from the smallpox. I trust that you have safely received my remittance of taels

50.00 sent, through Mr Meadows, on Saturday and that ere long you will be able to set out for (Taizhou) together . . . I feel more assured, the longer I pray about it, that the best thing for you to do, is to go at once and take possession of your future station, and there master the peculiarities of the local dialect. You had better try to get a house large enough to enable you to accommodate a colleague, and I would advise that it be in a *quieter* position than Stevenson's is. As to the rent it is difficult to advise, as I do not know what are the rates prevailing now in (Taizhou). But you have Mr Meadows with you and his experience will be your help in this respect . . . Six months' rental is the customary deposit here.

You will be wise in expending as little as is absolutely necessary in alterations and repairs, till you have been in the house long enough to prove that you are likely to be allowed to live there in peace. May the Lord be your guide in all things.

Duncan, McCarthy and I leave, D.V. this afternoon for the (Qiantang river region). We hope to visit and if possible open stations at (Yanzhou and Qu Xian), but having never visited these places our plans may possibly need modification. We have spent this morning in fasting and prayer for you and our selves. Surely our God will send us rich blessing . . .

With much Xtn. love, I remain,
Yours in Jesus,
J Hudson Taylor[11]

As part of his reformed attitude to Hudson Taylor, Jackson decided to travel in Chinese clothes, but urged Meadows to stay dressed as a foreigner! Soon after his flying visit, escorting Susan Barnes and Margaret McLean to Hangzhou at the end of June, Jackson, Meadows and Feng Nenggui, the basket-maker, set off together. On July 5 after an uneventful overland journey they reached Taizhou, 'perhaps the prettiest city I have ever seen . . . Fine hills rise, range after range, all around, and a river winds . . . below the city with its white-washed houses . . . The northern wall of the city (follows) the brow of the hills, on which stand many temples.'

When we entered the city, I at once saw the advantage of the native dress. I passed along the streets without being noticed, but not so with poor Mr Meadows. Men and women, boys and girls, called after him 'red-haired man,' 'white devil,' etc. As soon as we arrived at a temple on the top of a hill within the city, Mr Meadows began to upbraid me for advising him not to put on the native dress. My reason

JACKSON'S CITY WAS MORE BEAUTIFUL

for giving such advice was, because I had heard from so many quarters the danger of the road, and I thought the foreign dress would afford us more protection by the way; but in future I will never give such advice again . . .

The Abbot of the temple received us very kindly, brought us fruit, and ordered a man to bring us bedsteads, and put up bamboo partitions to our rooms, etc. Our luggage having arrived, we settled accounts with the (carriers), and then went to buy some articles of food. It was not long before we discovered, that many of the (Taizhou) people had never seen a foreigner before. Then a number of boys followed us, and began to throw stones at Mr M, but me they never so much as noticed. Having arrived at our quarters, and taken our evening meal, we kneeled down and thanked God for our safe arrival, and sought His protection through the night . . . [The next morning they went house-hunting and had 'plenty of offers'.] At noon we went to (salute) the (prefect) because we thought it the best thing to do, having received such rough treatment the day before. We sent in our cards, and, after waiting some time Nenggui (the evangelist) was called in. The (prefect) asked him some questions about us . . . He said we could go and dwell where we liked.[12]

Their upstairs room in the temple, only ten feet by eight, with three beds in it, had a frameless window-space 'twelve or fourteen feet' from the ground, safe enough while they slept, so they thought.

In the night I heard a noise like the falling of tiles; but as six or seven men belonging to the temple were lying outside . . . I thought all was right, and dropped off to sleep again. Mr Meadows also heard the noise, but he, as well as I, thought all was safe, and again lay down. . . . About six a.m., Sunday, 7th, we heard the (Chinese) talking about thieves, but little thought they had entered our own room. Just at this moment, Nenggui came and told us that my two boxes were gone, also Mr Meadows' best coat and waistcoat, white coat, bunch of keys, pocket-knife, and compass. I lost all my clothes, excepting those I have on. Nenggui lost clothes . . .

Jackson had brought all he needed for a long residence in Taizhou. The two boxes containing all his winter and some summer clothes and other personal effects worth a hundred dollars had vanished. Worse still, he thought, his shotgun and pistol close beside him for self defence had gone too! He was aping Carl Kreyer who often carried a weapon. Unaccountably his handbag containing their silver dollars had been left behind. The thieves had used a ladder and must have let the boxes down with a rope, all in perfect silence. Only in crossing broken tiles on the ground at the foot of the ladder had any sound been made.

The three victims returned at once to the prefect with an inventory of the stolen goods and asked for a proclamation for their protection. This time he received them and promised to do all he could to catch the thieves and restore their property. He sent an escort with them to the city magistrate or 'mayor' whose deputy invited them to move from the temple to the hospitality of his own home (merely a courtesy). Later on the prefect sent word that he had sent a posse of twelve men in pursuit of the burglars. Hundreds of sightseers came to gaze at them and commiserate over their losses. And, impressed by the attentiveness of the mandarins, many offered them premises for rental.

While James Meadows returned to Ningbo, Jackson and Nenggui stayed in Taizhou in a four-roomed house near the principal part of the city and began work.

> The robbery has all turned out for the good [Jackson reported]. I have recovered the greater part of my goods. I feel quite at home among the people, and they feel at home with me. I wear their dress, eat their food, and speak their language. I am fully persuaded in my own mind, that this way of living is the best way of getting near the people and winning their confidence . . .
>
> It is utterly impossible for me to describe to you my feelings, when Mr Meadows left me among a strange people, of whose language I understood but little. No one knows what it is to be left alone in a heathen land, but those who have gone through my experience. Oh, how I do long for the society of some godly person with whom I could converse and pray![13]

Nenggui filled that bill, but Jackson's Chinese was not up to it. After three months he had had enough of loneliness and felt suffocated by the endless talk about nothing in particular, and waste of time by his many visitors. The money he had brought with him had been enough to last many months, but already was exhausted. In spite of Hudson Taylor's advice he had had expensive alterations and repairs carried out and had found no way of having more funds transmitted to him through a bank or postal system or business house. Taizhou was too small and backward, he supposed. So he had run out of cash, borrowed to keep going, and began writing to Hudson Taylor for more. Then he panicked and in desperation travelled back to Ningbo to get help from Meadows.

His letter drew a reply from Hudson Taylor as instructive in timeless principles as in practical sense. As a demonstration of strong, sympathetic leadership it is an example of many such letters being written and in future to be written as the Mission grew. It urged Jackson to take stock of himself in the presence of God and go back to his post at once. Yet it was written only a few weeks after one of the most harrowing experiences Hudson Taylor himself had to pass through. Only an incomplete copy in Maria's hand remains. He was ill in bed and dictating to her. If quoted here to some excess, it is to represent those many which cannot be given space, especially as so much more happened. First he commented on Jackson's boredom with indolent callers, probably detectable in his behaviour,

(Make every effort) to acquire the language so as to make known to them the wonders of God's redeeming love. Never lose sight, even for a moment, of the all-important fact that it is as a messenger of His *love* that He has sent you. Now your best method of learning their language is by conversation with the callers; and the best opportunity of showing your love to them is afforded you when they so call. So instead of feeling impatient and fearing they will *mong* (stifle, suffocate) you to death, it would be happier and better to try and rejoice that God has given you such access to the people . . . We came here to serve them and not to please ourselves; and we ourselves should be very much inclined to question the value of a man's love and friendship, who, while talking much about it, showed most unmistakably that he considered our presence a bore and our company a nuisance . . . If you keep your ears open and your pencil at hand, you will soon be able to collect a large and valuable number of colloquial phrases, which will be of more worth to you than anything you can worm out of a teacher . . .

(He was sorry to hear that Jackson had been 'in need'. His greatest need was to learn from it.) I do trust that this may never occur again, that so trying a lesson will not be lost on you . . . As you know, I have been absolutely without food and without money, I have lacked clothing and suffered from the cold; and more than this, I have learned precious lessons from these adverse circumstances. On looking back I can see that my own imprudence has more than once been the cause of my trouble; but more frequently these trials of faith came apart from anything of this kind . . . God had, as it were, to shut me up to Himself before He sent deliverance.

[As for going into debt –] You have professed to me your ability to look to God for, and to trust in God for your support; that coming out to serve Him, you believed He would not forsake you. And I feel sure that you still have this confidence in Him, some clauses in your letter notwithstanding. But then, dear Brother . . . why borrow from a heathen man? Or why go to Ningpo? Is He the God of Ningpo and not of Taichow? . . . [Hudson Taylor here mentioned several expenses that Jackson could not afford, commitments for which he lacked the means.] Your going to Ningpo was caused . . . by your having less *realization* of the *presence* of a Brother and Friend, *able* and *willing* and *certain* to help you in your need, in Taichow than you had of the presence of those in Ningpo who you thought would so help you. I . . . know how much easier it is to lean on an arm of flesh than on the Lord; but I have learned too how much *less safe* it is. The broken reed always, sooner or later, runs into your hand; the Rock of Ages never fails . . . It is no precarious footing to stand on; it is no question of risk, of chances . . . Real trust in God *cannot* be confounded.

(John Stevenson) would be far *safer*, as well as far happier, without a cash in his pocket, than you were when you went to bed with above a hundred dollars' worth of things by your bedside, and your gun and your pistol by your side for your defence. Your gun was stolen; and had you happened to awake, would probably have been used to your own destruction; but God cared for you thro' all, and preserved you your dollars. Oh! for faith to trust Him more.

Had you used the means you have received with ordinary discretion and prudence, you would neither have run short of funds nor had to live on rice and salt fish. A dollar and a half a month will furnish better fare than that. We here are able to furnish a very comfortable table at from $5.00 to $6.00 per head, including all the fuel used by our servants, and in our washing. And if, living alone, your expenses had been double or three times that, you should have had enough and to spare . . . As to wages you had paid none. Your rent for a year in advance and the alteration agreed on by Mr Meadows and yourself, I had already refunded . . . But to get work done beyond your means to pay, when the Word of God says 'Owe no man anything'; and this too in a country where your life is more insecure than in England, and where you are labouring without guaranteed support; is a course which can only lead to and end in sorrow. I cannot be responsible for *any* expenses incurred without my own authorization or that of someone appointed to act in my stead.

Perhaps I should, too, say a word or two on the subject of your appeal to me for funds . . . Before the receipt of your note I had . . . allotted to you the $35.00 you have since received. The money would have been sent to you before the receipt of the note, had Mrs Nicol's confinement been a few hours later . . . How much more strengthening it would have been to your faith could you have told

your need only to God and received the supply from Him alone! . . .
Before we left England I warned you not to look to me as though I
were a storehouse, or the Lord would soon make it an empty one.
Such indeed I have almost been for some time, and even now the
funds at my disposal are very limited; while the home contributions
have fallen off for some months . . . If you find things more
expensive than you expected, by all means inform me of it . . . I have
penned a line to dear Mr Meadows requesting him to pay you $20:00
. . . apart from your ordinary maintenance (towards your losses by
theft).[14]

Jackson took this letter in good part, returned to Taizhou and his
so far unrewarding work, and was there to help George Stott when
to his surprise he turned up shortly afterwards (p 390). Hudson
Taylor also wrote to James Meadows that he had learned 'from an
incidental allusion' that on the Taizhou expedition he had incurred
personal expenses on behalf of the Mission. 'Now if you give your
valuable time and labour in the opening up of work in other parts, it
is not fair for you to be out of pocket too . . .' So would he kindly
accept $20 from Mission funds to cover that outlay and his loss
sustained by the robbery? In accompanying Stott to pioneer yet
another city, 'You *must* kindly let him be the paymaster.' Funds
would be given to Stott for the purpose.

In writing about Hudson Taylor forty years later, Griffith John
remarked that his 'firmness and love' gave him the 'moral sway' of
true authority over men. The observation reflected on Griffith
John's own understanding of Hudson Taylor after fifty years of
friendship. They were together one week before Hudson Taylor's
death.[15]

CHAPTER TWELVE

AT A PRICE
1867

Saint Hill   *August–December 1867*

While so much was happening to the CIM in China, William and Mary Berger in Britain were carrying their full share of the load. Ever since Hudson Taylor sailed away in the *Lammermuir* they had shouldered the responsibility. Receiving and remitting funds, rendering accounts, editing the *Occasional Paper*, and corresponding with supporters – often curious or excited by the news from China – were theirs to do. Fifty or sixty applicants, stirred up to offer their services by the 'pamphlet' *China: Its Spiritual Need and Claims*, the farewell meetings and the *Lammermuir* story, had to be assessed. For the *Occasional Paper* Mr Berger depended on reports and letters from the Taylors and members of the team. Editing the ill-expressed efforts of some of them to a reasonable standard of English was hard work in itself. He urged them to write objectively, not for effect. Reading and rendering legible for the printer the unfamiliar Chinese words could only be hit and miss and often ended wide of the mark. Where possible he offered a translation and eventually a glossary.

Judging what could be reproduced in print and what was confidential proved hazardous. Hudson Taylor, in saying he had bought land for a chapel at Hangzhou, went on to tell William Berger what he estimated to be the cost of building on it. Mistakenly this and similar information sometimes found its way into the *Occasional Paper*. Hudson Taylor had to urge more care. The Bergers were confident that the Lord would supply all needed funds – through themselves if necessary. But they wanted and expected to see them come in from the wide circle of sympathisers in many different congregations. Factual reports of what the young missionaries were doing were enough to fuel this interest. It was right to provide the information while not using it to appeal for funds. The vivid accounts quoted at length, and more pedestrian detail of day to day life provided ample material, even though to Mr Berger's distress Hudson Taylor was too pressed to send more of the formal statements needed to maintain the links with him. His personal letters to Saint Hill and his parents had to be drawn upon. As a result when Hudson Taylor did write he could stand back from pressing detail and assess the solid achievement, as in *A Brief Account of the Progress of the China Inland Mission from May 1866 to May 1868.*[1]

By May, word had come that single girls were harder to place in work outside Hangzhou than had been anticipated.

> This we greatly regret [Mr Berger wrote in the *Occasional Paper*], and we fear disappointment may be felt by several who have been earnestly desiring to go forth for some considerable time past. May this crossing of their wills be blessed to their souls' profit, and may they remember if it is God's will that they should go, He will yet bring it to pass in His own time.[2]

By then an incomplete report had arrived from Hudson Taylor. Mr Berger printed it as it stood, with the footnote, 'Here Mr Taylor breaks off, stating that he is unable to complete it at this time.' Neither of them said that he had been writing on the day following his return from Ningbo on hearing of Maria's fall down the stairs, just before Lewis Nicol arrived in foreign clothes and the Xiaoshan outrage took place. Hudson Taylor's letters to HBM Consul R J Forrest about the Hangzhou scare and Emily Blatchley's account of developments from hour to hour, ending with the governor's proclamation, provided readers with more food for thought. Each *Occasional Paper* was running to twenty, thirty or even forty pages.

On 20 November 1867, immediately after the riot at Huzhou and while ill with dysentery, Hudson Taylor addressed a letter to all members of the Mission in China, containing some surprising statements.

> For some months back the amount of home contributions has been very small, and by the mail just arrived I learned that the £2000 left in the banker's hands in London on May 26th/66 is now entirely expended, and that the funds in hand on current a/c were such as will by this time have been exhausted . . . These facts together with the prospect of a steadily increasing expenditure fill my own soul with joy in which I trust you will share. [!] . . . There can be no doubt as to the issue. This time it may be even more to the glory of God than before. None will be able to ascribe the answer to our prayers, to Mr Taylor's

lectures on China, or to the éclat of a new missionary enterprise.

Let us remember that after all our greatest needs are those of a spiritual nature; If we seek *first* the kingdom of God and His righteousness, He will to the spiritual blessings *we* require, *add* the supply of our temporal need . . . Let us also seek to husband the resources God has given us that should He be pleased to try our faith and patience and longsuffering we may not have to reproach ourselves . . . May I also request that no one not mentioned (on the appended list of the mission's members) be made acquainted with the facts here stated . . . I trust that we as a mission shall make our wants known only to God that the praise may be rendered to Him alone.[3]

Such positive leadership could not fail to produce more men of faith.

Warm friends of the Mission sometimes took it upon themselves to urge support or even to solicit donations for the CIM. The approved methods of the main societies, the only known approach to the need for funds, seemed impossible to dislodge from people's thinking. For all that had been said in launching the Mission, it was not enough. Jennie Faulding besought her mother to put a check on their minister, William Landels' zeal.

As to our mission I hope Mr Landels will not beg for it . . . We shall be sure to be supplied for God cannot fail us. He feeds the ravens because He is their Creator, how much more will He feed us who are His servants, His children? Our funds are low, and we daily look to God but without one fear or anxious thought that He will withhold any good thing from us.[4]

It was to take many years for Hudson Taylor's closest friends and even official representatives in Britain to understand and implement his convictions on this subject. Those close to him in China, hearing him reiterate his belief again and again, like Jennie, could share his faith and express it as their own. Others at home who had given evidence of understanding, had from time to time to be reminded, 'Don't beg! trusting God is far more reliable.' Entirely one with him in spirit, the Bergers did their best to follow him in practice.

No more women – yet *August 1867*

The strain of 'candidate selection and training' appears to have taxed the Bergers' strength as much as anything. They welcomed into their own home at first those men and women who seemed through correspondence and interviews to be most suited to the Mission. Supervising their reading, village evangelism and personal part in activities at Saint Hill, the Bergers hoped to judge their characters and potential as missionaries. As demands on time and space increased, their much-prized billiard room was given up to be an office. Shelves lined the walls, no longer as a library but to hold stocks of *China: Its Spiritual Need and Claims* and the *Occasional Paper*. Mrs Berger herself spent hours addressing and despatching them, helped by whoever might be available. The young men had to be housed in the village and their supervision taken over by trusted colleagues. William Berger felt less and less confident of sending the right reinforcements to a land he had never seen, for work which from multiplying accounts was unlike anything he had known.

News of the failings of so many accepted and taken by Hudson Taylor and Maria (as in other societies) added to his doubts of his own ability. Hudson Taylor tried to help. Work among Chinese women, carried on by Jennie, Mary Bowyer and Maria, and to a smaller extent by others as they saw what could be done, was proving so productive that no denunciations could reverse the policy that had led to it. Only the inability of the married missionaries to take unmarried ones under their wings dictated the halt to sending more. Once the early pioneers became experienced and older in years this difficulty was removed. It had been a 'teething trouble' of infancy. Even so when the team had been in China only one year, Hudson Taylor wrote in October 1867 to 'Friends and Fellow-Helpers' at home,

> . . . In every direction our sisters have free access to the women in their own homes . . . In its actual influence on the people at large, I am strongly inclined to consider it the most powerful agency we have at our disposal, and I would draw particular attention to it, being convinced that its value can scarcely be overrated. [He hoped that this principle, the part to be played by women, would become] as widely recognized with regard to missionary work abroad, as it is in our city missions at home.[5]

Nor was he overlooking his own crowd-drawing, confidence-building medical work. The uphill climb to success in implementing this insight about women was against difficulties imposed by his own missionaries. There were always the women willing to do the work. That he persevered until he saw the policy fully implemented and subsequently approved, is again the measure of his conviction at the beginning. For the present all unmarried reinforcements must be men.

'Think – before you come'   *August 1867*

Sell had died. Jackson at last meant well. As for Nicol, who could tell? After the first few months of almost devastating friction, the rest of the young men were finding their feet, soon to perform acts of heroism. Something had to be done to obtain the right reinforcements.

William Berger clearly needed guidance in sifting and directing the abundance of young men and women in touch with him. Hudson Taylor drafted a twenty-page letter for him to read to them and discuss at length until he and they were sure of what they were embarking on.[6]

> Difficulties attending the inauguration of our work here compelled me with no small regret to defer for a time the reception of reinforcements. Now, these difficulties are somewhat passing away . . . Much sorrow and disappointment may be avoided by persons proposing to identify themselves with a particular work, if they first thoroughly master the principles by which it is regulated and apprehend the line of practice resulting therefrom. Should these not commend themselves to them, they have still the option of standing aloof. If, on the other hand, they are led intelligently and heartily to concur in them, they will be likely to throw themselves into the work with an unvacillating energy which cannot be expected from those who, having first committed themselves to an undertaking, afterwards raise the question for the first time, as to whether it is conducted in a right and proper manner . . .
>
> (As to) the various points to which I am about to call your attention . . . while they represent our views and our practice, there is perhaps no one of them which may not at some time or other be called in question by persons whose piety is undoubted and to whose judgement in many respects, you might feel prepared to defer. Should you after prayerfully waiting upon God be led to adopt them, you will be

less likely to be startled or disconcerted when you meet with those who hold different opinions.

Referring them to *China: Its Spiritual Need and Claims* (1868 edn), to be studied carefully, he then drew attention again to the basic principles of the pact existing between members of the Mission in China, which they would enter upon of their own choice. He did not mince matters.

> That dear Mr *Berger* has kindly given himself to the management of the home department of the work;
> – that *I* have felt called to direct the work in China;
> – that *we ourselves* are seeking God's help in the faithful use of the funds entrusted to us by His people for the support and furtherance of the work;
> – and that it is as *helpers* in the work among the *Chinese* that we desire and pray for your co-operation and fellowship. We do not request you to assist us in the general direction of affairs of the mission, either at home or in China; nor do we ask you to share in our responsibilities as trustees for the funds committed to our care. Nothing is further from our thought than the formation of a committee or committees for the management of our affairs. There are many useful societies conducted in this way, and those who deem this the best mode of working, will do well to seek identification with them. But to attempt to graft them on to our work is impossible – even were it not so, would not be attempted, as we do not consider it, for such work as ours, the most excellent way . . . None of you will suppose that immediately on your arrival in China you will be in a position of such knowledge of the language, people, habits, etc, or of the local peculiarities of the work, as would enable you to give any real help in the direction of affairs.

He then enlarged upon the impracticability of widely scattered missionaries attending committee meetings. In this too the CIM was at first to be different.

> Travelling in this country being painfully slow and tedious . . . (they might) return in due course to their own stations, in some instances not improbably to find the work broken up, and further residence in the place impossible . . .
> I hope that it will be fully understood that both our work and our mode of conducting it avowedly differ from the ordinary missionary societies and that therefore no one will suppose that what these

societies or those connected with them may do will form any precedent for the carrying on of our work. Our work may be a humble one; but it is distinctive . . . .

Our effort is and will be . . . to minister towards the need of particular persons or departments of the work according to the best of our judgement and ability. With varying spheres of service, and varied wants, the needs of no two brothers or sisters will ever exactly correspond. If, therefore, one brother or sister is supplied with less than another, those unacquainted with the reasons which have led to this difference of ministration must not assume that either partiality on the one hand or neglect on the other, has been shown.

Again, our ability to minister may at times be greater and at times smaller, as God does not supply us uniformly with the same amount of funds; so that brothers and sisters must not expect a regular salary from us . . . In any case however, the funds of the mission will not be at the demand of helpers engaged in the work, whether at home or abroad. . . . Nothing is guaranteed and no claims can be made on the funds. Each one must abide by the stand he takes in joining this mission, of 'relying on the living God for all needed supplies both of pecuniary means and spiritual grace.' (At the same time everything in his own and Mr Berger's power would be done to help) in case of real need occurring in the course of faithful service. (They would try to supply outfits for the sea journey and on arrival in China, but) all and only what is really requisite.

After this, if anyone came to join them, they would surely be the kind he wanted. But the main problem still had to be faced, in the same spirit.

On becoming a Chinese to the Chinese[7]   August 1867

Twelve years ago Hudson Taylor had faced this great step for himself. Since then everything had convinced him, and others, of its rightness (Book 2, p 287). Looking back, and forward into inland China, he tried to set out the pros and cons of wearing Chinese clothes. Frankly stating that few other Protestant missionaries had adopted it, being near the treaty ports, he warned that some 'are positively hostile to it'. George Moule was already in Britain denouncing it, but there were others.

But as to work carried on at any considerable distance in the interior of such a nature as that which we contemplate, I am fully satisfied that the native dress is an absolute prerequisite. No foreign missionary to

the best of my knowledge ever has, in European costume, carried on
such a work: and my strong conviction is that at present no foreign
missionary could do so. He might travel, almost anywhere under the
protection of his passport; but quietly settling among the people,
obtaining free, familiar, and unrestrained communication with them,
conciliating their prejudices, attracting their esteem and confidence,
and so living as to be examples to them of what Christian Chinese
should be, require the adoption, not merely of their costume, but
also of their habits to a very considerable extent . . . I have never
heard of anyone who after having *bona fide* attempted to become a
Chinese to the Chinese that he might gain the Chinese, either
regretted the step he had taken or decided to abandon the course . . .
In seeking the co-operation of fresh helpers it is for work in the
interior that I desire it. Holding strongly the views just mentioned, I
should wish all those who desire to help me . . . not to join a work to
be so conducted unless prepared heartily and conscientiously to carry
out its principles. I repeat, it is as helpers in a work already designed
and in successful operation, and not as designers of a new work that I
invite your co-operation.

A close examination followed of Christ's example as set out in
Scripture (in *Hebrews* 2.9–18; 4.15–5.9; *Galatians* 4.4–6; *2 Corinthians* 8.9; *Philippians* 2.5–8) and of the apostle Paul (*I Corinthians*
9.19–23) making himself 'all things to all men that (he) might by all
means save some'.

Surely no follower of this meek and lowly One will be likely to
conclude that it is 'beneath the dignity of a Christian missionary' to
seek identification with this poor people, that he may see them
washed, sanctified, and justified in the name of the Lord Jesus and by
the Spirit of our God. Let us rather be imitators of Him (who washed
His disciples' feet).

His application of Biblical principles to the missionary is ageless.

We have to deal with a people whose prejudices in favour of their
own customs and habits are the growth of centuries and millenniums.
Nor are their preferences ill-founded. Those who know them most
intimately respect them most; and see best the necessity for many of
their habits and customs – this being found in the climate, produc-
tions, and conformation of the people. There is perhaps no country in
the world in which religious toleration is carried to so great an extent
as in China; the only objection that prince or people have to

Christianity is that it is a foreign religion, and that its tendencies are to approximate believers to foreign nations.

I am not peculiar in holding the opinion that the foreign dress and carriage of missionaries – to a certain extent affected by some of their converts and pupils – the foreign appearance of the chapels, and, indeed, the foreign air given to everything connected with religion, have very largely hindered the rapid dissemination of the truth among the Chinese. But why need such a foreign aspect be given to Christianity? The word of God does not require it; nor I conceive would reason justify it. It is not their denationalization but their Christianization that we seek.

Here he made a truly classic statement:[8]

We wish to see Christian (Chinese) – true Christians, but withal true *Chinese* in every sense of the word. We wish to see churches and Christian Chinese presided over by pastors and officers of their own countrymen, worshipping the true God in the land of their fathers, in the costume of their fathers, in their own tongue wherein they were born, and in edifices of a thoroughly Chinese style of architecture.

It is enough that the disciple be as his master (Jesus Christ) . . .

He then applied the principle to his policy, in another classic definition, making 'health and efficiency' the touchstone,

If we really desire to see the Chinese such as we have described, let us as far as possible set before them a correct example: let us in everything unsinful become Chinese, that by all things we may save some. Let us adopt their costume, acquire their language, study to imitate their habits, and approximate to their diet as far as health and constitution will allow. Let us live in their houses, making no unnecessary alterations in external appearance, and only so far modifying internal arrangements as attention to health and efficiency for work absolutely require.

Our present experience is proving the advantage of this course. We do find that we *are* influencing the Chinese around us in a way which we could not otherwise have done. We are daily coming in contact with them, not in one point, but in many; and we see the people becoming more or less influenced by the spirit, piety and earnestness of some of those labouring among them. But this cannot be attained without some temporary inconvenience, such as the sacrifice of some articles of diet, etc, etc. Knives and forks, plates and dishes, cups and saucers, must give place to chopsticks, native spoons and basins (and food) . . .

But there are other restraints and privations which to many will be far more trying than these trifling ones. Husbands and wives may not walk out together arm in arm, nor even walking separately may they be unattended. In walking out among the Chinese, persons of both sexes will have to adopt the slow, orderly, sedate gait of educated natives; otherwise they will lose influence with the people, and be thought ill-brought up, unmannered and ignorant. Ladies must remember that they cannot enjoy that freedom in public to which they have been accustomed; that they can never go out unattended; and that they will find their personal liberty in other ways more or less restricted.

But will any brother or sister reflect on what He gave up who left heaven's throne to be cradled in a manger . . . and yet hesitate to make the trifling sacrifices to which we have alluded? We give you credit, dear friends, for being prepared to give up, not only these little things, but ten thousand times more, for Christ's sake . . .

Some time ago I was walking at a little distance behind a missionary and his wife, in the streets of Ningpo, (a place where foreigners are perhaps better thought of than in any other part of China) and was not a little pained to hear the remarks made by the Chinese about the foreign missionary and his 'paramour' – if I may so far soften the expression used. A comparatively brief residence among the Chinese (I do not say *in* China) will convince the attentive observer that the prevalent opinion of the masses at the present time, is that the rite of marriage is unknown among the nations of Europe and America, which are believed to be appropriately styled, with regard to morality, 'barbarian'. Nor is it easy to conceive whence the Chinese could obtain more correct notions. Certainly not from the smuggling traffic of opium – so long carried on along the entire coast of China. Certainly not from the gangs of intoxicated seamen who frequent our open ports; nor alas! from the lives of too many of our countrymen, whose education and position, and in many instances, previous religious training might have led us to expect better things. Certainly not from the floods of filthy and obscene French and German prints and photographs which are sold in foreign stores at the Free Ports and are found adorning the walls of opium dens and lying on the shelves of native 'foreign goods stores' throughout the whole country; – in many places these being the only representation of life and customs ever seen by the people. Identification with *them* is not likely to heighten the esteem felt for the first Christian missionary who may visit such localities. It is no small boon to be as far as possible dissociated in the minds of the Chinese from their ideas of foreign customs and manners. Let a thoughtful observer visit a place in the foreign dress, and notice how carefully the younger and the more respectable females avoid him, and how quickly the doors and gates are closed and barred at his near approach. Let him then visit some place in native dress, and see how differently the people will receive him . . .

In (Chinese dress) the foreigner though recognized as such, escapes the mobbing and crowding to which, in many places, his own costume would subject him; and in preaching, while his dress attracts less notice his words attract more. He can purchase articles of dress and also get them washed and repaired without difficulty and at a trifling expense in any part of the country . . .

You will see that it is not without reason that I desire to see this principle thoroughly carried into effect . . . Let it not be a question with you as to whether *you* prefer the appearance of the European or the Chinese costume, nor yet as to whether your own personal appearance will be improved or deteriorated by the change in the eyes of others. And though I am well assured that if you heartily adopt the costume both your health and your comfort will be promoted thereby, I would say let not these considerations be the chief reasons which influence you. Rather let the love of Christ constrain you to seek to commend yourselves and your message to the Chinese, as becomes the followers of such a Master. Let there be no reservation; give yourselves up fully and wholly to Him whose you are and whom you wish to serve in this work; and then there can be no disappointment. But once let the question arise, 'Are we called to give up this or that or the other?' or admit the thought, 'I did not expect this or that privation or inconvenience,' and your service will cease to be that free and happy one which is most conducive to efficiency and success. God loveth a cheerful giver.

His own experiences were being repeated in his colleagues' daily life. Time and again the contrast could be seen. Some who thought they knew better were learning the hard way. Others who gave his advice a fair trial would not go back to alien ways for anyone.

Face up to the dark side   August 1867

He had more to say and he was 'pulling no punches', but he would persuade, not order his 'brothers and sisters' to follow him.

We have not thought it wise to encumber our work with a series of rules and byelaws. Should emergencies arise, I trust first to seek God's guidance and help, and then to act myself, or direct others to act, as the case may require. (You) will do well to remember that circumstances may sometimes require prompt and energetic action, the reasons for which it may not be possible or prudent immediately to disclose. In other instances inexperience or very partial acquaintance with the exigencies of the case, may lead some of my helpers to think that a very different course of action from that which I am led to pursue would sufficiently meet, or better meet its requirements. I need scarcely say that should such circumstances arise, I, as director of the work, must act according to the best of *my* ability, and shall hope to have the cheerful co-operation of my fellow-helpers even where they do not entirely see with me . . . I reserve to myself the right of locating them in such positions, and of appointing them to such work as it shall seem to me they are best suited for . . .

He warned them against magnifying details of a practical nature into matters of conscience, and against turning to the free ports and the hospitality there as an escape from the adopted life inland. And finally, anyone departing from the Mission's principles or from 'the great fundamentals of the Christian faith', or guilty of immoral behaviour 'will thereby *ipso facto* remove themselves from the Mission'.

I would far rather that you first saw all the dark side of the picture, and then were afterwards pleasingly surprised by finding it, as I believe all will find it, who enter into it with a proper spirit, a service replete with joys and pleasures, than that the reverse should be the case . . . 'Trust in the Lord with all thine heart; and lean not to thine own understanding. In all thy ways acknowledge Him and He shall direct thy paths.'

If he was offering them blood, sweat and tears, he would be in it with them. Who would join such a man on such terms? The answer was, hundreds!

The garden and the Gardener[9]   *August 1867*

At 102° Fahrenheit in Rudland's room and 98° in the coolest place at No 1, the summer heat became unbearable. No one could work. Even in the thinnest of Chinese gowns, so much better than Western clothing, the itching, burning rashes of 'prickly heat' broke out on everyone. Hudson Taylor sent some of the household to the relative coolness of Pengshan to prepare to receive the rest, and others to the Stevensons' hill retreat near Shaoxing. William Rudland made a river journey to Lanxi to encourage Duncan in his exile and when he returned brought with him another cow in milk for the children. When Grace Taylor had her eighth birthday on July 31 Maria was

HOW JENNIE AND GRACE WOULD HAVE DRESSED

asked 'whether she would be willing to make a (matrimonial) alliance (for Grace), and so bring about a relationship between some (Chinese) family and ourselves'. Hudson Taylor's conjunctivitis was still tying him to his room in semi-darkness. Jennie wrote to his mother for him. 'Despite all the trials connected with it, aye and perhaps because of the trials, this is a life of deep happiness,' she said. A year ago, on the day William Carron was crushed by the falling spar on the *Lammermuir*, Grace after a long talk with Jennie had shown such convincing signs of being a child of God that Hudson Taylor now baptised her. In many ways she was another 'Miss Happiness'. 'Since her conversion she had become quite another child . . . more sweet, more happy.' She had a favourite corner of the garden where she loved to play, a paved rock-garden with a pool among the shrubs and two or three shady trees.

On August 2 Hudson Taylor went out to hire canal and river boats to take all the household except Lae-djün and James Williamson to the foot of Pengshan mountain. Maria was so prostrate, 'I feared she was not likely to last long,' so often did her cough and fever reduce her to helplessness. Grace had been off her food, ailing and losing weight for some weeks, during and since her holiday with the Stevensons. But he was not anxious about her as he was for Herbert, aged six and febrile. Any hint of hydrophobia since his dog-bite on the cheek alarmed them all. Four-year-old Howard (Freddie) had been hot and drowsy recently, but not really ill until Hudson Taylor came home from hiring the boats, to find him in convulsions. By the time he had recovered in a tepid bath it was late in the day. And by the time the boats reached the water-gate through the city wall it was closed. Grace was tired and irritable so the McCarthys took her into their larger boat with more space to lie down. After a sweltering night and day they reached Pengshan on August 5 and on the cool hilltop, living 'a gypsy life for a few days' in the derelict temple, three tumbledown sheds and an open pavilion, all quickly improved. Maria had had to be carried up. She and the two boys 'were really ill', Jennie thought.

Grace complained of headache the next day and by the 8th had a high fever. Now Hudson Taylor was more worried about her. But a message had come from Hangzhou that Jungeng, the Ningbo Christian in their employ as head servant, had been discovered lining his own pocket when doing the household shopping and laying in stores for Mr Tsiu's approaching wedding. Leaving directions for treating Grace, Hudson Taylor made a quick visit to New Lane to deal with him. There he found a message from Shaoxing, that Jane McLean's dysentery had relapsed and Mrs Stevenson and her child were both ill. Would he please come? What should he do? Anxious about Grace and the two boys, he urgently wanted to get back to Pengshan. But dysentery killed so many and so quickly. He hurried to Shaoxing by fast footboat, dosed Jane McLean and brought her back with Emily to look after her. Headwinds slowed them up and it was Saturday night, the 10th, before they reached Pengshan.

Friday had been distressing for Maria. Freddie had had more fever and convulsions, but Grace, lying in the fresh air on Rudland's camp-bed, was incoherent when Maria struggled from her own bed to go and see her. George Duncan arrived in the evening from Lanxi and immediately found ways to help. Jennie wrote, '(I will) never forget seeing her . . . in (his) arms with her beautiful hair hanging carelessly about her shoulder and looking so pretty,' as he carried her up to the higher of the three sheds they were living in, and laid her on Maria's bed.

They passed an anxious night and day until her father arrived back again. One glance and he could see how ill she was. Typhus? Or meningitis? It mattered little, she was desperately ill with convulsions from time to time. He told them to cut off all her hair and apply cold compresses. 'I cut it off myself,' Maria wrote weeks later when she could bring herself to put the details into words, 'and said, "May she be spared for it to grow again."' Grace was delirious but in spite of high fever more comfortable after that. Again and again she repeated, 'Waited till my head grew worse and worse and worse . . . and my skin was half burned off, and my skin was half burned off . . .' And Emily heard her say, 'Yes, dear Jesus!' Maria lay down exhausted beside her while Jennie, after being with her all through the day, watched over them both for half the night and Emily the other half.

After his travelling in the extreme heat Hudson Taylor himself began to feel so ill that he told Jennie what to do if he became unable to help in the morning. An attack of pain had begun, the worst he had ever had, probably renal colic. Emily's journal for that awful night reads, 'Things all looked so terribly dark. Would God forsake us and this infant Mission? No, I don't think I feared that, but it was so very hard to be there and hear poor Mr Taylor moaning with pain, and little Gracie uttering incoherent words of raving.'

Mary Bell gave up her bed to Grace and did her share of nursing. Privacy was minimal in their circumstances. She too could hear Hudson Taylor's moans of pain and added, 'He was so broken-hearted he cried most of the day.' To talk privately with Maria he had had to take her out to a secluded rock-pool in a gulley where they sometimes bathed. There he had told her that there was no hope of Grace recovering. 'There and then we put her into our Father's hands, pleading with him to do the best for her and for us.'

Mary Bell and Rudland were looking after the three boys, Herbert, Howard and Samuel, until both Mary and William fell ill with 'ague'. Freddie's 'throbbing carotid arteries' suggested that he was getting worse. Typhus, if that was what it was, could have struck all of them at once. But the dreaded 'hydrocephalus' (meningitis) which had taken Hudson Taylor's two brothers, one at about the same age as Grace, seemed more likely. To relieve the congestion in

Freddie's head he decided to insert a 'seton' in his neck. James Williamson, always the Taylors' staunch friend, had also come to join them. While he held him on his lap imprisoning his arms and legs, Hudson Taylor picked up a fold of skin on the back of Freddie's neck and thrust a needle through it. 'A skein of silk' drawn after it and left in place to be worked to and fro served as a counter-irritant. Though accustomed to operating without anaesthesia, to do this to his son added to his own distress. It seemed to be effective, but was still in use late in October.

Maria could no longer feed her baby, so Jennie went twice to Hangzhou to find a wet-nurse, always travelling with an older woman, but although so young herself, playing the part of a mature traveller in China. The second time she succeeded.

From two a m until daylight on the 14th Hudson Taylor was writing to his mother. 'I have heavy news to tell you . . . It will run thro' you and dear Father like a dagger . . . It is *Hydrocephalus* . . . I fear the effect of the loss of Gracie on her Mamma.' And the next day as he sat beside them he wrote to William Berger,

> I seem to be writing almost from the inner chamber of the King of kings – surely this is holy ground . . . beside the couch on which my darling little Gracie lies dying . . . Dear brother, our flesh and heart fail, but God is the strength of our heart, and our portion for ever. It was no vain or unintelligent act when, knowing the land, its people and climate, I laid my dear wife and the darling children with myself on the altar for this service.

As soon as Mary Bowyer heard in Shaoxing of so much illness at Pengshan she too came to help. Inconspicuously efficient as always, Louise Desgraz had all along been catering and running the cooking and laundering for the whole party of twelve adults, five children and several Chinese. Alosao, their one-time 'lodger', now a Christian friend, and another were with them.

On the 19th Grace showed signs of pneumonia and pleural effusion. Straining to breathe, she lingered for four more days. Mary Bowyer described the last scenes for Mrs Berger. Maria sat bowed low over her dying child as all who were well enough stood around the bed singing hymn after hymn, led with a breaking voice by Hudson Taylor. At eight fifty p m on Friday, August 23, her breathing stopped and peaceful beauty spread over her face. 'When all was over, it was truly wonderful to see the calmness with which preparations were made for returning to Hangchow.' Hudson,

Maria and the two older boys, Emily and James Williamson packed up their possessions and prepared to leave. The others were to follow the next day.

The temple priests and Pengshan villagers, if they knew a death had taken place so near to them, could cause great difficulties from their superstitions about departed spirits. Idolatrous practices would be demanded. Refusal to comply could lead to violence. So secrecy must be preserved. Pillows were placed in the light tin bath, Grace's body laid on them, and more pillows and bedding piled over it. Travelling in the coolness of night was commonplace. Around midnight they started downhill, Hudson Taylor and Williamson carrying the bath between them. 'Oh that sad, sad moonlight march, but the Lord sustained us.'

Their own boat was waiting. At the riverside, lest boatmen or anyone suspect what was happening, Williamson casually took the bath on his shoulder to carry it on board, and the others followed. Five hours later, as the city gates opened for the day, they passed through and reached New Lane before the household were up.

Hudson Taylor and Wang Lae-djün went out and bought a Chinese coffin of hardwood, its walls six inches thick, and Lae-djün worked all night preparing it for use. On Sunday morning before the great heat, they laid Grace's body in it, dressed as always in Chinese clothes by Maria herself. A single flower lay in her folded hands. Then they closed the lid.[10]

John McCarthy had been in Pengshan recuperating until August 4 and was in Hangzhou preparing to return to Yanzhou. His memory of how Maria and Hudson Taylor bore up through these experiences stayed with him for many years.

> It is impossible to separate even in thought the husband and wife at the time [he wrote. They were] sustained and helped to glorify God and be an example to those around of submission and joyful acquiescence in the will of God . . . There was no desire to take back or keep that which had been so fully given to God.

But both were still far from well and when their presence was not needed they stayed in their room, grieving together.

That Sunday, August 25, Hudson Taylor himself preached at the Chinese service, referring to Grace's death and showing by his composure that none of the fears and hopelessness of the pagan have any place in the grief of a believer. 'The Chinese say that when

Grace died Hudson Taylor said, "The Gardener came and plucked a rose."[11]

Wang Lae-djün had been like a nurse to the infant Grace in Ningbo and on the voyage home to England in 1860, and at Beaumont Street and Coborn Street, delighting to hold her in his arms. As a painter and decorator by trade, lacquer work and gold-leaf decoration were among his skills. With love that comforted Maria, he would let no one else work on the coffin during the next three weeks, lacquering, polishing and gilding it 'day after day in his spare hours, until the surface shone like a mirror'. In the corner of the rock-garden that Grace had made her own, 'a little house' was built, a typical Chinese tomb above ground. When the coffin was ready all the household, Maria's 'industrial class' of women and other Chinese gathered for a service in the garden and the 'little house' was sealed. A pencilled note in Maria's hand described the occasion, ending with the words,

> Renew my will from day to day;
> Blend it with Thine, and take away
> All that now makes it hard to say
>   *Thy* will be done.

By then a great deal more had happened. In a blundering letter of sympathy Lewis Nicol said his pregnant wife's time was near. Would Hudson Taylor come and see her? But Nicol was mistaken. All through September and most of October either Hudson or Maria or both together came and went or lived with the Nicols at Xiaoshan until after the baby was born. Severe pain in Eliza's side and the desire to let bygones be bygones led the Taylors to go the second mile.

On August 29 Duncan and two Chinese companions, Tianfu and Zhumou, set out on a new venture, to explore the route to Nanjing and stay there as long as possible. On the day they reached the ancient capital, Hudson Taylor and James Williamson also at last fulfilled a dream and a plan made long before, to explore the possibility of occupying the hostile city of Huzhou (now Wuxing). And on the anniversary of the arrival of the disabled *Lammermuir* in Shanghai waters, on the day after Grace's tomb was sealed, six more men and one woman were added to the fast-expanding church at Hangzhou. If the price was high, the fruits were promising.

Duncan in Nanjing[12]   *September–December 1867*

In the last four months of 1867 so much happened that a coherent account again demands the separation of the main strands of the story. Duncan embarked on the first advance of the China Inland Mission to the great Yangzi river and its cities. To rescue him in unforeseen difficulties, Rudland won his spurs by covering the same route at top speed and concluded an epic chapter in the Mission's history. Hudson Taylor and James Williamson occupied hostile Huzhou. George Stott scorned his handicap and pioneered the coastal city of Wenzhou, by his courage overcoming initial hostility. At Hangzhou, while the progress of church-planting continued and reinforcements arrived from Europe, Hudson Taylor slaved on as administrator, medical man and general factotum. Profiting from the first year's experience he sent home a statement of the kind of person needed to expand the mission far into the interior. The year which could have broken him became the year when most of his team rejected the disruptive influences and proved their worth.

Lewis Nicol had set his heart on the city of Jiaxing (map, p 237). Now he yielded to a sister mission's plans to work there, and contented himself with Xiaoshan. The Ningbo team and Jackson were striking out southward. The Qiantang river reconnaissance had shown Yanzhou and Lanxi to be friendly, ready for occupation at any time. Further advance across provincial borders into Anhui and Jiangxi could be made from Lanxi and Qu Xian, but more strategic progress (on the lines of Hudson Taylor's plan to work outward from capital cities towards the borders) would be made by extending up the Yangzi to the main cities of those provinces. The growing churches and the Mission's work at Hangzhou, Ningbo and Shaoxing could be left, small as they were except to 'the eye of faith', to complete the expansion into southern Zhejiang. In Meadows, Stevenson and McCarthy he had men of the best quality to do it. With ambitious foresight Hudson Taylor was therefore looking north-westwards, to the remaining region that challenged him (p 322). Zhenjiang (Chinkiang) where the Grand Canal crosses the Yangzi river, and Nanjing fifty miles further inland, were the key to Wuhu and Anqing and Anhui province and to Jiujiang (Kiukiang) at the mouth of the vast Poyang Lake, fed by the great navigable rivers of Jiangxi province.

Hudson Taylor had been pleased with George Duncan's spirit on the Qiantang journey. Over a month without a foreign companion

NANJING: A WATER GATE

at Lanxi had made Duncan feel at home as a Chinese among Chinese. Thoroughly adapted to living simply, and becoming fluent in colloquial, idiomatic Chinese, with some acquaintance with three dialect variations (Ningbo, Hangzhou and the Anhui mandarin of Lanxi immigrants), he welcomed Hudson Taylor's suggestion that he should go with two Chinese Christians and occupy Nanjing itself. Lanxi could wait. Only eight days after returning ill from Lanxi and watching over little Grace at Pengshan, and little more than eleven months in China, he set off with Li Tianfu and Ling Zhumou to preach the gospel in the second city of the empire. 'Nanking was an important place when our Saviour gave the word "Go ye into all the world and preach the gospel to every creature,"' Hudson Taylor wrote. 'How many generations have been born, have lived and died within those walls since that command was given?'

Nanjing had been populated since 2400 BC and the capital of six successive southern dynasties between the third and sixth centuries after Christ. From AD 1368–1411 it was the capital of the Ming dynasty, full of palaces and cultural treasures. But the Taiping rebellion had reduced Nanjing to desolation. Acre upon acre of ancient mansions, parks and gardens were still derelict within its fourteen miles of city walls and the remains of outer walls, thirty-five miles in length. Houses and business quarters were fast being rebuilt as displaced inhabitants returned and new ones moved in. Already the population approached half a million. Duncan knew the significance of his objective and determined to hold on there as long as possible. His reports to Hudson Taylor, clear and to the point, showed how gifted as a pioneer this stone-mason was by nature, and how much more fluent and grammatical he was becoming in English as well as Chinese.

Leaving Hangzhou on August 29 and meeting headwinds on the Grand Canal they made slow progress, but reached Tangqi the next afternoon. Ten months before, Tangqi had defied all efforts by Hudson Taylor to rent premises. Li Tianfu and Duncan stood on the main bridge over the canal talking with passers-by until, he reported, 'In a few minutes a large congregation had gathered round me. I tried to speak to them, as God helped me, of the way of life by Jesus Christ.' To his delight they 'understood the greater part of it'.

The next day a strong wind carried them out of their course as they crossed a lake and led the boatmen to go by smaller canals instead of returning to the Grand Canal. When they moored at Xinshi (map, p 237) and Duncan went to have his head shaved in a busy part of the town, they met some Christians and found a little church of twelve served by a Chinese pastor of the American Presbyterian Mission. 'I had intended to pass the Lord's day at (Xinshi); but when I found there was a preacher there, I decided that we had better go to another town where there was none. So we set out for (Wuzhen), as the next place of any importance.' They had come to 'Black Town' (Book 2, p 326) where William Burns and Hudson Taylor had been attacked by salt-smugglers in 1856. Li Tianfu managed to make himself understood, but the dialect-Chinese Duncan had learned was unintelligible there. '(Tianfu) spoke a great deal; he is a very energetic man, and very willing to speak . . .'

Back on the Grand Canal again well north of Jiaxing, they made good progress and reached Suzhou on September 3. The great city walls, 'strong and secure' since being repaired, impressed George Duncan. 'The boat stopped outside the (granary gate) . . . There is a greater concourse of people going in and out than I have seen at any other place that I have yet visited; the masses are overwhelming as they pass, thousands upon thousands . . . Since I have come here

I . . . have realized more than ever the vast numbers who are without the Gospel.'

Charles Schmidt, the converted ex-officer of Gordon's Ever-Victorious Army, had not yet come to Suzhou. Duncan and his companion paid off their boatman and took 'a room above a teashop' for 'about eight or ten days', climbed a pagoda to get a bird's-eye view of the city and countryside, and visited a temple to assess the religious feeling of the people. 'I am told there is a Roman Catholic chapel here, and that foreigners from Shanghai come and go on business, but that none reside here. At present I should think that it is a more important place for a mission-station than Hang-chow.' At the temple more than a hundred women were worship-ping the idols, and priests were receiving offerings from them. 'It seems such heartless work talking to these men – they are so besotted and wrapt up in idolatry.' 'I have found a bank through which money can be sent from Hangchow . . . and also (the name of) one in Hangchow, with which they can transact business. They *said* that they could (send) through several others; but this you will be able to ascertain for yourself.'

On or about September 11 they hired a boat to take them to Zhenjiang on the Yangzi, and reported on each city they passed on the way. A new Catholic chapel had been built at Wuxi, and all along the way people knew about 'the religion of the Lord of Heaven'. 'O that the true doctrine of Jesus Christ were as well known!' Duncan said. But as the dialect was strange they could scarcely make themselves understood and so pressed on. He did not comment as another (Reid) did a few months later, 'I was struck by seeing so many human bones lying along the shore' – unburied corpses from the Taiping rebellion four years earlier.[13] His concern was for the living and for his own devotion to Christ. As the rain pelted down at Zhenjiang he wrote, 'The ambitious man may take the honours of the world, so I may but have Christ. He shall be enough for my soul!' From Zhenjiang to Nanjing they travelled on a Yangzi river junk and retained it until sure of a foothold in the city. It was well they did. September 18, 1867, well within a year of the arrival in China of the *Lammermuir* party, was the historic date of their arrival.

Acting on Consul Forrest's advice, George Duncan with Li Tianfu went to pay his respects to the mandarins and was well received by the prefect. After all, the unequal treaty had been wrested from the emperor at this very place following the diplomatic comedy between Qi Ying and Sir Henry Pottinger (Book 1, p 264). The prefect invited Duncan to stay for a meal and in his innocence of Chinese courtesies Duncan accepted. While he was being cheerfully entertained, the *yamen* runners were scurrying through the streets, spreading the word to minor officials and from them to every innkeeper and householder that 'dire penalties awaited them if they ventured to harbour the "foreign devil"'. As a result Li Tianfu and Ling Zhumou had no difficulty, but no one would take Duncan in. Yet the prefect had miscalculated. One of his subordinates failed him.

At first Duncan merely slept on board the boat; but that was costly. Searching everywhere he came to the priest in charge of the city Drum Tower, a kind of temple from which the night-watches and fire-alarms were beaten. There was no guest-room, but permission to spread his bed-mat in the loft was all Duncan wanted. No one had thought to include the priest in the warning against the foreigner but of his own choice he would have none of it. A day or two later he relented and took pity on the homeless traveller saying he could come from sunset to sunrise if he stowed his bedding away and left the place before any worshippers arrived. Tea shops and eating-houses were open to Duncan by day, but he and his companions were busy distributing tracts and Scripture, and finding audiences to listen to the gospel.

For three and a half weeks he made the Drum Tower his home, with (in Hudson Taylor's words) only 'a miserable little side-compartment formed by pieces of matting (as his suite) and where the noise of the drum at various hours of the night, and the multitude of rats which shared his little tent, in no way added to his comfort'. Duncan later wondered how he ever endured it, but physical conditions mattered little in a cause of such spiritual consequence. He worked to acquire the Nanjing Mandarin dialect and make himself well known in the city. Meanwhile Li Tianfu, the 'energetic preacher', and Ling Zhumou being less conspicuous were able to work steadily without interference.

When 'the authorities concluded that (Mr Duncan) was a harmless sort of man and ceased to take notice of him', he found an impecunious carpenter willing to divide his only upstairs room in two by a matting partition and let Duncan, Tianfu and Zhumou rent one half. They moved in on October 15. With every sound audible from the carpenter's family and customers, Duncan could not but soak up the everyday speech of the people. Soon they persuaded

THE NANJING DRUM TOWER WAS FAR MORE IMPRESSIVE

their obliging landlord to divide his living-room–workshop on the
ground floor too. Like Adoniram Judson's famous *zayat* in
Rangoon,[14] this strip of space six feet wide by twenty long became
their preaching hall by day, furnished with a bench down each side
and a table and a chair at the far end. He employed a Mandarin-
speaking teacher and sent particulars to Hudson Taylor of two
banks in Nanjing who had business dealings with others in Hangzhou.

Rudland to the rescue   *November–December 1867*

   Hudson Taylor had his hands full with Mary Bowyer ill at New
Lane and Eliza Nicol in difficulty at Xiaoshan. While he was away
others found that one of the banks in Hangzhou named by Duncan
had failed and the other had left the city. When they reported this to
Hudson Taylor he could find no other channel for remitting funds.

> All his efforts at Nankin, and mine at Hangchau, [Hudson Taylor
> wrote in retrospect] and those of a mutual friend at Shanghai
> (William Gamble) . . . proved unsuccessful. I urged him to come
> himself for a further supply . . . but he felt convinced that if he left
> the city the authorities who chose to ignore his stay would prevent his
> return . . . He would seek first the kingdom of God and trust to God
> in some way or other to supply him. I confess that I was not as happy
> about the matter as he was . . . Therefore, when for the last time the
> money I had sent off [probably through a trading company] was
> returned to me, I felt sure he must be in want.[15]

   So concerned for Duncan was Hudson Taylor that he rose and
knelt by his bed time and again during the night to pray for him.
Duncan was still twenty-three. The temptation to borrow money
would be great, with ample reason for bending the Mission's
principles in the circumstances. So Hudson Taylor asked William
Rudland to go posthaste as his courier to Nanjing with a supply of
money. On October 29 he set out, intent on covering the three
hundred and twenty miles as quickly as he could by public transport – the 'passage-boat'. Although he joined it at four p m it did
not start until the next morning and toiled slowly against headwinds
to reach Suzhou, the half-way point, five days later on November
3.[16]
   Exposure to life with fellow-travellers, without foreign compan-

ions, taught Rudland more useful lessons than he could learn by other means.

> One difficulty was to get a suitable (Chinese) to go with me, as there was not one who could well be spared; so Mr. N offered me his teacher. This offer I accepted, but afterwards regretted, as he was but of little use when he found himself a few miles from home . . . I soon found out that he was an opium-smoker, although he never let me see him take it. Not being able to trust him, I was compelled to fight my way myself. This made me exercise my speaking powers, and use what knowledge I had of the language; so . . . in the end it was profitable . . . The passengers made me as comfortable as they could. I wish you to notice closely – the way I was treated, being in the Chinese costume; one great objection made to it being that the people take more liberty with you in their own costume than in the European. Two of our number were literary men, and as soon as I entered the boat, according to Chinese custom, one of them asked me my honourable name, my age, where I came from, where I was going, and my honourable business. I answered his questions, telling him that I was not a trader, but a preacher of religion, and asked him if he had heard of the religion of Jesus, which made him think I was a Roman Catholic priest. This is another objection made to the costume, for since the priests wear the native dress, you will generally be taken for one by the natives. They did so all the way on my journey, but after looking at the matter in many ways, I have come to the conclusion that it is better to be taken for a Roman Catholic priest than for an opium merchant, as the former is respected, but the latter is hated most bitterly. Though the Chinese use the opium, they hate the opium traffic, because they know its results.[17]

At Suzhou Rudland went in search of Charles Schmidt, who had arrived since Duncan passed through. From his active service in Gordon's Ever-Victorious Army, Schmidt knew the whole area well and gave him useful advice about the long journey still ahead of him.

> He was brought to Jesus through our dear brother Meadows. He is not connected with any society, but has gone to make known the Gospel in the place where he had lived previous to his conversion . . . He has the [very high] honour of the red button from the Emperor for his services, and stands in the same rank as a Mandarin; this is likely to prove useful to him, as it gives him liberties which others cannot have (see Appendix 5). It is his intention shortly to adopt the Chinese

costume, and I think his judgement on the subject is worth something, since he has mixed for so many years (nine) among the
Chinese. He did not go to Soo-chow for want of employment, for he
had a good offer from the custom house, which he refused, in order to
preach Christ to the Chinese . . .[18]

Rudland pressed on, this time hiring a boat for himself, and
passing Wuxi and Changzhou in three days reached Danyang, thirty
miles by canal from the Yangzi, fifty from Zhenjiang and a hundred
miles overland from Nanjing. The easy way would have been to go
on by boat, round two sides of a triangle, but at the price of heat,
blisters, aches and pains, the overland route could get him to his
destination two days sooner. 'A strong current being against us' was
the deciding factor.[19] To Rudland fell the honour of starting the
CIM's reputation for using a wheelbarrow, for economy, not
comfort.[20] Before he set out from Danyang with his bedding and
bag on a wheelbarrow, Rudland found an eating-house and was
waiting for food to be brought when,

A Chinese gentleman by my side, having gone through the ceremony
of asking my age, etc, I answered him, he not knowing but that I was
(Chinese). Shortly after, however, one said that I was a foreigner;
this led to a discussion on the subject, which amused me not a little.
When the food which was all Chinese, came on the table, and they
saw me handling my chopsticks pretty freely, some of them seemed
to be confirmed in their opinion that I was (Chinese), but had come
from another province. Not until one of them came and looked at the
back of my head, and saw that my hair was not black . . . were they
satisfied that I was a foreigner . . . Had I been a (Chinese) in
England, I question much whether I should have been treated half as
well as I was on this occasion. They all treated me with the most
profound respect, listening attentively to all I said to them, and when
I left most of them rose from their seats, and wished me a prosperous
journey.

At noon on the second day he was again mistaken for a Chinese,
at Jurong. And again at night, the man with whom they lodged gave
him his own bed and himself slept on the floor, sending his wife and
children to neighbours. For such treatment Rudland rewarded him
with a New Testament and more money than he asked for. Stiff and
footsore they were glad to meet two boys with donkeys and rode
into the ancient city of Nanjing like Don Quixote and Sancho.
    Hudson Taylor had been right. George Duncan had come to the

end of his store of silver dollars and could give the cook Zhumou no more to feed them on. Knowing that Duncan would not borrow from him, Zhumou made him a gift of the five dollars he himself had. 'Few men know how to make money go further than Mr Duncan, and in this he was well seconded by his servant. Nevertheless, this money also came to an end.'[21] Not to be outdone, Li Tianfu contributed the ten dollars he still had, and they were living on the last dollar when William Rudland and his worthless companion arrived, on Saturday, November 9.

'When I dismounted I could hardly walk into the house,' Rudland told the Bergers. 'As soon as (Zhumou) saw me, he guessed my errand, and told me that God had helped them, and he knew that He would send them supplies by some means, for they had asked it of Him . . . One thing I must ask you to notice – that in the whole journey of 320 miles, only one mission station is in existence, and that has not been many months open; while in every city of any importance, a building may be seen having a cross on the top of it, showing that Romanism has made a footing there.'[22]

Soon afterward Duncan 'succeeded in renting a comfortable house near to the *yamen*, and might perhaps have remained there in peace had not the occurrence of a fire next door drawn the attention of the authorities to him, who brought so much pressure to bear upon his second landlord that Mr Duncan judged it wiser to retire to his humbler quarters . . .' Months later he tried again and secured a house which he made his base until he left China – the firm foothold of the CIM in Nanjing.

Not one person had yet responded to the gospel, but a big stride had been taken towards the millions of 'inland China'. Nanjing was the springboard for the next leap forward up the Yangzi in the coming year.

CHAPTER THIRTEEN

FOILED?
1867

The scholar-gentry of China

The mild opposition met with at Xiaoshan, Hangzhou and Nanjing had its origins deep in Chinese history. The more the missionaries moved away from the coast and in among the Chinese, the more they were to be obstructed. To understand the events it is necessary to turn briefly aside from the narrative and to look at their background. To do so is to sympathise with the literati, the scholar-gentry of this ancient culture.

At their best the literati were men of true, profound scholarship and culture, and more. Practising the Confucian principles which they had mastered in theory, their gentility was ingrained and genuine. All that was best in the heritage of their people and nation they understood and appreciated. Its matchless art and calligraphy, its priceless jades and porcelain, silks and lacquer, sculpture and carving in wood and ivory they enjoyed and conserved.

The effect upon the sincere Confucian was to produce in him a dignified, self-disciplined gentleman, considerate of others and capable of friendliness toward even the uncultured 'barbarian'. But for most the harsh realities of life involved earning a livelihood, preferment to office, status, the freemasonry and loyalties of association with colleagues, and coping with a recalcitrant people. Appointment conferred power, as magistrates and viceroys, to command armed forces, as in the case of Zeng Guofan, Li Hongzhang and others we shall meet. Belonging to the literati, however unsuccessfully, carried an obligation to defend the ancient institutions. On Hudson Taylor's first solo reconnaissance up the Yangzi river from Shanghai in May 1855, a friendly old mandarin and he had talked 'science', horticulture and morality together and exchanged books. Other missionaries often found common ground for friendship with the literati over the classics.

The ability to obtain education and to profit from it was the key to

SCHOLAR-GENTRY AT HOME

social advancement through the State examination system. Thousands of students of the classics converged annually on the provincial examination halls. Locked into individual cells like larvae in a hornet's nest they disgorged their knowledge on to paper, endlessly quoting from the sages and expounding one phrase by using others. Status, employment, preferment as mandarins, even immunity from punishment by flogging were at stake. Success meant celebration and congratulation, feasts and introductions to influential officials. Afterwards young graduates impatiently waited for appointment. From a livelihood as teachers up to the highest rank and honours, their future was assured.

Scholars bred scholars, so a social class of successful scholar-gentry developed over a thousand years. They were the élite. From them the ranking mandarins tended to be drawn. In the Ming dynasty, noted for its high degree of cultural development, this section of society became dominant. Conservatism became established through the centuries, devoted to the preservation of the ancient classics and the status quo after the manner of Richelieu's French Academy. But scholarship was not the only entrée to the brotherhood. A successful merchant could evade the examinations by purchasing degrees from the central government, a minor source of revenue.[1] He still had to conform and to acquaint himself with the protocol.

Confucianism preserved stability, the antithesis of change, making any challenge to the status quo appear subversive of the ancient order rather than contributory towards it. It encouraged obscurantism and closed the minds of its devotees to all change and therefore to external influences and the foreign presence. While Confucian thought motivated some mandarins to keep their treaties, whatever their feelings, it moved others to defensive action. While some of the literati recognised and welcomed what was good in Western knowledge and culture, others rejected and opposed even that. As the repository of ancient morals and precepts they saw their duty to be resistance to subversion.

The chagrin of examination failure could be vented in drunkenness and rioting. The season of examinations was no time for foreigners to be conspicuous in a provincial city. At other times, however, a pool of unemployed and disgruntled literati posed a similar threat. Disgraced and degraded mandarins fuelled each other's discontent. But many successful ones shared the resentment.

The ultra-conservative scholar-gentry abounded, and rightly saw in the challenge of Western ways the death-knell of their own way of life. Naturally they reacted against it and struck back. Barbarians were barbarians in that they were ignorant and blind to the glories of ancient China. The vandalism in 1860 of the irreplaceable treasures of the Summer Palace could only be the work of barbarous men. Pained, grieved and indignant, the true literati feared and resented every fresh incursion of foreign influences into the land of their wonderful forebears. The culture they had inherited from centuries and millennia ago, highlighted and codified by Confucius and the sages since, was pre-eminently worth preserving. What newfangled notions, like steam-power, telegraphs and world trade could compare with it? The old and proven must not be displaced.

The Christian gospel was also a threat. Its emphasis on the individual cut across the fundamental ethic that the family was superior to the individual. Personal conversion, against the will of the clan, undermined the fabric of society and should be prevented. Acceptance of a new religion meant rejection of the old and therefore of the authority of its protectors. The very nature of the Christian message was seen as anarchic. Stability and the status of the literati were being challenged and must be defended. Griffith John after many years of dealings with Chinese of every kind wrote of 'many thousands (of Chinese) who are warmly attached to us'. But of the literati he wrote, from his own point of view on the doorstep of the most resentful province of Hunan, 'It is impossible not to displease them. To preach is to insult them, for in the very act you assume the position of a teacher. To publish a book on religion or science is to insult them . . . This is the way the literati think and feel with respect to foreigners and everything that is foreign . . . The spirit of this class is *the* resisting medium in China.'[2]

'The Missionary Question' 1867

The so-called 'Missionary Question' (a continuing issue touched on in earlier volumes[3] and again in the Prologue of this book) needs to be considered at each historical milestone. The foreigner has become part of the establishment in China, in fulfilment consciously or unconsciously of the decision by the British, French and American governments to support the dynasty rather than to see so great an empire collapse into chaos. Hart (in charge of the Imperial Customs), Martin (promoting international law and Western education), and Burlingame (showing friendly statesmanship), all represented only one side of the subject. Ministers and consuls co-operated with the Zongli Yamen in Peking and with viceroys and governors in the provinces, in preserving peace, although their aggressive role has drawn more attention. Missionaries delved deep into Chinese folklore, classics, history and culture, as the pages of *The Chinese and Missionary Recorder* and the work of James Legge and many others demonstrate. But this side of the foreigner was seen by few of the literati, while most saw only the subversive influence of missionaries riding the war machine into the heart and soul of China.

To Hosea Ballou Morse, Wen Xiang's statement to Sir Rutherford Alcock held the key to 'the Missionary Question', 'Do away with your extraterritoriality clause and merchant and missionary may settle anywhere and everywhere; but retain it, and we must do our best to confine you and our trouble to the treaty ports.'[4] It tied the missionary to opium as 'two evils, upheld by foreign force, which . . . interfered with the proper administration of the provinces, and brought disorder in their train.' Not that the two were associated with each other except as antagonists. 'Opium' was associated with the merchant, whatever useful trading he also engaged in. Both merchant and missionary enjoyed exceptional privileges. If the missionary were to be protected in the interior, the merchant and his activities must also be safeguarded. Even in the treaty ports the merchant 'interfered through his treaty rights with the taxing power of the officials . . . The taxing authorities were debarred from levying dues which might be levied on Chinese owned goods; and when, as too often happened, he lent the cloak of his name to purely Chinese trade . . . indignant resentment' was the natural outcome. When consuls referred complaints to high provincial authorities, the inferior local magistrates under whose jurisdiction the matter had arisen tended to be blamed.

As for the missionary, his teachings stirred up dangerous notions of human rights and justice as every man's due at the hands of the mandarins. Dark currents would gain strength if such teaching continued. From prince to underling the whole system of government rested on venality, while the missionary and Robert Hart and others like him including some merchants, were seen as a yardstick of integrity, to the discomfort of the corrupt. Socially the Christian gospel was divisive, challenging the ancestral rites and denying the validity of Buddhist-Taoist religion and Confucianism. Even if it smacked of truth, its condemnation of evil came too close to the bone to be welcomed by most men. The erection of large buildings in Western styles of architecture, with towers and spires, in locations offensive to *fengshui* (the mystical influences of nature associated with ancestral worship) cut deeply. (*See* Appendix 8)

The implementation of the French treaty enforcing the imperial edict of 1846, which ordered the return to the Roman Church of property confiscated during past persecutions, had begun. Other Catholic actions also provoked resentment. Chinese litigants found that by representing their cases to the missionary as being due to persecution for their interest in Christianity, the priest might approach (and intimidate) the magistrate on their behalf. Some people feigned conversion for what they could gain. For the sake of prestige the French government tended to support its missionaries who interfered in lawsuits, so earning the epithet 'the French protectorate'.[5] Far more serious was the Catholic practice of baptising children in danger of death, and of rescuing abandoned infants (Book 2, p 283), for not only lurid rumours but serious suspicions of malpractice endangered the whole missionary community, Protestant as well as Catholic. The lives of Hudson Taylor's family and friends were to be jeopardised in city after city by rumours about this practice. The massacre of priests and nuns at Tianjin in 1870 was the culmination of popular protest.

Consuls, merchants and newspapers did not hesitate to advise the missionaries, Catholic and Protestant, on how to conduct their work. Only occasionally did the missionaries respond by pointing to factors the critics had overlooked or were ignorant of. On February 10, 1868, for example, the Foreign Office in London advised the LMS to 'inculcate circumspection in regard to their own (missionaries') conduct, and with the utmost consideration for the feelings and character of the people among whom they dwell'. Foreign armies and outrages seemed to be overlooked in this homily to those who were the leaders in respect and consideration for the Chinese. 'The missionaries will do well to follow in the wake of trade, when the people have learnt to see in it material advantages to themselves', it continued! What trade? Opium? – was the natural retort. And what material advantages? Imperialism, colonialism and opium trading were British government policy. A strong riposte was given a year later by Bishop Magee in the House of Lords, 'Should the missionary wait till the beneficent influence of fire-water or opium has made the people amenable to the gospel?' But perhaps a clearer indication of the Foreign Office writer's remoteness from the issues involved was the sentence, 'In all cases of a doubtful nature, where a British missionary desires to receive counsel or directions, his safest course would be to apply to HM Minister at Peking and be guided by his advice.' Consultation with Peking, presumably through a consul, would involve at least a month's delay before a reply would be received. Even a telegram from Peking to London took two weeks, being carried on horseback to Kiahkta in Russian Manchuria to be sent across Siberia. The emergency requiring advice could blow up in a matter of minutes, as at Xiaoshan or Huzhou. And the minister's advice was well known – stay in the treaty ports out of harm's way. Who wanted safety? Freedom to work for China's good was what the missionaries craved.

London's ignorance was pardonable. The opinions of ministers and consuls, who sometimes travelled up country and had a passing acquaintance with life outside the treaty ports, while better informed, were coloured by their diplomatic and consular prejudices. They were good men and some were like-minded Christians, but in understanding missionary motives and policies they were at a disadvantage. 'The Missionary Question' in Chinese eyes at this stage of history was to Hawks Pott, historian of Shanghai, one of missionaries being foreign and unnecessary. Hudson Taylor's statement to prospective members of the Mission (on becoming a Chinese to the Chinese in order to preserve the essentially Chinese nature of the Church in China [pp 354ff]) was crystal clear about the effects of foreignness – of foreign appearance and behaviour, 'Its tendencies are to approximate believers to foreign nations . . . and indeed, the foreign airs given to everything connected with religion have very largely hindered the rapid dissemination of the truth among the Chinese.'[6]

It branded Christianity as an alien, European religion, but there was more to it than that. It was a matter of missionaries having a job to do, of many methods still being of necessity experimental, of their teaching inescapably being subversive, of abuses and indiscretions by some besmirching the good name of the innocent. It was also a matter of pioneers meeting situations of which they had no previous experience, of people and governments responding blindly as best they knew how – but from it all of new principles, new Churches and major new trends developing in Chinese thought. It would be decades before reform movements and the overthrow of the dynasty would result, as result they would. Sun Yat-sen, the reformer and father of the republic, was an infant not yet two years old. (*See* Personalia) But at the same time the power of the Industrial Revolution and the spread of democracy and scientific knowledge – factors distinct from any missionary issue – were having the identical result they would have had with or without missionary involvement. Missions were deeply implicated but the upheavals already in evidence in 1867, as Hudson Taylor and his Mission embarked on their innovations, sprang from 'the Barbarian Question' of which 'the Missionary Question' was a facet. In 1867–8 this became all too apparent.

'The Barbarian Question'   *October 1867*

On October 12, 1867, the Zongli Yamen issued a circular to all viceroys and provincial governors. It is to be distinguished entirely from that of April 1872 known as the Zongli Memorandum or Chinese Circular. The Circular of October 12, 1867, began with the words: 'The barbarian question is one of old standing.'[7] Prince Kong and his fellow mandarins at the foreign office were still smarting under the insults of 1860 and before. Under duress they had conceded extraordinary privileges to the Allied intruders, and as Hosea Ballou Morse said, 'They dreaded the future and were fearful that they might be driven to make still further concessions' when the treaties came up for reconsideration. The imperial Manchu administration knew their own weakness at this time, a legacy of panic and flight in the face of the Allied advance on the capital. Weak in relation to the barbarians, they also knew how weak they were towards their own powerful provincial nobility. By drawing the viceroys and governors into the international arena they would strengthen internal cohesion while confronting the foreigner.

So the Zongli Yamen consulted the provincial viceroys and governors. With steamships and modern armaments the barbarians need stop at nothing. With over a dozen open ports the merchants could not now be properly controlled. Foreign envoys had been admitted to the capital and consuls to the ports. Even a *daotai* of the fourth rank in the hierarchy had to enter a viceroy's expansive and illustrious *yamen* by a side entrance. But foreign consuls were demanding and being given, as their sovereign's representative, the right to use the main entrance. The nation was watching these humiliations. What should be done when the envoys made the expected demands for audience of the emperor, for Chinese embassies abroad, for freedom to construct railways and telegraphs and mines in China, and the right for foreign merchants and missionaries to reside and extend their activities anywhere in the interior?[8]

Prominent among the responses were memorials from the two victors of the Taiping campaign, Zeng Guofan and Li Hongzhang. Among the honours loaded upon Zeng had been the titular viceroyalty of Nanjing and appointment to be generalissimo of all imperial forces, with the task of suppressing the Nianfei.[9] These marauding forces, thousands in strength since their reinforcement by defeated Taipings, were more a mounted banditti than a revolutionary army. They did almost as they pleased in the provinces of Shandong and Henan, extending their threats into Anhui and Zhili.

In Zeng's absence from Nanjing, Li Hongzhang became the acting viceroy in spite of being a native of Anhui, one of the three provinces he ruled, while still holding his post as Commissioner for Foreign Affairs. 'Nanking became alive with troops camped round it in the most favourable positions to command the river Yangtze, whilst the artillery was held ready for action . . . Foreigners became convinced "that Li contemplated the insane folly of armed resistance to a foreign force in some possible eventuality" . . . Everyone at that time was full of the idea that Tseng and Li together could become masters of Central China . . .'[10] After a year the court in the capital began to fear the power of these two men, backed as they were by Hunanese troops from Zeng's home province and Anhui men loyal to Li. An arsenal and dockyard were started at Fuzhou to counter the threat of Li's arsenal at Nanjing. And in 1867 Zeng was promoted to the presidency of the ministry of war, in the capital and under the eye of the court, while retaining his post at Nanjing.

Li was promoted to titular viceroy of Hubei and Hunan but given command of the campaign to eradicate the Nianfei. He marched at the head of his forty thousand troops, drove the Nianfei out of Henan into Shandong and cornered eighty thousand in the peninsula with their backs to the sea. He then employed sixty thousand men to build a wall, fronted by a ditch, a hundred miles long, and a cordon of forts one mile apart, each garrisoned by five hundred men. Employing a feint, the mounted Nianfei broke through the line of forts and a race for the only other defensible position, the Grand Canal, ensued. Li succeeded in reaching and holding it. He was degraded three steps in nominal rank, but not for long. When a force of Muslim rebels crossed from Shanxi into Zhili and the

Nianfei invaded Zhili from Shandong, frantic appeals to save the capital and the sacred tombs of the imperial family brought him back. On September 5, 1867, all the honours of which he had been stripped were restored to Li and he became the substantive viceroy of Hubei and Hunan. In August 1868 he finally routed the Nianfei.

To glance ahead – on the death of the viceroy of Zhili, Zeng Guofan was promoted to succeed him, with Ma Xinyi of Hangzhou, governor of Zhejiang, designated to replace Zeng at Nanjing. Preparations were in train at Nanjing for Zeng to hand over to Ma, when Hudson Taylor became the centre of the major furore which brought Zeng into conflict with Britain. It anchored Zeng to Nanjing against his will. Before he could leave to assume one of the highest posts in China he had the deep humiliation of being forced to concede all Britain's demands. 'The Barbarian Question' had been shown to be as live an issue as ever.

In complete contrast, back in Tianjin and Peking three men, one English and two American, had established very different relations with the imperial authorities. Robert Hart, Anson Burlingame and W A P Martin (pp 30–1, 219–20) true friends of China, had won the confidence and friendship of court and council. Broad generalisation about barbarians and missionaries was seen to be misleading.

The Huzhou riddle[11]   *September–October 1867*

Ever since April when Hudson Taylor had been with George Duncan to Huzhou 'for the purpose of exploring', he had been looking for an opportunity to go again, this time with James Williamson. 'We want to plant out,' was his horticultural phrase. Well knowing Huzhou's reputation he was grasping the nettle. Would the Chinese authorities, could the authorities, support an attempt to occupy and evangelise a city known for its wickedness?

> This city, almost on the southern confines of the Great Lake, is inhabited by a people peculiarly turbulent and irritable. Their situation in a district infested by such lawless hordes as the notable Great Lake robbers, may in part account for this. Their own magistrates seem to have but little power over them, and are, indeed, as they confess to us, afraid of the people whom they nominally rule.

In May the Nicol rumpus, Sir Rutherford Alcock's investigations, and John Sell's death prevented this advance. In June Hudson

Taylor took Duncan and McCarthy up the Qiantang river – as much to take them out of the company of foreigners, (for the sake of their language learning, and to give them experience of living alone with Chinese) as to preach the gospel. As soon as he reached Hangzhou again in July, his conjunctivitis, the induction of Wang Lae-djün as pastor of the church, and a fortnight of consular despatches and Ningbo proclamations tied him down. The great heat and Grace's illness and death filled August. It looked as if September was going the same way as the last four months, after Duncan left for Nanjing and Eliza Nicol, suffering severe pain in her side, called for help. Hudson Taylor had been in Xiaoshan on the 3rd. He answered the call at once on the 8th, came back for Maria on the 10th, left her there to reassure the Nicols, and on the day Duncan reached Nanjing, September 18, at last set off for Huzhou with Williamson.

James Williamson had meanwhile carried out a preliminary reconnaissance with Liu Jinchen, a Ningbo Christian living in Hangzhou. At Tangqi they had preached and talked with interested people from six in the morning to six at night, until Liu was hoarse. Some had even brought stools to sit and listen more comfortably. Williamson's report to Hudson Taylor was reminiscent of the Gospels, about Galilee where the common people heard Jesus gladly. But he had gone on to Huzhou, found Ningbo men ready to be helpful, and learned that houses were available for rental. Returning to Hangzhou he waited for Hudson Taylor and together they set off again.

This time they followed the consul's advice[12] and, 'taking a copy of the Treaty proclamation and of course our passports', called first at the prefect's *yamen*. Referred to the two district magistrates, they were granted an interview and the assistance of a *dibao* or constable, 'without which we could not have (made progress)'. They found 'a nice little house near the south gate', with a large guest-hall to be used as a chapel, agreed the terms, signed the documents in the name of Liu Jinchen as instructed, and paid the deposit. Possession was promised for 'the 1st day of the 9th month' of the Chinese calendar, in October.

Within an hour or two Hudson Taylor was on his way home by passage-boat, leaving Williamson and Liu Jinchen living in a boat and going ashore to preach, until they could take possession. It was 'with the *help* of the authorities' that the house had been found and rented so expeditiously. But better still, Williamson was showing more promise than even McCarthy and Duncan. 'Williamson is perhaps the best helper I have got. Thoroughly devoted, of very respectable ability, loving the Chinese, and most unselfish. Add to this that he is cautious, courteous, and economical, and you may judge of his value to me.'

This was encouraging. He could now say that Hangzhou and Ningbo were occupied together with other missions, but Shaoxing, Xiaoshan, Fenghua, Taizhou and Huzhou 'we are alone in'. Had he known it at that moment he could have added Nanjing. 'Thus of the eleven Fu cities (prefectures) . . . five, nearly one half, are still destitute of the gospel; I hope, if spared, to see some of them supplied.' One of the five was Wenzhou, and he had plans to send George Stott and James Meadows there very soon. Could he have seen a century ahead he might have caught a glimpse of this province of Zhejiang with some counties claiming eighty to ninety per cent of the population under a communist regime professing to be Christian, with fifty thousand at Wenzhou alone.[13] He could not. Faith supplied the resolution to work with that end in view.

By September 30 clouds were gathering over Huzhou. 'Since I left, difficulties have arisen from the hostility of some of the people, which, for the time being, are preventing our obtaining possession of the premises . . . I have had to propose to Mr McCarthy to defer his return to (Yanzhou) for the present, as in Mr Williamson's absence I need his help . . . The work here is extending on every hand . . .' On October 19 Williamson was still being denied possession and the riddle was, Why? Why, when the authorities themselves had helped to arrange the deal? Then in early November word came that Williamson, still in his boat, had 'ague'. Hudson Taylor prepared to go to him before keeping his promise to Jackson to visit Taizhou as soon as possible. Jackson had written on October 9 pleading with his usual hyperbole for him to come soon. 'The people are flocking by multitudes to our chapel, and we have no one able to preach to them a full Gospel. I do the utmost in my power to communicate to them that Gospel which alone is able to turn them from darkness to light, and from the power of Satan unto God.' He and Aseng were doing their best but it was not enough, the people wanted more. 'In fact, the whole of Tae-tsiu (ie Taizhou) are pleading for (your) arrival.' Jackson felt isolated and frustrated by lack of fluency. But that night Hudson Taylor himself went down with his old enemy dysentery. The disease could be light and transient, very painful, or little short of cholera. This time he had 'more severe suffering' than ever. For two weeks he was helpless and for a time in danger of his life. John McCarthy went to take Williamson's place at Huzhou and Williamson arrived at Hangzhou with malaria.[14] His passport was expiring and well or ill he could not stay at Huzhou without it. So McCarthy was there when violence erupted.

Wenzhou: Stott's 'prey'[15]   November 1867

Only two years before, John Stevenson and George Stott had sailed from London. Already Stevenson had had his own work at Shaoxing since September 1866, but Stott had quietly played second fiddle to James Meadows in Ningbo and to George Crombie at Fenghua. He was too good for that, and well able to rise above his lameness. The spirit in which this one-legged schoolmaster had written from Scotland offering his services to Hudson Taylor, quoting *Isaiah* 33.23, 'The lame take the prey', had been the spirit which had made light of his riding accident (p 307). He had the qualities of a pioneer. At last they were to be proved.

He arrived at Hangzhou on November 9 while Hudson Taylor was ill with dysentery. Stott's zeal did him good. 'We have had a very pleasant visit' from him, Hudson Taylor still felt ten days later, though it had been for no more than a short weekend. Sitting by his bedside, Stott had proposed going without delay to stake a claim in Wenzhou, well knowing the risks. James Meadows had volunteered to help.

Wenzhou was another ancient city, the chief city of southern Zhejiang, steeped for centuries in idolatry and confirmed in arrogance by the failure of the Taiping rebels to touch it. What reception he would be given was unpredictable. Soon he was to write, 'The idolatry here is dreadful . . . In this proud city of glittering temples, they reckon their gods are of a superior order, since they saved the city of Great-Good-Luck and Golden-Glory from the ravages of rebellion.' The city stands near the mouth of a great river like the Qiantang. Both spring from the same mountainous watershed far to the west. Midway between the treaty ports of Ningbo and Fuzhou, Wenzhou was paid scant attention by foreign merchants. Stott lived there for over a year before he met another Westerner. But a brisk coastal trade in silk, tea and agricultural products existed between Wenzhou and Ningbo.

The Chinese merchants' ocean-going junks had to pass through the Nimrod Sound between the Zhousan (Chusan) islands and the mainland. An archipelago of small islands made it a notorious haunt of pirates 'not only numerous but almost numberless', Meadows claimed. Only large armed convoys attempted the journey down the coast, calling at Taizhou and Wenzhou. Meadows and Stott, with a Ningbo evangelist named Mr Zhu Xingjun and the faithful basket-maker Feng Nenggui, proposed to board a merchant junk at Zhenhai, at the mouth of the Ningbo river, and join a convoy. Meadows set out with a fever, but on the twelve-mile journey downstream from Ningbo developed serious symptoms. He had to be sent back at once to John Parker's hospital at Ningbo, while Stott, Zhu and Nenggui boarded the junk without him.[16]

Nenggui's story has been told in part (Book 3, Index), but deserves to be told again. His father had died when he was small and his mother had deserted him. Stunted in growth by cold and hunger, all his life he remained weak and sickly yet his zeal and achieve-ments were heroic. Soon after Hudson Taylor and Maria set up their house at Bridge Street in 1858, Nenggui came into their preaching hall with two other young basket-makers and responded to. the gospel. His refusal to make an incense basket for a customer amazed the painter Wang Lae-djün, working up a ladder, and led directly to his conversion. Unemployed because he would not work on Sundays, Nenggui went into a tea shop and sat talking to other customers. An elderly farmer named Wang Queyao (Ch'üo-yao) from a neighbouring village listened carefully, moved into Neng-gui's lodgings to learn more, and was introduced to Hudson Taylor. When Dr William Parker's hospital was to close if Hudson Taylor could not run it, Wang Lae-djün, Nenggui and Wang Queyao joined him to help in every way they could. Nenggui became a humble colporteur, Wang Queyao an evangelist and Wang Lae-djün first an evangelist and then pastor of the Hangzhou church.

On May 1, 1866, when seven women and three men were baptised at Kongpu, between Ningbo and Zhenhai, six of the women and one man had been led to Christ by Nenggui, in spite or because of strong opposition by which he was unshaken. By early 1867 his own converts at Kongpu formed a congregation of fourteen with himself as their unofficial pastor. The wealthiest and most influential family in the village were among them. He had helped John Stevenson to get started at Shaoxing. In Feng Nenggui George Stott had as reliable a companion as he could want.

Mr Zhu's background was very different. Educated, and moving in the business world, he had longstanding links with the merchants of Wenzhou. When he was converted he too forsook his source of livelihood to become a preacher. He and Nenggui had another strange experience in common. When the Taipings ravaged Ningbo and its countryside in 1862 and were driven off eventually, they compelled Nenggui to go with them far beyond Hangzhou. At last he escaped and found his way home. Zhu Xingjun had been less fortunate. Merchants and scholars suffered more than the common people. Hundreds of thousands were slaughtered but he survived with the four characters for *Tai Ping Tian Guo* branded on his cheek.[17] To rid himself of their taint he burned them out. The Bridge Street church in Ningbo had asked James Meadows to be their pastor with Zhu Xingjun as evangelist.

Nimrod Sound was navigated peacefully and at Taizhou Josiah Jackson joined them to go on to Wenzhou where they landed before the end of November.[18] Stott was in foreign clothes and all Zhu's influence with his acquaintances was needed even to find an innkeeper who would take them. Not until January 18, 1868, did they succeed in renting a house. Jackson then left him to return to his own city, and George Stott stayed to face mobs and stoning alone until February 1870 when he left for the first time – to meet his bride-to-be at Shanghai. For two years he had been three hundred miles from Hudson Taylor at Hangzhou, and six hundred from Duncan, by the shortest route.

Hangzhou still the hub[19]   *September–December 1867*

Grace Taylor had died on August 23. Ten days later Hudson Taylor had gone to Xiaoshan in answer to the Nicols' call, and again on Sunday, September 8. Thinking Maria with her own experience of seven pregnancies might help him to reach a diagnosis of Eliza's pain he had come back to Hangzhou and escorted Maria to Xiaoshan for a week, leaving Jennie Faulding to do Maria's work and mother the children. In a record of many more notable events there is little space for family life, but this week was exceptional.

On Sunday evening Jennie was with the intelligent Howard (Freddie) when he knelt at his bedside before going to sleep. 'He asked as he has always done of late for "a new heart",' she reported. 'When he got up, as I kissed him he said, "Has Jesus given me a new heart then?" . . . I told him that Jesus had always been willing to give him a new heart, and had been waiting till Freddie was willing

. . . "Then I needn't ask Jesus for a new heart any more." ' Three nights later, on the day Hudson Taylor set off with James Williamson for Huzhou, Mary Bell, the nurse, accidentally set the mosquito net on fire and, petrified, could only scream. Emily Blatchley ran in, rescued Freddie from the bed and extinguished the flames. Barely awake, he was quite unmoved. He had been wanting to tell everyone about his new heart lest 'a bright angel might take me away in the night'! So started Frederick Howard Taylor, MD, MRCP, FRCS Edin., his father's biographer, on his 'pilgrim way'.

After Hudson Taylor's return from Huzhou and the burial of Grace's coffin in 'the little house' in her corner of the garden, he continued to visit the Nicols at Xiaoshan, staying as long as he could afford to be away from Hangzhou. Still Eliza Nicol's long-expected confinement failed to materialise. Supervising all his missionaries, scattered over an area as extensive as England, trying to keep in touch with Duncan, sending Rudland off with money, corresponding with the Bergers, the consul and a hundred and one others, and running the local Hangzhou missionary work, was all difficult in the circumstances. When Mary Bowyer fell ill with rheumatic fever, what Jennie called 'inflammation of the heart', and pleurisy, he had to come back to Hangzhou to treat her. John McCarthy, wanting to illustrate a statement about Hudson Taylor's 'tenacity of purpose and steady perseverance in spite of all obstacles', recalled,

> He travelled by the quickest means available, crossing the river opposite Hangchow late in the evening when it was almost dark. The city gate was as he feared already closed, and not to be opened except by order of the Governor . . . We had given him up for the night, being especially thankful that there had been some abatement of the dangerous symptoms . . . On his way towards the gate he had noticed a government messenger who passed him . . . Knowing that this man would be sure to get an entrance Mr Taylor kept close to him, though in the deepening darkness not noticed by the man. Arrived at the gates, the messenger called out and the soldiers on guard let down a basket in which, by means of a rude windlass, the man was to be hoisted up on the wall. As the basket ascended Mr Taylor noticed that a good piece of rope hung down from the basket. This he was not slow to seize, so that as the basket was raised he was raised also, and carried to the top. The men who were at the windlass all the time railing at the weight of the messenger, when they saw the foreign devil at the top of the wall, they seemed at first almost inclined to throw him down again. He was enabled to prove to them that it was more profitable for them to allow him to remain, and

quickly left them behind . . . When asked how he managed to get in so late . . . Mr Taylor replied that he had given the man 'two hundred reasons' why he should let him pass . . . It was after all only a question of handing the man two hundred cash (for his efforts).[20]

It was Saturday, October 19. He had left Maria with the Nicols. On Sunday he was summoned to Xiaoshan again. Eliza was at last in labour. On the 23rd he wrote to 'Dr Miss F' ('Dear Miss Faulding'), 'Mrs N was confined on Monday eve[g] after a very trying and somewhat dangerous time. The infant never breathed. I was very anxious about Mrs N but now I hope she may do well, tho' I am far from comfortable about her.' His postscript about printer's proofs was no mere afterthought. Work was work. There was always something more.

He brought Maria home for the next weekend to be present for six more baptisms. The courtyard at No 1 was filled with a hundred and sixty people for the service. The number baptised in Hangzhou had reached twenty-five. Then he hurried away again, this time to Shaoxing, to rent a house for Susan Barnes as a rendezvous for Chinese women, and a girls' school. But Emily Blatchley developed erysipelas, a severe and dangerous 'inflammation', and he had to return. That day, November 2, McCarthy wrote, 'Mr Taylor's hands are full. We do so love him for his unselfish, constant love to us, and for his zeal in his Master's service.' Maria had written to her brother, Samuel Dyer, hinting that he might come and help. 'Superintendence (of the work) threatens to preclude almost entirely (Hudson's) engaging in direct mission work. (Emily Blatchley) has come out partly as our governess, partly for the purpose of assisting him in writing, etc; but there is still a great deal that can only be done by himself, or by a private confidential secretary.' Nothing came of it, until later Samuel succeeded Alexander Wylie as the Bible Society representative in China.

Hudson Taylor arrived home on the evening of November 2 and the next day Jennie noted that he himself was ill. 'He has not been so ill since our return to England,' Maria wrote. He had intended going back to Huzhou to help James Williamson again, but his 'enteritis' was so severe that John McCarthy went instead with the teacher Yi Zewo (Tse-ngoh).

In this hub of action at Hangzhou, Hudson Taylor had his office, entered easily through its own small yard from the main courtyard and working area. (*See* diagram, p 247) Another door led to the staircase of the upstairs living quarters. In the office he interviewed people, dictated letters to Maria or Emily Blatchley, prayed and planned, walking up and down, to and fro, as he found most conducive to thought. There he read William Burns' warm letter of October 9 from Newchang (now Yingkou) on the Liaoning coast north-east of Tianjin and Peking, six weeks after he had arrived there.

It is a much larger place than Swatow, as you and I found it in 1856, and, besides, is the door of access to the whole of the province of Mantchooria, in which, as also in the provinces of Kirin and Amour beyond it, Mandarin, little differing from the language of the capital, is the spoken language. How sad to think that, in a region so extensive and populous, so open and so healthful, there should yet be, if I except myself, no Protestant missionary . . . The Rev A Williamson, formerly of Shanghai, and now agent of the National Bible Society of Scotland, is going over the whole region in detail, and he is much impressed with the importance of this as a field for missionary operations. When the members of your mission are ready to leave Hangchow and its vicinity for distant places, I could not imagine a more suitable destination for a few of them than some of the many cities and villages of Mantchooria. Should any of your number be guided in this direction, I need not say that I would do all in my power to help them on their way . . .[21]

Access to western China through Burma had stirred his imagination and suggested co-operation with the CIM. This invitation to send missionaries to Manchuria was the second such possibility. It was not to be. By the time Dr James Cameron, a pioneer of the CIM dubbed 'the Livingstone of China', reached Manchuria, William Burns had died, for he only survived one winter.

The first Huzhou riot[22]   *November 1867*

When John McCarthy took James Williamson's place at Huzhou in the first week of November, the wise actions of the Muslim governor, Ma Xinyi, had apparently contained the unrest in his province of Zhejiang. The consuls' indignation over Xiaoshan and elsewhere had been mollified. And although delay in obtaining possession of the premises rented in Huzhou with the magistrate's help was inconvenient, there was no apparent reason to doubt success, given patience. That is, until a series of scurrilous placards was posted in public places, denouncing missionaries in the vilest language. Anti-foreign resentment was never far below the surface. A visit by Carl Kreyer in foreign clothes was greeted by a fresh wave of them.

On Wednesday, November 13, McCarthy and his companions Yi Zewo and Liu Jinchen were walking to a tea shop where they sometimes sat talking with other customers, when they were met in a narrow lane by two or three men. 'One apparently the worse for liquor' struck at McCarthy, jostled them, spoke 'derisively' of Christianity and seized hold of Mr Yi. McCarthy was ahead. Seeing that his friends were not following, he turned back. An unruly crowd surrounded them, but he walked through it and returned to the boat for his passport and a copy of the treaty proclamation, 'an exhibition of which has hitherto always induced respect'.

He asked Mr Liu to alert the *dibao* (constable), who came too late to influence events. By then McCarthy and Mr Yi had reached the tea shop. Again a crowd gathered yelling abuse. Seeing one of the former troublemakers accusing them of crimes usually held against the Catholics, Yi angrily went across to protest. 'You compel us to appeal to the authorities,' he said, and insultingly seized him by his *bianzi* (queue), 'upon which there was a regular uproar' – led by underlings from the prefect's *yamen*! The ringleader slapped Yi on the mouth and cheek two or three times and went out. Bedlam ensued, with the onlookers roaring and waving their arms about. But a few attempted to make the peace.

Hoping to pacify the mob McCarthy, Liu and Yi sat down at a table and called for tea. But soon an official arrived and told Mr Yi to go with him. He could but comply, and was beaten all the way to the *yamen*. When the crowd tried to prevent McCarthy going too, he struggled through them and followed to the *yamen* entrance. By then the mob was howling for Yi's blood. Realising that one of the posters had called for bloodshed, Yi followed Chinese custom crying out aloud to the prefect for justice.

Passport and proclamation in hand, John McCarthy tried to enter the *yamen* to claim the prefect's protection, but 'a whole crowd of (the magistrate's) servants opposed our entrance.' Whereupon, seeing that the *yamen* itself was closed to the foreigner, the mob at the door set on Yi again. Some tried to drag McCarthy away, but 'for a time I managed to protect him, for unfortunately they seemed determined *not* to hit me, but in the dragging and pulling a man caught hold of my (queue) nearly pulling me on my back, when they dragged (Yi) away, knocked him down and kicked him.' This understatement covered a ferocious attack with weapons, leaving Mr Yi scarcely able to move when they stopped. The proclamation was snatched away and several tried to tear the passport also out of McCarthy's hand as he made his way back through the roaring mob to Yi, calling upon God to protect him.

Apparently thinking Yi was dead, 'the most furious' leaders turned away. Liu Jinchen was nowhere to be seen. McCarthy tried to find someone to help him take Yi back to their boat but none would help. So being a muscular man he alone half-carried him through the streets. Sending Yi home by boat for treatment, he wrote a quick note to Hudson Taylor in which his own state of mind was apparent: 'Wednesday evening (Nov.13/67). The devil has at length I believe overreached himself in this place. The seeming quiet of which I wrote last has been somewhat rudely broken today.' Believing it to be 'the path of duty to remain' at Huzhou, McCarthy briefly described events and waited for advice. 'I do not think there is any danger to me . . . I do not yet know where Liu is.'

A battered and bruised Yi Zewo arrived at New Lane the next day with a partial story of what had happened. He did not know what had become of John McCarthy or of Liu Jinchen. Immediate action was vital. Consulting with Carl Kreyer, Hudson Taylor, still weak in bed from dysentery, drafted a petition to the provincial governor and had it written by a calligrapher trained in the right conventions. Dressed in his most formal Chinese costume he was carried to a sedan chair, so arranged that he could almost lie in it. Accompanied by Carl Kreyer and their 'teachers' they went first to the *daotai* who was away superintending the repair of the Qiantang river embankments, and then to the governor's *yamen*. Both the consul and (on the previous occasion) the governor himself had advised this course of action. 'Amity' between the nations could best be preserved by such co-operation. The document read:

Petition to the Fu-tai (Governor)

The Petition of J Hudson Taylor, British missionary, and Superintendent of the China Inland Mission, on account of a most urgent matter, and with a view to the preservation of life:

Some time ago your petitioner sent the British missionary, James Williamson and others to the city of Hu-chow, to distribute good books and disseminate the true religion; and there a house had already been rented. But . . . they have been prevented from entering into it, and at the present time are staying in a small boat, unable to move the one way or the other. Mr Williamson petitioned the Wu-hsing (ie Huzhou) magistrate, and received the reply that the matter would be attended to in a short time, etc, etc. Therefore the only course was to wait patiently.

But suddenly and unexpectedly yesterday a multitude of the people . . . became uproarious, took the British missionary John McCarthy and others, and dragged them to the gate of the Hu-chow Prefect's *yamen*, shamefully disgracing them, snatching at the passport and the treaty proclamation. Moreover they took the Assistant Yi (and others) and cruelly beat them with various articles, severely wounding them. Mr McCarthy sought the help of the (Prefect) but in vain. It appears as if the Treaty of Amity had become a dead letter. The matter being most important, your petitioner urgently begs Your Excellency graciously to interpose, and without delay to do justice, repressing the evil-doers, preserving life, and showing hospitality to strangers from a distance.

Presented the sixth year of T'ung-che (Tong Zhi), the 10th month . . .[23]

Ma Xinyi was conducting military examinations, but a deputy listened courteously as Hudson Taylor urged action to prevent loss of life. Realising it would be some hours before a reply could come from the governor, Hudson Taylor then decided to make an immediate appeal to the prefect of Huzhou before more violence broke out. Even that would have to be carried the fifty miles between them. As soon as the 'petition' was written, in reality a protest, Carl Kreyer left for Huzhou with another Chinese companion for McCarthy. Hardly had they gone than the evangelist Liu Jinchen arrived at New Lane (on Friday 15th) in as bad a state as Yi had been and with no news of McCarthy. Bit by bit Hudson Taylor pieced the story together.

Liu had been on the edge of the crowd vainly trying with some well-disposed townsmen to pacify the mob. But when the ringleaders had left Yi for dead they had recognised Liu and set on him. Severely beaten, somehow he had escaped to the boat to replace the shoes he had lost in the affray, and then bravely made for the *yamen* of the county magistrate who had helped them to rent a house. The mob had anticipated his move and he ran into them at the entrance. Again they beat him. Dragging him to the canal they tied a heavy stone to him and only the intervention of bystanders saved him from being drowned. A friendly *dibao* lent him money and Liu found his way to Hangzhou, like them not knowing what had become of the others.[24]

The last appeal *November 1867*

By Sunday, November 17, Hudson Taylor felt he had enough of the facts to report to Consul Fittack at Ningbo 'a serious disturbance (at Hu-chow-fu) which compels me to appeal to you for assistance'. It was expected of him. He had not yet seen the better way he soon preferred. So he echoed the conventional sentiments once again. Beginning with James Williamson's first visit to Huzhou in September and his own success in renting premises, he outlined how opposition had been fomented, how John McCarthy had taken Williamson's place, and how Yi Zewo had come back suffering severely from injuries received. He reported his appeal to the provincial governor and to the Huzhou prefect, and Kreyer's departure to support McCarthy.

> Liu Kin-ch'en (ie Jinchen) arrived in Hangchou yesterday, having succeeded in making his escape; he has been very brutally treated and is much shaken . . . his head and face were frightfully swollen . . . In all probability both he and Yi would have lost their lives but for the interposition of the better disposed inhabitants, most of whom continue well affected towards us. [After an account of the outrage at Huzhou he continued:] Two facts . . . appear to make this outrage particularly aggravated. The first is that these deeds of violence were perpetrated, not so much by the people at large, as by the immediate servants of the (prefect) himself, and at the very gates of his *yamen*. The second is that a British subject in immediate danger of his life, when presenting his passport and claiming help and protection was rudely repulsed, and the attempt made by the underlings of the very magistrate to gain possession of and destroy the document which empowered him to seek such aid. We also greatly regret the loss of the proclamation, and fear it may have been destroyed, in which case we cannot replace it.
>
> The result of our appeal to the (governor) and to the Huchow Fu (prefect) remains to be seen; in the meantime, as British subjects with passport and treaty in hand, we have been publicly insulted and abused. May I therefore beg of you to take such prompt measures as shall secure our protection, and vindicate our rights as British subjects.
>
> I have the honour to remain,
> Your obedient servant,
> (Signed) J Hudson Taylor.[25]

For the last time he had taken his stand firmly on nationality and treaty rights in appealing for protection and for vindication of violations of the treaties.

The governor's reply arrived too late to be quoted. He had had time to consult the prefect of Huzhou first.

> Ma, Governor of the Province of Che-kiang (ie Zhejiang)
>
> In reply to the petition of the English missionary J Hudson Taylor:
> When Missionaries travel in the interior authorized by passport, provided they confine themselves to their legitimate functions of propagating their faith, the people cannot be allowed to collect in mobs and be uproarious. And the Prefect and District Magistrate ought *bona fide* to protect them, and not to look on unconcerned.
> I will send down an officer who in conjunction with the Prefect and magistrate will thoroughly and without delay adjudicate upon the matter. The two (nations) must live in amity, and unintelligent people cannot be suffered to make mischief.
> The three passports, having been examined, are returned.[26]

So favourable a reply drew from Jennie the sigh of relief in her next home letter, 'To dare to trouble him at all was a bold step to take.'

In Huzhou Carl Kreyer and McCarthy presented the protest to the prefect and after a satisfactory interview with him Kreyer returned at once to Hangzhou. On November 18, therefore, Hudson Taylor reported again to Consul Fittack that not only had the response of the governor been satisfactory, but the prefect of Huzhou had issued this reply to Hudson Taylor in a tone of injured innocence:

> It appears on examination that foreign preachers of religion are already clearly recognised by the Treaty of Amity. All persons, whether soldiers or private citizens, not wishing to join this religion are of course at liberty to follow their own inclinations, why then should there be riotous disturbances?
> As to the matter about which you have petitioned me, I will command the magistrates to investigate them thoroughly.
> The petition is accepted.[27]

The prefect had arrested and beaten the two innocent *dibaos* in whose districts the disturbances had taken place and ordered his two subordinate magistrates to punish the offenders and take appropriate action. But this statement made it appear that the riot had been without his knowledge, that he acknowledged the right of missionaries and their Chinese colleagues to live and work safely in Huzhou, and that they could therefore return. The facts were very different. The riot had been instigated and led by a certain 'Sing Tsin-si', one of the Huzhou literati with the equivalent of a D.Litt., superior in academic rank to the prefect, and therefore beyond his reach.

After all the comings and goings of the past week, Hudson Taylor's enteritis relapsed on the 19th and, still unable to get to Huzhou himself, he asked Mr Tsiu to go instead. Did he realise what courage it required for him to go? Memories of the Xiaoshan flogging were still fresh. Yi and Liu, recovering at No 1 New Lane, had been the victims only a week ago. But Tsiu went, specifically to search in Huzhou for proclamations by the mandarins. All he found were two unsatisfactory ones put out by the district magistrates, not by the prefect. But McCarthy quickly saw from Tsiu's taciturn manner how apprehensive he was there, and asked him to take a letter to Hangzhou. Some advice on how to proceed now would be useful. In this new climate of affairs should he try to gain possession of the rented house? And could Mr Yu, the travelling 'doctor' they had met on the Qiantang journey, now teaching in the New Lane school, come up instead of Tsiu? The uneducated servant Kreyer had brought to him was no more use than McCarthy himself in any dealings with officials which might arise.

Incredibly perhaps, Hudson Taylor had a different, bolder plan. John McCarthy ought to come back to his family and work in Hangzhou. He himself with Maria and the children, Emily, at last recovering from her long illness, and Louise Desgraz would take a break from work and see what they could do in Huzhou!

Try women and children!　　　　　　　　*November–December 1867*

Within a week Hudson Taylor's relapse was over and he felt fit to travel. Kreyer, Williamson and McCarthy were all beginners. Maria's fluency and his own experience might make the difference. At least he would make his own assessment of the Huzhou situation. After the weekend when Rudland returned from Nanjing, they set out, on November 26, the women in a houseboat and Hudson Taylor following in the sleek footboat – with Mr Berger's shotgun –

to enjoy the holiday and bag food for the family. The leisurely canal journey did them all good, and on arrival they chose to moor the boats inside the city rather than outside the walls where the danger from robbers was greater.

When Hudson Taylor called on their landlord, he was willing for him to take possession if only the prefect would put out a proclamation strong enough to protect him against the instigators of the outrage. After all, it had been with official help that the agreement had been made in the first place. The Huzhou riddle had not yet been solved. Living on their boats they tried to find alternative premises. No one would have them.

McCarthy left at the beginning of December and they stayed on. But after two weeks the waterways began to be very busy as rice-junks brought tribute-rice from the countryside, to be sent north to the emperor. At such times brawls and riots were commonplace. The mandarins advised Hudson Taylor to withdraw 'until the spring'. He read between the lines. They could not guarantee the safety even of harmless women and children. By mid-December he learned that 'only the year before (the mandarins themselves) had been dragged from their (sedan) chairs and beaten . . .' and were afraid for their own safety.

Huzhou was closed to foreigners after all. 'We were now satisfied that in any trouble which might arise no help would be afforded us by the rulers.' This was food for thought. Even a good governor like Ma Xinyi with the best intentions could not alter the mood of hostile literati and an intimidated prefect. The lesson was to be driven home three years later when Ma himself became the victim of attack.

The Huzhou story did not quite end there. During the first weeks of James Williamson's time at Huzhou before he fell ill, a local barber had claimed to be believing in Jesus. The riot had been the test of his sincerity. 'He stood by us all through,' McCarthy wrote. And later the barber came to Hangzhou for teaching.[28] So when the consul asked McCarthy in February 1868 to go back to Huzhou to test the effects of diplomatic protests, he went, as much to see the barber and several 'inquirers' as to oblige the consul. On February 19 he wrote to Hudson Taylor that he had reached Huzhou after the city gates were shut, but they had been opened for him! People had been surprised to see him back, 'but nothing, so far, disrespectful'. Nowhere even now could he find any sign of the prefect's proclamations which should have been posted up. To tread carefully with the populace mattered more to the mandarins than to please the foreigner. From then on missionaries made no attempt to live in Huzhou until 1874 when a second riot occurred. If the moral of this tale was apparent, it failed to prevent attempts in other directions.

POSTSCRIPT

Life did not end as this book must. It surged on inexorably, a multicolour kaleidoscope of the unpredictable. Christmas was coming and the New Year, but first the wedding of Mary Bell and William Rudland.

With Huzhou written off for the present, the family party withdrew. 'The return to Hangchou was almost too much for (Hudson Taylor); there were such a multiplicity of affairs for him to attend to.' Work he was never afraid of. It was finding the household at odds again that was hard to take. Encouraged by Nicol, the McLean sisters in spite of renewing their pact with their leader were insisting on eating their Chinese food with knife, fork and spoon, whatever the others did. A small thing in itself, it declared their unwillingness to adapt or to throw in their lot with the Mission. The disharmony it caused again sapped happiness from the scene. Nicol himself, restless at Xiaoshan, was off on his own to visit Jiaxing in a second futile attempt to live there instead. . . . 'Jackson does not settle at Taichow,' Jennie noted, 'and is the cause of a good deal of uneasiness just now.' After overspending on his premises and travelling to Ningbo to borrow from his colleagues, he had dallied there until the firm letter from Hudson Taylor sent him back to work, and to the money which had reached Taizhou in his absence. Hardly had he arrived than Stott and Mr Zhu passed through, and Jackson joined them unnecessarily for three months at Wenzhou before returning to his own place. Anything but the work he had asked for seemed to consume his time. How Hudson Taylor shepherded him with the rod and staff of rebuke and sympathy is one of the incidental highlights of this continuing history – and how Jackson found the solution to his innate weakness in an ideal wife.

The rest of the team were measuring up more closely to Hudson Taylor's hopes of them. Some of the girls were becoming experts.

Others might one day find their feet. Duncan was doing well at Nanjing. Banned from Huzhou, James Williamson spent a fortnight with a Chinese fellow-missionary in the city of Linghu, ten miles away, but his future movements were undecided. Such promise as Williamson showed deserved the best, a challenge and a prospect as good as George Stott's at Wenzhou. The Yangzi valley advance would be right for him. James Meadows was offering to join in that too. In fact, the 'Ningbo five', Meadows, Barchet, and the Crombies, as well as the Stevensons and Stott, had caught the spirit and felt as fully parties to the pact as the *Lammermuir* team itself.

The first reinforcements sent by the Bergers were due at Shanghai, Henry Cordon and his wife, and Henry Reid, another Scotsman. Rudland had gone ahead to make arrangements for them and for his wedding. Anxious to be there to welcome the newcomers before the strong influences of Shanghai and opposition to the principles of the CIM could unsettle them, Hudson Taylor and Maria left the children with Emily and Jennie again, and Maria set off with Mary Bell on December 18. Hudson Taylor followed in the footboat the next day and caught them up. Between Hangzhou and Shanghai his bag of sixty wild duck and other game stocked the larders of their friends.

Comedy took over at this point. Rudland was to wait in Shanghai for his bride, and the Taylors were to take the Cordons and Reid to Hangzhou after the wedding. When their ship arrived on the 14th, a week earlier than expected, William Rudland, no less eager to shelter them from disruptive influences, thought he could reach New Lane with them before the bridal party left. He saw them quickly into canal boats and hurried them away to Hangzhou, only to find he was too late. Instead of escorting Mary he had passed her on the way and had to race back as fast as he could. Meanwhile she and the Taylors reached Shanghai to find no bridegroom or travellers. On December 23 Hudson Taylor scribbled a quick line to Jennie, '*We* are well, but the birds have flown . . . Give my love and sympathy to Rudland.' But that bird had flown too and was halfway back to Shanghai. He married his buxom Mary on Christmas morning and was away again the same day, honeymooning in a houseboat, this time on a leisurely return, he to supervise his printing presses and workmen, and Mary to continue as nurse to the Taylor children until her widowed sister, Mrs Bohannan, arrived to take her place. Annie Bohannan was already on the high seas with another couple named Cardwell and Charles H Judd, Tom Barnardo's friend. On the same ship came Edward Fishe of Dublin, but independently. Barnardo stayed to continue his medical course, his heart becoming as much drawn to the children of London's East End as to China.

After the wedding party had all left Hangzhou, the household at New Lane unpacked the boxes brought by the Cordons from families and friends at home, to enjoy a snowy Christmas with its own hilarities. There was something for everyone from the Bergers. 'A splendid (tin) bath!' for Jennie from her parents was to live under her bed, perfect for use in hot weather. And a Christmas pudding, mouldy and needing to be pared away until she reached good pudding. A displaced paperweight had somehow sunk into it. Hammers and other tools were powdered with sherbet. Broken jam pots compounded the mess. Emily's keys had been kept from rusting by sardine oil leaking over them.

Both No 1 and No 2 New Lane were full. No 1 still housed the married couples and single girls; only the McCarthys had moved into No 2 with the single men. At No 1 the printing presses, the clinic, Maria's 'industrial school and women's class' – 'suddenly trebled' – and the church activities, continued until the chapel was built, on the land bought during December, large enough to seat two hundred. Jennie's boys' school now consisted of seventeen boys, 'nine of whom are written (ie committed) to us for five years,' she wrote, referring to the customary contract by which the parents were bound to leave pupils under control for long enough to be worthwhile. Even so, there was space and to spare within the two walled premises for all the comings and goings of Chinese and foreign missionaries looking to Hudson Taylor for direction. For all alike this Christmas season meant feasts, celebrations and services of worship and rejoicing. Soon they would scatter again.

The Taylors arrived back at Hangzhou at one a m on December 31, in time to join in the annual day of prayer and thanksgiving. Their first full year in China as a Mission was ending. They had obtained premises and begun work from which they would never be forcibly dislodged, in the six prefectural cities of Nanjing, Hangzhou, Shaoxing, Ningbo, Taizhou, and Wenzhou – as far apart as Edinburgh, York, Birmingham and London – or Boston, New York, Philadelphia and Washington – and in two county and three market towns. But for setbacks Huzhou, Xiaoshan, Yanzhou and Lanxi could have been included.[2] The largest Protestant mission in China at the time was the LMS with thirty members. With the addition of the Cordons and Reid, and in spite of the loss of Jean Notman and John Sell, the China Inland Mission had reached thirty also, with five more soon to arrive. It had been a hard and often disappointing year, but by the standards of any period before or since, and in spite of difficulties, this, their first full year in China, was no failure. It had to end with thanksgiving to God.

Riots, illness, death; new suffering, new cities and new churches – all was but a rehearsal of things to come in the next three years.

THE NINGBO ROMANISED VERNACULAR NEW TESTAMENT
1866–68

After Hudson Taylor left Britain on May 26, 1866, Frederick Gough carried on the revision but made slow progress. In November when he announced to the Bible Society his marriage to Mary Jones, and his hope of their continuing the work together, the Committee resolved to urge on him the necessity of advancing more rapidly. A year later, however, he reported that he was free to leave England if the Bible Society would relieve him of the revision, and in January 1868 George Moule declined to help unless in so doing Gough was set at liberty to return to Ningbo. On January 28, the Editorial sub-Committee resolved that Mr Gough's services should cease at the end of the Epistle to the Hebrews, and George Moule, whose Greek tutor Gough had been at Cambridge, was asked to finish the New Testament. Finally, on September 2, 1868, only seven months later, a Minute recorded the completion of the last sheet. At long last the whole vernacular New Testament was available to the Ningbo churches. The Goughs returned there in 1869.

In *The Story of the Cheh-Kiang Mission*, Arthur E Moule was to describe it as 'a work which has been of the greatest value to Christians throughout the province', and in the Bible Society's *Historical Catalogue of Holy Scriptures*, of 1911, the whole story was summarised:

> 1865 *The Gospel* and *Acts* . . .
> 1868 *The New Testament* . . . with marginal references. In the earlier books the text was thoroughly revised; but in the latter portions only obvious mistakes were corrected.

By 1911 the earlier facts had been obscured by subsequent entries, and few if any knew that Hudson Taylor had not only originated but done most of the work, daily devoting long hours to it from 1861–6. Since greater claims had reduced the time he could give, in 1865, progress through the epistles had been painfully slow. But in the end the millions of Ningbo-speaking people had the Scriptures in the language they used among themselves, the Christians could understand and expound it, and the missionaries who had initiated its revival and seen it through to completion were back in China among them.

(BFBS Minutes of Editorial sub-Commitee, Oct. 18, 1865, Minute 3; Dec. 6, 1865, Minute 3; June 13, 1866, Minute 11; Nov. 28, 1866, Minutes 25, 26; April 24, 1867, Minute 21; Nov. 27, 1867, Minute 39; Jan. 28, 1868, Minutes 27, 30; Feb. 26, 1868, Minute 25; Sept. 2, 1868, Minute 39.

BFBS Editorial Correspondence, Inward, No 4 pp 119, 175; *Historical Catalogue* Vol. II p 241; cf. *BFBS Minutes of (General) Committee,* No 49; April 1, 1861, Minute 54; April 15, 1861, Minute 98; June 17, 1861, Minute 55; *Minutes of Editorial sub-Committee,* No 6: July 17, 1861, Minutes 29–31 (Resolution); Nov. 27, 1861, Minute 17; *Minutes of Editorial sub-Committee, No 7: July* 15, 1863, Minutes 8–10; Oct. 21, 1863, Minutes 41–43; Moule, A E: *The Story of the Cheh-Kiang Mission,* 2nd Edn. 1879, p 87.)

THE CHINA TEA CLIPPERS

Like the *Jubilee* (Book 3, p 207), the *Lammermuir* was a 'ship' – that is, a sailing vessel square-rigged on three masts. Confusion and contradictions have arisen from the existence of two *Lammermuir*s, both built by Pile on the Durham coast for the 'legendary' Captain John ('White Hat') Willis, son of John ('Old Stormy') Willis of the sea shanty 'Stormalong'. (Captain John Willis, Jr, became very favourably disposed to the CIM after this voyage of the *Lammermuir*.) The first, built at Sunderland in 1856, left Wusong (Shanghai) on December 17, 1863, for London, and on the 31st was wrecked on the Amherst reef in the Gaspar Strait between Bangka and Belitong islands, off Sumatra (map, p 195). The second, built at Hartlepool in 1864, was listed in *Lloyd's Register* as 'iron', meaning at that date a wooden construction on an iron frame, 1054 tons, two hundred feet in length over all, 'engaged, London to China, Capt. M. Bell' in 1866, with which Lloyd's record ends. But C T Fishe and T P Harvey of the CIM sailed in her, from July 14 to November 9, 1869. The figure of 760 tons in the biography by the Howard Taylors was true of the *Jubilee*, not the *Lammermuir*. The *Lammermuir* had a well deck between the mainmast and forecastle, with a low poop-deck extending aft above the saloon and cabins to the wheel, open to the elements. The *Cutty Sark* had no well deck. In having so much passenger accommodation, occupying all space aft of the mainmast, the *Lammermuir* was also different. In no sense were they sister-ships. The sleek *Cutty Sark*, of 963 tons gross, was launched on November 22, 1869, by Scott and Linton on the Clyde and finished by William Denny (Book 3, pp 413, 416, 423) when her builders went bankrupt. Built to challenge the fastest tea clippers and averaging one hundred and fifteen days on eight runs from Shanghai to Britain, she handsomely outpaced the famous *Thermopylae*. The *Lammermuir* was to take a fortnight longer, a hundred and twenty-eight days, going out. 'Of all her lovely sisters that roamed the seven seas in the golden age of sail, only the *Cutty Sark* remains to show the world in which we live what a thing of grace and beauty was a clipper ship in the fulness of her glory' (Carr, F G G: *The Cutty Sark*, Pitkin Pictorials Ltd © 1973). To get the feel of this voyage of the *Lammermuir* readers should visit the *Cutty Sark* at Greenwich.

(MacGregor, David R: *The Tea Clippers, Sailing Ships of the Nineteenth Century*; Lubbock, Basil: *The China Clippers* (1924); Woodcock, George: *The British in the Far East*, pp 27–31, 117–18; *Milestones of History*, p 40 f.)

OFFICERS AND MEN OF THE *LAMMERMUIR*

Captain M Bell; First Officer J Brunton; Second Officer W Tosh; Apprentices J B Lewis; N H Saunders; H Fickling; G Carter; Bo's'n R Mills; Carpenter J Stewart (West Indian); Joiner J Forbes; Sailmaker Harris; Cook Dennis; Steward C Russell; Cabin boy Geo. H Hartley.

21 Foremast hands: 4 Swedes, 1 German, 1 West Indian, 1 South Sea Islander

H Bennis	Robert Dummelow	J McDougall
H Betler (German)	D Edmonds	J Patterson/Peterson
Benjamin Buchan	Henry Elliott	Charles Pryor
James Byolds	W Henderson	J Robinson
William Carron	J Johnson (Swedish)	– Svenson (Swedish)
Peter Chalmers	Robert Kane	G Williams (South Sea Is)
J Dixon (St Vincent Is)	J McDonald	J Young
	(spelling as in sources)	

THE NATURE OF TYPHOONS

A typhoon is a tropical cyclone, a destructive hurricane of force 12 and more on the Beaufort scale, such as occurs in the western Pacific and China seas, but also in the Caribbean, the Bay of Bengal and Arabian Sea, western Australia and elsewhere. Winds of 75 or as much as 150 miles per hour whirl round an intense depression only a few miles in width. Anti-clockwise in the northern hemisphere, they rotate clockwise south of the equator. The whole cyclone advances at only 15 to 25 miles per hour, so that in the age of radio enough warning is received for ships to evade its expected path. But it can change direction. Arising in the western Pacific, successive seasonal typhoons sweep across the Philippines and Taiwan to the coast of China, even as far north as Peking, and may curve away over Korea and Japan.

Before the advent of radio, only the premonitory signs gave warning, difficult to interpret. At sea a growing swell extends for hundreds of miles beyond the typhoon, haloes appear round the sun and moon, oppressive stillness, and the dense, dark 'bar of the storm' itself all give evidence of its approach. The roaring, howling and shrieking wind builds up huge waves with overhanging crests. It whips the spume, the spray and the torrential rain almost horizontally. Thunder adds to the uproar of flapping canvas and cracking shrouds, but only startlingly close thunderclaps can be heard through the infernal din, and the impenetrable darkness of night is split by lightning flashes. As the typhoon advances, changing wind directions create changing wave patterns. Great breakers clashing with each other in confusion give the impression that the sea is boiling, and toss a ship about and smash it to pieces. On land, trees, roofs and houses are demolished and may be hurled long distances, scything through whatever stands in their path. In October 1881 three hundred thousand Chinese lost their lives, mostly by drowning, in a typhoon which struck Shantou. Famine may follow the widespread destruction.

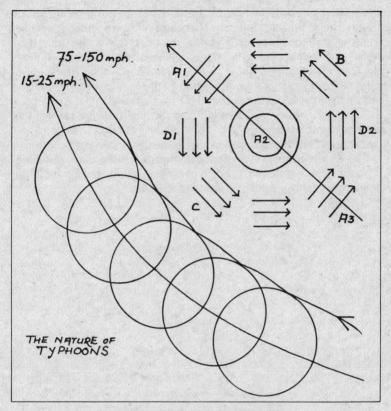

THE NATURE OF TYPHOONS

By the wind direction the relative position of an observer to the vortex or eye of the typhoon may be judged. At the centre a deceptive calm is usual and even blue sky may be seen, but to be there after enduring the full force of the leading half of a typhoon means inescapably having to endure the second half. Lives are often saved by studying the wind and taking shelter in the lee of stable objects.

Initial winds at right angles to the path of the typhoon will indicate to an observer that he is in its direct line and will experience its full force. Assuming a north-westerly path, the winds will come from north-east to south-west (A 1) then (after the lull A 2) from south-west to north-east (A 3). Initial winds in the same direction (B) as the main path indicate that the typhoon is passing on the south-west of the observer. They will not be repeated unless another typhoon follows. Similarly, initial winds directly against (C) the track of the typhoon show that it is passing on the north-east. Intermediate positions on the broad path receive correspondingly oblique winds, first from one side (D 1) and then from the other (D 2) with little or no lull between. The farther from the centre, the stronger (in general) the wind force and its effects. But the capriciousness of typhoons is no less characteristic.

The *Lammermuir*'s experience demonstrates the passage of two typhoons, each time to the north of them, so that she met head-on winds, becoming westerly as she progressed.

PROVINCIAL MANDARINS

(following Hosea Ballou Morse)

Each rank was recognisable by the wearer's cap 'button' or globe, 'the size of a pigeon's egg'.

Rank:		
1st degree	Ministers of State	plain red globe
2nd degree	Viceroy: Governor-general of two or three provinces; equivalent of duke, marquis or earl;	plain or engraved opaque red stone or coral
	Provincial Governor (*futai*), equivalent of baron or knight	deep blue gem (R Morrison and others include provincial governors in the 1st rank, wearing a red button, cf Book 2, Appx. 3 inferior red button.)
3rd degree	Provincial Judge and Treasurer (*fantai*)	deep blue gem
4th degree	Provincial Intendent of Circuit (*daotai*); Superior Prefect	light blue gem (so Morse, but cf Book 2, Appx. 3)
5th degree	City Prefect (*zhifu, zhizhou*)	crystal globe
6th and 7th degrees	District Magistrate (*xian zhang*)	opaque white stone
8th and 9th degrees	Magistrates' subordinates; educated civilians	gold or gilt button

Military mandarins were graded in nine equivalent degrees of rank.

(continued)

Hudson Taylor's 1865 comparisons (from *China: Its Spiritual Need and Claims*) to indicate the magnitude of viceroys' and governors' roles.

Zhili	territorial size of England and Wales; population then 31 millions
Shandong	size of Scotland and Ireland; 32 millions
Jiangsu	three times the size of Switzerland; 43 millions
Zhejiang	30 millions
Fujian	16.5 millions
Hubei	30.5 millions
Hunan	20 millions
Anhui	'twice the population of England'
Shaanxi	11 millions
Gansu	16 millions

Clearly by any criterion governors were able and powerful men, and viceroys even more so.

THE PACT AFFIRMED
(verbatim)

Hangchou
May 10, 1867

'On the occasion of the meeting at 30, Coborn St, Bow, on the 2nd of Feb 1866, to decide who were to go to China on or about the 15th May, in connection with the China Inland Mission; Present W T Berger Esq; Mess. Williamson, Rudland, Nicol, and Duncan, and J H Taylor, the principles of the Mission were fully stated, and assented to by all present.

'In the first place, it was stated that *I* was feeling called of God to do a work in China, in which I desired helpers.

'That such helpers must be satisfied that God had called them individually to labor in China for the good of the Chinese; must go to China on *their own* responsibility; and must look to *God* for their support, and trust *Him* to provide it, and not lean on me. That they must be prepared to labor without guaranteed support from man, being satisfied with the promise of Him who has said, "Seek ye first the kingdom of God and His righteousness, and all these things shall be added unto you."

'That such being the case, they promising to work under my guidance and direction, I would in the event of my having funds at my disposal, minister to their need as the Lord might direct me.

'As to the guidance and direction it was stated that in every respect what I deemed requisite must be complied with. That *where* we should go to, where and when different individuals should be located, the positions they should occupy, etc, must be left to me to determine. Should I think one person fit for the superintendence of a school, he must be prepared to accept my decision on this point. Should I deem another fitted for pioneering work, he must be prepared to go and open up work, not necessarily remaining permanently; while another I might permanently locate in any station I deemed suitable. That it was not for the brethren themselves to decide what they were fit for, or where they were to go, but that in all points save those matters of conscience on which Christians of various denominations differ, it was to be fully understood that I should direct.

'That it was most needful for all to seek to assist me in the great work contemplated in every way in their power, above all supporting my hands by prayer, seeking especially from God that I might be directed by Him in my direction of the affairs of the Mission. That in the event of any one being dissatisfied with, and so unable to continue in, the position which I allotted to him; or to acquiesce in the plans that I might devise, he must pray God to change my views on the subject, or to give him to see that it was his right path. That, furthermore, if any one were dissatisfied with the funds which I might be able, or deem sufficient to supply him with, he was to look not to me, but to God, to send him more through such channel as He might see best, seeing we were building on the promise "Seek ye first the kingdom of God and His righteousness, and all these things shall be added unto you."

'And that finally, in the event of anyone being unable to work longer under my direction, he must quietly resign his connection with the Mission and all expectation of further co-operation. In that event there would be no claim on me or on the Mission for further support or expenses, seeing that each one was going out to China on his own responsibility. That the relation between us was this – that as far as possible they should feel responsible for affording me all the help in their power in the work of the Mission, and that I should feel myself responsible for guiding, directing and helping, pecuniarily and otherwise, as I might be able and deem advisable, those so assisting me. It was laid down that no human foresight could anticipate the various contingencies which might arise, but the fact that those going were going as helpers in my work, threw on me the responsibility of deciding according to the best of my ability on the course to be adopted, and that my decision, *as such*, was to be accepted whether those helping me could or could not see the necessity of the step.

'In explanation of the extent to which I expect those in their own stations to consult with me about their work, and to submit to my direction in the affairs of the Mission, I would now, May 10th 1867, add, that, to the extent to which I personally (or the Mission) am involved in any proposed step – to the extent to which I am responsible for the results whether pecuniary or otherwise of such a step – to that extent I must be consulted before it is taken, or be understood to be at liberty to confirm or disallow the step in question.

J Hudson Taylor

'By the above mentioned principles of the Mission, we the undersigned, intend by the help of God to abide in our mutual intercourse.

J Hudson Taylor
Lewis Nicol'

(OMFA 331Bg; 3411; E431.15)

WILLIAM BERGER AND MISSION FUNDS

In the development of what has jocularly been called 'the conspiracy of silence' about material needs, some statements in the *Occasional Paper* of 1867 are of interest. Without Hudson Taylor to consult, William Berger trod an untried path. In the fourth *Paper* of October 1866, he ventured on to thin ice. As the representative of a mission which on principle made no appeals for funds, he said,

> In consequence of Mr Stephan Barchet . . . suffering so frequently from fever and ague, through sleeping on the ground floor, it has been thought advisable by friends in Ningpo, to build him a two-storied house; the upper part to be used as a dwelling, and the lower as a place for preaching, etc. The cost will be about £200. Friends desiring fellowship in the above, may send their contributions to Thos D Marshall, 192, Oxford Street, London; or to W T Berger, Saint Hill, East Grinstead, Sussex.

From this and other statements and from his correspondence it is clear that Mr Berger had not moved as far as Hudson Taylor had from the position of 'ask the Lord and tell His people' (as Sir Henry Kennaway, PC, put it in 1893). William Berger had long since abandoned the methods of the Chinese Evangelization Society. While he did not publish needs in order to raise funds, he was incautious in advising those who already wished to give what help they could. In the case of Stephan Barchet at least two strong factors gave him a free hand, but he took them for granted. He barely mentioned them. Dr and Mrs E C Lord, to whom Stephan had been seconded in Ningbo, intended to build this simple frame-house with upstairs rooms safely above the miasms of fever at ground level. They did so at their own charges. Thomas Marshall and the congregation of Bryanston Hall in London's West End had assumed full responsibility for Stephan's support as a member of the CIM.

William Berger was doing the Lords and Marshall a favour. But Barchet was a member of the CIM and a hundred and twenty pounds came in to the Mission account toward the building.

In the *Occasional Paper* he reported the amounts remitted to Hudson Taylor and his balance in hand, treating his readers as self-declared supporters. In the fifth *Paper*, largely given to letters about the *Lammermuir* typhoons, he wrote,

> Though the funds in hand are little more than half what they were when Mr Taylor left, you will perceive that there is a balance of £1,092, 4s – sufficient for a time to carry on operations with all comfort; trusting, as I think we may, that God will continue to put it into the hearts of His dear people to send in aid from time to time, as required . . . [In this confidence he was interviewing candidates with a view to sending them when ready to go. In March he stated,] The balance of funds in hand is £1123.15s.2d., upon which we shall at once draw largely for the coming outfits, passage money, and remittances to China . . . Still we are happy, feeling sure that sufficient means will be provided to meet every necessary expense of thus sending the gospel to the perishing millions of China.

The balance sheet for the first full year since the *Lammermuir* sailed on May 26, 1866, showed an income of 'little short of three thousand pounds; for which we give God and the kind donors our sincerest thanks', and a balance carried forward of a little over one thousand pounds. News of John Sell's death and the start of the Qiantang river journey introduced *Occasional Paper*, No 9, with the passing statement,

> You will be glad to learn that hitherto the funds for carrying on the Mission in China and at home have been supplied. The balance in hand £620.4s.11d., will suffice, I trust, not only for sending forth Messrs Cardwell and Judd (both of whom expect to be married before leaving) . . . but also for making the next remittance to China, and defraying the home expenses to that date.

Balances in England were a different matter from remittances received in China, and sometimes William Berger had to write to Hudson Taylor that his funds were too low to permit the transfer of all he would have wished.

(Stock, E: *The History of the CMS*, Vol. III p 677; *Occasional Paper*, No 4 p 14; No 5 p 5; No 6 p 4; No 8 pp 1, 32; No 9 p 2; No 13 p 155.)

(For further references to this subject, see succeeding volumes.)

FENGSHUI AND EARLY CUSTOM

This vital factor in the tensions between China and the West was too often disregarded by foreigners. No Chinese would build a house, dig a grave or indeed undertake any project of consequence, without consulting a geomancer or necromancer, the learned practitioner of *fengshui*, 'wind and water'. The importance of an auspicious site and an auspicious time was paramount. Disagreement with or scorn for the practice and its underlying beliefs could not absolve the foreigner from the need to respect the host country's convictions. He was barbarous if he did not. Anti-foreign riots were the predictable outcome of their abuse or neglect.

The concept of *fengshui* was and is no more scientific than the superstitions of sixteenth-century Britain, of which it is an equivalent, or of more than one modern philosophy. A concept of the equilibrium of the elements, the harmony of the two forces responsible for the serenity and balance of nature, *Yin* and *Yang*, it links ancestor worship to daily living. It identifies good and evil influences and so maps the hazardous way between good luck and bad. *Yang*, the bright, warm, active force personified in the blue dome of heaven and *Shangdi* the supreme ancestor, has its counterpart in *Yin*, the dark, cold, static element of earth. *Yang*, the genial animation of spring and summer, life and beauty, emanating from the south, and *Yin*, the cold, dying nature of autumn and winter from the north hold the balance of human happiness. Wind is chilling and parching. Water is life-giving. The forces of *fengshui* clearly flowed due north and south, the tide path of happiness and prosperity.

Only a professional geomancer can fathom the complexities of the subject. It is far too complicated for lesser mortals. Using a compass he determines the true direction of the influences. A coffin must lie in line with the currents, never athwart them. Surveying the scene he pronounces on the presence of objects obstructing the south or shielding from the north. On his word sites may be rejected, decisions postponed and endless litigation begun, for one man's north may be another man's south if the first builds in front of the other. The foreigners' telegraph poles and lines, tall and straight, his railways slashing through hill and field, graves and groves, his tall buildings dwarfing even the mandarin's *yamen*, and his mines penetrating deep into the realms of darkness could not but set the offended spirits against the living. Calamities could be traced directly to bad *fengshui*. The most delicate diplomacy was needed to evade the consequences of a false step. Feelings ran high and riots ensued.

But bad *fengshui* could be corrected. Disaster was predictable and could be circumvented. When it occurred, disaster revealed the fatal flaws which once recognised could be remedied with the geomancer's aid. If his pronouncement at any time was unwelcome, a 'better' geomancer could be found. Missionaries, not prepared to employ or to tolerate the wiles of geomancy, often fell foul of the system. W A P Martin wrote,

> Within (the walls of Fuzhou) rises a hill, covered with trees and rocks, with here and there a small house hidden in the foliage. This is the palladium of the city, an elevation which draws propitious influences from the four winds and pours them down on the people below . . . English missionaries built on that hill, and the populace became so excited lest their presence might disturb its good influences that they rose *en masse*, and demolished church, school-house, and dwelling.
>
> In Hangchau, a magistrate having died suddenly, his death was believed to have been caused by a mission building on a hillside overlooking the *yamen* . . . The missionaries were courteously invited to accept another site in exchange, to which they acceded rather than have their house pulled about their ears.

The premises and location provided for E B Inslee of the American Presbyterians were superior to those he vacated in exchange.

In the Chinese city of Shanghai a church had been built due north of the magistrate's *yamen*. That in itself was all right, but the tower dominated the scene. When the Triads executed the magistrate and sacked the *yamen*, the bad *fengshui* was attributed to the church tower. When Matthew T Yates the missionary, protected by the foreign settlement, declined to demolish it, the geomancers were undismayed. The new *yamen* was built at an angle to the north–south meridian so that malign influences from the north would be divided and flow past it. No other magistrate died, but in 1868 Hudson Taylor was to suffer from the animosity of one resentful incumbent.

A Shanghai temple known as the Guang Fu Si had been built by Guangdong and Fujian men, and financed by the keeper of a house of ill fame. When the Triads, mostly from those two provinces, brought devastation to the city, the temple would have been demolished after their defeat, but for its occupation by the gods and spirits. Ingeniously the geomancers showed that four little bridges over its moat, and a main bridge at its entrance were the limbs, head and neck of a tortoise of which the temple was the body. Two wells were its eyes! Brothel-keepers were known as tortoises. The bad *fengshui* had been identified. Its name was changed, the wells were blocked to extinguish its eyes, and good *fengshui* was restored.

There were loopholes through the difficulties, at a price, but *fengshui* could always be invoked by anyone wanting to accuse the barbarian of provocation.

(Chinese Recorder, June–July 1868, pp 39–43, M T Yates; Du Bose, H C: *The Dragon Image and Demon*, 1886; Smith, A H: *The Uplift of China*; Martin, W A P: *A Cycle of Cathay.)*

A CHRONOLOGY

1865–67

1865

Feb 20	Robt Hart to Peking as Inspector-General of Customs
March	President Lincoln assassinated
April	Prince Kong degraded (first time)
May 10	American Civil War ends
June 25	Hudson Taylor agrees to lead CIM in China; 2000 Protestant communicants in China
July 24	Benjamin Hudson dies
July	Barchet and Crombie reach China
Aug 21–24	JHT, Stott and Stevenson at Bristol
Aug 28–Sept 13	JHT in Scotland
Sept	Anne Skinner (Crombie) arr. Ningbo
Sept 5–7	Perth conference
Sept 26–Oct 2	JHT in Norfolk
Oct 3	Stevensons and Stott dep. UK
Oct 4	No 34 Coborn St rented
Oct 18	Lord Palmerston dies; Lister introduces anti-sepsis
Oct 25	*China: Its Spiritual Need and Claims*, 1st edn. published
Oct 25–27	Second Mildmay Conference
Nov 25	A Macpherson brings W D Rudland to Coborn St
Dec 6–7	Maria confined, Jane Dyer Taylor born, dies
Dec 30	First CIM Day of Fasting and Prayer

1866

	Muslim rebellion in Ili
	Yakub Beg takes Kashgar and Yarkand
	Dungani Muslim rebellion in Xinjiang and Gansu
Feb 6	Stevensons and Stott arr. Shanghai

Feb 8–14	JHT to Barnsley, Liverpool, Manchester
Feb 14	JHT meets H Grattan Guinness
Feb 19–28	JHT in Ireland
Mar 6	JHT to Birmingham
Mar 8	Radstocks' soirée
Mar 12	*Occasional Paper* No 1 published
Mar 22	JHT to Brighton
Mar 31	Thomas J Barnardo to CIM, Coborn St
Apr 4–25	JHT West Country tour
Apr 21–22	JHT at Exeter
May 2	Colonel Puget's meeting
May 3	*Lammermuir* accommodation chartered
May 26	*Lammermuir* sails
July 31	Cape of Good Hope rounded
Aug 27	*Lammermuir* at Anjer
Sept 10–14	First typhoon
Sept 14–19	Stormy detour round Taiwan
Sept 20–24	Second typhoon
Sept 29	*Lammermuir* arr. Wusong
Sept 30	arr. Shanghai
Oct 1–26	*Lammermuir* party at Shanghai and Longhua
Oct 27	dep. Shanghai
Oct 31–Nov 4	Wu Joohoon joins at Songjiang
Nov 22	*Lammermuir* party arr. Hangzhou
Nov 28	No 1 New Lane occupied
Dec 6–17	MJT to Ningbo and back
Dec 19–29	MJT to Ningbo and back

1867

	Campaign against Muslims of north-west begins
	Agitation at Hangzhou follows Hunan rumours
Jan 4	Xiaoshan house rented
Jan 5–20	JHT at Shaoxing, Ningbo, Fenghua
Jan 9	Maria falls down stairs
Jan 28	Xiaoshan outrage, Mr Tsiu flogged
Feb 3	Maria Hudson Taylor born
Feb 19	G Moules dep. Hangzhou
Feb 23	McCarthys and M McLean arr. Hangzhou
Mar 7	CIM women's declaration
Mar 14	Nicols, Williamson to Ningbo consul
Mar 21–27	Hangzhou disturbances

Mar 29	Anatomy specimens to Ningbo
Apr 5	Moules dep. Shanghai to UK
Apr 23–28	JHT and Duncan to Huzhou
May 7	First CIM Hangzhou baptisms
May 10	Nicol signs the pact
May 14–18	John R Sell with smallpox, dies
June	France annexes three Indo-Chinese provinces
June 12–July 12	Qiantang expedition
June 21	G E Moule and W T Berger meet with Henry Venn
July 5	Jackson with Meadows occupies Taizhou
July 12	Wang Lae-djün arr. Hangzhou; 16th becomes pastor
August	Stott's riding accident
Aug 4–23	Pengshan hill resort and illnesses
Aug 23	Grace Taylor dies
Aug 29	G Duncan dep. Hangzhou to Nanjing
Sept 18	Duncan arr. Nanjing
Sept 18–25	JHT and Williamson to Huzhou
Oct 12	Zongli Yamen 'circular' issued
Oct 19	Rudland to Nanjing
Nov 13	Huzhou riot; 14th, JHT to provincial governor
Nov late	G Stott occupies Wenzhou with Feng Nenggui
Dec 22	Cordons and Reid arr. Hangzhou
Dec 25	W D Rudland and Mary Bell married
Dec 31	Anson Burlingame commissioned as Envoy Extraordinary for China

NOTES

Page Note

Preface

10   1   Latourette, K S: *A History of Christian Missions in China*, p 389; *A History of the Expansion of Christianity*, Vol VI, pp 326–7, 329

Prologue

25   1   Latourette, K S: *Christian Missions*, p 303; Martin, W A P: *A Cycle of Cathay*

25   2   1860 ports: In the south, Qiongzhou (now Haikou), on Hainan island; Shantou (Swatow) and Fuzhou; on Taiwan, Tainan and Danshui; on the Shandong coast, Dengzhou, then Yantai (Chefoo); on the southern coast of Manchuria, Niuchuang (now Yingkou); between Tianjin and Peking the river city of Tongzhou, instead of Tianjin itself; and on the Yangzi River, Nanjing. Three other ports 'for loading and discharge' without 'extraterritorial concessions', were Hankou, eight hundred miles upstream, Jiujiang (Kiukiang) and Zhenjiang (Chinkiang). After 1870 Tianjin superseded Tongzhou.

28   3   The *Chinese Recorder and Missionary Journal*, July 1869, pp 50–1

29   4   Morse, Hosea Ballou: *The International Relations of the Chinese Empire*, Vol II, xxiii, Chronology; p 25

30   5   Woodcock, G: *The British in the Far East*, p 69; *Chambers Encyclopaedia*, Vol 3 p 474b

30   6   *Chamb. Encycl. ibid*

31   7   Woodcock, G: *British in the Far East*, pp 154–7

32   8   Broomhall, M: *The Chinese Empire*, p 85; *see* HTCOC Books 2, 3

32   9   op. cit. p 141; Taylor, J H: *China: Its Spiritual Need and Claims* (1866), p 52

32   10   Woodcock, G: *British in the Far East*, pp 165–74, 188; race club since 1850; cricket club 1860; exclusive Shanghai Club in 1860s; Pott, F L Hawks: *A Short History of Shanghai*, p 79; Morse, H B: *International Relations*, pp 121–2

33   11   Woodcock, G: *British in the Far East*, p 18; Latourette, K S: *Christian Missions*, p 410

33   12, 13   *Chamb. Encycl.* 3.451, G E Hubbard

36   14   Stock, Eugene: *The History of the Church Missionary Society*, Vol I pp 285–9; II.12

36   15   Universal suffrage: 1870 France and Germany; 1874 Switzerland; 1884 United Kingdom except women.

36   16   Precursors of Sinn Fein, Irish for 'ourselves alone', the nationalistic movement founded 1905.

36   17   Morris, E W: *The London Hospital*
37   18   *Milestones of History*, Weidenfeld and Nicolson: Africa 12,000; South
            America 26,000; Asia 37,000
37   19   Humble, R: *Marco Polo*, p 213; cf Yule, H: *The Book of Ser Marco
            Polo*, 2 vols.
38   20–24   Stock, E: *History of the CMS*, Vol II p 337; II. 645, 648; II.299;
            II.582, 598; I.468
39   25   op. cit. I. 71–2
40   26   Latourette, K S: *Christian Missions*, p 384. Characteristically W A P
            Martin wrote that Peking 'swarms with Jesuits'.
40   27   op. cit. pp 40–44
41   28   Broomhall, M: *The Jubilee Story of the China Inland Mission*, p 23
42   29, 30   *China's Millions*, 1876, p 157, Tenth Anniversary Meeting, May 26

Chapter 1
47   1   Taylor, J H: *A Retrospect*, 18th edn p 112
47   2   op. cit. p 114
50   3   No 30 Coborn Street, later renumbered No 1.
50   4   HTCOC Book 3, pp 413–20, 423
51   5   OMFA 3Bk4. 10, Hudson Taylor's Journal
52   6   Stock, E: *History of the CMS*, Vol II. pp 340–1
53   7   Taylor, J H: *China*, p 12 footnote
56   8   op. cit. p 12
58   9   HTCOC Book 2, pp 353–9
60   10   Stock, E: *History of the CMS*, Vol II. p 343
.62   11   op. cit. II.61
63   12   James Vigeon and his wife are in the 'second group' photograph of
            August 10 and again on September 15.
66   13   Philip Gosse had been married from Robert Howard's home: Coad, F R:
            A History of the Brethren Movement, p 222; on November 1, 1852,
            Anthony Norris Groves 'stayed with dear Miss S. who, with the
            Howards, were most kind to me.' He died, May 20, 1853 at G Müller's;
            Groves, Mrs: *Memoir of the Late Anthony Norris Groves*, 1857 edn
            p 488
66   14   *The Revival*, No 303
67   15   Latourette, K S: *These Sought a Country*, Tipple Lectures, 1950 edn.
67   16   'Undenominational' would have been as imperfect a term, for members
            of all Protestant denominations were welcomed. 'Supra'- or
            'trans-denominational' would be a better description.
68   17   Taylor, J H: *China;* Broomhall, M: *Jubilee Story*, p 30. The inclusion of
            three or four men with little education or cultural refinement in the party
            Hudson Taylor took with him to China has contributed – but by a
            shallow reading of the records – to a misconception that he chose or
            preferred to enlist such men and was even 'anti-intellectual'. His use of
            the King James (AV) word 'labourers' for Christian workers may have
            been misleading. Alexander Michie's strongly biased *Missionaries in
            China* is no source for factual comment.
68   18   Latourette, K S: *Christian Missions*, p 385
68   19   *China's Millions*, 1875, p 31
69   20   OMFA: F115

69 21 Taylor, Dr and Mrs Howard: *Hudson Taylor and the China Inland Mission*, Vol 2 p 54, quoting JHT

69 22 Guinness, M Geraldine: *The Story of the China Inland Mission*, Vol 1 p 453

70 23 Taylor, J H: *After Thirty Years*, OMFA 3Bk5 p 3; Broomhall, M: *Jubilee Story*, p 41

70 24 Taylor, J H: *Thirty Years*, pp 3–5; *China's Millions*, 1875, *Plan of Operations*, pp 31–2; *A Summary of Operations*, OMFA 441.11 p 7

71 25 Scotland: OMFA 3Bk4.11; 3221m; 3223a–g; E444; FHT Reconstruction N5 pp 466–78

73 26 Guinness, M G: *Story of CIM*, 1.246

73 27 OMFA 3Bk4.11 Sept 5

75 28 Norfolk: OMFA 3Bk4.12; 3222d; 3223h

77 29 OMFA 3222d; FHT N5.478

79 30 Family circumstances necessitated Wm Lockhart's return to Europe. After retiring from the LMS he practised as a surgeon in Blackheath, dying in 1896 aged 85. His famous medical paintings by Lam Gua, pupil of George Chinnery, now hang in the Gordon Museum of Guy's Hospital. (*Guy's Hosp. Gazette*, centenary number)

Chapter 2

81 1 In *A Retrospect* JHT wrote of 'the adjoining house'. This supposes the absence of a No 32, but the No 34 is definite. No 33 was on the opposite side of the road.

82 2 Fount or font (esp. N America) from Old French for a casting or founding of metal.

84 3 *The Revival*, October 9, 1865; OMFA N5.484

85 4 Neill, S C et al: *Concise Dict. of Christian World Mission*, p 82; Latourette, K S: *Christian Missions*, p 328

85 5 Neill, S C: *A History of Christian Missions*, p 334, not in direct reference to JHT's book.

85 6 Stock, E: *History of the CMS*, Vol III p 21

85 7 Mildmay: they met in The Iron Room, a hall he had built, and in the garden outside. A larger venue was soon needed. Henry Reed of Tasmania guaranteed the entire cost of erecting the Mildmay Conference Hall, seating 3000, first used in 1870. *See* Book 3, p 389. OMFA 3Bk4.12

86 8 Demy 4vo 11×8½ cut. OMFA JBk1, Preface.

87 9 OMFA 3222e–o, 3224b, 3331a, E429; Collier, R: *William Booth: The General Next to God*

88 10 Not Timothy Richard, a later candidate referred to the BMS and soon to be famous in China. In 1865 TR was only 20, a student at Haverfordwest theological college, Pembrokeshire; Soothill, W E: *Timothy Richard of China*, pp 21f

90 11 OMFA 3222e, 'the haemorrhage now scarcely ever ceases and is at times serious. She is very thin and weak (and) sometimes has a hectic flush on her cheeks.'

91 12 Ergot at 11 p m, the foetus' right femur fractured in fast forcible delivery because of the *placenta praevia*; without contractions Maria 'lost a fearful lot of blood' – a grim sequence.

92 13 Day of prayer: 1865–1984, 119 years.

93	14	OMFA 3231a–e, G429g WDR's reminiscences.
98	15	*Directory of Protestant Missions*, 1866; OMFA 3Bk3
100	16	*China Inland Mission Occasional Paper*, No 2 p 25
101	17	OMFA 3222piii
101	18	*Occ. Paper*, No 2.9–11
102	19	James Laidlaw Maxwell, MD, English Presbyterian Mission

Chapter 3

104	1	OMFA 3234
106	2	Stott, G: *Twenty-six Years of Missionary Work in China*, pp 2–4
106	3	OMFA 3231f
108	4	OMFA 3235.7, 8; 3325; F211d; N5.523
109	5	Accounts: *Occ. Paper*, No 1.4–8, 15; No 2.5
110	6	Taylor, J H: *China*, 2nd edn pp 112–13
112	7	Stock, E: *History of the CMS*, Vol II p 36; *CMS Report*, 1853
113	8	OMFA 3235 p 9; N5.525; 3232c
114	9	HTCOC Book 3 pp 251–2; 126 present including 37 missionaries.
116	10	OMFA 3231h,i,t; 3235.9,14; N5.530; *China's Millions*, 1880, p 105
117	11	HTCOC Book 1 pp 88, 140. Strictly, Maratha.
117	12	Orr, J E: *The Second Evangelical Awakening in Britain*, p 232
118	13	OMFA 4133; N5.532
119	14	Marchant, J and Mrs Barnardo: *Memoirs*, p 29; OMFA 3234a,b, reminiscences of C T Fishe, J McCarthy.
120	15	Fenians: A legendary band of Irish warriors of the second and third centuries AD, called Fianna, were the folk heroes of a revolutionary organisation that had originated in the United States to fight for an independent Ireland. To be distinguished from Sinn Fein, Irish for 'ourselves alone', founded 1905 and linked to the Irish Republican Army (IRA).
123	16	Rowdon, H H: *The Origins of the Brethren*, p 188; McKay, Moira J; M.Litt.thesis, University of Aberdeen, p 232 ref 56, citing F Boase and V Gibbs. £7000 may be thought of as perhaps £140,000 a century later.
125	17	Cavan: McKay, M J: op. cit. p 230; Taylor, F Howard, biography, 1927 edn p 7
126	18	OMFA 3232*l*
126	19	Stock, E: *History of the CMS*, Vol III p 295
127	20	OMFA 3231y; 3232e–h
127	21	Was this the first step towards the formation of German associate missions linked with CIM? No evidence found.
127	22	OMFA 3231x
127	23	*China's Millions*, 1876, p 202; *Occ. Paper*, No 1 p 5
130	24	Broomhall, M: *Jubilee Story*, pp 31, 36
130	25	Rudland: She herself long afterwards was described as 'a woman of remarkable Christian character and faith' who at 91 still kept 'a keen eye on everything connected with missionary work'.
130	26	JHT was known to many from his sermon on the Great Commission on June 25, 1865. By this time George Pearse had sold his house preparatory to evangelism among French soldiers, which led to his becoming a missionary to the Kabyles of the Atlas Mts. and from that to the founding of the North Africa Mission.

131 27 Aberdeen: her husband, the 5th earl, son of the Prime Minister of
1852–55, had died in 1864.

133 28 *China's Millions*, 1876, p 202

134 29 Care of Maw, and two days care of Cobbold.

135 30 Orr. J E: *Second Awakening*, p 131f

135 31 Blatchley: born January 24, 1845

138 32 OMFA 3235 p 32

140 33 OMFA 3235 p 36

140 34 OMFA 3231 V,X

141 35 OMFA N5.574

142 36 *China's Millions*, LVII No 5 p 91f; Henrietta Soltau reminiscences;
OMFA 3235 p 39

Chapter 4

148 1 MacGregor, David R: *The Tea Clippers*, *Sailing Ships of the Nineteenth
Century*; Lubbock, Basil: *The China Clippers* (1924); Woodcock, G:
British in the Far East, pp 27–31, 117–18; *Milestones of History*, p 40f.

149 2 *See* Ch 1, note 17

149 3, 4 Groves: *Memoir of the late Anthony Norris Groves*, by his widow (1856);
Groves, A N: *Christian Devotedness* (1825)

149 5 Stock, E: *History of the CMS*, Vol I pp 265–6; II.46, 70, 336, 391; III.45

150 6 Taylor, J H: *China*, 1866 edn p 109; JHT to Theodore Howard,
November 21, 1902. As JHT's use of the word 'labourer' to mean
'Christian worker' has been misunderstood, so has his phrase 'of humble
origin' for any who were not 'middle class'. None of the artisans among
his first missionaries were 'manual labourers' in the sense of being
unskilled. After a marked reaction against one whose conduct in 1867–68
betrayed Hudson Taylor's trust, he again welcomed 'working class' men
and women, but only if skilled, literate, intent on improving their
education and, above all, of proven value as evangelists.

150 7 OMFA F425, WDR's report for 1909; N5.496

150 8 Stott, G: *Twenty-six Years*, p 11

151 9 *China's Millions*, 1876, p 215

153 10 Taylor, J H: *A Retrospect* (1954 edn) pp 118–19

154 11 Puget: 'probably a five-pound note'; Taylor, J H: *Retrospect*, p 119;
OMFA 3235 p 42

154 12 OMFA N5.586. Stilted language tended to replace it on formal
occasions.

158 13 Judd: reminiscences, OMFA 3428; N5.202

159 14 Broomhall, M: *Jubilee Story*, p 39, says Mrs Jones, 4 Montague Terrace;
CIM Occasional Paper, No 2 p 9 says 7 Montague Terrace. Possibly F F
Gough at this time was in one and Mrs Jones in the other.

160 15 Receipt No 3231. No contributions to the CIM from FES were recorded
after July 13, 1865, when they paid for the passages of J W Stevenson and
G Stott.

162 16 OMFA F212; 3Bk1a (JHT Journal); 3234c,e,f; 3242a,f,g; 3243b–e;
3423 0

165 17 OMFA F215; 3428

165 18 *Occ. Paper*, No 2.8, 9

166 19 Barr, P: *To China with Love*, p 6; McKay, M J: thesis pp 211–12. Moira

McKay's analysis of CIM receipts for January–December 1865 put to rights others' well-intentioned errors by pointing out that while one gift was of £160 and one of £650, these amounts and the occasions of them were exceptional, the rest being mostly for small sums. Wm. Berger's own contributions of £30 twice, £36, £70, £100, £170 and £300, amounting to £760 in all, were generous but not basic to the Mission's income. The five others who gave £100 did not repeat this amount. One hundred and eight donations of £5 or more accounted for 17% of the total receipts; 83% were for £50 or less. Fifty-eight were for £1 or £2 and sixty-one for £4 or £5. Three hundred and sixty-four donations were for less than £1, of which most were for less than 8s, half the weekly wage of an artisan. Analysis of receipts during the succeeding years has yielded similar findings.

168   20   OMFA 3428
169   21   Stott, G: *Twenty-six Years*, pp 7, 8

Chapter 5
175   1   Main sources: OMFA 3Bk1, JHT's *Journal*; letters, 3242, 3243 and
           F212, 213c; *Occasional Paper*, No 4 pp 4–9
191   2   Krakatau: further eruptions forty-four years later, in 1927, produced a
           smaller island, Anak Krakatau, 'child of Krakatau'.
193   3   Thomas, Griffith: *Principles of Theology*, p 374 citing Goode, W: *The
           Effects of Baptism in the Case of Infants*.

Chapter 6
194   1   Main sources: OMFA 3Bk1, (JHT: *Journal*); 3Bk5, *A Brief Account of
           the Progress of the China Inland Mission from May 1866 to May 1868;
           Occasional Paper*, No 5; F212; 3242, 3243g
194   2   HTCOC Book 1 pp 159, 182. Pontianak was occupied by the Mission
           (CIM-OMF) ninety years later.
197   3–7 Sources as in Note 1

Chapter 7
209   1   Main sources: 3Bk5, *A Brief Account of the Progress of the China Inland
           Mission from May 1866 to May 1868*; 3314a; *Occasional Paper*, No 6;
           F311
213   2   Ningbo: J J Meadows, CIM; G and A Crombie, CIM; S P Barchet,
           CIM; W R and Mrs Fuller, UMFC; J and Mrs Mara, UMFC; J Notman,
           Independent; G Stott, CIM; J W and A Stevenson, CIM
215   3   Broomhall, M: *John W Stevenson: One of Christ's Stalwarts; passim*;
           F328a
216   4   Stock, E: *History of the CMS*, Vol II p 825
216   5   The *Chinese Recorder*, 1874, p 206
216   6   HTCOC Book 3 p 152
217   7   *Chinese Recorder*, 1875, p 418
218   8   *Chinese Recorder*, 1868, pp 65–68; op.cit. 1875, p 113; Broomhall, M:
           The Chinese Empire, p 65
218   9   *Chinese Recorder*, 1877, p 380ff
218   10   op.cit. p 385
219   11   op.cit. p 385f

219   12   Martin, W A P: *A Cycle of Cathay*; Covell, R; *W. A. P. Martin, Pioneer of Progress in China* (1978), pp 21, 59, 90–145 *passim*
219   13   Martin, W A P: op.cit. pp 238, 240
220   14   op.cit. pp 221–2
220   15   Covell, R: op.cit. pp 233–4
220   16   OMFA 3Bk3
221   17   *Occ. Paper*, No 2.10
221   18   Thailand: called Siam until 1939; Latourette, K S: *Expansion*, Vol VI pp 242–4; *The Directory of Protestant Missions in China, June 15th, 1866*, included *a list of Protestant missionaries in Japan and Siam* (publ. Am. Meth. Episc. Mission Press, 1866). In Japan at Kanagawa, eight; at Nagasaki, two. In Siam at 'Bankok', eighteen; at Petchaburi, four. (OMFA 3Bk3)
221   19   OMFA 3Bk3 *Directory* op.cit., at long last excluding Siam and Malaysia from the general term 'China'. (*See* HTCOC Book 1 pp 137, 187, 310, 388 note 25)
221   20   Main sources: OMFA 3243 gii; 3312; F324, 326 Rudland reminiscences.
224   21   Crew: *Occ. Paper*, No 6.16
226   22   Woodcock, G: *British in the Far East*, p 105
226   23   cf. *China's Millions*, May 1932, Vol 57 no 5: no verbatim report preserved, and no record of this recollection in the abridged report of proceedings.
227   24   Fool or knave: Smith, A H: *The Uplift of China*, 1909, p 172
227   25   OMFA 3Bk3 *Directory*, 1866
227   26   Main sources: OMFA *Occ. Paper*, No 6 pp 5, 28; 3312b; 3314f
231   27   HTCOC Book 1, pp 229, 273, 305
232   28   Latourette, K S: *Christian Missions*, p 234; *Encyclopaedia Sinica*, The Christian occupation of China, p 460
233   29   *Occ. Paper*, No 6.18
233   30   OMFA 3312D
234   31   Guinness, M G: *Story of CIM*, Vol I p 292 quoting OMFA 3312e
235   32   Main sources: OMFA 3Bk5, *Brief Account*: *Occ. Paper* No 6. 19, 21, 28, 34; 3312e; 3314c; F315 p 23
241   33   Flowers of silk: The emperor Hui Cong (Hui Ts'ung) formed the *Hua Yuan* (Academy of Arts) at Kaifeng, Henan. When Kaifeng fell to the Mongols in 1127 his collections were lost. When Hangzhou became the capital of the Southern Song dynasty, the academy was partially revived under the artists Li Tang, Zhao Be-zhu (Chao Po-chü) and Li Di (Li Ti). The Ma Xia (Ma Hsia) school continued the monochrome tradition, but the panoramic tradition changed with Ma Yuan (*c* 1190–1225) to focus on single motifs eg. boat on stream, trees in rain, huts on shore. (Ha, S H: in *Chambers Encycl.* 3.448b)
243   34   Moule, A E: *The Story of the Cheh-Kiang Mission*, p 79 note; Garside, E: *China Companion*, pp 18, 165–71; Broomhall, M: *The Chinese Empire*, p 75; Williams, Wells: *China*, p 98; CES *Gleaner*, March 1852, pp 73–4
243   35   Moule, A E: *Cheh-Kiang Mission* loc.cit.; *Chinese Recorder*, 1876, p 344; OMFA 3Bk3, *Directory*, 1866
243   36   OMFA 3313; *Occ. Paper*, No 6.34
245   37   Guinness, M G: *Story of CIM*, 1.295

246 38 OMFA 3Bk5, *Brief Account*, p 14; 3314h; 3315. JHT said 5 or 6; Maria said 4 families, probably following Chinese custom in treating families of brothers as one.
249 39 *Occ. Paper*, No 6.34–5
250 40 op.cit. No 7.4; OMFA 3Bk5, *Brief Account*, p 13

Chapter 8
251 1 *CIM Occasional Paper*, Nos 6, 7; OMFA 3314d; 3317a–d
254 2 OMFA 3Bk5, *Brief Account*, pp 23–4; *Occ. Paper*, No 6; 3315; 3412a, b
256 3 OMFA 3312b; 3314j; 3315; 3321
258 4, 5 OMFA 3316a, b
259 6 OMFA 441.11, *A Summary of Operations*, p 8
261 7 Broomhall, M: *Jubilee Story*, pp 41–2; *China's Millions*, 1875, p 31f
261 8 OMFA 8Bk1: Taylor, J H: *After Thirty Years*, pp 29–32
262 9 OMFA F32.10; 12Bk10 pp 65, 68, 71; 3315; 3321a; 3332b, kii
265 10 OMFA 12Bk10 p 65; 12Bk11 pp 68, 71; 3315; 3321a; 3332b, kii; Guinness, M G: *Story of the CIM*, Vol I pp 300–1; Broomhall, M: *John W. Stevenson*, p 5

Chapter 9
271 1 Main sources: OMFA 12Bk11 p 72ff; 3315; 3321a; 3324; *Occasional Paper*, No 7
272 2 Broomhall, M: *Jubilee Story*, p 56
274 3 OMFA F41.11
277 4 Main sources: OMFA 3Bk5, *Brief Account*, pp 24–5; *Occ. Paper*, No 7.12–15; No 11.69–70; No 13.27–8; No 31.21–3; 3331Bb; 3332h; 3Bk4 p 25; 12Bk11 pp 76–83
282 5 OMFA 12BK11 pp 76–83
282 6 Therefore this and other material should be cited only in its chronologically correct context.
282 7 OMFA 3332h,l; 4118a,b,e; *Occ. Paper*, No 7.15; No 11.67–70; No 31.21–23
286 8 OMFA 3414 J McCarthy recollections
287 9 OMFA 3234; 3311; 3315; 3322A23; 3332a,f,m; 3413d; N7B.89–98
289 10 OMFA 3332a
293 11 *Occ. Paper*, No 8.4–6
294 12 OMFA 3331Bb; F32.10
295 13 OMFA 4118f
296 14 OMFA 3311, 3332d
296 15 OMFA 3332i
297 16 OMFA 3413f
298 17 OMFA 3332kii

Chapter 10
299 1 Main sources: OMFA 3311; 3315; 3323; *CIM Occasional Paper*, No 8 pp 311–13
300 2 Moule, A E: *Cheh-Kiang Mission*, p 136f
301 3 *Occ. Paper*, No 8.11–13
302 4 *Occ. Paper*, No 8.10–16, 21–6; OMFA F312.9,10; 3311; 3315; 3322A13; 3323a–c
303 5 OMFA 3323a–c; *Occ. Paper* No 8.10–16
303 6 OMFA 3315

305 7 OMFA 3323c
306 8 Contrary to a published error, the 'separation' they lamented was not a rift between themselves or between them and the Taylors. It referred to their reluctantly discreet avoidance of Hudson and Maria while the Nicols and their friends were still in the house.
306 9 Stock, E: *History of the CMS*, Vol III p 26
306 10 op.cit. II.579–94
307 11 op.cit. II.579–81
308 12 *Occ. Paper*, No 10.47–9
310 13 OMFA F32.10,11; 3315; 3322A15,20
311 14 OMFA F425
313 15 OMFA 3321e
313 16 OMFA 3315; 3321e; 3322A16; 3331Bd,h,i,p; 3332p,q; *Occ. Paper*, No 13.129
315 17 *See* pp 417–19; OMFA 3331Bg; 3411
317 18 The net result is to demonstrate again how JHT coped with criticism.
318 19 CMS Archives: G/AC 1/17 pp 157–58
319 20 OMFA 3332r
320 21 OMFA 3332s; 3412c, d; F315.24
321 22 OMFA 3412d
321 23 *Chinese Recorder*, 1877, p 316f

Chapter 11
322 1 Main sources: OMFA 3Bk1, Journal; 3Bk5, A Brief Account, 3234b, 3321g,h; 3322A20; 3414; F313; *Occasional Paper*, No 9 pp 9,20–31; No 32. 32–3
324 2 Fuchun Jiang above Hangzhou
327 3 Yanzhou: confusingly spelt Nyin-Choo-Fu and Nyin-tsiu in the romanisation of two different dialects. To be distinguished from Yangzhou in Jiangsu.
330 4 *Proceedings of the Royal Georgraphic Society*, August 1879, pp 489–509; map p 544; OMFA I128. Journey, January–August, 1877; lecture April 28, 1879, in the presence of Marquis Zeng, Chinese Ambassador, son of Zeng Guofan.
330 5 OMFA 3311; 3315; 3321n; 3322t; 3322A20,21; F32.11,14; F411
333 6 OMFA 3322A20,21
335 7 All from OMFA 3315
338 8 Dodd: British, probably Canadian, serving with the American Presbyterian Mission. The Dominion of Canada was constituted during 1867.
338 9 OMFA G124 p 75
340 10 OMFA G124 pp 76–7; *Occ. Paper*, No 10.39–40
341 11 OMFA 3332s; N7B.163
343 12 OMFA N7c.216a; *Occ. Paper*, No 9.32–5
344 13 *Occ. Paper*, No 13.150–2
347 14 OMFA 3415; G123; 3321q
347 15 *Chinese Recorder*, 1905, pp 392, 423

Chapter 12

349   1   OMFA 3Bk4, *A Brief Account*
349   2   *Occasional Paper*, No 7 p 1
350   3   OMFA 3324D
350   4   OMFA 3423a
351   5   Women: *Occ. Paper*, No 13.124ff, 131
352   6   OMFA 3311, 3325: letter dictated to Jennie Faulding or perhaps Maria.
          Their handwriting is very similar. While JHT was confined to his room
          with conjunctivitis, Maria was also 'poorly'. Jennie's day-book for July
          24 reads 'wrote for Mr T', for July 27 'copying for Mr T', and for July 29
          'copying letter to candidates for Mr T.' Emily had gone to Shaoxing on
          the 26th.
354   7   op.cit.: *Occ. Paper*, No 13.131; Taylor, J H: *China*, (1868 edn)
358   8   'classic': defined as 'a standard or model of its kind . . . characterised by
          simplicity (and) balance . . . for lasting interest or significance.'
359   9   OMFA 3322Ba,d,g; 3322C; 3414; 3421; 3234b; 3322Bk; *Occ. Paper*,
          No 10.44–5; N7C.243; F312.19,20; F314; 12Bk11 p 122; G124.74
364 10   The death certificate which JHT sent to the consul gave the cause of
          death as 'tubercular hydrocephalus' with terminal 'double
          pneumo-pleuritis (effusion in the thorax)' OMFA 3Bk1. Today the term
          'meningitis' would be used instead of 'hydrocephalus'.
365 11   Personal communication by the third James Hudson Taylor, grandson of
          Herbert.
366 12   This account is intended only to supplement that told by the Howard
          Taylors in *Hudson Taylor and the China Inland Mission* (Vol II p 121ff),
          introducing material they did not use. OMFA 3423e; F312.10.
          N7C.247–8; *Occ. Paper*, No 10.52–7; No 11.67–9; *China's Millions*,
          1888, pp 25–6
369 13   Morse, H B: *International Relations*, Vol 2 p 107. 'The whole countryside
          was found to be ravaged and desolate, and the inhabitants reduced to
          feed on human flesh . . . The country was reduced to a mere desert, the
          villages totally uninhabited, and their vicinity strewn with bleached
          skeletons of their former inhabitants.'
372 14   Judson: preached for five years in a Burmese shack before baptising the
          first convert, as difficult as 'drawing the eye-tooth of a live tiger', he said.
          (Neill, S C: *A History of Christian Missions*, p 293)
372 15   *China's Millions*, 1888, p 25
372 16   In 1893 Geraldine Guinness quoted at length in her *Story of the CIM*
          from Hudson Taylor's account in the March 1888 issue of *China's
          Millions*, of this Duncan–Rudland episode. Memories of different
          journeys appear to have become confused, for JHT wrote: 'They were
          remarkably prospered on their way, to the surprise of the boatmen, who
          remarked to . . . Rudland, that his God must be the god of the winds, for
          whichever way the Grand Canal turned they had a fair wind!' But
          Rudland's own account of December 3, 1867, after the journey said,
          'Having the wind ahead, we made little progress.'
373 17   *Occ. Paper*, No 11.84–6
374 18   op.cit. The red cap button showed him to have the equivalent rank of a
          provincial governor.
374 19   Here again memory was unreliable. The retrospective account made

Changzhou the city at which they found 'that the bank of the Canal had given way, that the water had flooded the low lands . . . and that they were unable to proceed.' The boatmen said they might have to wait a month before the canal would be made usable. JHT's frequent travels by this route in the coming years seem to have linked another experience with Rudland's.

374 20 Woodcock, G: *British in the Far East*, p 183. Dr Woodcock equally truly attributed the practice to the policy of being Chinese to the Chinese.

375 21, 22 *China's Millions*, 1888, p 26; *Occ. Paper*, No 11, 89–90. A fuller account is given in the Howard Taylor Biography.

Chapter 13

378 1 *China: The Country, History and People*, RTS, pp 57–9; Morrison, R: *Memoirs*, Vol 2 Appendix p 22. According to J K Fairbank: *China Notes*, (Division of Overseas Ministries, NCC–USA) p 39, 'about a third of those who had degrees got them by purchase.'

379 2 Thompson, R W: *Griffith John*, pp 255–6

379 3 HTCOC: Book 1, pp 274–5; Book 3, pp 240–3

380 4 Morse, H B: *International Relations* Vol 2 p 220, citing Hart, Robert: *These from the Land of Sinim*, p 68; Martin, W A P: *A Cycle of Cathay*, p 449; *North China Herald*, Jan 25, 1872

381 5 Latourette, K S: *Expansion*, pp 267f, 290

382 6 Taylor, J H: *China*, 1868 edn, Appendix

383 7 Morse, H B: *International Relations* Vol 2, p 206 following A Michie: 'it referred to the difficulties and dangers to the state resulting from the aggressiveness of foreign powers . . . if a rupture could not be avoided, what course to follow . . . The points . . . likely to be brought up by the foreign envoys were: 1. Audience of the emperor; 2. a Chinese embassy abroad; 3. the construction of railways and telegraphs; 4. the admission of foreign salt and the opening of coal mines in China; 5. the right of foreign merchants to reside and trade in the interior; 6. increase of privileges to missionaries.'

384 8 op.cit.

384 9 op.cit.

384 10 Little, Alicia Bewicke: *Li Hung-chang, His Life and Times*, p 52

385 11 OMFA 3Bk5, *Brief Account*, p 26; 12Bk11.143–4; 3311; 3315; 3322Bi; F32.10; 3413j; 4115; *Occ. Paper*, No 8.31; No 10.57, 63; No 11.74,77

386 12 Consular notification E.84, p 304

387 13 Personal communications; cf Three Self Patriotic Movement, *Tian Feng* Magazine, No 13, Jan. 30, 1983, quoted by *China News and Church Report* No 2, April 29, 1983.

388 14 OMFA 3311, 3315: John McCarthy dep. Hangzhou Nov. 4; J Williamson arr. Hangzhou Nov. 8

388 15 *Occ. Paper*, No 9.82; No 12.100; *China's Millions*, 1878, pp 140–3; OMFA N7C.275–81

389 16 Dr John Parker dep. to UK 1867; *Chinese Recorder*, 1874, p 142

390 17 OMFA 3413m

390 18 Stott, G: *Twenty-six Years*, p 10; N7C, p 277

390 19 OMFA 3311; 3315; 3321; 3413i; 3414; 3423d; N7C.245; *Occ. Paper*, No 11.73, 76–7

392	20	OMFA 3414
393	21	*Occ. Paper*, No 11.73
393	22	OMFA 12Bk11 pp 132–56; 3Bk5, *Brief Account*, pp 26–8; 3311; 3413j–1; N7C.288, 290
396	23	OMFA 12Bk11 pp 134–6
396	24	3Bk5, *Brief Account*, pp 26–8
397	25	OMFA 12Bk11 pp 142–55
398	26	OMFA 12Bk11 p 136; 3315
398	27	OMFA 12Bk11 p 142; 3315
400	28	OMFA 3421; 3423e

Postscript

| 403 | 1 | OMFA 3315; 3322A28; 3416; 3423a; 441.11 *Summary of Operations*, p 10; 3Bk5 *Brief Account*; 8Bk1 p 6; F423 *Report of the Hangzhou Branch of the China Inland Mission; Occasional Paper*, No 11.77, 84; No 12.103 |
| 405 | 2 | OMFA 441.11 *Summary of Operations*, p 10; 8Bk1 p 6; 3416; F423 *Report of Hangzhou* |

PERSONALIA

ABERDEEN, Lady; Widow of George John James Hamilton-Gordon, Lord Haddo, 5th earl (1816–64) son of Earl of Aberdeen (1784–1860) Prime Minister 1852–55; 5th earl and Lady A influential evangelicals, supported CMS, T J Barnardo.

AITCHISON, William; Am. Board; 1854 Shanghai, Pinghu; travelled widely; d. 1861.

AITKEN, Canon W M Hay; curate to Wm Pennefather (qv) St Jude's, Mildmay; leading missioner of 1870s influenced by D L Moody 1875; an initiator of Keswick Movement, patterned on Mildmay Conferences.

ALCOCK, Sir John Rutherford (1809–97); MRCS at 21; 1832–37, surgeon Marine Brigade and Spanish Legion, Peninsular Wars, Dep.-Director of Hospitals; 1835 partially paralysed; 1843 Diplomatic Service; 1846 HBM consul Fuzhou; Xiamen (Amoy), Shanghai; 1858 Consul-gen. Japan; 20 June 1862 knighted, KCB; 1859–65 HBM minister, Japan; 1865–71 HBM minister, Peking; 1876 Pres. RGS.

ALLEN, Young J; Am. Meth. Episc. (South); 1860 Shanghai; edited reform publications read by Chinese from peasants to emperor; 1868–74 *Church News*, *Globe News*, *Review of the Times*; 1882 founded Anglo-Chinese College, Shanghai; 1887 Member, Socy. for the Diffusion of Christian and General Knowledge among the Chinese; consulted by reformers.

ARTHUR, William (1819–1901); 1839 Methodist mission to India; 1858–60 CES Board; 1861–68, 1871–88 Secy. WMMS; 1866 Pres. Wesleyan Conference.

AVELINE, Mr; one-time missionary to Demarara (Br. Guyana); personal secy. to Wm T Berger (qv).

BAGLEY, Paul; Am. Meth. Episc. local preacher; 1865 independently, Peking, travelled to Sichuan-Tibet border.

BALFOUR, Major-Gen. Sir George, CB; Capt 1840 opium war; 1843–46 first consul Shanghai; 1865 nominated JHT for FRGS; knighted after 1865.

BARCHET, Stephan Paul; German-born; 1865 Ningbo, sent by JHT; m. Mary Bausum (qv); CIM, then Am. Baptist with E C Lord (qv); later doctor of medicine, American.

BARING-GOULD, Rev A; Wolverhampton; assoc. with Hay Aitken (qv) missions.

BARING-GOULD, Rev B; St Michael's, Blackheath; 1882 CMS Assoc. Secy; 1894 to Japan, China.

BARNARDO, Thomas John (4 July 1845–19 Sept. 1905); 1862 converted; 1866 met JHT in Dublin; April 1866 to London; 1866–69 CIM candidate; became CIM Referee.

BARNES, Susan; 1866 met JHT, Limerick; CIM *Lammermuir* party, Hangzhou, Shaoxing; 1867 resigned.

BATES, Rev J; CMS Islington College; 1867 Ningbo; 1884–89 B & FBS NT revision committee; 1895 still active in China.

BAUSUM, J G; independent, Penang; 1845–46 m. Maria Tarn Dyer, mother of Maria Jane.

BAUSUM, Mrs; 2nd wife of J G Bausum; mother of Mary; 1856 Ningbo; 1861 m. E C Lord (qv); d. Jan. 15, 1869.

BAUSUM, Mary; daughter; on *Lammermuir*; 1868 at 18 m. Dr S P Barchet (qv).

BAXTER, Robert Dudley (1827–75); parliamentary lawyer in father's firm Baxter, Rose & Norton, chief Conservative election agents; cousin of C R Alford, Bishop of Victoria, Hong Kong; CES Board; chairman FES; declined nomination to stand for parliament.

BEAUCHAMP, (Rev Sir) Montagu Harry Proctor-, Bart, MA (Cantab) (1860 –1939); son of Sir Thomas (qv); Cambridge Univ. oar; 1885 member of CIM 'Cambridge Seven' to China; pioneer, Shanxi, Sichuan; travelled '1000 miles' with JHT; World War I Hon. Chaplain to Forces, Egypt, Greece, Murmansk; 1915 inherited baronetcy; Oct. 1939 d. Langzhung, Sichuan.

BEAUCHAMP, Sir Thomas Proctor-, Bart; Langley Park, Norwich, 4th baronet; m. Hon Caroline Waldegrave, daughter of 2nd Baron Radstock and Dowager Lady Radstock (qv); friend, supporter of JHT, CIM, d. 1874.

BELL, Capt M; Master of John Willis and Son tea clippers; 1864 converted; 1866 voyage of *Lammermuir* with JHT and CIM party.

BELL, Mary: Malvern, Glos.; 1866 CIM, *Lammermuir*, Hangzhou, 1867 m. W D Rudland (qv); 1868 Yangzhou riot, Zhenjiang; 1871 Taizhou; d. Oct. 23, 1874.

BERGER, William Thomas (c 1812–99); director Samuel Berger & Co, Patent Starch manufacturer, St Leonard St, Bromley-by-Bow; CES supporter; early donor to JHT; 1865 co-founder and UK director, CIM; generous life-time donor; home at Hackney village, then Saint Hill, East Grinstead, devoted to Mission.

BERGER, Mary; wife of WTB; (c 1812–Feb 16, 1877)

BERGNE, Samuel Brodribb; Independent minister, 1854–79 co-Sec. B&FBS.

BEVAN, Francis Augustus (1840–1919); son of Robert Bevan (qv); donor to CIM; 1896 first chairman of Barclays Bank.

BEVAN, Robert Cooper Lee (1809–90); a founder of LCM; friend of CMS; first chairman of YMCA; CES Gen. Committee.

BEWLEY, Henry (1814–76); Dublin printer, built Merrion Hall, Brethren; supporter and Referee of CIM.

BISMARCK, Prince Otto Eduard Leopold von (1815–98); leading German statesman; 1862–90 Foreign Affairs; 'Iron Chancellor'; PM of Prussia; 1865 Count, 1867 Prince; defeated Austria, France; united Germany; first chancellor of Reich; 1890 'old pilot dropped'.

BLAKISTON, Capt; adventurer; 1860 attempted Shanghai to India via Tibet, forced back.

BLATCHLEY, Emily (1845–74); 1865 Home and Colonial Training Coll. grad.; 'rt.hand' secy., governess to JHT, family; 1866 CIM, *Lammermuir*, Hangzhou, 1868 Yangzhou, riot; March 1870 UK with three JHT children; 1870–74 London, guardian, secretary; d. July 25, 1874.

BLODGET, Henry, DD (1825–1903); Am. Board; 'massive build and commanding presence', 'the soul of country and good breeding'; 1850–53 tutor, Yale; 1854 Shanghai with Aitchison (qv); 1860 to Tianjin with Br. forces, first Prot. to preach in streets; 1864 Peking 30 years; translator, Mandarin NT with Burdon (qv) Edkins (qv) W Martin (qv) Schereschewsky (qv), revised W H Medhurst's

Southern Mandarin NT; 1870 Shanghai Vernacular NT with W J Boone, T McClatchie *et al*; 1889 'easy *wenli*' NT with Burdon (qv) Groves, J C Gibson, I Genähr; 1890 Union Mandarin NT committee; 1890 with others submitted memorial to emperor 'setting forth the true nature of Christianity'; 1894 retired ill.

BOHANNAN, Annie; widowed sister of Mary Bell (qv); nurse to JHT children; 1868 m. Edward Fishe (qv).

BONAR, Andrew; Scottish divine; friend of W C Burns.

BONAR, Horatius (1808–89); Scottish divine, hymn-writer.

BONHOURE, M/Mme; Paris Prot. Mission; 1861 Tianjin, Yantai, Mme died. M retired.

BOOTH, Catherine (née Mumford) (1829–90); m. Wm Booth (qv) June 16, 1855; Salv. Army.

BOOTH, Evangeline; b. 1865 C'mas Day, to Wm and Catherine (qv); famed SA evangelist; US Natl. Commander SA; 1934–39 General, SA.

BOOTH, William (1829–1912); Methodist evangelist; June 16, 1855 m. Catherine Mumford (qv); Methodist New Connexion; 1865 'found his destiny' in London's East End and with Catherine formed The Christian Mission; 7 Aug 1878 changed name and form to Salvation Army; son Bramwell, daughter Evangeline (qv) among successors as 'General'.

BOWYER, Mary; 1865 Wm Pennefather's training school; 1866 CIM, *Lammermuir*, Hangzhou; 1868 Nanjing; 1875 m. F W Baller, CIM Sinologue.

BRIDGMAN, Elijah Coleman, DD (1801–61); Am. Board (ABCFM); 1830 Canton; 1832 first editor *Chinese Repository* with R Morrison; 1843–44 US treaty interpreter-negotiator; 1845–52 translator, Chinese Bible, Delegates' Committee, 1847 Shanghai.

BRIDGMAN, Mrs; 1845 Canton; 1847 Shanghai; 1864 Peking.

BROOMHALL, Benjamin (1829–1911); m. Amelia Hudson Taylor (1835–1918); 1878–95 Gen. Sec. CIM London; editor, *National Righteousness*, organ of anti-opium trade campaign, to 1911 (*see* Maxwell).

BRUNTON, John; first officer, *Lammermuir*.

BUNSEN, Baron Chevalier; 1839 emissary of King Fredk Wm IV of Prussia to London; with Lord Ashley (Shaftesbury) worked for natl. home for Jews, toleration for Christians in Holy Land; warned King Fredk Wm of Gutzlaff's hyperbole; urged by king to arouse C of E to vigorous evangelisation of China; friend of Hy Venn; studied Chinese lang.; helped Ld Shaftesbury create Bp. of Jerusalem.

BURDON, John Shaw (1829–1907); CMS, 1853 Shanghai; pioneer evangelist; 1857 m. Burella Dyer, sister of Maria Taylor (qv); 1862 Peking; 1874 3rd bishop of Victoria, Hong Kong; Bible translator (*see* Blodget).

BURLINGAME, Anson (1820–70); barrister, Congressman, Methodist; 1861–67 US minister, Peking, appointed by Abraham Lincoln; 1867–70 ambassador-at-large for China; d. St Petersburg (Leningrad).

BURNS, Prof Islay, DD (Glas.); biographer of brother, Wm C Burns (qv).

BURNS, William Chalmers (1815–68); first English Presby. to China; 1847 Hong Kong; Amoy; 1855 Shanghai; 1856 Swatow; 1863 Peking; 1867 Niuchuang (now Yingkou), d. Niuchuang; translated *Pilgrim's Progress*; close friend of JHT.

BUXTON, Sir Edward North, Bart, MP (1812–58); son of Sir Thomas Fowell Buxton, 1st baronet; CES Gen. Committee.

CALDER, Eliza; Arbroath, Aberdeen; 1866 m. Lewis Nicol (qv), CIM, *Lammermuir*, Hangzhou; 1867 Xiaoshan, outrage; 1868 left CIM.

CALDWELL, John R; Glasgow silk merchant, influenced by JHT, faithful CIM supporter.

CARDWELL, J E; CIM, 1867 Hangzhou; 1868 Taizhou, Zhejiang; Dec 30, 1869 Jiujiang, pioneered Jiangxi.

CAREY, William (1761–1834); Baptist Miss. Soc. founder; 1793 India, Serampore; 1800–30 Prof. of Oriental Languages, Calcutta.

CASSELS, William Wharton (1859–1925); St John's College, Cam.; 1882 ordained; one of the 'Cambridge Seven'; 1885 Shanghai, Shanxi; Sichuan; 1895 consecrated Bishop of West China, as a member of both CIM, CMS.

CAVAN, Fredk John Wm Lambart, 8th earl of, (1815–87); Lt Col 7th Dragoon Guards; CES Gen. Committee; supporter of CIM, Mildmay Conf., D L Moody; Welbeck St Brethren.

CHALLICE, John; director of six companies, deacon, Bryanston Hall, Portman Square; 1872 member, first CIM council; hon. treasurer UK; d. 1887.

CHAPMAN, Robert Cleaver (1802–1902); High Court attorney; C of E; 1832 Strict Baptist minister; Brethren; 2nd Evang. Awakening evangelist; 1872 CIM Referee; JHT's friend.

CIGGIE, Grace; Glasgow, 1865 influenced by JHT, 'China's Need', recruit for Ningbo; 1866 CIM *Lammermuir* party, deferred by ill health; 1866–69 Glasgow slums; 1870 m. Geo Stott, Wenzhou.

CI XI, (Ts'u Hsi) (1835–1908); Empress Dowager; Yehonala, the Concubine Yi; 1860 empress regent to Tong Zhi; 1860–1908 supreme power in China.

CLARENDON, Earl of (1800–70); Foreign Sec. to Lord Aberdeen 1853, Lord Palmerston 1855, Lord Russell 1865, Gladstone 1868.

COBBOLD, Robert Henry; CMS, 1848–62, Ningbo; translator, Ningbo romanised vernacular NT; 1863 Rector of Broseley, Staffs; 1871–1909 Rector, Ross on Wye.

COLLINGWOOD, R G; Oxford philosopher, expert on Roman Britain; grandson of Wm Collingwood (qv).

COLLINGWOOD, W G; biographer of Ruskin; son of Wm Collingwood (qv).

COLLINGWOOD, William (1819–1903); Fellow of Royal Watercolour Society; Oxford; 1839 Liverpool; C of E until Brethren; 1850 responded to C Gutzlaff, supported CES; met JHT Sept. 1853 and supported JHT/CIM; 1872 CIM Referee.

COLLINS, W H, MRCS; 1858 CMS Shanghai; 1863 Peking.

CONGLETON, John Vesey Parnell, 2nd Baron, (1805–83); 1830–37 with A N Groves (qv) Baghdad, m. Iranian Christian widow of Shiraz; Brethren leader, Teignmouth, London, Orchard St, Welbeck St; travelled widely; donor to JHT/CIM.

COOPER, T T; adventurer, Sichuan, Tibet; agent, Calcutta Chamber of Commerce; 1862 Rangoon; 1867 Shanghai; 1868 Hankou–Tibet in Chinese clothes, forced back; 1871, author, *Travels of a Pioneer of Commerce*; proposed Yangzi–Bhamo (Irrawaddy) railway.

CORDON, Henry; 1867 CIM, sent by Berger (qv); Hangzhou; 1868 Suzhou.

COX, Josiah; 1852 Wesleyan MMS, Canton, joined G Piercy (qv); 1860 invited by Taipings (by Hong Ren) to Suzhou, Nanjing, visited, disillusioned; 1862 invited by G John (qv) Hankou, began Hubei, Hunan Miss. of WMMS; 1863 first Prot. miss. to enter antagonistic Hunan; 1865 Jiujiang; 1875 invalided to UK, d. 1906.

CRANAGE, Dr J Edward; Anglican, Old Hall, Wellington, Shrops; 1859–62 Evangelical Awakening leader (*see* Bk 3).

CROMBIE, George; Aberdeen farmer; 1865 JHT's second recruit, to Ningbo; 1866 CIM Fenghua.

CULBERTSON, M S, DD; Am. Presbyterian; 1850 Shanghai; co-translator of Delegates' Version, Chinese Bible (NT); with Elijah Coleman Bridgman of OT, completed 1862; d. 1862, cholera.

DAVIES, Evan, LMS Malaya; author, 1845, *China and her Spiritual Claims*; 1846 *Memoir of the Reverend Samuel Dyer*.

DAVIS, President Jefferson (1808–89); Confederate leader and president at start of Am. Civil War.

DELAMARRE, Abbé; Paris Mission; 1858–60 chief interpreter, French treaty; falsified Chinese version; 1860 dep. Peking carrying tricolor and 27 passports for SW provinces.

DENNISTON, J M; Presby. minister, London, Torquay; associated with W C Burns revivals and JHT founding CIM; co-founder Foreign Evangelist Soc.

DENNY, William; Glasgow ship-owner/builder, Wm Denny and Brothers, Dumbarton; 1865 gave free passages to China to Barchet and Crombie (qv); 1869 completed *Cutty Sark*.

DESGRAZ, Louise; Swiss governess to Wm Collingwood (qv) family, as a daughter; 1866 CIM, *Lammermuir*, Hangzhou; 1865 Yangzhou, riot; 1878 m. E Tomalin.

DEW, Capt Roderick, RN; 1862 commander, Ningbo front, against Taipings.

DISRAELI, Benj (1804–81); 1st Earl of Beaconsfield; son of Isaac d'Israeli; statesman, social novelist; 1837 MP; 1868, 1874–80 Prime Minister, bought Suez Canal shares, friend of Queen Victoria, made her 'Empress of India'.

DODD, Samuel; Canadian in Am. Presbyterian Mission; 1861 Ningbo; 1867 Hangzhou; 1875 translated *Hebrews* into *wenli*.

DOOLITTLE, Justus; Am. Board; 1850 Fuzhou; 1862 Tianjin, editor *Chinese Recorder*.

DOUGLAS, Carstairs, LL D (Glas.) (1830–77); English Presby. Mission; 1855 Amoy with W C Burns; Amoy vernacular dictionary; advocated occupying Taiwan; 1865 enlisted J L Maxwell (qv), with Maxwell began at Tainan; 1877 chairman General Miss. Conference, Shanghai; 1877 d. cholera.

DUDGEON, J, MD; 1863 LMS Peking.

DU HALDE, P J B; author *The General History of China* (Ldn. 1736, 1741); *A Description of the Empire of China and Chinese Tartary . . . Korea, Tibet, etc*, 2 vols (Ldn. 1741).

DUNCAN, George; Banff, Scotland, stone-mason; 1865 CIM; 1866, *Lammermuir*, Hangzhou; 1867 Lanxi, Nanjing; 1868 Yanzhou riot, m. Catherine Brown; 1872 UK; 1873 d. TB.

DYER, Burella Hunter; b. 31 May 1835; elder daughter of Samuel Dyer Sr (qv); 1857 m. J S Burdon; d. 1858.

DYER, Samuel Sr (1804–43); Cambridge law student; 1827 LMS, m. Maria Tarn, daughter of LMS director; 1827 Penang; 1829–35 Malacca; 1835–43 Singapore; d. Macao.

DYER, Samuel Jr; b. 18 Jan. 1833, son of Samuel Sr.; brother of Maria Taylor (qv); 1877 agent of B&FBS, Shanghai, after Alex Wylie (qv); expanded staff, distribution.

EDKINS, Joseph (1832–1905); LMS evangelist, linguist, translator, philologist, expert in Chinese religions; 1860 visited Suzhou Taiping rulers; 1862 Nanjing; 1848–60 Shanghai; 1860–61 first to Shandong, Yantai; 1862 Tianjin (wife died *aet*.

22) Peking; 57 years in China, 30 in Peking; 1880 retired from LMS, attached to Imperial Maritime Customs; author 1853 *Grammar Shanghai dialect*; 1857 *Mandarin Grammar*; 1859 *The Religious Condition of the Chinese*; 1878 *Religion in China*; 1880 *Chinese Buddhism*; 1875 DD (Edin.); 1877 second wife died; *aet.* 80 survived typhoid; *aet.* 81 still writing, d. Easter Sunday.

ELGIN, Earl of; son of Thomas Bruce, 7th earl (Elgin marbles); 1857 Indian mutiny; 1858 envoy, Treaty of Tientsin; treaty with Japan; 1860 second opium war, captured Peking, burned Summer Palace, negotiated Peking Convention.

FAN QISENG (Vaen Kyi-seng); evangelist, Fenghua.

FARNHAM, J M W; Presby.; 1860 Shanghai with Wm Gamble (qv); friend of CIM.

FAULDING, Jane (Jennie) Elizabeth (1843–1904); Home and Colonial Training College (with E Blatchley (qv)); 1865 assist. to JHT, London; 1866 CIM, *Lammermuir*; Hangzhou; m. JHT 28 Nov. 1871; 1877–78 led CIM team, Shanxi famine relief, first Western woman inland.

FAULDING, William F and Harriet; parents of Jane E Faulding (qv) and Ellen (Nellie); piano frame and fret manufacturer, 340 Euston Road; Regent's Park Chapel.

FENG NENGGUI, Ningbo basket-maker, member of non-idolatrous Buddhist sect; became evangelist, pastor, Fenghua, Wenzhou.

FISHBOURNE, Capt. RN; rescued Amoy victims; strong supporter of missions and anti-opium soc.; later, evangelist; CES Gen. Committee.

FISHE, Colonel; Dublin; HEIC Madras Horse Artillery (retd.); father of Edward and Charles (qv).

FISHE, Charles Thomas; son of Col Fishe, Dublin (qv); influenced by H G Guinness (qv), JHT; 1867 asst. to W T Berger (qv); 1868 CIM, Yangzhou; 1871 CIM China Secy.; 1875 m. Nellie Faulding (qv).

FISHE, Edward; elder son of Col Fishe, Dublin (qv); 1866 influenced by H G Guinness (qv), JHT; 1867 to China independently; attached to CIM; m. Annie Bohannan (qv); 1868 Zhenjiang.

FITTACK, W H; HBM consul, 1867 Ningbo.

FLEMING, T S; 1860 CMS recruit taught by JHT; Ningbo, Hangzhou; 1863 invalided home.

FORREST, R J; 1860 HBM consular interpreter, later consul, Ningbo.

FRANCKE, August Hermann; pietist, 1696 founded Orphan Houses, extensive by C 19; prof. divinity, Halle Univ. Germany; d. 1727.

FRASER, John; Scottish missionary to Egypt; initiated movement resulting in Foreign Evangelist Society.

FULLER, Wm R; first United Meth. Free Ch. missionary to China; trained by JHT; 1864 Ningbo; 1867 invalided to UK.

GAINFORT, Mrs; Dublin; influenced students to join CIM.

GAMBLE, William; Am. Presby. Mission Press; 1858 Ningbo; 1860 Shanghai; friend of JHT; 1866 received *Lammermuir* party, served as CIM business agent.

GARDNER, Christopher T; 1867 HBM consular interpreter, Ningbo.

GARIBALDI, Giuseppe (1807–82); with Mazzini and Cavour created united Italy; 1860 freed Sicily, took Naples; Victor Immanuel proclaimed King.

GAULD, Dr Wm; Engl. Presby. Mission, c 1863 began med. work at Shantou (Swatow), largest in China for years; 1867 new hospital.

GILMOUR, James (1843–91); LMS; 1870 Mongolia for 20 years.

GLADSTONE, Wm Ewart (1809–98); 1832 MP; Liberal PM 1868–74, 1880–85, 1892–94.

GORDON, Lt Col Charles George (1833–85); 1860 Tianjin, Peking campaign; 1862 Shanghai, commanding Ever-Victorious Army; 1864 Taiping Rebellion ended; emperor awarded Order of the Imperial Dragon, and Queen Victoria the CB; 1865–71 London; donor to JHT; 1880 adviser to Chinese govt.; 1883–5 Major-Gen., Sudan.

GOSSE, Philip Henry (1810–88); naturalist, author: 1855–66 *Manual of Marine Zoology*; 1860–62 *Romance of Natural History*; through W T Berger joined Hackney Brethren; early donor to CIM.

GOSSE, Sir Edmund Wm (1845–1928); (aged 15–20 while JHT at Mile End); 1867–75 asst. librarian British Museum; poet and critic, 1904–10 librarian, House of Lords; author, histories of literature, and *Father and Son*, biographical.

GOUGH, Frederick Foster, DD; CMS 1849–61 Ningbo; Mary, first wife, d. 1861; 1862–69 London, Ningbo vernacular romanised NT revision with JHT; 1866 m. Mary Jones (qv); 1869 Ningbo.

GRANT, Gen. Ulysses Simpson (1822–85); commander in chief Union forces in Am. civil war (1864–65); 1869–76 President USA.

GRANT, Hay Macdowell; laird of Arndilly; 1865 chairman Perth Conference.

GREEN, D D; Am. Presby.; 1859 Ningbo; 1865 Hangzhou.

GRETTON, Henry; CMS 1867 Hangzhou, alone without Chinese companion after G E Moule dep.; 1870 Shaoxing.

GROVES, Anthony Norris (1795–1853); early exponent of 'faith principle'; brother-in-law of G Müller; missionary to Baghdad, initiator of Brethren movement.

GUINNESS, H Grattan, DD, FRAS (1835–1910); 1855 left New Coll. Lond. to become great evangelist of Evangelical Awakening; 1859 Ulster revival, drew thousands; 1865 offered to CIM, JHT advised continue UK; became JHT's friend; 1872 CIM Referee; 1873 founded East London Miss. Training Institute (Harley College); trained 1,330 for 40 societies of 30 denominations; 1877 Livingstone Inland Mission, 1888 Congo-Balolo Mission, 1898 initiated RBMU; NAM founded on his advice; greatly influenced Barnardo, John R Mott; author, astronomy, eschatology; 7 children, grandchildren in Christian ministry.

GUINNESS, M Geraldine (1862–1949); daughter of H Grattan Guinness (qv); 1888 CIM; 1894 m. F Howard Taylor (qv); author, biography of JHT and others.

GULICK, J T; Am. Board 1864 Peking; 1865 Kalgan (now Zhangjiakou) outside Gt. Wall.

GUTZLAFF, Charles (Karl Friedrich Augustus) (1803–51); DD Groningen 1850; 1826–28 Netherlands Miss. Soc., Batavia (Jakarta), Java; 1828 independent, Bangkok; 1929 m. Miss Newell, Malacca, first single Prot. woman missionary to E. Asia d. 1831; 1831–35 voyages up China coast; 1834 m. Miss Warnstall d. 1849; 1839 interpreter to British; 1840, 1842 governor of Chusan Is.; 1842 interpreter-negotiator, Nanking Treaty; 1843–51 Chinese Sec. to British govt. Hong Kong; initiated Chinese Union, Chinese Associations and missions; 1850 m. Miss Gabriel.

HALL, Charles J; 1857 CES missionary Ningbo; 1860 Shandong; d. 1861.

HALL, William; manufacturer of footwear, deacon, Bryanston Hall, Portman Square; 1872 member of first CIM London council.

HALL, William Nelthorpe; Methodist New Connexion; 1860 Shanghai; 1861 April Tianjin with J Innocent (qv); d. 1878.

HANSPACH, August; Chinese Evangelization Soc. of Berlin (Berlin Missionary Soc. for China); 1855 Hong Kong; 11 years' extensive inland travel.

HARPER, Andrew P, DD; Am. Presby. 1844–46 Macao (debarred from Canton); 1847 Canton; 1887 first president, Canton Christian Coll.

HART, Sir Robert; b. 1835; 1854 Ningbo, consular interpreter; 1857 Canton; Nov. 1862 Inspector-General, Chinese Imperial Maritime Customs; 1865 Peking.

HILL, Richard Harris, FRIBA; civil engineer, evangelist; helped build Mildmay Miss. Hosp. CIM Newington Green; m. Agnes, daughter of Henry W Soltau (qv); 1872 Hon. Sec. London CIM.

HOLMES, J L; Am. Southern Baptist; 1860 pioneer of Shandong, Yantai (Chefoo); Oct. 1861 killed with H M Parker (qv).

HOUGHTON, John; son of Richard (qv) Liverpool; Feb. 1866 host to JHT; introduced to H Grattan Guinness.

HOUGHTON, Richard; father of John (qv); 1866 as 'perfect stranger' read JHT's China, donated £650 (modern equiv. ?£13,000).

HOWARD, John Eliot (1807–83); quinologist, 1874 FRS, Fellow of Linnaean Soc.; manufacturing chemist; early leader of Brethren, Tottenham; member of B&FBS committee and CES Board; JHT's close friend and supporter; 1872 CIM Referee.

HOWELL, Alfred; Dent & Co, Japan; 1866 donor to CIM in approval of Chinese dress.

HUDSON, Benjamin Brook (c 1785–1865); Wesleyan Methodist minister; portraitist; grandfather of JHT.

HUDSON, T H (1800–76); General Baptist Mission; 1845 Ningbo, remained till death; 1850–66 translated NT into wenli (literary Chinese).

HUTCHINSON, Sir Jonathan (1828–1913); 1859 general and ophthalmic surgeon, London Hospital; 1882 FRS; 1889 President RCS; Nov. 1908 Knight Bachelor; benefactor of JHT.

INNOCENT, John (1829–1904); Methodist New Connexion evangelist; 1860 Shanghai; 1861 Tianjin with W N Hall (qv) till 1897; 1864 visited Mongolia.

JACKSON, Charles; 1862–79 Anglican Sec. of B&FBS with J Mee (qv); (cf John Jackson, B&FBS 1823–49).

JACKSON, Josiah Alexander; carpenter, draper, Kingsland, Stoke Newington; 1865 CIM cand., 1866 Lammermuir, Hangzhou; 1867 Taizhou, Zhejiang; d. Shanghai 1909.

JENKINS, Horace; ABMU; 1860 Ningbo, joined Knowlton (qv), Kreyer (qv).

JOHN, Griffith (1831–1912); LMS; 1855 Shanghai; pioneer evangelist; 1861 Hankou; 1863 Wuchang; 1867 Hanyang; 1888 declined chairmanship, Congregational Union of Eng. and Wales; 1889 Hon. DD (Edin.); Sept. 24, 1905 jubilee in China; April 1906 retired ill.

JONES, John; CES; 1856–57 Ningbo; independent, 1857–63; early exponent of 'faith principle', influenced JHT; d. 1863.

JONES, Mary; wife of John; 1863–66 with Hudson Taylors, London; 1866 m. F F Gough; 1869 Ningbo; 1869–71 fostered Chas Edw Taylor; d. Nov. 1877.

JUDD, Charles H Sr (1842–1919); 1867 CIM through influence of T J Barnardo; 1868 Yangzhou; 1869 Zhenjiang; 1872–3 UK; 1874 Wuchang, with JHT; 1875 with two Chinese rented house at Yueyang (Yochow), Hunan, forced out; 1877 with J F Broumton via Hunan to Guiyang, Guizhou; Broumton settled, Judd via Chongqing to Wuchang; 1879 built at Yantai before school and sanatorium.

KENNAWAY, Sir John Henry, Bart, MP, PC; 1887 President of CMS; 1897 PC; 1893 coined phrase, 'Ask the Lord and tell His People' (Stock III.677).

KENNEDY, Rev; Congregational minister, Stepney.

KERR, John G M D, LL D; Am. Presby. North, 1854 Canton, took over Dr Peter Parker's hosp. for nearly 50 years, treated over 1 million, 480,000 surgical operations, 1300 urinary calculus, incl. US Minister, Peking; 1870 trained 260 Chinese medicals; pioneered care of insane, 1898 opened Canton Refuge for the Insane; 1887 first Pres. Med. Miss. Assn. of China; author-translator *Chinese Materia Medica*, other med. books.

KINNAIRD, Hon Arthur Fitzgerald, 10th Baron (1814–87); supported CMS, LCM, Barnardo. Son, of same name, 11th baron m. niece of Hon and Rev Baptist W Noel (qv); she helped found Foreign Evangelization Socy, 1871, and Zenana Bible and Medical Mission (now BMMF).

KLOEKERS, Hendrick Z; Netherlands Chinese Evangelization Soc.; 1855–58 Shanghai; 1862 BMS; 1862–65 Shandong, Yantai.

KNOWLTON, Miles Justice (Feb. 8, 1825–Sept. 10, 1874); ABMU; 1854 Ningbo; stalwart friend of JHT, rebutted slander.

KOCH, Robert (1843–1910); German bacteriologist, discovered *B. tuberculosis*; cholera, and others.

KONG, Prince (Prince Kung) (1833–98); brother of Xian Feng (Hsien Feng) emperor; 1860 *et seq*, leading statesman.

KREYER, Carl T; ABMU; 1866 Hangzhou; lent his home to *Lammermuir* party; assisted CIM in Hangzhou, Huzhou crises.

LAM GUA; student of George Chinnery (oriental artist); Canton works now in Gordon Museum, Guy's Hospital, London (Book 2, p 405).

LANCE, Henry; pastor, Berger Hall, Bromley-by-Bow (*c* 1865–70); trained first CIM candidates, later opposed JHT's principles, esp. Chinese dress.

LANDELS, William, DD (1823–99); minister Regent's Park Chapel (Baptist); 1872 CIM Referee.

LATOURETTE, Kenneth Scott; late Willis James and Sterling Prof. of Missions and Oriental History, Yale Univ.; author, *see* bibliography.

LAUGHTON, Richard Fredk; BMS; 1863 Shandong, Yantai; d. 1870.

LAY, Horatio N; son of George Tradescent Lay, B&FBS (1836–39) and HBM consul; HBM consul, Fuzhou, Canton; 1860 first Inspector-General, Imperial Maritime Customs; negotiated 'Lay-Osborne fleet'; 1862 dismissed; succeeded by Robt Hart (qv).

LECHLER, Rudolf (1824–1908); Basel Mission pioneer; 1847 Hong Kong, Guangdong (Kwangtung) Hakkas, under Gutzlaff, with Hamberg (qv); 52 years in China, to 1899.

LEES, Jonathan; LMS; 1862 Tianjin, many years; d. 1902.

LEGGE, James, DD, LL D (1815–97); LMS; 1835 MA (Aberdeen), Congregational; 1839–43 Anglo-Chinese College, Malacca; 1843–70 Anglo-Chinese College, Hong Kong; 1861–86 translator, Chinese classics; 1875 Fellow, Corpus Christi, Oxford; 1877–97, first Prof. of Chinese, Oxford Univ.

LEWIS, William Garrett; Baptist minister, Westbourne Grove Ch., Bayswater, London; a founder of London Baptist Assn.; urged JHT to publish *China: Its Spiritual Need and Claims*; 1872 CIM Referee.

LIANG AFA (1789–1855); Canton engraver-printer; 1815 to Malacca with W Milne; 1819 Canton, colporteur; arrested, flogged; 1821 Malacca; 1828 Canton; 1834 arrested, escaped, betrayed, escaped; 1839 returned, tolerated by Lin Zexu (qv); first Prot. pastor; 1845 mobbed; d. 1855.

LI HONGZHANG (Li Hung-chang) (1823–1901); holder of the highest academic degrees, highest honours after defeat of Taiping rebels; enlightened liberal but failed in modernisation of China; 1895 forced to cede Taiwan to Japan; the Grand Old Man of China, leading statesman until death.

LI LANFENG; 1867 printer employed by CIM, Hangzhou; converted per W D Rudland (qv).

LI TIANFU; 1867 Ningbo Christian; 1868 Nanjing evangelist with G Duncan (qv).

LI ZHUGUI; 1871 evangelist at Xiaoshan.

LINCOLN, Pres. Abraham (1809–65); US anti-slavery congressman; 1861 President; 1863 Gettysburg speech; 'government of the people, by the people, for the people'; 1865 assassinated.

LINDSEY, Gen Sir Alexander; 1865 host to JHT, Perth.

LING ZHUMOU; Ningbo Christian; 1868 cook-evangelist at Nanjing with G Duncan (qv) and H Reid (qv).

LISTER, Joseph, Lord, PC, OM, FRS (1827–1912); father of asepsis and antisepsis; 1895–1900 Pres. Royal Soc.

LLOYD, E R; Anglican relative of Howards of Tottenham.

LOCKHART, William (1811–96); surgeon, FRCS; LMS; 1839 Macao; 1840 and 1843 Shanghai; 1840–41 Chusan with Gutzlaff, first British missionary Hong Kong; 1848 mobbed in 'Qingpu (Tsingpu) Outrage', Shanghai; 1861 first Prot. missionary in Peking; 1864 to UK; 1867 retired from LMS; surgeon, Blackheath.

LOMAX, Mr; Berger Starch Works executive; elder, Berger Hall, Bromley-by-Bow.

LORD, Edward Clifford, DD (1817–87); ABMU; 1847 first Am. Baptist to Ningbo; 1853 NT Baptist version, with Dean and Goddard; 1863 independent Am. Bapt. Mission, Ningbo; 1887 still there; appointed US consul by Abraham Lincoln; JHT's friend; d. with wife, of cholera.

LORD, Mrs; (1) d. Jan. 1860; (2) Jemima (Bausum) m. 1861, d. 1869.

LOWE, Miss Clara M S; daughter of Lt-Gen Sir Hudson Lowe (1769–1844) (Governor of St Helena, custodian of Napoleon Bonaparte); English tutor to Russian nobility; early friend of CIM; pension on acct. father.

LUSH, Lady; wife of Sir Robert (1807–81) (Lord Justice, CES Gen. Committee); attended Regent's Park Chapel; donor to CIM.

MACKENZIE, Francis A; philanthropist of Dingwall, Scotland; donor to CIM.

MACKINTOSH, William; with J Fraser (qv) initiator of FES; missionary to Cairo.

MACPHERSON, Miss Annie; mid-19th-century schoolteacher, social reformer, evangelist; 'ragged schools'; organised emigration to Canada; firm friend of CIM; introduced W D Rudland (qv).

MARA, John; United Meth. Free Ch.; trained by JHT; 1865 Ningbo; Aug. 1869 invalided to UK.

MARJORIBANKS, Charles, MP; ex-Chief, East India Company, Canton.

MARKHAM, Sir Clements R (1830–1916); explorer, Arctic, S.Am., Ethiopia, India; Secy. and Pres. Royal Geog. Soc. (1893–1905).

MARSHALL, Thomas D; minister, Bryanston Hall, Portman Square.

MARTIN, Samuel N D; older brother of W A P Martin (qv); Am. Presby. Mission; 1850 Ningbo, i/c boys' school founded by R Q Way (qv).

MARTIN, William Alexander Parsons, DD LL D (1827–1916); Am. Presby. Mission; educationalist; 1850–60 Ningbo; 1858 with S Wells Williams (qv) interpreter, Am. treaty; 1862 Peking; 1869 president, Tongwen Imperial College; 57 years in China; book on Christian evidences had huge circulation, China, Japan.

MARX, Karl (1818–83); German Jew, Univs. of Bonn, Berlin, law, philosophy, history, economics; 1848 *Communist Manifesto*; 1849 lived 28 Dean St, Soho; 1864 helped found Comm. International; 1867–83, *Das Kapital*.

MA XINYI; Muslim; 1865–68 Gov. of Zhejiang; 1869 Viceroy of the Two Jiangs, Jiangsu, Anhui, Jiangxi; 1869–70 Nanjing; August 1870 assassinated.

MAXWELL, James Laidlaw, MD (b. 1836); English Presby. Mission; 1863 Amoy; 1865 Taiwan pioneer, Tainan, Dagao; 1871 invalided to UK, 8 years on his back; publ. vernacular NT; 1883 Taiwan again; 1885 founded Medical Missionary Association (London), Secy; 1888 co-founder with B Broomhall (qv), 'Christian Union for the Severance of the Connection of the British Empire with the Opium Traffic'.

McAULAY, Alexander (1818–90); Wesleyan minister, missionary; 1876 Pres. Wesleyan Conf., Gen.Sec. Wes. Home Miss.; CIM Referee.

McCARTEE, Divie Bethune, MD (1820–1900); Am. Presby.; 1844 Ningbo 28 years; 1845 organised first Prot. church on Chinese soil; 1851 extended work beyond treaty ports; 1853 m. Juana Knight, first single Presby. woman to China; adopted Yu Meiying, orphaned daughter of pastor as own daughter, first Chinese woman doctor educated abroad, returned as missionary to China; 1861 met Taiping leaders, Nanjing, negotiated protection Am. citizens, Chinese Christians; Dec 1861–April 1862 earliest Prot. miss. in Japan; McC's tract translated into Japanese was first Prot. lit. in Japan; 1862–5 Shandong, Yantai; 1864 Ningbo again; 1872 Japan with Chinese envoy negotiated release of coolie prisoners on *Maria Luz* (Macao-Peru), received gold medal; 1872–77 Prof. of law and natural science, Tokyo Univ; 1877 secy. foreign affairs to Chinese legation, Japan; 1880 USA; 1889 Presby. Miss. again, Tokyo; good scholar in Greek, Chinese, Japanese; 1899 invalided USA; d. July 17, 1900. (*Chinese Recorder* 1902 Vol 33 p 497f).

McCARTHY, John; Dublin, member H G Guinness (qv) training class; Feb. 1866 influenced by JHT; 1866 CIM; 1867 Hangzhou; 1877 Jan–Aug Hankou to Bhamo, Burma on foot.

McLEAN, Jane; Inverness 'Bible-woman'; 1866 Wm Pennefather's training school; CIM, *Lammermuir*; Hangzhou; 1867 engaged to John Sell (qv); 1868 resigned, worked for LMS Shanghai.

McLEAN, Margaret, twin of Jane; 1867 CIM, Hangzhou, 1868 resigned, worked for LMS Shanghai.

MEADOWS, James J (1835–1914); JHT's first recruit to Ningbo Mission, 1862, and CIM; wife Martha d. Ningbo 1863; 1866 m. Eliz. Rose (qv); 1868 began pioneering; 1869 Anqing.

MEADOWS, Elizabeth; née Rose; friend of Martha Meadows; d.; 1866 CIM, *Lammermuir*, Ningbo, m. Jas Meadows (qv); 1869 Nanjing, Anqing, riot.

MEARS, Mr; works manager, Berger's Starch Works, Bromley-by-Bow; helped CIM crating, freighting.

MERRY, Joseph; Cambridgeshire farmer; brother-in-law of Annie Macpherson (qv).

MILL, John Stuart (1806–73); Engl. philosopher; author, *On Liberty*; *The Subjection of Women*; *Principles of Political Economy*.

MILNE, John; Scottish divine; organiser, Perth Conf.; friend of Wm Burns, JHT.

MOODY, Dwight Lyman (1837–99); 19th century's greatest evangelist; 1873–75 first Br. mission; 1882 Cambridge Univ. mission stimulated 'Cambridge Seven'; 1886 first Northfield student conference led to Student Volunteer Movement.

MORRISON, John Robert (1814–43); son of R Morrison; aged 16 official translator, East India Co.; Canton; 1842 interpreter-negotiator to Sir H Pottinger, Treaty of Nanking; 1843 Chinese Sec. to Gov. of Hong Kong; chairman, first LMS and General Missions Conferences, Hong Kong.

MOULE, Arthur Evans; CMS; 1861 Ningbo; 1876 Hangzhou (Hangchow); archdeacon.

MOULE, George Evans (b. 1828); CMS; 1858 Ningbo; 1864 Hangzhou (Hangchow); 1880 Bishop in Mid-China; over 50 years in China.

MOULE, Henry; Anglican minister; father of Handley, Bishop of Durham; George (qv) Bishop in Mid-China; and Arthur (qv) archdeacon, Ningbo.

MUIRHEAD, William, DD (1822–1900); LMS; evangelist, renowned preacher, translator, like a son to W H Medhurst; 'a gigantic worker'; 1846–90 (53 years) at Shanghai; 1848 victim of 'Qingpu (Tsingpu) Outrage', Shanghai; 1877–79 organised famine relief funds; warm friend of JHT, CIM; 'passionately fond of children'. (*Chinese Recorder* 1900 Vol 31 pp. 384, 625; 1902 Vol 32 pp 1, 42).

MÜLLER, George (1805–98); German-born; married sister of A N Groves (qv); 1832 read biography of A H Francke; 1835 founded Orphan Homes, Bristol, 2,000 children, financed 'by faith in God'; 1872 CIM Referee.

NAPOLEON I, Bonaparte (1769–1821); 1799 proclaimed himself First Consul of France; 1804 Emperor; 1805 virtually dictator of Europe; 1814 abdicated, sent to Elba, 1815 escaped; 18 June 1815 Waterloo; exiled to St Helena.

NEVIUS, John Livingston (1832–93); Am. Presby. Mission; 1854 Ningbo; 1859 Hangzhou; 1860 Japan; 1861 Shandong (Shantung); 1864 UK, USA; 1867 DD; 1869 Shandong, Denglai; Bible translator, author; 1890 Moderator, Shanghai Miss. Conf.; Korea, exponent of 'indigenous church' policy.

NICOL, Lewis; blacksmith, Arbroath, Aberdeen; 1865 CIM candidate; 1866 m. Eliza Calder (qv), *Lammermuir*, Hangzhou; 1867 Xiaoshan, outrage; 1868 dismissed.

NIGHTINGALE, Florence (1820–1910); pioneered hospital reforms; 1854–56 Crimea, 'lady with the lamp'.

NOEL, Rev and Hon Baptist; Anglican clergyman; 1848 became Baptist; revivalist, 21 Sept. 1859 drew 20,000 at Armagh.

NORTH, Brownlow (b. 1809); grandson of bishop successively of Lichfield, Worcester, Winchester, whose brother, Lord North, was Prime Minister to George III; roué converted aged 45, studied Bible and prayed for two months, then began as evangelist; Free Church of Scotland; drew thousands.

NOTMAN, Jean; recruit sent by JHT to Ningbo, 1864; assistant to Mrs Bausum (qv); 1866 resigned to marry.

OLIPHANT, Laurance, MP (1829–88); novelist, traveller, secy. RGS.

OSBORNE, Capt Sherard; 1861 engaged by H N Lay (qv), commanded 'Lay-Osborne fleet' to China debacle.

PALMERSTON, Viscount (1784–1865); Tory, Whig statesman, 1808–65; 1830–51 periodically Foreign Sec.; 1855, 1859–65 Prime Minister.

PARKER, H M; Am. Prot. Episc; 1861 Shandong, Yantai; Oct. killed with J L Holmes (qv).

PARKER, Dr John; brother of Dr Wm Parker; 1863 Ningbo, independent; 1865 United Presby. Ch. of Scotland Ningbo.

PARKER, Dr Peter, MD (1804–88); Am. Board (ABCFM); 1834 Canton; first medical missionary in China (not first Western physician); 1835 Ophthalmic Hospital after T R Colledge; 1838 formed 'Medical Missionary Soc. in China';

1838, 1843–4, semi-skilled interpreter-negotiator for US treaty; 1850 General Hosp., Canton; several times US chargé d'affaires and minister.

PARKER, Dr William; CES 1854–61; Shanghai, Ningbo; wife (1) d. 26 Aug. 1859 of cholera; m. wife (2) UK 1861; 1862 to Ningbo; d. injuries 1 Feb. 1863.

PARKES, Sir Harry Smith (1828–85); cousin m. C Gutzlaff (qv); 1841 sister m. Wm. Lockhart (qv); 1841 Macao; 1842 asst. to J R Morrison (qv); 1842 July 21 with Sir H Pottinger at assault on Zhenjiang, *aet.* 14; present at signing of Treaty of Nanking; 1842–43 Zhoushan (Chusan) Is. with Gutzlaff; 1843 Canton consulate asst.; 1845 Fuzhou, interpreter with R Alcock (qv); August 1846 Shanghai with Alcock; 1852–54 Canton; 1853 author Parl. Paper No. 263 on *Emigration* (Coolie trade); concluded first Br. treaty with Siam for Sir John Bowring; 1856 vice-consul Canton; Oct., *Arrow* incident; 1858–60 Br. Commissioner, Canton; 1861 Hankou Feb.–Apr. with Adm. Sir Jas Hope; May 20 1862 KCB knighthood *aet.* 34; intimate friend of Col Gordon; strongly opposed by Li Hongzhang (qv); 1865 Br. minister, Japan, 'won the most signal victory Br. diplomacy ever gained in the Far East' (Dickens, F V: *Life of Parkes*, II.44); 1871 UK; 1872–79 Japan; 1879–82 UK received KCMG, to Japan; 1883 Br. minister Peking, after Sir Thos Wade; treaty with Korea opened ports; d. March 22, 1885 'Peking fever'. (*Dicty. of Nat. Biog.* Vol XV; H B Morse).

PEARSE, George; London stockbroker; CES foreign sec.; co-founder Foreign Evangelist Soc.; friend and adviser of JHT's; later missionary to Kabyles, N. Africa, initiated N. Africa Mission.

PENNEFATHER, William (1816–73); vicar, Christ Church, Barnet; convener, Barnet and Mildmay conferences; hymn-writer, friend of JHT; 1864 St Jude's, Mildmay, N. London; director, Mildmay Mission Conf. centre and hospital; deaconess and missionary training school; 1872 CIM Referee.

PERBOYRE; Lazarist priest; 1836 Fujian, Wuchang; 1840 executed; 1846 his sister arr. Hong Kong, Sisters of St Paul. (Book 1, pp 229, 273, 305).

PETRIE, David; 1866 Shanghai, Jardine, Matheson agent; friendly to CIM.

PIERCY, George; 1850 to China at own expense; 1851 Canton; 1853 adopted by Wesleyan Meth. Miss. Soc.; joined by Josiah Cox (qv).

PILLANS-SMITH, Helen; from 1866 longtime friend of CIM.

PUGET, Colonel John Henry; brother of Dowager Lady Radstock (qv); generous donor to CIM.

QIAN LONG, (Ch'ien Lung); sixty years (1736–96) 4th emperor, Qing (Ch'ing) dynasty; after Yong Zheng, before Jia Qing; d. 1799.

QUARTERMAN, J W; Am. Presby.; 1847–57 Ningbo; smallpox, nursed by JHT; d. 1857.

RADSTOCK, Lord; Hon Granville Augustus Wm. Waldegrave (1833–1913); 3rd (qv), Hon Miss Waldegrave (qv); sister of Col J H Puget (qv); Welbeck St Brethren; friend and supporter of JHT.

RADSTOCK, Lord; Hon Granville Augustus Wm. Waldegrave, (1833–1913); 3rd Baron; converted at Crimean War; raised, commanded W. Middlesex Rifles for 6 years; evangelical Anglican evangelist in aristocratic Russian, E. European society; closely associated with Brethren; friend of JHT and CIM; 1872 CIM Referee.

RANYARD, Mrs; née Ellen White; means of conversion of M S Alexander, Prof. of Hebrew, Arabic, Bishop of Jerusalem; founded London Bible Women's Assn. and Ranyard Mission.

RAO, O; Paris Prot. Mission; 1861 Yantai, Tianjin.

REID, Henry; 1867 CIM, Hangzhou; 1868 Yangzhou riot, eye injury; 1873 retired.
RICHARD, Timothy (1845–1919); converted in Evang. Awakening 1859–60, Wales; offered services to JHT, referred to BMS; 1870 Shandong; 1875 sole survivor of twelve; 1876–79 Shandong, Shanxi famine relief; educationalist, views changed, left BMS, founded Univ. of Shanxi, Taiyuan (8 years), 1891 Soc. for Diffusion of Chr. & Gen. Knowledge; 1906 Christian Literature Soc.; his policies to Christianize China akin to the techniques of Ricci (qv); adviser to emperor, Chinese govt. and Kang Yuwei; translated *History of the Nineteenth Century* (1 mill. copies); 1885 proposed a Christian college in every prov. capital; 1901 with Boxer indemnity funds founded Taiyuan Univ. College; received two of the highest honours of the empire.
RIDGEWAY, Joseph; CMS Assoc. Sec.; editor CMS *Intelligencer*, *Record*, *Gleaner*; 1869 opposed C R Alford's proposed CMS Mission for China; d. 1871.
ROBERTS, Issacher Jacocks; eccentric Am. Bapt.; 1833–67 Canton, Shanghai; 1837 Canton, taught Hong Xiuquan (qv), Taiping leader; 1842 first missionary in Hong Kong, with J L Shuck.
ROSE, Elizabeth; 1866 CIM, *Lammermuir*; m. J Meadows (qv).
RUDLAND, William D; Eversden, Cambridgeshire blacksmith/farm mechanic; 1856 CIM; 1866 *Lammermuir*, Hangzhou; 1867 m. Mary Bell (qv); 1868 printer, Yangzhou riot; 1869 Taizhou, Zhejiang many years; 1874 UK, wife died; translated (adapted) Taizhou vernacular romanised NT; 1878 m. Miss Brealey, d.; later m. Miss Knight; d. 1913.
RUSSELL, Lord John (1792–1878); 1st earl; 1832 Reform Bill; 1846, 1865–66 Prime Minister.
RUSSELL, William Armstrong; CMS; 1847 Ningbo; 1872–79 first bishop in N. China; d. 1879.
RYLE, John Charles, DD; 1880–1900 Bp. of Liverpool; uncompromising Evangelical leader, writer, C H Spurgeon's 'best man in the Ch. of England'; author *Knots Untied*, *Holiness*, *Practical Religion*.
SCHERESCHEWSKY, Samuel Isaac Joseph (1831–1906) (pron. *Sher-e-sheff-skie*; called 'Sherry'); Russian Lithuanian rabbi, converted; 1854 USA Gen. Theol. Seminary, NY; 1859 ordained Am. Prot. Episc. Church by Bp Wm Boone Sr (Book 1, p 393); 1860 Shanghai; 1862–75 Peking, began Dicty. of Mongolian; alone translated OT into Mandarin while committee trans. NT; 1865 with J S Burdon (qv) trans. Anglican Book of Com. Prayer; 1875 nominated bishop, declined; 1876 consecrated; 1878 founded St John's College, Shanghai, and St Mary's Hall for girls; 1879 *wenli* Prayer Book, Wuchang; 1881 paralysed limbs, speech, to Europe; 1883 resigned episc. office; 1886 USA, began OT revision – impaired speech excluded Chinese help, typed with one finger, 8 hours daily – 1888–95 easy *wenli* OT, NT romanised; 1895–97 Shanghai, romanised into Ch. character; 1897 Japan, to supervise printing; 1902 OT revision publ.; sole object 'to make plain the Word of God to the Chinese'; d. Tokyo, Sept 15, 1906, *aet.* 75 in working chair. (*Chinese Recorder* 1906 Vol 37 p 615f).
SCOTT, William; Dunedin, Edinburgh, manufacturer; staunch friend of CIM.
SELL, John Robert; Romford, Essex; 1866 CIM, *Lammermuir*, Hangzhou; 1867 engaged to Jane McLean (qv), Ningbo, d. smallpox.
SHAFTESBURY, Lord Anthony Ashley-Cooper (1801–85); 7th earl; evangelical philanthropist; legislated to relieve ill effects of industrial revolution.
SIMEON, Charles (1759–1836); King's Coll., Cambridge; 1738–1836 Holy Trinity, Camb.; 1897 a founder of CMS; encouraged Henry Martyn to go to India.

SKINNER, Anne; Cornwall fiancée of Geo. Crombie (qv); 1865 Ningbo; m. Crombie; 1866 Fenghua; 1882 retired.

SMITH, Elizabeth; first CMS single woman to China; 1863 Fuzhou; 1864 Peking; 1869 not listed.

SOLTAU, George; son of Henry W (qv); Lamb and Flag Mission and schools, London; 1872 on first CIM London Council.

SOLTAU, Henrietta E; daughter of H W Soltau (qv); 1873 London, asst. to Emily Blatchley; Tottenham home for children of missionaries; later, CIM Women's Training Home.

SALTAU, Henry, Jr; son of H W Soltau (qv); Aug. 1872 Hon. Sec. CIM, London with R H Hill (qv); 1875 to Bhamo, Burma with J W Stevenson (qv); 1880 with Stevenson first Westerners to cross China W. to E., Burma, Chongqing, Wuchang, Shanghai.

SOLTAU, Henry W; Chancery barrister, Plymouth and Exeter Brethren; sons George, Henry Wm, daughters Henrietta, Agnes, (m. Richard Hill qv), all in CIM.

SOLTAU, Lucy; daughter of H W Soltau (qv), d. young, 1873.

SOLTAU, William; son of H W Soltau (qv); 1875 Asst. Secy. CIM, London, with R H Hill, B Broomhall.

SPURGEON, Charles Haddon (1834–92); renowned Baptist preacher, Metropolitan Tabernacle; lifelong friend of JHT.

STACEY, Miss; one-time Quaker, member of Brook Street chapel, Tottenham; CES Ladies' Assn.; long a friend of JHT, CIM and T J Barnardo; d. 1876.

STEVENSON, John Whiteford (1844–1918); son of laird of Thriepwood, Renfrewshire; m. Anne Jolly; with G Stott (qv) first of CIM after Crombie (qv); Oct. 1865 dep. UK; 1866–74 Ningbo, Shaoxing; 1875–80 Burma; 1880 with H Soltau, Jr. (qv) crossed China W. to E., Bhamo–Chongqing–Wuchang then Shanghai; 1,900 miles, 86 days; 1885–1916 deputy director, CIM.

STOCK, Eugene (1836–1928); CMS UK staff; editor Dec. 21, 1875–Dec. 11, 1906; historian, author *The History of the Church Miss. Soc.*, Vols I–III; warm friend of CIM.

STOTT, George; Aberdeenshire schoolmaster, one leg; Oct. 1865 dep. UK; 1866 Ningbo; 1869–89 Wenzhou (Wenchow); 1870 m. G Ciggie (qv); d. 1889.

STRONACH, Alexander; LMS; 1838–39 Singapore; 1839–44 Penang; 1844–46 Singapore; 1846 Amoy.

STRONACH, John; LMS, 1838–76, 30 years without furlough; 1838–44 Singapore; 1846 Amoy; Bible translator, Delegates' Committee, 1852; S Dyer Sr's friend.

SUN YAT-SEN (1866–1925); Chinese statesman; 1891 first medical graduate, Hong Kong; 1905 founded China Revolutionary League, in Europe, Japan; 1911–12 founder and first president Republic of China; m. descendant of Paul Xu, (SOONG QINGLING, dep. chairman Nat. People's Congress till d. 1981).

TARN, William Jr; son of William Sr (qv); cousin of Maria Taylor; Secy. RTS.

TARN, William Sr; brother of Samuel Dyer Sr's wife; guardian of Burella (Mrs J S Burdon qv) and Maria Dyer (Mrs JHT qv).

TAYLOR, Frederick Howard (1862–1946); b. Beaumont St, London, Nov. 25, 1862; second son of JHT and Maria Jane (qv); 1888 MD (Lond.); 1889 MRCP; FRCS(Edin.); Jan. 1890 to China; 1894 m. M Geraldine Guinness; CIM missionary, biographer of JHT; d. Aug. 15, 1946.

TAYLOR, Grace Dyer; daughter of JHT and Maria (qv), b. Ningbo July 31, 1859; *Jubilee*, *Lammermuir* voyages; d. nr. Hangzhou, Aug. 23, 1867.

TAYLOR, Herbert Hudson; son of JHT and Maria, b. Bayswater, London,

April 3, 1861; Jan. 1881 CIM, to China; c 1886 m. Jean Gray, CIM 1884; father of James Hudson Taylor II.

TAYLOR, James Hudson (21 May 1832–3 June 1905); 1853 dep. UK; 1 Mar. 1854 arr. Shanghai; 20 Jan. 1858 m. Maria Jane Dyer; 1857 with J Jones (qv) began Ningbo Mission; June 1865 founded China Inland Mission; 28 Nov. 1871 m. Jane E Faulding; 3 June 1905 d. Changsha, Hunan.

TAYLOR, Maria Jane, née Dyer, (1837–70); daughter of Samuel Dyer (qv); wife of JHT; mother of Grace, Herbert Hudson, Frederick Howard, Samuel, Jane, Maria, Charles, Noel; d. Zhenjiang, July 23, 1870.

TAYLOR, Maria Hudson, daughter of JHT and Maria; b. Hangzhou, Feb. 3, 1867; 1884 CIM to China *aet.* 17; m. J J Coulthard; d. Sept. 28, 1897.

TAYLOR, Samuel Dyer, son of JHT and Maria; b. Barnsley, June 24, 1864; d. Zhenjiang, Feb. 4, 1870.

TIDMAN, Dr Arthur; Foreign Sec., LMS; member CES General Committee.

TONG TIANXI; destitute Shanghai boy, 1857 adopted, educated by JHT; worked with CIM.

TONG ZHI (T'ung Chih) (1856–75); 1862 succeeded Xian Feng emperor.

TRESTRAIL, Frederick; BMS Secretary with E B Underhill (qv).

TSIANG ALIANG (*see* ZIANG).

TSIU KYUO-KWE; 1858 Ningbo Christian; evangelist; 1866 Hangzhou; Xiaoshan outrage victim; 1868–71 Zhenjiang, Nanjing; 1872 Taizhou, Hangzhou; m. En-sing, adopted by Maria Taylor.

UNDERHILL, C B; Sec. BMS; friend of JHT, nominated him for FRGS.

VALENTINE, Jarvis Downman; CMS recruit taught by JHT; 1864 Ningbo; 1870 Shaoxing; d. 1889.

van SOMMER, James; member, Hackney Brethren circle with W T Berger (qv) (brother-in-law) and Philip H Gosse (qv); editor, *The Missionary Reporter*.

van SOMMER, John; brother of James.

VENN, Henry 'the elder'; vicar of Huddersfield, leading promoter of first evangelical revival; grandfather of Henry Venn 'Senior'.

VENN, Henry 'the younger', known as 'Senior' (1796–1873); son of John Venn, grandson of Henry 'the elder'; St John's, Holloway; 1841–73, Hon. Sec. CMS; sent 498 clergy overseas.

VENN, Henry 'Junior'; second son of Henry 'Senior'; c 1869–72 Assoc. Sec. CMS.

VENN, John; rector of Clapham, member of 18th century 'Eclectic Socy.'; a founder, first chairman of CMS; father of Henry 'the younger' or 'Senior'; d. 1813.

VIGEON, James, accountant, and Mrs; 1865 recruits for Ningbo, prevented from sailing with J W Stevenson (qv) and then *Lammermuir* party.

WALDEGRAVE, Hon Miss; daughter of Dowager Lady Radstock (qv); friend, supporter of CIM.

WANG GUOYAO; 1864 peasant convert, irrepressible evangelist, village pastor, 1867 Fenghua outstations many years.

WANG LAE-DJÜN, (Ch. characters not found); Ningbo Mission convert; 1860–64 with JHT London; 1867 pastor, Hangzhou, remainder of life.

WARD, Hon John E; 1859 US plenipotentiary; 1860 at capture and Convention of Peking.

WAY, R Q; Am. Presby.; 1844–59 Ningbo; established schools; brother-in-law of J W Quarterman (qv); friend of JHT; d. 1896 (*Chinese Recorder* 1896, Vol 27 p 35).

WEATHERLEY, Joseph; early CIM supporter; 1872 first chairman, CIM London Council, met in his home, 51 Gordon Sq.

WEIR, Thomas; Shanghai merchant, 1865 influenced by JHT Glasgow; long a friend.

WILLIAMS, Samuel Wells DD (1812–84); Am. Board, printer, scholar; 1833 Canton; 1847 author *The Middle Kingdom*; 1851 succeeded E C Bridgman (qv) as editor, *Chinese Repository*; 1856 interpreter and Secy. to US minister, Peking; 9 times chargé d'affaires to 1876; 1884 *Syllabic Dicty. of Chinese Language*, 12,527 characters; prof. of Chinese, Yale Univ. 8 years.

WILLIAMSON, Alexander, LL D (1829–90); Falkirk, Scotland, b. Dec. 5, 1829, eldest of seven sons; Glasgow Univ.; 1858–63 invalided UK; 1863 National Bible Soc. of Scotland, Shandong, Yantai; 1864–69 travelled extensively distributing Scripture, Peking, Mongolia, Manchuria; Aug. 1869 brother, James Williamson, LMS, murdered near Tianjin; 1869 UK; 1871 LL D Glasgow, 1871–80, 1881–83 Yantai, NBSS and United Presby. Soc. of Scotland; 1883–85 Scotland ill, founded Book & Tract Socy. for China, later (1887) Socy. for Diffusion of Christian and General Knowledge among the Chinese (Christian Lit. Soc.); 1886 Shanghai, wife d.; 1890 d. Yantai. Author, *Natural Theology*, and others. 'Very tall, striking in appearance; intellectually also among the giants'.

WILLIAMSON, James; younger brother of Alexander W (qv); 1863 LMS Tianjin; 1869 murdered.

WILLIAMSON, James; Arbroath, Aberdeen, carpenter; 1866 CIM, *Lammermuir*, Hangzhou, JHT's assistant pioneer; 1869 Anqing riot.

WILLIS, Capt John, Jr; 'Jock' Willis, son of 'Old Stormy', clipper master and owner, known in London as 'White Hat' Willis; *Lammermuir*, *Cutty Sark*; favoured CIM.

WILLIS, Capt John, Sr; clipper master and owner, 'Old Stormy' of sea shanty 'Mr Stormalong'; founder of John Willis and Son.

WINNES, Ph; Basel Mission; 1852 joined Theodore Hamberg (qv), Guangdong, after R Lechler died.

WU JOOHOON; Singapore Chinese, converted after Sept. 1866 typhoon danger; baptised by JHT.

WYLIE, Alexander (1815–87); LMS; 1847 Shanghai, printer, Delegates' version of Bible; 1863 Bible Soc. (B&FBS); one of the greatest Sinologues; completed distribution of the million NTs provided 1855 by Bible Soc. special fund; 1877 retired with failing eyesight; succeeded by Maria Taylor's brother Samuel Dyer, Jr (qv).

XIAN FENG (Hsien Feng) (1851–61); 7th Qing (Ch'ing) dynasty emperor.

YAKUB BEG; Muslim conqueror, 1864 captured Kashgar, Yarkand; appointed ruler by Emir of Bokhara; added Urumqi, Turfan to his kingdom; 1872 independence recognised by Russia, GB, Turkey; honoured with title only used by caliphs of Baghdad; great Muslim revival predicted, with conquest of China; but 1876 Urumqi fell to Zuo Zongtang (Tso Tsung-t'ang) (qv); May 1877 Yakub Beg died suddenly; Dec. 1877 Kashgar taken, kingdom ended.

YATES, Matthew T (1819–88); Am. S. Baptist; 1847 Shanghai; Sinologue, learned contributor to *Chinese Recorder*; Am. vice-consul; translator, Shanghai vernacular NT.

YÜ XIANSENG (Mr); 1867–68 Hangzhou schoolmaster; 1869–71 Yangzhou, Suzhou, Qingjiangpu, Zhenjiang; 'doctor', Chinese materia medica.

ZENG GUOFAN (Tseng Kuo-fan) (1811–72); scholar, provincial governor; 1854 defeated Taipings; viceroy of the 'Two Jiangs' (Jiangxi, Jiangsu and Anhui), then of Zhili (Chihli); 1870 after Ma Xinyi (qv) assassination returned Nanjing; d. March 11, 1872.

ZHU XINGJUN; Ningbo evangelist, pioneered Wenzhou with Stott (qv).

ZIANG ALIANG; Hangzhou laundryman; with his brother LIANGYONG became evangelist; Taizhou, Yangzhou.

ZUO ZONGTANG (Tso Tsung-t'ang); native of Hunan; successful imperial general vs. Taipings in S. China; 1860s built naval dockyard at Fuzhou; 1870 appointed to suppress Muslim rebellion in NW, completed Dec. 17, 1877, at fall of Kashgar (*see* Yakub Beg).

BIBLIOGRAPHY

	British Library ref.
BIBLE SOCIETY, *History of the B&FBS*, vols 1, 2	3129.e.76
BREDON, Juliet, *Sir Robert Hart*, Hutchinson & Co 1909	010817.de.10
BRIDGEMAN, Mrs E J G, *The Life and Labors of Elijah Coleman Bridgman*, 1864	
BRIDGMAN, Elijah C and Eliza J G, *The Pioneer of American Missions in China*, 1864	4985.aaa.27
BROOMHALL, Benjamin, *The Evangelization of the World*, CIM 1889	
BROOMHALL, Marshall, *John W Stevenson: One of Christ's Stalwarts*, Morgan & Scott/CIM 1919	4956.aa.33
The Jubilee Story of the China Inland Mission, Morgan & Scott/CIM 1915	4763.g.4
Hudson Taylor's Legacy, Hodder & Stoughton 1931	10823.a.16
The Chinese Empire: A General & Missionary Survey, Morgan & Scott/CIM 1907	4767.eeee.4
BURNS, Islay, *Memoir of the Rev William Chalmers Burns*, London 1885	
CARR, F G G: *The Cutty Sark*, Pitkin Pictorials Ltd 1973	
CHINA MAIL (Hong Kong)	British Library Colindale
CHINA'S MILLIONS, Magazine of the China Inland Mission 1875–1951	
CHINESE RECORDER AND MISSIONARY JOURNAL: Vols 1–3, 5–12	
May 1868– May 71, editor Justus Doolittle; Vol 5	
bi-monthly Jan–Dec 1874 (after 2-year interlude) – Vol 12, 1881	
CLARKE, A, *The Boy from Shoreditch*, OMF Books; Clipper Series	
CMS, *CM Gleaner, Intelligencer, Register, Reports*, Church Missionary Society	
COAD, F Roy, *A History of the Brethren Movement*, The Paternoster Press 1968	
COLLIER, Richard, *William Booth: The General Next to God*, Collins 1965	X.100.1629
COLLIS, Maurice Stewart, *Foreign Mud*, 1946	9059.df.15
CORDIER, Henri, *The Life of Alexander Wylie*, 1887	10803.cc.4/6
COVELL, Ralph, *W A P Martin, Pioneer of Progress in China*, Wm B Eerdmans Publishing Company 1978	
DAVIES, Evan, *China and her Spiritual Claims*, John Snow 1845	1369.b.24

Memoir of the Reverend Samuel Dyer, John Snow
1846   1372.c.20
FAIRBANK, John King, *Trade and Diplomacy on the China
Coast*, 2 vols 1953 Edn. Cambridge, Massachusetts   Ac.2692.10
FORBES, Archibald, *Chinese Gordon*, George Routledge &
Sons 1884
FOREIGN OFFICE LIBRARY, Public Records Office, *A Century
of Diplomatic Blue Books*, China FO/17
FULLERTON, W Y and WILSON, C E, *Report of the China Missions
of the Baptist Missionary Society*, BM House, London 1908
GLEANER, CES, *The Gleaner in the Missionary Field
    The Chinese & General Missionary Gleaner
    The Chinese Missionary Gleaner*, Chinese
Evangelization Society 1850–60
GROVES, Mrs, *Memoir of the late Anthony Norris Groves*,
2nd Edn, 1857
GUINNESS, M Geraldine, *The Story of the China Inland Mission*,
2 vols, Morgan & Scott, London 1893
GUY'S HOSPITAL GAZETTE, Centenary Number
HALDANE, Charlotte, *The Last Great Empress of China*,
Constable 1965
HART, Sir Robert, *These from the Land of Sinim*   8022.cc.48/01
                                                                                           and 0817.d.10
HOLT, Edgar C, *The Opium Wars in China*, 1964 edn.   X.709–581
HOOK, Brian, *China's Three Thousand Years*: Part 4
The Modern History of China, *The Times* Newspaper
(publishers)
HUMBLE, Richard, *Marco Polo*, Weidenfeld and Nicolson 1975
KNOLLYS, Sir Henry, *Incidents in the China War, 1860*   9056.bb.19
    English Life in China, 1885   10058.e.31
LATOURETTE, Kenneth Stott, *A History of Christian
Missions in China*, SPCK 1929   4763.g.4
    *A History of the Expansion of Christianity
1800–1914*, Eyre and Spottiswoode   4533.ff.22
    These Sought a Country: Tipple Lectures,
1950 edn, Harper & Brothers   4807.e.25
LEGGE, Helen E, *James Legge (1815–97)*, Religious Tract
Society 1905   04429.1.37
LITTLE, Mrs Archibald, *Li Hung-chang, His Life and Times*,
Cassell & Co Ltd 1903
LOCKHART, William, *The Medical Missionary in China*,
1861 edn   10058.d.16
LUBBOCK, Basil, *The China Clippers*, 1914
LYALL, L T, *A Passion for the Impossible*, Hodder
& Stoughton 1965; OMF Books 1976
MacGILLIVRAY, Donald, *A Century of Protestant Missions
in China* (Centennial Conference Historical Volume),
Shanghai 1907   4764.ff.11
MacGREGOR, David R, *The Tea Clippers; Sailing Ships of
the Nineteenth Century*, London 1952

MARTIN, W A P, *A Cycle of Cathay*, 1896   010056.g.7

MEDHURST, W H, Sr, *China: Its State and Prospects*,
John Snow 1838   571.g.10
    A Glance at the Interior of China in 1845,
Shanghai Mission Press 1949   10055.c.25

MEDHURST, Sir Walter H, *Curiosities of Street Literature
in China*, 1871   10057.aaa.16
    The Foreigner in Far Cathay, Edward Stanton 1872   010058.ee.35

MICHIE, Alexander, *Missionaries in China*, Edward Stanford
Ldn. 1891; 2nd edn Tientsin Press 1893   4767.ccc.10
    *The Englishman in China: as illustrated in the
Career of Sir Rutherford Alcock*, Wm Blackwood & Sons,
Edin. 1900 2 vols   09057.d.3

MORRIS, E W, *The London Hospital*, Edward Arnold
1910

MORSE, Hosea Ballou, *The International Relations of the
Chinese Empire* (9 vols), vols 1–3 1910   2386.c.17

MOULE, Arthur E, *The Story of the Cheh-Kiang Mission*,
CMS 1879

MÜLLER, George (ed. G F Bergin), *Autobiography:
Narrative*, J Nisbet & Co, Ltd 1905

NEILL, Stephen C, *A History of Christian Missions*
(Pelican History of the Church), Penguin Books 1964;
    Colonialism and Christian Missions, Lutterworth Press:
Foundations of Christian Mission 1966

NEILL, S C *et al*, *Chinese Dictionary of Christian World
Mission*, United Society for Christian Literature,
London 1971

NEVIUS, Helen S C, *The Life of John Livingston Nevius*,
Revell 1895   4985.eee.5

NORTH CHINA DAILY NEWS (newspaper)   British Library, Colindale
NORTH CHINA HERALD (newspaper)   British Library, Colindale

ORR, J Edwin, *The Second Evangelical Awakening in
Britain*, Marshall Morgan & Scott 1949

PARLIAMENTARY PAPERS: Foreign Office Blue Books,
Official Publications Office

PIERSON, A T, *George Müller of Bristol*, Jas Nisbet
& Co, Ltd 1905

POLO, Marco, *The Book of Ser Marco Polo, The Venetian,
1298*, First printed edition 1477 (see YULE)

POTT, F L Hawks, *A Short History of Shanghai*,
Kelly & Walsh 1928   010056.aaa.46

ROWDON, H H, *The Origins of the Brethren*, Pickering
& Inglis 1967

SELLMAN, R R, *An Outline Atlas of Eastern History*,
Edward Arnold Ltd

SMITH, Arthur H, *The Uplift of China*, The Young
People's Missionary Movement of America 1909

SOOTHILL, Wm E, *Timothy Richard of China*, Seeley,
Service & Co, Ltd, London 1924

STOCK, Eugene, *A History of the Church Missionary Society*, Vols I–III 1899–1916   4765.cc.28

STOTT, Grace, *Twenty-Six Years of Missionary Work in China*, Hodder & Stoughton 1897

TAYLOR, Dr & Mrs Howard, *Hudson Taylor in Early Years: The Growth of a Soul*, CIM and RTS, 1911
    Hudson Taylor and the China Inland Mission: The Growth of a Work of God, CIM and RTS, 1918
    Hudson Taylor's Spiritual Secret, CIM, 1932

TAYLOR, Mrs Howard (M Geraldine Guinness), *The Story of the China Inland Mission*, 2 vols, 1892, Morgan & Scott
    Behind the Ranges: A Biography of J O Fraser, CIM
    Pastor Hsi: One of China's Scholars (2 vols), CIM

TAYLOR, J Hudson, *China: Its Spiritual Need and Claims*, 1st–6th edns 1865 et seq, CIM
    China's Spiritual Need and Claims, 7th edn. 1887, CIM 8th edn. 1890, CIM
    Brief Account of the Progress of the China Inland Mission, May 1866 to May 1868, J Nisbet & Co 1868
    A Retrospect, 1875, CIM
    After Thirty Years, 1895, Morgan & Scott and CIM
    Occasional Paper Vols 1–6, Jas Nisbet & Co
    Summary of the Operations of the China Inland Mission, 1865–1872, J Nisbet & Co 1872

THOMAS, W H Griffith, *The Principles of Theology*, Church Book Room Press, London 1945

THOMPSON, R Wardlaw, *Griffith John: The Story of Fifty Years in China*, The Religious Tract Society 1907

WALEY, Arthur David, *The Opium War through Chinese Eyes*, London 1958   09059.pp.30

WILLIAMS, Fredk Wells, *The Life and Letters of Samuel Wells Williams, LL D, Missionary, Diplomatist, Sinologue*, G P Putman & Sons, New York and London 1889

WILLIAMS, Samuel Wells, *The Middle Kingdom*, 1847

WOODCOCK, George, *The British in the Far East*, Weidenfeld & Nicolson 1969 (A Social History of the British Overseas)

YULE, Sir Henry, *The Book of Ser Marco Polo the Venetian*, 1878, 2 vols.

INDEX